WITH US MORE THAN EVER

SPIRITUAL PHENOMENA
TANYA MARIE LUHRMANN and ANN TAVES, Series Editors

WITH US MORE THAN EVER

MAKING THE ABSENT REBBE PRESENT IN MESSIANIC CHABAD

Yoram Bilu

Translated by Haim Watzman

Stanford University Press
Stanford, California

STANFORD UNIVERSITY PRESS
Stanford, California

English translation © 2020 by the Board of Trustees of the Leland Stanford Junior University. All rights reserved.

With Us More Than Ever: Making the Absent Rebbe Present in Messianic Chabad was originally published in Hebrew in 2016 under the title *Itanu Yoter Mitamid: Hankha'hat HaRabbi BeChabad Hameshihit* © 2016, Open University Press.

No part of this book may be reproduced or transmitted in any form or by any means, electronic or mechanical, including photocopying and recording, or in any information storage or retrieval system without the prior written permission of Stanford University Press.

Printed in the United States of America on acid-free, archival-quality paper

Library of Congress Cataloging-in-Publication Data
Names: Bilu, Yoram, author.
Title: With us more than ever : making the absent Rebbe present in messianic Chabad / Yoram Bilu.
Description: Stanford, California : Stanford University Press, 2020. | Includes bibliographical references and index.
Identifiers: LCCN 2019046791 (print) | LCCN 2019046792 (ebook) | ISBN 9781503608344 (cloth) | ISBN 9781503612419 (paperback) | ISBN 9781503612426 (ebook)
Subjects: LCSH: Schneerson, Menachem Mendel, 1902-1994—Cult. | Habad—Customs and practices. | Hasidism—21st century. | Jewish messianic movements.
Classification: LCC BM755.S288 B55 2020 (print) | LCC BM755.S288 (ebook) | DDC 296.8/3322—dc23
LC record available at https://lccn.loc.gov/2019046791
LC ebook record available at https://lccn.loc.gov/2019046792

Cover design: Rob Ehle

Typeset by Kevin Barrett Kane in 10/15 ITC New Baskerville

In memory of MEL SPIRO,
mentor, friend, *mensch*

CONTENTS

Figures ix
Preface xi

Introduction xvii

PART I: CHABAD'S MESSIANISM

1 Chabad and the Messianic Idea 29
2 Meshichist Sociology 37

PART II: MESHICHIST PHENOMENOLOGY

3 Writing to the Rebbe: The Holy Letters Oracle 47
4 Sensing the Rebbe: Traces and Practices of Embodiment 74
5 Seeing the Rebbe I: Chabad's Visual Culture 98
6 Seeing the Rebbe II: Dream and Waking Apparitions 135

PART III: MESHICHIST COSMOLOGY

7 Schneersoncentrism: The Rebbe Steers the World 175
8 The Apotheosis of the Rebbe 188
9 "To Make Many More Menachem Mendels": Creation and Procreation in Messianic Chabad 197
10 Holy Place and Holy Time in Meshichist Chabad 206
11 The Omnipresence of Absence: Messianism in the Technological Age 215

PART IV: THE MESHICHISTS FROM A COMPARATIVE PERSPECTIVE

12 Meshichists, Christians, Sabbateans, and Popular Culture Heroes   229

13 From *Tzadik* to Messiah: Comparing Chabad and Bratslav   241

   Conclusion   258

   Notes   267

   Bibliography   297

   Index   309

FIGURES

Figure 1	Poster of the Rebbe on a shop door.	3
Figure 2	*Sichat Hage'ulah* (Discourse on Redemption): The Weekly Bulletin for the Days of the Messiah.	13
Figure 3	*Beis Moshiach* (House of the Messiah) magazine.	14
Figure 4	The author at a Messiah and Redemption Rally.	19
Figure 5	Pocket-sized volume of the Holy Letters.	69
Figure 6	Replica of "770": In Kfar Chabad (above); the original building in Crown Heights (below).	76
Figure 7	Replica of "770": Facade of a private house.	76
Figure 8	Replica of "770": Torah ark.	78
Figure 9	Replica of "770": Clock.	78
Figure 10	The advertisement for the photocopied dollars.	89
Figure 11	Soldier with a *Chitat* safety kit on the front page of *Sichat Hage'ulah*.	92
Figure 12	The Rebbe's iconic image: On a poster in Tel Aviv.	103
Figure 13	The Rebbe's iconic image: On stickers.	104
Figure 14	The Rebbe's iconic image: On the Partition Wall between Israel and the Palestinian Authority.	104
Figure 15	Calendar displaying the Rebbe's iconic image.	106
Figure 16	Keychains, card, and candle box displaying the Rebbe's image and his abode.	107

Figure 17	Clock with the Rebbe's image.	108
Figure 18	Car-window shade with the Rebbe's image.	108
Figure 19	Typical cover of *Citizens in the Messiah's State* magazine.	110
Figure 20	Meta-iconization 1.	112
Figure 21	Meta-iconization 2.	113
Figure 22	At Oro shel Mashiach (Light of the Messiah) summer camp.	114
Figure 23	The Rebbe's image in the wall.	122
Figure 24	The Rebbe's photograph from 27 Adar 5752 (2 March 1992).	132
Figure 25	A photograph from *Open Your Eyes*.	155
Figure 26	The boy with the Rebbe in 2004.	156
Figure 27	A bride holding the Rebbe's photo.	199
Figure 28	Portrait of Che Guevara as Jesus.	237
Figure 29	Cherry Guevara. Magnum ice cream.	239

PREFACE

My first encounter with Chabad emissaries was unplanned. During the second week of the 1973 Yom Kippur War, after the Israel Defense Forces had established a bridgehead on the far side of the Suez Canal, I was placed at the head of a company of tankers; we were assigned to cross the canal to fuel IDF armored units on the western bank. We made our preparations under Egyptian bombardment. While the artillery fire was sparse, it was very dangerous because of our flammable cargo. Suddenly I heard Hasidic music. It turned out to be blaring from speakers that had been attached to the roof of a civilian pickup truck. High-strung as we were from the danger we were under, we first thought that we were hallucinating. But the two Hasidim who jumped out of the truck turned out to be entirely real. They eagerly handed out small plastic bags containing a copy of the traditional wayfarer's prayer, printed on parchment-colored paper, along with two ten-agorot coins that, they said, bore the Rebbe's blessing. They were old-style Chabad Hasidim ("Lubavitchers"), a type you hardly see anymore—they wore everyday clothing and had newsboy caps on their heads. I don't know how they got so close to the front, but I vividly remember that all of us, religious and nonreligious alike, shoved the precious charmed coins into our pockets or into the pouch holding our dog tags.

A later memory comes from an organized tour of Peru and Bolivia in 2007. When we reached Cusco, the Andean capital of the Inca Empire, our group, which included both observant and nonobservant Jews, decided to enjoy a Friday-night Sabbath meal at the local Chabad House. To our surprise, we found ourselves sitting among about a hundred Israeli trekkers at tables that had been set up under the sky in the courtyard of the house. The local Chabad emissary, who offered an animated talk on the weekly Torah portion, displayed the garb, speech, and the body language of a man born into a Chabad family. We were thus surprised to learn that, just a decade before, he and his wife had been trekkers themselves. They had encountered Chabad for the first time on the beaches of Goa in India. From his discourse on sacred matters, the rabbi segued straight into the profane. First he cautioned the trekkers against swindlers who rent motorcycles without providing full insurance policies. Then he invited the crowd to come back a couple of days later to watch Brazil play Argentina in the Copa América soccer championship. When he said that he had ordered a giant screen especially for the occasion, dozens of trekkers drummed on their tables and cheered "*Yesh Elohim!*" ("God exists!").

A year and a half later, I visited India. I arrived in Mumbai a few weeks after an Islamist organization staged a terror attack in the city, in November 2008; one of the targets was the city's Chabad House. The sight of the bullet-pocked building nauseated me. A few days later I made my way to Varanasi, where, on the banks of the Ganges, I saw numerous signs, in Hebrew and English, pointing the way to a new Chabad House. Following the signs, I discovered that the house—where there were no security guards—had been opened just weeks before by an emissary couple. Like their counterparts in Cusco, they were *ba'alei teshuvah*—young Jews who had become religious (the Hebrew term translates as "masters of repentance" or "those who have returned"). The man was absorbed in his prayers when we arrived, so we were greeted by his wife, a very young woman with a baby in her arms. I asked her if she did not fear for her life, given the recent events in Mumbai. In reply, she pointed, with a smile, to the large picture of Rabbi Menachem Mendel Schneerson, Chabad's late spiritual leader (*admor*),[1] whose followers, and many beyond them, know him simply as "the Rebbe," as I will refer to him in this book. "He protects us," she said with conviction. "You see, even she [the baby] knows who he is." Indeed, the baby seemed fascinated by the Rebbe's face.

Many Israelis and Jews have had similar encounters in recent years, in Israel and throughout the world. Who hasn't run into the cheerful Chabad emissaries who stand in airports and at busy city intersections, urging passersby to put on *tefillin*, the phylacteries that religious Jews wear on their arm and head during morning prayers? What Israeli backpacker has not gone to a Chabad house in some remote part of the world to enjoy a kosher meal, the company of fellow Hebrew-speakers, and to get important information about his surroundings? Who has not seen the omnipresent photograph of the Rebbe gazing at him or her from billboards or leaflets? No other Haredi (ultra-Orthodox) group has such a public presence; no other sect's adherents and leader are so ubiquitous. Chabad turned outward, toward the Jewish people as a whole, even before Rabbi Menachem Mendel became its leader. But its revolutionary project of sending emissaries throughout the world was his initiative. Its purpose is to return Jews to their roots and to better the ways of non-Jews, so as to achieve the most noble and demanding goal that any religious system can place before its believers—to bring the Messiah and the dawn of the final redemption.

The first of my three encounters with Chabad emissaries, on the banks of the Suez Canal, took place when the Rebbe was still alive and at the height of his strength. The two other meetings occurred during the second decade following his passing on June 12, 1994 (3 Tammuz 5754 on the Jewish calendar), without leaving an heir and successor. Despite the painful shock caused by "the Event of Gimel Tammuz" (gimel, the third letter of the Hebrew alphabet, represents the number three), the Rebbe seems to have lost none of his capacity for infusing his followers with messianic fervor and motivating them to spread Chabad's teachings and message of redemption. On the contrary, his potency may be even greater than it was in his lifetime. The central puzzle this book seeks to solve is the fact that Chabad has thrived in the post-Gimel Tammuz period. My most fundamental question is: What makes this Hasidic movement so vital and popular precisely when it is leaderless? After all, a leaderless Hasid is almost an oxymoron. One central tenet of that religious movement is that the *tzadik*, the righteous leader, mediates between his flock and heaven. True, there is a debate within Chabad regarding the ontological status of the Rebbe—did he go the way of all flesh, or is he alive but hidden from human eyes? The latter view is held by the more radical Hasidim who are at the center of my study; but either way, for members of all factions of the movement, the vacuum the Rebbe left behind him is unbearable. How can a connection between the *tzadik* and his disciples be maintained? How can the Hasidic body function without a head, especially when the head in question was such a charismatic and revered leader whose activity stretched around the world, who was considered by his followers to be not just their leader but the "president of the generation," the "head of the Jewish people" (the Hebrew words for the latter phrase form the acronym "Rebbe"), a wonderworking saint, a farsighted prophet and, ultimately, the King Messiah himself?[2]

In seeking to account for these puzzlements, I was first seized by an acute sense of urgency, a fear that Chabad's messianic surge—a relatively rare moment in Jewish history—would soon dissipate. Thus far, as the book you are about to read documents, this has not been the case.

While I alone remain responsible for the contents of this volume, I am deeply grateful to many who helped me along the way. Insights from the article I coauthored with Michal Kravel-Tovi on the construction of messianic temporality in Chabad, based on her master's thesis, found their way into this book. A book chapter I coauthored with Zvi Mark, which compared the Hasidic sects of Chabad and Bratslav, gave rise to Chapter 13 in this book. Aside from allowing me to make use of our joint texts in my work, Kravel-Tovi and Mark helped me with fruitful comments. I also profited from two other master's theses on messianic Chabad by Sagiv Elbaz and Shlomo Reinitz. Elbaz also served as my research assistant, and his high work ethic combined with intimate knowledge of Chabad proved invaluable to the project. The late Rabbi Yehoshua Mondshine, a historian of Chabad and a Chabad Hasid himself, generously gave me access to his private collection of documents associated with the messianic ferment in the movement. The text was enriched by discussions and exchanges with Henry Abramovitch, Benjamin Beit-Hallahmi, Kimmy Caplan, Alon Dahan, Rachel Elior, Immanuel Etkes, Menachem Friedman, Jonathan Garb, Galit Hazan Rokem, Samuel Heilman, Boaz Huss, Moshe Idel, Haviva Pedaya, Tomer Persico, Ada Rapoport Albert, Ariel Rot, and Gadi Sagiv.

I would also like to thank the Eshkol Institute at the Faculty of the Social Sciences at the Hebrew University of Jerusalem for funding my research and the Open University Press for publishing the Hebrew version of this book and for granting it the Goldberg Prize.

I am deeply indebted to Tanya Luhrmann and Ann Taves, the editors of the Spiritual Phenomena Series at Stanford University Press, for their encouragement and comments. The constructive comments of Shaul Kellner and a second, anonymous reviewer helped me to improve the manuscript in various ways. Emily-Jane Cohen, SUP executive editor, lavished me with thoughtful suggestions that contributed significantly to the book's outline and coherence. After she had left SUP, Faith Wilson Stein, Kate Wahl, and Gigi Mark accompanied me in the last phases of production with dedication and care.

In this volume I revisit some of the material I have published elsewhere and gratefully acknowledge the publishers for granting me permission to use this material. These publications appeared as "To Make Many More Menachem Mendels: Childlessness, Procreation, and Creation in Messianic Habad," *Contemporary Jewry* (2012) 32:2, pp. 111–134; "We Want to See Our King: Apparitions in Messianic Habad," *Ethos* (2013) 41:1, pp. 98–126; and "Between Tsaddiq and Messiah: A Comparative Analysis of Chabad and Breslav Hasidic Groups," in *After Spirituality: Studies in Mystical Traditions* (2012), Jonathan Garb and Phillip Wexler, eds. (New York: Peter Lang), pp. 47–78 (coauthored with Zvi Mark).

WITH US MORE THAN EVER

INTRODUCTION

Messianism Here and Now

The messianic fervor that has electrified the Hasidic movement of Chabad-Lubavitch in recent decades, and in particular the departure in the summer of 1994 of Rabbi Menachem Mendel Schneerson, Chabad's charismatic leader and the designated Messiah in the eyes of his followers, offers a rare opportunity to study the way the religious imagination is fueled in transitional states. In such historical moments the religious horizon shatters but can also expand. When routines are shaken and the conventions of normative religious behavior crack, new or revived beliefs, practices, and patterns of experience can gain entry. These practices are meant to reestablish an adequate system of meaning for believers and to provide them with an updated agenda. We still lack the necessary historical perspective to evaluate the results and consequences of Chabad's messianic ferment, but we can certainly point to its not insignificant similarities to constitutive events in the histories of other religions, in which crises born out of a seemingly spectacular messianic failure proved to be fertile ground for religious renewal. This is what happened to the early Christians after Jesus's crucifixion,[1] to Shi'ite Islam in the ninth and tenth centuries following the disappearance of the twelfth imam,[2] and to the devotees of the Jewish Messiah Shabbetai Zvi in the seventeenth century following his conversion to Islam, and then again after his death.[3] Such historical moments are characterized by energetic religious activity manifesting the presence of the departed messianic figure, so as to secure his privileged status. Chabad's messianic awakening offers a convenient platform for gaining understanding of key processes in the way religious thinking and experience are shaped.[4] Every religious belief system, after all, involves some sort of attempt to imbue metaphysical entities with concreteness and vitality—in other words, to transform them into a presence in the world of the believer.[5] Denial of the Rebbe's death, a central tenet of the radical messianic circles in Chabad, can also be seen as a radicalization of fundamental and common religious claims about the endurance and eternity of the soul and life after death.

Beyond the broad religious issues it illustrates, Chabad messianism also needs to be considered in terms of the implications that the idea of redemption has for contemporary Judaism, in Israel and outside it.[6] The uniqueness of messianic figures lies in the vision of redemption that they embody and preach, but such a vision does not necessarily require a personal messiah. Utopian and apocalyptic ideas of a secular cast, lacking a specific messianic figure, have been a feature of the modern world. The role played by such ideas in the great ideological movements of the twentieth century, such as communism and fascism, is common knowledge. Utopian values and the concept of redemption have been part of Zionism as well, and the establishment of the state of Israel was perceived by many Zionists, not just religious ones, in such terms.[7] Religious Zionists view the establishment of the state in 1948, and later its decisive victory in the Six Day War in 1967, as the "first manifestation of the approach of our redemption."[8] But the messianic scenario accepted in such circles, even as embodied in the most potent language used by the Gush Emunim settler movement at its height, never publicly and explicitly said that a particular person was the Messiah. Yet that is exactly what Chabad has done. Chabad reverts to the classical concept of the messianic era, with its two essential elements. First, it centers on a personal Messiah, descended from King David, and claims to know who that Messiah is—the Rebbe himself. Second, it imbues in its believers an intoxicating conviction that they live on the verge of redemption. It is a concept that has not been current in Judaism for more than three hundred years, since the messianic tide set in motion by Shabbetai Zvi.[9] It would be difficult to exaggerate the

FIGURE 1. Poster of the Rebbe on a shop door. The note reads: "I will soon return." Courtesy of the Association for the True and Complete Redemption.

significance of this phenomenon, even if we cannot yet take a long historical view of it.

It is hard to think of a more stirring and noble religious ideal than that realized by the coming of the Messiah. In Jewish history, with its string of calamities, the belief in the coming of the Messiah is an inseparable part of religious life, one that offers comfort and hope. Yet that same belief is tied up with apocalyptic prophecies that "have always contained interwoven elements of terror and comfort."[10] The shift from the historical present to the messianic future involves a cosmic upheaval of a catastrophic nature, known in Jewish lore as *chevlei mashiach*, the birth-pangs of the Messiah. It is no wonder therefore that the Jewish religious establishment takes an ambivalent view of acute messianic visions. Jewish society has paid a heavy price following the appearance of messianic figures in its midst, beginning with Jesus and Bar Kokhba in ancient times and ending with Shabbetai Zvi and Jacob Frank in the early modern age. These failures did not cause the mainstream to reject the messianic idea, but they intensified suspicion of flesh-and-blood messiahs. Jews continued to believe with perfect faith, as Maimonides admonished them to, in the last of his Thirteen Principles of Faith, in the coming of the Messiah, even, and perhaps especially, in times of crisis and catastrophe. But Judaism's messianism remained beyond the horizon of actual life, set in some undefined future. Given that, in an unredeemed world, past messiahs are by definition false messiahs, the messianic scenario generally refrains from putting the idea to a critical test by pointing to a specific messianic figure or setting a proximate date for redemption.[11] Chabad's message of redemption, which identifies the Rebbe as the Messiah and claims that the ultimate redemption is impending, has created a heated and active messianism that defies the rabbinic establishment's caution and ambivalence. The Rebbe's boldness in fostering the messianic idea and disseminating tidings of redemption is worthy of special note given these attitudes of apprehension and reserve, the products of a manifestly passive messianic ideology. On the one hand, this displayed resolute faith and theological courage—unlike most other rabbis, the Rebbe was not afraid to grapple with the charged messianic idea and to try to realize it here and now (even if he avoided explicitly declaring that he himself was the Messiah). On the other hand, it testifies to his authority and charisma as a religious figure. The Rebbe was able to enthuse his followers and mobilize them for his messianic project with hardly any remonstration from any central figure in the Jewish public.[12] The nearly negligible opposition to his initiative seems to be due, in part, to the difficulty of coming out firmly against an admired leader who, with his disciples, was seeking to achieve a central principle of faith while strictly observing Jewish law. Beyond that, however, it has been difficult to stand against the power and influence Chabad wields in Israel and the world. Here, too, lies the phenomenon's importance.[13] This contemporary messianic ferment has not occurred on the margins of Jewish society but within a large and influential Hasidic movement that has a considerable public presence.

Twenty-five years have passed since Chabad's new era began, and the future is foggy. That fog puts me in an inferior position in comparison with historians who study outbreaks of messianism from the past, examining how they played out and what effects they had, from beginning to end. I deal with the here and now. But the messianic tempest taking place before my eyes offers me a rare opportunity to document systematically and in real time a rich skein of processes and events connected to the phenomenon, and to do so in a prospective rather than retrospective way. Using this method, my aim is to analyze the ways in which Chabad Hasidim try to make the absent rabbi present in their lives. Their ways of doing so are many and varied, and together form a behavioral environment that I call a messianic ecology, in which the Rebbe is an active participant. The Rebbe vanished in the summer of 1994—even his most extreme adherents have to acknowledge that. But all his Hasidim continue to see him as their leader, and would never think of proposing that an heir or successor should take his place. That being the case, the movement's endurance depends in large measure on his disciples' capacity for maintaining the sense that he continues to live among them, attentive to their requests and acting for their sake. In this book I want to show how that capacity is realized—how the Hasidim maintain ties with the Rebbe, the presence of whom they experience with their senses, and how they "live the Rebbe" and with the Rebbe. My focus, then, is not the classic Chabad movement and its theosophy, nor the messianic teachings of the last Rebbe,[14] but rather the means that his followers developed in the past generation to make the Rebbe manifest in their world. This is a system of practices that has developed in connection with an absent-present leader and has come into regular use by his Hasidim, many of whom never knew him in his lifetime. While the phenomenology that this system of practices engenders is my primary concern, I also seek to show how the multiform experiences of the Rebbe's presence constitute Chabad messianic cosmology.

In redirecting my spotlight from Chabad's teachings and theosophy to its ways of making the Rebbe present, this book joins a cluster of recent works which share a conceptual framework that has come to be called, in the study of religion, "the media turn."[15] These works center on the means of mediating the gap that religious thinking presumes between the real world of the senses and the unseen world that lies beyond it. The claim that the material means that serve this mediating purpose actually constitute religious experience challenges the traditional distinction between religion and the media. It also challenges the presumed superiority, in classic scholarly approaches (influenced by Protestant tradition) of spirit to matter, theology to technology, faith to practice, inner experience to external ritual, and sacred text to ritual object. With the media turn, means of mediation are no longer seen as secondary to the ostensibly primal transcendental experience of the encounter with the divine. Quite simply, such an encounter cannot take place without them.[16]

The emergence of this new paradigm at this time has to do with the connection between, on the one hand, the growing strength of religion and its prominence in the public sphere, and on the other, the appearance of new audiovisual and digital media technologies.[17] But the claim that religion and the media constitute each other relates to mediating mechanisms in their broadest sense. They are not just the sophisticated mass communications media of recent years, but anything that bridges over gaps. Media in this broader sense includes, for example, the body of the shaman-medium in tribal societies, the stones on the high priest's breastplate in ancient Judaism, the icons and relics of Catholicism and Orthodox Christianity, and the sacred text in the book-based faiths. Contemporary society is replete, even flooded, with different types of media, which has led scholars to address not only mediation processes themselves, but also the mediatization processes through which a religion, like other social institutions, assumes new guises under the influence of new media channels, reformulating itself in their terms.[18]

One important source of inspiration for this line of research is Jacques

Derrida's assertion that the links between religion and media need to be examined in an open way, without distinguishing ontologically between religion as a transcendental realm and the media as a purely technological one.[19] Derrida's claim that mediation creates presence is also the starting point for the present work, which maps out the means of manifestation aimed at making the vanished Rebbe into a concrete presence. The conceptual system of researchers working in this new paradigm is derived in part, explicitly or implicitly, from the theoretical framework proposed by Jay David Bolter and Richard Grusin for understanding the ways in which the new media work.[20] Their opening argument has two components. First, they claim, the real world is always mediated—that is, it is dependent on media in the broadest sense. Second, it is structured and continually restructured on the basis of previous mediations, with new forms of media engaging in dialogue and basing themselves on previous forms. Bolter and Grusin's key concept is therefore not mediation but rather remediation.[21]

Remediations characteristically seek to obviate media technologies while at the same time highlighting them. Bolter and Grusin call the first aspect "transparent immediacy." Communications technologies tend to be expunged from the representations they produce such that the representations seem to offer direct, immediate, and unmediated access to the real world. The medium becomes transparent in a process that creates a sense of authenticity and presence. The sense of involvement and realism produced when watching a realistic feature film, which erases the fact that this "reality" is actually being projected onto a two-dimensional screen, is an example of the effect of a transparent medium. Likewise, in the religious context, a sacred text becomes the word of the living god, an authentic and authoritative religious experience that conceals the material mediating object, the printed book. This sense of authentic media contributes to the empowerment of religious mediating practices in general, and in particular to those used in Chabad. The Rebbe's presence is manifested when the medium that provides communication with him itself melts away. This happens, for example, when Hasidim sense that a letter the Rebbe wrote in his lifetime is addressed to them directly even though they have taken it from a printed collection of letters that were sent to other petitioners in the distant past. It also happens when they feel that the Rebbe's gaze is directed at them and meant to guide them even though the gaze comes from a photograph taken many years before and reproduced endless times since.

The opposite of transparency is hypermediacy. In this experience, the user is exposed to a varied set of channels of information, to many forms of representation, such that the medium itself does not vanish but is instead highlighted. Examples of hypermediacy are collage or photomontage in the plastic arts, hypertext such as the Talmud, and Microsoft Windows. This is the ostentatious aspect of the media in which technology becomes real and a second nature.[22] The connection between this postmodern logic and Chabad's means of making the Rebbe present is less clear,[23] but it corresponds to the multiplicity and even redundancy of the means of mediation to which believers in a messianic environment are exposed simultaneously, to the dialectical nature of Chabad mysticism, and perhaps also to the Rebbe's own interest in sanctifying technology in general, and the mass media in particular.

In the mediation model there is tension between the mediated and the immediate as the central characteristic of religious systems, with an awareness of the paradox inherent in this dynamic. The believer's experience in encountering the transcendental is hugely powerful because of the sense of authenticity, directness, and immediate presence, but these feelings can be created only by indirect representational means mediated by the media. Given this tension, there is no way of being certain that new communications media and information will in fact appeal to believers. Studies based on the mediation paradigm grant much weight to struggles between users of new and old media in the conceptualization of religious change, conflict, and revolutions. Different types of media shape the religious subject in distinct ways, in part because they affect different sensory pathways.[24] In this spirit it would not be out of line to argue that the many uses that Chabad makes of photographs of the Rebbe and videos in which he appears, based on an entire system of visual culture, affect the shaping of the religious experience of Chabad Hasidim today.

The media turn in the study of religion has taken place in part as a counterresponse to simplistic theories of modernism, progress, and secularization which predicted that religion's hold on the subjects who live in modern nation-states would loosen and contract into the private sphere alone.[25] Works of this type stress that new media technologies contribute to strengthening the influence of religions in the public space and augment the dissemination of their messages beyond local communities, often leading them to adopt a global orientation. The new media-mediated face of religion can be seen, for example, in the blurring of the religious-secular distinction. The blurring can be seen in the use of information technologies and advanced communications technologies for religious purposes, as well as in aspects of commercialization, consumerism, and entertainment that become integrated into and even enhance religious experience. These new technologies make it possible to create imagined communities and new religious identities, but the turn to the public space is also liable to undermine the sense of community and to threaten the religious establishment's control over believers.

Chabad is an excellent example of religion's new face. Its public activity and prominence in Israel and the world are unprecedented; its orientation is transnational and even global. Its regular use of communications media and visual and digital information contains within it aspects of commercialism, with an eye toward popular culture. Chabad has adapted well to the modern post-secular world and thrives there, but it is not immune to the dangers that this world holds for religious authority and community cohesion.

Having offered the study's theoretical framework, I now turn to its research population. All Chabad Hasidim maintain a connection with the vanished Rebbe, but his presence is especially prominent among that group of Hasidim who are called the Meshichists (Messianists, from the Hebrew word for Messiah, *mashiach*). The common trait of all these Hasidim is not their adherence to the belief that the vanished Rebbe is worthy of being considered the Messiah even today, but rather their position on his ontological status. Chabad can be roughly divided into two major groups. The first is the movement's central current, consisting of Hasidim who are prominent in large Chabad communities, first and foremost in its home base in Crown Heights, Brooklyn and in Kfar Chabad in Israel, but also in major American and European cities. Many of these people were born into the movement to established Hasidic families. Most Chabad emissaries belong to this group. The members of this central group have accommodated themselves to the fact that the Rebbe died on Gimel Tammuz 1994. Most of them retain, however, the hope that he will return from the dead to lead his people into redemption. The second group, the Meshichists, are prominent in Israel, especially among young new adherents to the movement and *ba'alei teshuvah*. It includes many Mizrachim—Jews whose ancestry lies in the Islamic world, far removed from the East European orbit where Hasidism emerged. The Meshichists deny that the Rebbe ever died; instead, they maintain, he is "alive and well in body and spirit, in the full sense."[26] It is only the limits of the flesh that prevent people from seeing him now. In their view, he continues to live in his home, called Beit Hayenu (The House of Our Lives), at Chabad's international headquarters at 770 Eastern Parkway in Crown Heights, which believers refer to simply as "770." The Meshichists uphold the belief that the Rebbe will reveal himself "soon and *mamash* immediately" to lead the Jewish people on the path to redemption. Note that *mamash*, "in fact" or "really" in Hebrew, is read by believers as an acronym for *Mashiach Menachem shmo*, meaning "Menachem is the name of the Messiah," or as the initials of the Rebbe's name, Menachem Mendel Schneerson.

This study focuses on the messianists, who are ostensibly on the margins of the movement, although they see themselves as the vanguard of redemption. But the boundaries between the Meshichists and other Chabad Hasidim are not as sharp as one might expect, and the view that there are two distinct and conflicting camps is oversimplified, even if it is based on Chabad's internal discourse. It is true that the two groups have found themselves at odds many times, especially during the early years after the Rebbe's departure. The adherents of each side vilified and stridently condemned their opponents, and at times even attacked each other physically or sued each other in secular courts. But the truth is that the differences within each of the groups are almost as great as the differences between them. Among the moderate Hasidim there is a broad spectrum of positions regarding the Meshichists, ranging from ambivalent acceptance or disregard to active opposition and even accusations that the Meshichists are mentally ill. The Meshichists are divided into a large number of sects, some of them ephemeral. They lack a common agenda or uniform ideology. The most radical of them—those who explicitly attribute divine status to the Rebbe or consider the possibility of annulling halakhic strictures and prohibitions on the ground that the era of redemption has already begun—are a small minority. Most of the activists I interviewed refrain from visiting the Ohel, the shrine marking the Rebbe's grave in the Old Montefiore Cemetery in Queens. Instead, they go to 770, where, they claim, the Rebbe continues to live as in the past. But I also met Meshichists who visit both sites and explain the apparent contradiction in the spirit of Chabad's dialectical mysticism.[27]

In the last twenty-five years, Meshichist communities have been founded within larger Chabad communities, where they maintain separate synagogues and educational institutions and print their own publications. The men in these communities wear distinctive dress, including a *kipah* with an inscription that declares the Rebbe to be the Messiah, and a lapel pin displaying a yellow flag emblazoned with the crown of the King Messiah. Nevertheless, many Meshichists continue to be part of the larger fabric of life in the Chabad movement and its operations, in which they work and study with non-Meshichists. In any case, since the distinction between Meshichists and non-Meshichists is part of Chabad's internal discourse, and because my research interest led me to the more hard-core and distinctive Meshichists, I will also apply this distinction despite its oversimplification.

Between the Researcher and His Subjects

I spent more than a decade researching the Meshichists, beginning in 2003. My means were textual analysis of Meshichist literature, interviews with activists, and participant observations at the movement's central events. Chabad has produced a wide range of messianic literature in recent decades, in a quantity estimated to be double that of everything previously written on Jewish messianism.[28] Faced with this plethora of texts, I chose to focus on periodicals, among them popular weeklies and monthlies aimed at a broad readership. My reason for choosing them is that, unlike books and one-off pamphlets and other texts, periodicals offer the possibility of systematically examining, over a period of months and even years, the way in which the Meshichist imagination works and the changes it undergoes. Since most of these publications began to appear immediately after "the Event of Gimel Tammuz" (as the Meshichists designate the date of the Rebbe's departure) and as a direct consequence of it, they display the ways in which the Meshichists responded to the painful vacuum left by the Rebbe's disappearance, and how they cultivated the means of communication through which he is made present in the world of his believers.

The most prominent of these periodicals, *Sichat Hage'ulah*, which labels itself as "The Weekly Sheet for the Days of the Messiah," follows the format of a weekly Torah-portion pamphlet, one of the myriad examples of this genre that has blossomed in Israel in recent decades. *Sichat Hage'ulah*, along with the weekly *Beis Moshiach* (House of the Messiah), are the most widely read organs of Chabad's Meshichists. At the beginning of the 2000s at least thirty thousand copies of *Sichat Hage'ulah* were distributed in Israel.[29] It first appeared on July 8, 1994, less than a month after the Event of Gimel Tammuz. It evinced a fierce expectation that he "who had been revealed to [the people of] Israel and the entire world and announced the tidings of redemption and then once again was concealed—will now return and be revealed to them, Israel, and redeem them."[30] By the end of August 2018, a full 1,210 issues had come out in a slickly designed and professionally produced four-page format. The leaflet is divided into different sections, most of which address the Messiah and the redemption. The section titled *Nifla'ot Achshav* (Wonders Now), which offers detailed testimonies of miracles performed by the Rebbe, in the language of witnesses who are identified by name and sometimes with a photograph, provided me with a particularly fertile inventory of the means commonly used to make the Rebbe's presence felt. The sheet also appears online, on the website of the Association for the True and Complete Redemption, haGeula.com, headquartered in the city of Bat Yam just south of Tel Aviv. The sheet's editor, until his death in 2018, was the association's chairman, Rabbi Zimroni Tzik.

Rabbi Tzik grew up in a religious-Zionist home and attended a

FIGURE 2. *Sichat Hage'ulah* (Discourse on Redemption): The Weekly Bulletin for the Days of the Messiah. Courtesy of the Association for the True and Complete Redemption.

yeshiva boarding high school associated with the national-religious youth movement, Bnei Akiva, where he later served as a spiritual counselor. He grew close to Chabad during his military service. Tzik was privileged to have several private audiences with the Rebbe. At the first of these, in 1971, he addressed the Rebbe as the designated Messiah, and he claims that the Rebbe did not deny this. With the Rebbe's blessing, Tzik established the first Chabad House in Israel, in Bat Yam, and made it into a vibrant center for disseminating the gospel of the redemption. Since the Event of Gimel Tammuz he has maneuvered himself into being a leading figure in the Meshichist camp, and has not been afraid to confront mainstream Chabad rabbis. Convinced that we are in the first stage of the era of redemption, actively led by the Rebbe despite his concealment, Tzik and the association vigorously—with *shturem*, as the Hasidim say in

FIGURE 3. *Beis Moshiach* (House of the Messiah) magazine. Courtesy of Avraham Rainitz.

Yiddish—campaign to spread the doctrine, not just with the weekly sheet but also at conclaves, conferences, and fairs around Israel.

Another publication I used is the weekly *Beis Moshiach*, published by the Chabad World Center for Welcoming the Messiah, headquartered in Crown Heights in Brooklyn; a subsidiary editorial office operates in Kfar Chabad in Israel. It began to appear in 1994, in response to the moderation of the messianic line in Chabad's official publication in Israel, *Kfar Chabad*, following the Rebbe's disappearance, and became the most important voice of the Meshichist camp. Unlike *Sichat Hage'ulah*, which is restricted in scope and focuses on the Messiah and the redemption,

Beis Moshiach is broad and varied in its content. Alongside articles on the Rebbe and the redemption, it also publishes pieces in Hebrew and English on the movement's history and the lives and teachings of former Chabad leaders. With its large stable of writers, who represent a spectrum of views, *Beis Moshiach* is somewhat more moderate than *Sichat Hage'ulah*, even though both are Meshichist and overlap in many ways. *Beis Moshiach* also appears online, on the Chabad.info website.

In addition to these two publications, I also examined other Meshichist publications that disseminate the gospel to the public, among them *Baruch Haba Melech Hamashiach* (Welcome, King Messiah), *Ezrachim Bimedinat Hamashiach* (Citizens in the Messiah's Country), *Or Hamashiach* (Light of the Messiah), *Hage'ulah* (The Redemption), *Peninei Hage'ulah* (Pearls of the Redemption), *Dvar Melech* (The Word of the King), and *Acharit Hayamim* (The End of Days). This is hardly an exhaustive list of the large number of periodicals that have been put out by Meshichists over the last twenty years.

Interviews and conversations with Hasidim from the Meshichist camp, along with participant observations at the camp's central events, have enriched the material I drew from texts. Over my years of research, I had many conversations with Meshichists, activists, and ordinary Chabad Hasidim in Jerusalem, Kfar Chabad, Bat Yam, Bnei Brak, Kiryat Malachi, Safed, Beitar Illit (all in Israel), and in Crown Heights in Brooklyn. I conducted comprehensive interviews with twenty Meshichists, and I participated in Hasidic gatherings held on days of special significance in Chabad, Messiah and Redemption Rallies held by the Association for the True and Complete Redemption, weddings of Meshichists, and activities at a Meshichist summer camp.

I made contact with the first Meshichists I interviewed through information about them published in *Sichat Hage'ulah*; they in turn referred me to additional interviewees. I had many apprehensions about the move from studying Meshichist publications to conversations with Hasidim. While I had no trouble accessing Meshichist publications, I was not at all certain that activists would want to speak with a nonreligious researcher pursuing a skeptical examination of the project that was the essence of their lives. I was happy to find that my fears were groundless.

At the beginning of each interview I made a point of mentioning that my conceptual system for examining the messianic turbulence in Chabad originates in the social sciences and not Hasidic teachings, but that, as an anthropologist, I seek to understand the point of view of the Hasidim and to portray it in a nonjudgmental way. This statement of purpose generally satisfied my interviewees. They cooperated with me and were not put off by the difficult and challenging questions I sometimes posed as I sought to test the limits of their faith.

In retrospect, the Hasidim's positive response should not be surprising. Chabad Hasidim are united by a sense of mission that induces them to connect with and engage in dialogue with Jews who are entirely outside Hasidic circles. In the view of the Meshichists, who devote all their efforts to disseminating the ideas of the Messiah and the redemption, the interest of a university professor furthers their cause. Since the Rebbe, the King Messiah, steers the world, everything happening in this world testifies to his existence. This includes my research project which, some of my interviewees surmised, was in fact instigated by the Rebbe as a way of spreading the news of the redemption. The Hasidim have grown ever more confident, thanks to the Rebbe's achievements during his lifetime and as a result of the movement's robust health since his departure. The Hasidim's sense of mission and election makes it easier for them to speak with academic researchers without feeling any sense of inferiority. Their capacity for accepting sometimes critical academic findings and even to adapt that work for their own purposes stems from the fact that Chabad teaching as a whole, and the messianic faith in particular, equip them with a comprehensive system of meaning. All Chabad Hasidim believe that the divine presence can be found in every aspect of concrete experience, including academic research. Furthermore, the Meshichists are convinced that the world, under the leadership of the Rebbe, the King Messiah, stands on the threshold of redemption; academic research and its achievements are simply taken as further evidence of this.

The Meshichists are indeed attentive to research about them, and have no hesitation about publicizing it, while using it for their own needs. This tendency is especially notable when it comes to those subjects on which scholars agree with the Hasidim—for example, the question of whether the Rebbe believed himself to be the Messiah. Meshichist publications quote extensively from the works of academic writers on Hasidism, declaring that "all academic figures who have studied and objectively researched the Rebbe's teachings on the subject [the Rebbe's messianic self-awareness] have reached a single conclusion about it [affirming his awareness of his messianic vocation]. And that must certainly constitute food for thought for us on the whole subject of explaining this matter to all strata of society."[31] When interviews with scholars are included in Meshichist publications, their personal connections to Chabad, their appeals to the Rebbe in times of trouble, and their esteem for him are stressed. In this way the Meshichists seek to enlist the academy's authority and prestige in extolling the Rebbe.

The extent to which the Meshichists are eager to use academic research for their own purposes can be seen in a collection of academic articles published by a Meshichist, *The Academy Welcomes the Messiah*.[32] The book is divided into two parts: "The Academy as Seen by Hasidism" and "Hasidism as Seen by the Academy." The two parts are symmetrical in a way that intimates a dialogue between them. But the cover copy leaves no doubt about who has the upper hand: "As time passes, the teaching and doctrine of the great leader [*nasi*] of this generation rings inside the walls of universities and scientific institutes, and even more importantly, science proves and itself concludes that the Rebbe is the King Messiah."

This summary disregards, of course, the epistemological gap between the Hasidim's faith that the Rebbe is the King Messiah and the claim by scholars that, at some point, the Rebbe began to see himself in this role. No less than six scholars with academic titles including myself—are represented in this anthology, either in the form of printed versions of lectures we have given, selections from articles we have published, or interviews we have given to the media.[33] When, in an interview, Yitzhak Kraus, an expert on contemporary Chabad, evaded answering a question on whether the Rebbe was indeed the Messiah, his interlocutor, a Chabad rabbi, hastened to conclude: "Kraus as an academic researcher . . . opened up a road, but did not finish it; he did not have the courage to follow it to its end. In his study, he did not point with his finger and say:

'This is Menachem, our righteous Messiah.'"[34] Just as Kraus uses scholarly paradigms to plumb Chabad Hasidism and the Rebbe's teachings, so the Hasidim parse and judge Kraus's work in accordance with the uncompromising standards of messianic faith.

As noted, I too am represented in the anthology, and am cited in other Meshichist publications as well. The connection thus created between me and the Hasidim during my work illustrates the way in which they relate to research about them and the uses they make of it. Following the interviews I conducted with members of the Association for the True and Complete Redemption, they invited me to speak at their Messiah and Redemption Conferences. I debated whether to acquiesce, fearing that negative responses to my lecture might put an end to my ties with the Hasidim. But my research has taught me that such encounters-confrontations between a researcher and his subjects can be fertile ground for gaining sharper knowledge of the views of the latter and new insights about them.[35] I was also encouraged by the hope that the self-confidence and openness to my research displayed by the Hasidim whom I met with would help them assimilate the findings I would present to them, even if they did not sit well with their beliefs. As it happened, my talks at two such conferences were well-received. I presume that this reception was partly due to the respectful and sometimes even admiring way in which I presented my material. But, while I made sure to use a conciliatory rather than polemical rhetorical style, I did not feel as if I were misrepresenting my true thinking. In these cases, and when I was asked to write an article on Chabad emissaries for a special supplement to the weekly *Beis Moshiach*, I gave voice to the very real admiration I had for the faith, courage, and determination of these emissaries.[36] In addition, despite the fact that I cast the findings of my research in skeptical terms, many of them were consistent with the beliefs of my research subjects. A claim that will run throughout this book is that, as a result of the actions taken by the Hasidim to make the Rebbe present in their lives, the absent leader became *more* accessible than he had been before he departed. That finding pleased the Hasidim. When I summed it up at the end of one of my talks by citing the ubiquitous Meshichist slogan, "[The Rebbe is] with us more than ever," my audience applauded loudly.

FIGURE 4. The author at a Messiah and Redemption Rally. Photographer: Sagiv Elbaz.

On top of this, the Hasidim had no trouble finding my academic articles and lectures, in which I did not write and speak with the restraint I exercised when speaking to them. And they demonstrated that they were able to accept my work even if it was not always to their liking. This capacity, too, derived from their self-confidence and their firm conviction that the redemption is inevitable. It is also attributable to the media expertise they have acquired as a part of their enterprise of spreading their ideas. In keeping with Marshall McLuhan's classic adage that "the medium is the message," they understand very well that scholarly interest in their activities itself amplifies their importance and that of their teachings. In any case, Meshichist publications present scholarly findings in a manner that fits in with and supports the Rebbe's doctrine of redemption.

At the first conference of the Association for the True and Complete Redemption at which I spoke, I turned to Rabbi Zimroni Tzik and noted, jokingly, that when he began spreading the news of the Messiah with his weekly *Sichat Hage'ulah* sheet, he probably had not imagined that he would be supplying academic researchers with valuable material that would enable them to track, in real time, the messianic idea and the practices it engendered. In retrospect, I can see that my words were colored with the condescension commonly employed by scholars, who believe that they have a monopoly over the manufacture of knowledge.[37] But this position is rather anachronistic in today's social research, and all the more so before an audience of the Meshichist activists who constituted my research subjects and were firm and confident of their ideas. In contrast with the underprivileged subjects that classic ethnographic work documented, the voice of Chabad rings loud and clear. It is a determined and self-assured voice, projecting moral authority deriving from the ultimate truth of the gospel of redemption and sense of religious duty to disseminate the news; and it is quite widespread thanks to Chabad's proficiency with a broad range of mass media platforms. Chabad's communications systems enable it to adapt research findings and to integrate them into Meshichist publications. In other words, they can write about and discuss the scholars and their findings no less than scholars can write about what is going on in Chabad.

In fact, when I explained to Rabbi Tzik and his Meshichist activists the extensive use to which I had put *Sichat Hage'ulah*, I had no idea that I would very soon thereafter find my name in issues of the pamphlet, where I was presented as living proof that the redemption is at hand.[38] In the second of these items, a photograph of me was included, captioned "The Messiah from an academic point of view." It opens by stating that:

> It would be difficult to estimate the physical and, especially, spiritual influence the Rebbe *shalita* [may he have a long and good life], the King Messiah has had on all members of this generation, including people from far-flung places.... A concrete example of this, reaching to "the lowest of the low," can be found in the words of Prof. Yoram Bilu, who has in recent years followed the Chabad movement from an academic point of view.... When he is asked, precisely as a person who considers himself to be looking in "from the outside" he opens with a description of the revolution initiated by the Rebbe ... through the emissaries around the world.

Having attended one of my academic talks, the author of this piece in

Sichat Hage'ulah concludes that it "demonstrates . . . the King Messiah's huge influence today on everyone, even in the eyes of a scholar who as yet does not observe the Torah and commandments. . . . His talk shows again that, following the work of our generation, the world is now prepared for the epiphany of the Rebbe *shalita* the King Messiah."[39]

When I read the praises lavished on my work by Meshichist writers—notwithstanding the inferior position they put me in ("the lowest of the low")—I felt as if they were coopting me into their community as a kind of court anthropologist, using me to promote their cause. I was especially impressed by the fact that the detailed account of my work was a fairly accurate portrayal of the way I myself present the goals of my research. It even used some of my phrases, such as "messianic fervor," "making the Rebbe present," and "channels of communication," not phrases that the Hasidim themselves ordinarily use. This may well indicate that these concepts are not remote from the believers' experience. Furthermore, the use of scholarly terms on Meshichist websites is consistent with their inclination not to hide or expurgate the scholarly language but rather to use it for their own purposes. Academic research, despite its skeptical positions and foreign terminology, is in the final analysis further evidence that the world is ready for the Rebbe's epiphany and the full redemption.

My dialogue with the Hasidim was protean. On June 13, 2014, issue 1,000 of *Sichat Hage'ulah* appeared. I was asked to contribute to the special issue, which appeared in an expanded and elegant format, and wrote a short article on the publication's great importance to scholars as a source for data and insights into the Meshichist movement. I did not see this piece as a violation of research ethics so long as my piece was published as I wrote it. The text I submitted was indeed printed in full. But there was a catch—every time I mentioned the Rebbe, the editors added the abbreviations *shalita mh"m* [may he have a long and good life, the King Messiah]. These two recurring acronyms turned me from an empathetic observer into a committed Meshichist. I was surprised and angry at the way I was coopted into the camp that denied the Rebbe's death—all the more so as a number of my acquaintances asked me whether I had changed my views and way of life. In retrospect, however, it was naïve of me to have expected that the editors could allow the

Rebbe to be mentioned in this central Meshichist publication without these titles that deny his death.

Some readers may see my involvement as crossing a red line and my attempt to defend my behavior as simple rationalization. I believe, however, that the difficulty the Hasidim have faced in assimilating my research—in which, for example, I compare apparitions of the Rebbe to his believers to those related by believers in Jesus or those who maintain that Elvis Presley never died[40]—is on the same level as my difficulty in accepting that I was turned into a Meshichist despite myself. I am not sure that this argument will satisfy all my readers, but perhaps it would be best to reserve judgment until completing the book. Then each reader can decide whether the goal I set myself at the beginning of this chapter—presenting the beliefs and practices of Meshichist Chabad Hasidim as they are currently in the process of formation—indeed justifies the means, which involved the charged interrelationships that I established with the Hasidim.

In order to bring my readers as close as possible to the experience of the Meshichists, I will offer, in the rest of this book, numerous examples of the discourse of the believers, deliberately suspending the skeptical gaze that challenges their initial assumptions. The suspension is of analytic importance—a precise mapping of the experiential world that constitutes the Meshichist ecology is absolutely necessary for understanding the processes and mechanisms that maintain it. But since the channels of making the Rebbe's presence felt are replete with miracles, a large portion of which I document by quoting directly from those who have had such experiences, it is important to stress that my research interest is not miracles themselves but *miracle stories*.[41]

An epistemological abyss yawns between the view of these events as miracles in an ontological sense and their narrative and rhetorical framing as miracles.[42] These two levels of investigation—the event as it happened, and the event as it was told—are mediated by an intermediate level—the event as it was experienced. Did the narrators really and truly experience as a miracle a complete cure of their disease or a sudden improvement in their economic fortunes? This intermediate level too is not directly accessible to the researcher. In principle, one could argue that the miracle stories are nothing more than a conventional literary genre that has nothing to do with the way the recounted events were subjectively experienced. But I am prepared to make the leap of faith between the miracle story and its experience as a miracle, on the basis of the assumption that these two levels are largely correlated. My cumulative impression from my interviews and encounters with those who have experienced miracles is that most of them are ordinary believers who sincerely believe, as the Hasidim put it in rabbinic Aramaic, that "*bedidi havah 'uvda*," it really happened to me.

Admittedly, the claim for subjective authenticity regarding the experiences of miracles is weakened by the fact that Meshichist publications provide many of the miraculous accounts. The published stories are presented as eyewitness testimonies rendered verbatim, but it would be naïve to assume that they remained unedited. This overreliance on textual sources significantly limits the license to discuss disappointments, ambiguities, doubts, and failures. What the publications amply display is the extent to which the messianic ecology is saturated with miracle stories, and how these stories are rhetorically rendered and disseminated. Partly due to this effective rendering and distribution, the dual notion that miracles do occur and that they originate from the Rebbe is shared by most of the Meshichists as a phenomenological constant in their life-world.

Nevertheless, setting aside the ontological status of the miracle as inaccessible to scholarship does not mean that I seek only to document the experiential world of the believers in this regard. The chapters that follow are replete with such documentation, presented nonjudgmentally and sometimes with real wonder. That, as I have already noted, has led some Meshichist activists to take my work as further evidence that the world is ready for redemption. But beyond my description of the operation of the means of making the Rebbe present from the point of view of the believers, I try, in places where the material makes that possible, to explain the ostensibly miraculous phenomena using concepts and tools that are not consistent with the metaphysical explanation offered by my subjects. Taking cognitive models such as dissonance and signal-detection theories as my point of departure, I seek to enrich, and problematize, them by attending to the mystical-messianic ecology that constitutes the experiential world of the Meshichists.

Finally, since this book does not address Chabad's position on social and political issues that are current in Israel, I want to remark on something that remains silenced in these pages. The focus on how the absent Rebbe's presence is made felt, which has been constitutive of Chabad messianism since the Event of Gimel Tammuz, means that I address a liminal time, a waiting period "between the ages."[43] This book does not address the past, neither the distant past of Chabad as a historical movement nor the recent period of the Rebbe's leadership. More importantly, it does not address the sublime future of the Messiah's arrival and the coming of the final redemption. This disregard for the messianic future, especially for the eschatological and political tinderbox that it bears within it, was useful for me in my encounters with Hasidim, but this future has menacing implications. Like many others who have encountered them all over the world, I was indeed charmed by Chabad's emissaries. I could hardly dislike most of the Meshichists I met during my research, fervent in their beliefs yet also attentive and kindly to others. Neither could I help admiring how they face up to the test of faith placed before them by the "hot" messianic scenario, in which the redemption is imminent, "immediately *mamash*." But I found their channeling of all their energies toward the eschatological idea, and their tendency to see the world solely through the messianic prism, to be discomfiting and sometimes even terrifying. Even without adducing the catastrophic consequences of messianic eruptions, as chronicled in the history of the Jews and other religions, I have a great deal of trouble with the extreme political positions that the Meshichists derive from their faith. This is particularly true with regard to the Israeli-Palestinian conflict, a subject that came up again and again in the Meshichist publications. Their arrogance and vitriolic intolerance toward the other in this conflict, which contrasted so sharply with their pleasant demeanors, are clearly fueled by their messianic faith.

Messianic visions are by nature universal. The glowing future that they promise is meant to apply to all of humanity. But the apocalypse leading up to the redemption is often washed by rivers of blood, the blood of heretics and sinners who do not accept the kingdom of heaven that is offered to them.[44] Such a violent scenario does not appear in Chabad discourse. Under the Rebbe's inspiration, the movement replaced the catastrophic messianism preached by the Rebbe's predecessor, Yosef Yitzchak

Schneerson, which viewed the Holocaust as the tribulation that precedes the Messiah's arrival, with a messianism of success. In this view, the world progresses toward the dismantling of the barriers of alienation and enmity that separate nations, toward the establishment of world peace in the spirit of the biblical prophets.[45] But it is impossible to ignore the dichotomy and tension between the universal elements of the messianic vision and the particularist nature of its Jewish version. This is especially troubling in the Meshichist discourse. On the one hand, Chabad also campaigns among non-Jews, urging them to observe the seven Noachide laws that, according to Jewish tradition, all humans must obey. In the spirit of this inclusive messianism, Salim Jabar, mayor of the Israeli Arab municipality of Abu Ghosh, opened a massive Meshichist assembly by shouting its slogan, "May our Lord, Teacher and Rabbi the King Messiah live forever and ever," in Arabic. In the same spirit, Arabic-language billboards in the West Bank call on the Palestinians to observe these seven laws. On the other hand, the Chabad messianic vision stresses the Jewish people's chosen status—they will be at the top of the new world order. In this view, Jewish superiority is an "ontological constant" along the historical and metahistorical path that leads inexorably to the redemption, and other nations cannot deny it. The Palestinian people, in this view, is meant by its very nature to obey the chosen people. If it deviates from the progress of history, it must be forced with an iron hand to obey it, by whatever means are necessary. The Meshichists invoke the story, from Chapter 34 of Genesis, in which Jacob's sons Simeon and Levi take bloody revenge on the city of Shekhem (today's Palestinian Nablus) because the son of its chieftain raped their sister Dinah. "Our neighbors will be forced into line before the redemption," the editor of *Sichat Hage'ulah* declared. The blood of the Christian Apocalypse is liable to flow in the Jewish one as well.

But, as I have stressed, the present book does not deal with this unfinished business. In my conversations with the Hasidim I managed to sidestep eschatological-political debates. But it is important to me to mention that hole in my story, one that requires a study of its own.

PART 1

CHABAD'S MESSIANISM

CHAPTER I

CHABAD AND THE MESSIANIC IDEA

The messianic fervor that sustains Chabad's sense of election and vocation is founded on a highly honed historical consciousness. It is a product of the sect's origins in the early years of Hasidism, when it developed a distinct theosophy and identity. The process began in the Belorussian towns of Liozna and Liadi, and continued thereafter in Lyubavichi, the town that gave the group its alternative name, Lubavitcher Hasidism. Any contemporary discussion of Chabad must take its history, and especially its messianic doctrines, into account. Nevertheless, it is best not to oversimplify by "drawing an unambiguous linkage of ideas between the Chabad of then and the Chabad of now."[1]

Hasidism emerged in part as a reaction to the messianic crisis that erupted in the Jewish orbit in the seventeenth century after the conversion to Islam of Shabbetai Zvi, the proclaimed Messiah (see Chapter 12). Scholars debate the extent to which a messianic consciousness pervaded the early leaders of the Hasidic movement.[2] Without delving into that debate, it is clear that most scholars agree that nationalist messianism did not lie at the center of the Hasidic world.[3] The exalted position of the *tzadik* (holy man), who mediates between heaven and earth by bringing down God's bounty to his community and sees to the material and spiritual needs of his disciples, led to his being identified with Yesod (foundation), the ninth of the ten *sefirot*. These emanations of the Godhead signify the forces or qualities through which God creates and maintains the world. Such a divine standing could ostensibly have turned the *tzadik*, in times of crisis, into a natural candidate for the role of the Messiah.[4] But among the second and third generations of Hasidic leaders the role of *tzadik* became institutionalized. The *tzadik* whose standing grew out of his personal charisma was replaced by one who received the position as a matter of dynastic succession; he no longer potentially marked the end of history and thus could no longer easily be thought of as a possible Messiah.[5] This nonmessianic model also characterized Chabad, which was led from its founding at the end of the eighteenth century through the twentieth century by seven *admorim* (sing. *admor*, acronym for "our master, teacher, and rabbi") or, as Chabad terms them, *nesi'im* (sing. *nasi*, "president"), all of them members of the Schneerson dynasty.

Chabad was founded by Rabbi Schneur Zalman of Liadi (1745–1812), whom Chabad Hasidim refer to in Yiddish as the "Alter Rebbe" (the "Elder Rebbe") and by the acronym of his name, RaShaZ. A member of the third generation of Hasidic leaders, he was the youngest student of Rebbe Dov Ber, the Maggid of Mezeritch, himself a disciple of the founder of Hasidism, Rabbi Israel Ba'al Shem Tov. His charisma soon became legendary, and Hasidim began to gather around him, attracted by his immense learning, spiritual inspiration, and organizational acumen.[6] He categorically opposed the popular view of the *tzadik* as a miracle worker, maintaining that such a figure's principal tasks were education and spiritual guidance. His intellectual proclivities were evidenced by the name he gave his method—Chabad, an acronym for the highest of the *sefirot* in the divine world according to Chabad teaching: Hochmah (wisdom), Binah (understanding), and Da'at (knowledge). Under his leadership, Chabad grew into the largest and most tightly organized Hasidic movement in Eastern Europe. The Chabad court was a very orderly one, with rules and customs that clearly defined the relationship between the *tzadik* and his Hasidim. There was also a system of emissaries and local leaders, constituting a hierarchy that enabled the *admor* to keep tabs on distant communities. Rabbi Schneur Zalman fashioned a unique spiritual-religious ethos that included substantial exposure to Kabbalah, in an effort to cleave to God—a psychic and spiritual state called *devekut*—through meditative-contemplative prayer and religious study. Rabbi Schneur Zalman's major work, *Sefer Hatanya*, which offers detailed instructions on how to serve God, was accorded canonical status by his followers.[7]

The common wisdom among earlier scholars who studied Chabad was that the radical nature of the movement's theoretical-mystical teachings meant that it had less messianic tension than other Hasidic sects.[8] An account of Chabad's mystical theosophy lies beyond the scope of this book, but many who have written about it have emphasized its a-cosmic nature. Chabad doctrine denies ontological status to matter and the universe; on its face, it views the sensible world as an illusion.[9] According to its sweeping dialectical logic, the true and spiritual reality lies beyond the reach of the senses; humans must become part of it by means of a contemplative process in which the self is negated. Chabad mysticism is of a manifestly individual nature. It downplays the interaction between the *tzadik* and his flock and views history, and all the other phenomena of the real world, as nothing but deception.[10] Such a theosophy seemingly conflicts with the messianic idea. A number of scholars have argued that Chabad's a-cosmic position is mitigated by panentheistic features that grant ontological status to the sensible world.[11] Dov Schwartz argues that Chabad's paradoxical dialectics—the doctrine of the unification of opposites—makes it possible for its adherents to hold both these positions simultaneously, without feeling a need to resolve the contradiction between them.[12]

Chabad's paradoxical dialectic can be seen in its complex take on the world. On the one hand, Chabad fosters a "hermeneutics of suspicion" toward empirical reality, on the ground that human perception is limited. On the other hand, the movement has always been characterized by activism and involvement in the affairs of the world, and under the leadership of the seventh and last *admor* this activism became overwhelming, sometimes even frantic. Perhaps the contradiction can be made less stark by arguing that Rabbi Schneur Zalman aimed his teachings at the masses, "middling" people as he put it. His theosophy thus underwent a significant process of routinization and standardization. The movement's integral reality-based attitude and tight-knit organization, which led Jacob Katz to call it "Judaism's first [monastic] order,"[13] can be seen as part of the Alter Rebbe's efforts to draw in the masses.[14] Recent scholarship offers a fairly complex picture of the connection between Chabad's theosophy and the messianic idea, stressing the great interest in eschatological questions that the movement has displayed from its very beginnings. But Naftali Loewenthal reflects the general rule when he says that while early Chabad teachings were grounded in an eschatological framework, "there is little evidence that the Chabad fraternity was in a state of messianic tension."[15]

Chabad's messianic turn grew out of a confluence of historical and biographical-personal factors. Rabbi Shalom Dovber (1860–1920), the fifth *admor*, began fostering messianic ideas in the face of the crisis faced by Jewish traditional society as a whole and by Chabad in particular as a result of secularization and the Haskalah (Jewish Enlightenment) that swept through Jewish communities in Eastern Europe during the second half of the nineteenth century. Movements calling for change and revolution, most notably Zionism and the Bund, were attracting young Jews. Rabbi Shalom Dovber came out against Zionism early on, seeing it as a threat to Chabad. No less a danger, in his view, were the Lithuanian yeshivot, which represented traditional Judaism's principal response to the challenges of secularization, enlightenment, and nationalism. These yeshivot were fashioning a universal form of religious Judaism, one no longer based on local communities and their leaders. This innovative religious movement was based on an ideal of scholarship, principally the study of Talmud. It was a concept that challenged the particularist religious identities of the Hasidic courts. Chabad was especially vulnerable because of its geographic proximity to Lithuania. In 1897 Rabbi Shalom Dovber founded his own yeshiva, Tomkhei Temimim, to serve as a counterweight to the Lithuanian seminaries. Its students were called "soldiers of the house of David" and served as a spiritual-religious vanguard in the battle for the hearts of Jewish youth. Messianic rhetoric was used to energize and fuse the Chabad "soldiers" into a unified force that could withstand competing ideologies.[16]

Rabbi Shalom Dovber's son and heir, Rabbi Yosef Yitzchak Schneerson (1880–1950), employed explicitly messianic rhetoric in reaction to the Holocaust, which he argued was the "birth-pangs of the Messiah," the tribulations that, according to tradition, were to befall the Jews and the world as a whole just prior to the Messiah's arrival. Rabbi Yosef Yitzchak's messianic orientation seems to have had two sources. One was Chabad's radically immanent conceptualization of the world, according to which all of material reality, including the Holocaust, reflects the presence of the divine. This concept accords with the declaration, contained in the classic work of Jewish mysticism, the Zohar, that "there is no place devoid of Him [God]." The second, apparently, was the ordeals that the rabbi suffered in his own life, under the most tyrannical regimes of the twentieth century, communist and Nazi, which he survived by the skin of his teeth.[17]

Under the leadership of the seventh *admor*, Rabbi Menachem Mendel Schneerson (1902–1994), the messianic idea became the motivating force in Chabad. His path to the leadership of Chabad was not a direct one. As a man of great talent named after and a direct descendent of the third *admor*, Rabbi Menachem Mendel, known also as the Tzemach Tzedek, he had little trouble making his way into the court of his relative, Rabbi Yosef Yitzchak, and into the heart of his relative's second daughter, Chaya Mousiya (Mushka). The marriage did not, however, dampen his eagerness to acquire an academic education at universities in Berlin and Paris during the 1920s and 1930s. During this period the couple was distant from the Chabad court, which had moved to Riga and then moved on to Otwock near Warsaw. Nevertheless, Rabbi Menachem Mendel resolutely maintained his Hasidic identity and his ties with his father-in-law. In 1938 he was certified as a mechanical and electrical engineer, but World War II put an end to his professional aspirations. Rabbi Yosef Yitzchak and his son-in-law were reunited in the early 1940s in New York, to which they had fled from the Nazis. During the ten years that followed, Menachem Mendel transformed himself from an immigrant engineer to a Hasidic *tzadik*. His father-in-law's followers gradually came to appreciate the talents and spiritual standing of the young outsider who had pursued "foreign wisdom." Rabbi Yosef Yitzchak did not have a son, so when he died his two sons-in-law were the candidates to succeed him. The Hasidim preferred Menachem Mendel to Rabbi Shmaryahu Gourary, the older son-in-law, who had for many years served as Rabbi Yosef Yitzchak's closest aide. On the tenth day of the month of Shevat, 5711 (1951), precisely a year after Rabbi Yosef Yitzchak's death, Rabbi Menachem Mendel was proclaimed the seventh *admor* of Chabad.[18]

Despite his personal charisma and authority, which transformed Chabad into a transnational movement and a leading force in the Jewish world, Rabbi Menachem Mendel always presented himself as the servant and emissary of his predecessor, Rabbi Yosef Yitzchak.[19] He carried on his predecessor's projects and established a worldwide network of schools and religious institutions meant to serve all Jews, communities and individuals, and to bring them back to their origins. These institutions were run by emissaries (*shluchim*) personally connected to the Rebbe and totally devoted to him.[20] In the very first spiritual message he issued after ascending to the leadership, the Rebbe proclaimed that the Messiah's arrival was imminent and would take place in his own generation, the generation of the seventh Chabad *admor*. He quoted the words of Midrash Vayikra Rabba: "All sevens are beloved." The Rebbe viewed the wide-ranging religious and educational activity that he initiated as a means of disseminating his ideas and hastening the redemption. Their success was for him a clear sign that the labor has been completed for the reception of the Messiah. His messianic rhetoric grew ever more intense as the years went by, sweeping up his followers into countless initiatives, activities, and "operations" meant to speed the Messiah along his way.[21] Chabad Hasidim were guided by a spiraling sense of urgency growing out of the Rebbe's clear-cut statement that "all inquiry into the time of the Messiah's arrival had been completed and all the dates predicted for it had passed." The world was ripe for redemption, he said; all that remained was simply "to welcome our Righteous Messiah in practice *mamash*."[22]

In contrast with the catastrophic messianism of his predecessor, the Rebbe fostered a "messianism of success." He viewed historic events of the second half of the twentieth century, among them the Six Day War, the collapse of the Soviet Union and the Jewish exodus from that country, the First Gulf War, and the efforts to mitigate the global arms race as omens of the impending redemption. The expectation that the Messiah would arrive any day, encouraged by the Rebbe, was eventually focused on him. His admiring Hasidim, who conducted an unprecedented cult of personality around him, began to point to him as the designated Messiah.[23] Two Chabad traditions reinforced this conclusion. First, the Schneerson family was traditionally believed to be descended from

King David, the forefather of the Messiah-to-be (a claim made by other Hasidic dynasties as well). Second, another tradition prophesied that Chabad would be led by seven leaders, culminating in the arrival of the Messiah.[24] Even though the Rebbe did not explicitly say that he was the Messiah, and at first even castigated those who addressed him as such, many scholars believe that, at the acme of his success, he was inclined to see himself in those terms.[25]

Messianic expectations reached new heights in the 1990s, the years that in the Hebrew calendar were marked by the letter *nun*, signifying the number fifty, but which is also the first letter of the word *nifla'ot*, meaning "wonders." The first of these years was 1990, 5750 on the Hebrew calendar, which the Hasidim read as the initials of "It will be a year of wonders." The year that followed, 5751, was predicted by many of them to be the year of the redemption. As the holiday of Pesach, marking the redemption from Egypt, approached, the atmosphere in the community grew taut and electrified. When the holiday passed and the redemption was late in coming, as they saw it, the elderly Rebbe, for the first time ever, evinced disappointment and doubt. On the eve of Thursday, 28 Nissan (April 18, 1991), he returned from his father-in-law's grave and gathered his disciples for an urgent talk. He acknowledged that everything he had done had not been effective and that he was handing over responsibility for the redemption to them. His bluntness and frustration shocked his followers and the date became a fateful one for Chabad.[26] The Hasidim conducted fevered ad campaigns in which they crowned the Rebbe as King Messiah and demanded that he immediately reveal himself. But less than a year later, on 28 Adar I 5792, their hopes were dashed when the Rebbe suffered a stroke that left him paralyzed and speechless. As is common when messianic hopes are disappointed,[27] the Hasidim found ways to explain what had happened. The Rebbe's tribulations, they claimed, were the birth-pangs of the Messiah, and the calls for the invalid Rebbe to reveal himself became even more impassioned. But they did not help cure the Rebbe, who died on 3 Tammuz 5794 (June 12, 1994).[28]

The childless Rebbe left no successor. Nevertheless, the vacuum generated by his passing did not lead to any large-scale desertions by Hasidim. The movement's institutions and emissaries, overseen by the executive committee of Agudas Chassidei Chabad (the Association of Chabad Hasidim), remain hugely active throughout the world. Despite infighting between different factions, all the indications are that Chabad is still going strong; the number of its members and those who are influenced by it has grown steadily since 1994.[29] But this raises a question: How long can the headless movement keep this up? Menachem Friedman, one of the most important scholars of Haredi Judaism as a whole and of Chabad in particular, writes:

> The future that a Hasidic movement without a living rebbe can expect is not promising. . . . Hasidim who have become accustomed to a rebbe who was in daily contact with his followers through letters, in person . . . or via video broadcasts; Hasidim who have become accustomed to ask the rebbe for advice and instructions in all areas, including the most intimate parts of life—such Hasidim now have to live alone, to live off the living memory, and no one can know how long this can be maintained as a unifying force and symbol of identity.[30]

Without challenging the sociological logic behind Friedman's argument, the subject of this book is precisely that heterogeneous set of tools that the Hasidim use to get around the obstacles presented by a headless movement, and to make the absent *tzadik* a presence in their lives.

CHAPTER 2

MESHICHIST SOCIOLOGY

The beliefs and the practices of the Meshichists, which I will present in the chapters that follow, do not form a coherent system detached from classic Chabad heritage, and are certainly not disconnected from the legacy crafted by the Rebbe during his leadership of the movement. Meshichist beliefs and practices thus cannot be granted the standing of a new religion, neither theosophically nor sociologically. The belief that the Rebbe is the Messiah, which has captured the minds and souls of the Meshichists, has been current in mainstream Chabad as well, even after the Event of Gimel Tammuz. The fact that the mainstream has come to terms with the Rebbe's death does not mean that they now reject his messianic status. Rather, many of them have come to accept an idea somewhat akin to the Christian model of a Second Coming.[1]

On the sociological side, the picture of a messianic religion that has put down roots almost solely on the margins of Chabad, sharply separating the Meshichists from the mainstream, is exaggerated. There are many Meshichists in Chabad's American and Israeli heartlands, in Crown Heights and Kfar Chabad; they can be easily identified by the yellow Messiah flags that fly proudly above their homes. They can be found both among the Hasidic rank and file and among the rabbis who hold posts in the movement's institutions, teaching and wielding influence in the movement's yeshivot. The boundaries separating the different subgroups within Chabad are fuzzy. That said, it would hardly be wrong to say that the beliefs and practices I will present here are peculiarly characteristic of the Chabad periphery. Furthermore, it is a phenomenon that has more of a presence in Israel than in the United States; in Israel it is more common in the towns and urban settlements on Israel's margins, among young Hasidim and new adherents to the movement, both those who have become religious and "immigrants" from other religious communities. Mizrachim are especially conspicuous.

Chabad is a peculiarly Israeli Hasidic movement. Unlike other Hasidic groups, which generally stand apart from the country's larger society, Chabad Hasidim are relatively integrated. Most Hasidic movements do not seek new adherents and accept newcomers reluctantly. Chabad preaches its message all over Israel and accepts any Jew who wants to join. Chabad Hasidim are involved in and speak out on the country's most pressing social issues and political controversies, and take part in election campaigns. Furthermore, they are also highly visible and part of the landscape in public spaces, including Israel Defense Force bases, educational institutions, and at Ben-Gurion Airport. As the Rebbe's emissaries, they offer warm hospitality and a variety of services, far beyond merely religious ones, to Israeli travelers throughout the world. And they speak up-to-date Hebrew, using the latest expressions, references, and idioms. The Meshichists are prominent in all these activities, a direct product of the fact that, as people who came to Chabad from all walks of Israeli life, they are intimately acquainted with the country and its people. Their messianic enthusiasm lends added clout to their activity.

Another specifically Israeli characteristic of the Meshichists is their familiar use of military language. Chabad used military terms prior to the Rebbe's accession to its leadership.[2] But the use of this type of speech reached new heights at his initiative, culminating in the organization of Chabad children into Tzivot Hashem (Armies of God) and using the word *operations* for Chabad campaigns, carried out with the help of "Mitzvah Tanks" (vans or trucks fitted out to serve as mobile synagogues and outreach facilities). These originated in Crown Heights, of course, not Bat Yam.[3] But this military language, used by the Meshichists in Israel, connects intimately with the Israeli ambience, replete as it is with terrorist attacks, military threats, and personal experience of army service. In using it, the Meshichists partake of the IDF's aura.[4] The Rebbe saw his Hasidim as an army with the mission of offering the Hasidic approach to life to the public at large.[5] He believed that, like soldiers, his Hasidim should devote all their energies and time to carrying out their orders and their mission to disseminate Judaism and teach Torah. The use of military language is amplified by Chabad's messianic fervor because the King Messiah, in Chabad's view, based on Maimonides, is meant to be a military commander who will fight the wars of God.[6] Chabad emphasizes, however, that the Rebbe's wars are spiritual ones. In practical terms, the battles waged in Israel aim to ensure that conversions to Judaism are allowed only in accordance with the halakhah and that the country not cede any territory. But in a social environment where children are issued "warrior ID cards" as soldiers in the Armies of God, and the Torah's commandments are termed "orders of the day," the metaphors are hugely influential.

One of the best examples of military socialization in Meshichist circles is the Oro shel Mashiach (Light of the Messiah) summer camp that Chabad boys attend during vacations.[7] The camp (the English word is used instead of the Hebrew equivalent) is termed "an anvil on which Hasidim are forged" and serves as a kind of extended initiation ceremony, a kind of basic training awash with IDF slang and military practices. *Sichat Hage'ulah* describes it: "As part of the challenge, the camp is run along military lines, with the children becoming soldiers . . . and the counselors—commanders." Upon arrival at the camp the children are "inducted," given a "uniform," a camp shirt and hat, and obey the rules of the camp, which is divided into groups with names expressing different aspects of Hasidism and its customs.[8] Each morning all the soldiers are lined up for "inspection," in which they recite the twelve verses[9] and "Yechi Adoneinu"[10] and salute the army commander in chief, the Rebbe King Messiah.

> In one field trip last year the children were taken to the traditional ceremony at the Kotel [Western Wall]. It was a moving and powerful sight, seeing hundreds of soldiers filling the entire plaza in front of the Kotel, fervently singing the camp songs, all of which express the anticipation of the coming redemption and the construction of the Temple immediately *mamash*, with hundreds of onlookers gathering to watch the scene.[11]

This description does not fully portray the military atmosphere at the camp. It includes rigorous physical activity to improve the children's physical fitness as well as paramilitary exercises, from marching and saluting to "special forces' actions in the enemy's rear," which means manning Chabad stands where the children hand out Meshichist literature in non-religious neighborhoods and passersby are encouraged to put on *tefillin*. The military atmosphere is further bolstered by the songs the child soldiers sing to their Rebbe-general and in films made at the camp which extol daring commando operations by volunteers (who defeat the enemy, the "evil impulse"). Prior to a concluding ceremony at the Kotel (modeled after the swearing-in ceremonies for IDF soldiers that are often held there) the camp generally holds its climactic event—a reenactment of Napoleon's invasion of Russia. Campers are assigned to the French and Russian armies, but the ultimate purpose is to demonstrate the superiority of the Armies of God, that is, the youngsters of Chabad, the vanguard of the messianic revolution. They defeat both the French revolutionary forces and the Bolshevik revolutionary forces that took over Czarist Russia.[12]

The liberal use of militant terminology in Meshichist publications and how it fits in well with the military discourse that pervades the Israeli media can be seen in the following examples. The first example comes from a piece in *Sichat Hage'ulah* describing "Messiah activity on the northern border":

> As soon as the IDF's response to the events on the northern border began, Hasidic activity in the Kiryat Shmonah area was reinforced under Rabbi Yigal Tzipori. The command of the tanks—the Chabad mobile centers for disseminating Judaism, headed by Rabbi David Nahshon also reinforced the number of tanks acting in the sector. Rabbi Shemariya Harel, the tanks' operations officer, reports on wide-ranging activity among IDF soldiers, including putting on *tefillin*, handing out flyers with the Shema prayer, and distribution of pictures of the Rebbe the King Messiah, may he live forever. In the settlements along the front lines, the tank crews are conducting patrols among the bomb shelters and buoying children by conducting meetings of the Armies of God.[13]

If one omits the explicit references to Chabad, the text sounds just like an account of an IDF operation produced by the official army spokesman.[14]

A report on "Chabad mobile units in the southern sector" during the IDF's Operation Pillar of Defense in the Gaza Strip in November 2012 uses a similar military vocabulary. It describes in detail the activities of a fleet of Chabad's mobile tanks at the front—from enabling soldiers to put on *tefillin* to handing out cold drinks and snacks—and reports "a huge spiritual awakening among the soldiers."[15] The Chabad force also played its part in the war effort during Operation Protective Edge in Gaza in July–August 2014. "The guys got to every place it was possible to get to with Chabad tanks." The IDF soldiers responded by saying "Bravo for giving us the strength to defend the country!"

These accounts from Chabad's self-styled exploits on the battlefield show how deeply embedded the Meshichists are in the military-security style of discourse that is so integral a part of Israeli culture. Beyond its decidedly Israeli face, however, Chabad's military discourse is also nurtured by deep theosophical roots. At a cosmological level, the Rebbe is not just the commander in chief of Chabad youth's Armies of God but the King Messiah, the omnipotent military leader, who presides over the world and directs all its affairs.

Geographically, more Meshichist strongholds lie on Israel's periphery than in its central region. The city of Bat Yam, where the Association for the True and Complete Redemption is located, is just a few minutes by car from Tel Aviv but far removed from it socioeconomically; yet it is designated "the city of redemption." Meshichist communities can be found all over Israel, but, as a rule, the most vibrant focal points of messianic radicalism lie in places that seem otherwise lacking in allure, such as Kiryat Malakhi, a development town in the south; Kiryat Shmuel, north of Haifa; Nazareth Illit, in the Lower Galilee; Afula Illit, a neighborhood of the city of Afula, in the Jezreel Valley, and Givat Olga on the Mediterranean coast between Tel Aviv and Haifa.[16] Sociologically, this dispersion can be attributed to the particularly strong appeal that messianic ideas have for people living in marginal areas, who seek to make their voices heard and to underline their distinctiveness from the elites in the country's center. Ideologically, the Meshichists view these locations that ostensibly lack any religious aura as the most appropriate ones for a global messianic revelation, no less, and perhaps even more, than traditional holy sites.

There is no official data on the numbers of *ba'alei teshuvah* or the number of Mizrachim in Chabad, and it is very difficult to arrive at an estimate. Indirect evidence indicates that the numbers are very significant. It seems reasonable to presume that, among the Meshichists, the number of Hasidim who were not born into the movement exceeds those who were born to Chabad parents. A quantitative analysis of stories about people seeking the Rebbe's assistance, taken from two hundred issues of *Sichat Hage'ulah*,[17] indicates that only about a third of them are from Hasidic families. A third are *ba'alei teshuvah*, a fifth nonobservant, and more than a tenth religious Jews who are not Chabad Hasidim. The fact that nonreligious Jews engage in practices connected to the Rebbe shows just how open the boundaries of popular messianic religion are, especially in the periphery and among Mizrachim.

The prominence of the newly-religious among the Meshichists is hardly surprising. The transformation they have undergone was brought on, in many cases, by a search for spiritual experience and uplifting religious meaning. Messianic fervor, combined with an uncompromising test of faith in immediate redemption, provides that in abundance. Withstanding that test can also provide them a way of extricating themselves from the marginality imposed on newcomers by traditional frameworks. In much the same way, the messianic fervor ignited by Shabbetai Zvi was particularly intense in communities of Conversos who had previously returned to Judaism.[18] Today's *ba'alei teshuvah*, who came to Chabad from the secular world, are not unlike the Conversos of the seventeenth century; it was argued that Chabad's messianic wakening can be attributed in large measure to this group.[19]

Most Hasidic groups are unenthusiastic about welcoming new members, especially non-Ashkenazim. Chabad, in contrast, opens its doors wide to such people, and this is particularly evident among the Meshichists. The number of typically Mizrachi family names among those people who report miracles resulting from an appeal to the Rebbe in *Sichat Hage'ulah* is larger than non-Mizrachi names. According to a rough estimate, about a third of new adherents to Chabad Hasidism are Mizrachim.[20] These new Hasidim generally assume an Ashkenazi Chabad identity and tend to set aside their Mizrachi identities. The first names that these families give to their children and grandchildren testify to their "Chabadization." For example, one issue of *Sichat Hage'ulah* mentions a Rabbi Shneur Zalman Yomtovian, whose last name is clearly Mizrachi but whose first and middle names are classic Chabad Ashkenazi ones. His children are named Menachem Mendel, Chaya Mushka, and Shalom Dovber. Other such combinations that appear in the same publication are Chaya Mushka Abutbul, Menachem Mendel Vaknin, and Chaya Mushka Ma'atuf.[21] Hasidim of Mizrachi origins can also be found among the authors of messianic literature, emissaries, and rabbis; many of them have assimilated fully into the movement's Ashkenazi milieu.

The Hasidim and texts at the center of my work have a very specific and demarcated character. I am interested in the Meshichists, many of whom are relatively young Hasidim, including *ba'alei teshuvah* and Mizrachim. Most of them never met the Rebbe in person. The Meshichists believe that the Rebbe, the King Messiah, resides, alive and well, in his home in Crown Heights in Brooklyn, even if he is presently invisible to others. And they believe that he will redeem the world "immediately *mamash*." In reading texts, my interest lies not in the Rebbe's complex messianic teachings,[22] or the Hasidic-mystical ideas of Chabad rabbis and scholars, but rather in popular publications written for a large and varied public, people who quiver at the messianic message of redemption and who extol the Rebbe as the leader of the world and as an omnipotent miracle worker. My work focuses on the experiential world of ordinary and marginal Hasidim, a world centered on the Rebbe. In the chapters to come I will analyze the practices and beliefs that are constitutive of and constituted by Chabad's messianic ecology. This ecology, which enables the impressive transformation of the Rebbe from an absence to a presence, has been shaped and enhanced before our eyes since the 1990s. Precisely because my study lacks a historical perspective that would make it possible to assess the vitality and vicissitudes of the movement, I am duty-bound, to every extent possible, to document and understand the present historical moment.

PART II

MESHICHIST PHENOMENOLOGY

CHAPTER 3

WRITING TO THE REBBE

The Holy Letters Oracle

Of all the privations that the Rebbe's disappearance caused, the most excruciating for his Hasidim was the loss of the opportunity to request his guidance on the dilemmas they face and his blessing for their actions and decisions. The personal connection between the *tzadik* and his followers is central to Hasidism, both on the communal-material and the spiritual-mystical plane. When the *tzadik* disappears, the question of how his followers may contact him becomes acute. True, even during the Rebbe's lifetime the average Chabad Hasid did not usually have an opportunity for *yehidut*—a face-to-face audience with him. If they did, it was a rare and brief event that generally took place late at night. Furthermore, the Rebbe ceased to meet with supplicants individually in the early 1980s.[1] But Hasidim could always write to the Rebbe and receive a reply. In fact, this avenue of communication was open to people outside Chabad as well. A huge volume of correspondence was received and sent out by the Rebbe's court each month until his stroke in 1992, some two years before the Event of Gimel Tammuz.

Can one conduct an epistolary dialogue with an absent addressee? An answer to this difficult question took form during the publication of the Rebbe's replies to the letters he received. As of this writing, Chabad's Kehot publishing house's Otzar Chasidim (Hasidic Treasury) project has issued thirty-two volumes of *Igrot Kodesh*, replies the Rebbe wrote to letters he received from 1938 to 1977. It was a simple process to turn these letters from the past into a text in which answers to current problems could be sought and found. The use of a mediating text might at first glance seem to make direct, concrete, and unmediated manifestation of the Rebbe's presence difficult, in contrast with, for example, his appearance in dreams or in daytime revelations. The fact is, however, that divination by means of the *Igrot Kodesh* grants Hasidim, and others, quick and handy access to the Rebbe in a way that can even produce an ongoing dialogue.

Bibliomancy, the use of sacred texts to tell the future or reveal answers to theological and mundane conundrums, is a technique with a long history of practice, both among Jews and other nations.[2] In Judaism, the Five Books of Moses have been used in this way, for example, in the practice known as *Goral HaGR"A*, the Oracle of the Vilna Gaon, attributed to the eighteenth-century Rabbi Elijah of Vilna. Chabad Hasidim have long used their canonical text, *Tanya*, for this purpose at times when they have found themselves distant or without contact with their leader. The Rebbe himself instructed that the collected letters of his predecessor, Rabbi Yosef Yitzchak Schneerson, should be used in this way. The current version of the technique is easily learned and can be used even by believers who lack a religious education (although they sometimes need the assistance of facilitators). The petitioner writes a letter to the Rebbe and then sticks it randomly into an available or arbitrarily chosen volume. A relevant answer is then sought on one of the two facing pages between which the letter has been inserted. *Sichat Hage'ulah* frequently reports on the use of *Igrot Kodesh* to receive a blessing or information from the Rebbe, or to obtain his assistance in solving a problem. The practice is mentioned in a full 70 percent of the pamphlet's first three hundred issues.[3]

My discussion of this practice is based largely on an intertextual relationship—that is, a dialogue between *Igrot Kodesh* and *Sichat Hage'ulah*. In every sense of the term, it is a dialogue between the center and the periphery. The volumes of *Igrot Kodesh* are issued by Chabad's longstanding institutions in Brooklyn, specifically its central publishing house, Kehot, and are catalogued in the Library of Congress under the name Schneerson. In contrast, *Sichat Hage'ulah* is published in the plebeian Israeli town of Bat Yam, and many of its staff members, writers, and readers are new Hasidim and *ba'alei teshuvah*. A comparison of the two texts shows that the Hasidim in Bat Yam refuse to acquiesce to what those in New

York regretfully accept. In the Library of Congress's database, the latter volumes of *Igrot Kodesh* display the years of the Rebbe's birth and death, 1902–1994. Volumes 20–22, published during the Rebbe's final illness of 1992–1994, include a prayer for the Rebbe's full recovery. But Volume 23 instead has a prayer for the awakening of the dead with the Rebbe at their head. Furthermore, the epithet *shalita*, the acronym for "may he have a long and good life" traditionally used when referring to a living rabbinical figure, which appeared in the first twenty-two volumes, was replaced with an acronym meaning "may his memory protect us, amen." In contrast, the Association for the True and Complete Redemption of Bat Yam, which publishes *Sichat Hage'ulah*, enthusiastically adopts a ruling made by some Chabad rabbis that forbids the use of terms referring to the Rebbe's death, adding after his name the acronym *shalita* or *shilo*, "may he live forever and ever." When the association's members refer to people who say that they once wrote to the Rebbe but since Gimel Tammuz have ceased to do so, their response is that it is now easier than ever to write to him: "The Rebbe responds and blesses even more than before."

It is this channel of communication with the Rebbe, by means of *Igrot Kodesh*, that I will examine, diachronically and systematically, in this chapter. My examination is based primarily on how this practice is presented in *Sichat Hage'ulah*. The oracle was not immediately drawn out of the Hasidic toolbox after the Rebbe's occlusion, as a preexisting medium, ready for use. Indeed, it makes no appearance at all in *Sichat Hage'ulah*'s first six months, which coincided with the first six months following the Event of Gimel Tammuz. Rather, those issues display a search, in different directions, for a way of answering the need for something to fill the vacuum left by the Rebbe's disappearance. What would in time become "wonders now" began as "wonders then." The second issue contains a story about a miracle performed by the founder of Hasidism, Rabbi Israel Ba'al Shem Tov. But the third story already shows evidence of direct evocation of memories of the Rebbe, and the same is true of the nineteen issues that follow. In the great majority of these stories—all of them telling of events *prior* to the withdrawal—medical, financial, family, and religious problems are resolved by sending letters and faxes to the Rebbe or by face-to-face audiences with him, group or individual. But these methods of communication cannot continue as before after the Event of Gimel Tammuz.

The opening of the story in the twenty-second issue of *Sichat Hage'ulah*, reported on December 9, 1994—close to half a year after the Rebbe's withdrawal—proves that the idea of communicating with the Rebbe by means of a text of his was not a new idea. The first person to do this who is mentioned in *Sichat Hage'ulah* is Rabbi Shaul Axelrod, an organizer of gatherings of Chabad children held in Givat Olga. A local man approached him, saying that he urgently needed a blessing but did not know whom to turn to after the Event of Gimel Tammuz. The case is a paradigm-setting one, as it provides the first testimony of using a written text as a means of contacting the Rebbe. Nevertheless, it is not the origin of this practice, as Axelrod's reply indicates: "You should know that . . . we continue to write to the Rebbe, King Messiah. . . . You should know that the Rebbe replies and blesses us even more than before."[4]

The pioneer in making *Igrot Kodesh* the preferred text for communication with the Rebbe seems to have been the rabbi of the Chabad community in Rehovot, Menachem Mendel Gluckowsky. He says that the idea came to him immediately after the Rebbe's stroke, "when written responses ceased to come from the Rebbe and the public was in great consternation."[5] At that juncture, Rabbi Gluckowsky took upon himself the daily study of five of the Rebbe's letters. As he studied, he found, to his surprise, that the contents of the letters he examined corresponded to issues that were preoccupying him and questions sent to him at the time. Following this discovery, he began to advertise the possibility of approaching the Rebbe through the letters collected in *Igrot Kodesh*. The new practice spread quickly. Rabbi Herzl Borochov learned the practice from Rabbi Gluckowsky a short time after moving to Rehovot from New York, about a month after the Rebbe's withdrawal. Borochov wrote: "I knew that the Rebbe had not left his flock, and even though physically there is no way of receiving replies from the Rebbe in the previously accustomed way, other new ways have opened up."[6] Rabbi Gluckowsky allowed Herzl and his wife, Hagit, to open an *Igrot Kodesh* Center in his city, the first of many institutions which offer instruction in how to write to the Rebbe and assistance in locating the answer to the question posed. In fact, the Borochovs themselves asked the Rebbe's advice about opening the center by means of *Igrot Kodesh*, and found an answer in a letter that discusses the opening of a post office in Kfar Chabad—which they saw as clear sanction for their initiative.

In this twenty-second story in *Sichat Hage'ulah*, Rabbi Axelrod says that the request he received brought on an inspiration. An hour after he had met with the supplicant, he was scheduled to open a convocation of Chabad youngsters in Givat Olga, but heavy rains threatened to spoil the celebration. "Why shouldn't I ask the Rebbe to fix the weather right now?" he asked himself, and then "put on his coat, tied his sash, readied his hands and sat down to write: 'Long live *admor* King Messiah forever and ever, a *pidyon nefesh* [lit. "redemption of the soul," a plea from a Hasid for the help of his *tzadik*], please awaken much [divine] mercy on the children's assembly . . . so that it be a great success, and so that the weather improves.'" He read out his letter, "trembling with sacred awe . . . as if he were standing before the Rebbe King Messiah, handing him his request." He placed the letter within a volume of the Rebbe's *Sichot Kodesh*[7] and quickly set out from the building. "The sight outside astounded him: the rain had ceased and the clouds looked as if an invisible hand were scattering them in all directions, the sun was shining in its full strength, and it was hard to believe that just a few minutes ago the lord of winter had ruled here."[8]

At the center of this paradigmatic case stands a Chabad functionary with a problem touching on the younger generation, the Soldiers of the Armies of God, who had been left without their commander in chief. Control of the forces of nature gives the story a mythic cast that makes it an appropriate overture to further miracle stories that appeared in its wake. Several elements deserve attention. Note the ritual preparations that Rabbi Shaul makes before composing his plea, the same ones that precede prayer—dressing himself in specific garments, ritually washing his hands, and opening his letter with a formulaic salutation. The Rebbe's presence is stressed ("as if he were standing before the Rebbe King Messiah, handing him his request"). The need is urgent, and the immediacy of the response also testifies to the Rebbe being close by. Note, however, that the ritual of opening a volume of *Igrot Kodesh* has not yet crystallized. The Rebbe's response to Rabbi Shaul's request does not come from a text but rather is seen in a dramatic shift in the weather. In later stories, however, finding the supplicant's answer in the text will become the core of the process of revelation.

This initial story already displays a characteristic sociological template, that of the hierarchy of the request made to the Rebbe. In many cases the supplicants, both men and women, come from Israel's urban periphery. Many are not Chabad Hasidim, and some are not even religiously observant.[9] In many cases, the petition to the Rebbe is mediated by a Meshichist functionary, who may play a very significant role. Sometimes it is this mediator who initiates the petition and who provides or chooses a volume of *Igrot Kodesh* for this purpose. He also interprets obscurities in the response, and translates the answer into Hebrew when the text that contains the answer is in Yiddish. Over the years the chain of mediation in the process has become institutionalized with the establishment of other branches of the *Igrot Kodesh* Center, which offer advice and counseling by this method in other locations outside Rehovot.

In the second such story, which appeared in the following issue of *Sichat Hage'ulah*, the results are also seen "in the field" rather than in a text. The protagonist is a former air force pilot who has become a *ba'al teshuvah*. A friend has been unable to sell his apartment, and the pilot advises him to write to the Rebbe. The petition is effective—the apartment is sold.[10] Three weeks later *Sichat Hage'ulah* reported the first case of an answer being found in the text of *Igrot Kodesh* before appearing as a change in the world. This story testifies to how energetically the practice was being promoted and disseminated, far beyond Chabad itself. A Meshichist proposes to his fellow students in a gardening course that they submit personal questions to the Rebbe. One of them, a Muslim Bedouin who was facing a court trial, asked if he too could ask for the Rebbe's help, and the Hasid encouraged him to do so. The Bedouin was told to recite the Chabad mantra "Yechi Adoneinu" and then to insert his request for an acquittal into a volume of *Igrot Kodesh*. The answer he received was: "But the explanation of these matters is that this goy [non-Jew] in himself, in his inner being and root, knows and senses that he must add holiness." In the wake of this response, the Bedouin took upon himself to observe the seven Noachide commandments that, according to Jewish tradition, are incumbent on non-Jews.

Another participant in the course disparaged the idea of appealing to the Rebbe but nevertheless gave it a try. He received a response in the form of a comment by the Rebbe on a passage in the Zohar (Kabbalah's canonical text): "And Sarah died in Kiryat Arba [literally, the City of Four] and Abraham came to weep for Sarah." The cynic turned pale. His name was Abraham and he was one of four brothers whose mother's name was Sarah, and she was about to undergo a heart operation in France. The Meshichist reassured the startled supplicant with another Chabad mantra, "Think good and it will be good."[11] He suggested that the petitioner submit the letter to the Rebbe one more time—a common practice when a negative answer is received—but while at the same time making a "good decision" (a phrase that generally means committing oneself to better observance of the Torah and commandments). The second answer was a sentence expressing the joy of liberation from slavery that was felt in particular by Israelite women at the Exodus, when they were no longer subject to Pharaoh's evil decrees. Shortly thereafter Abraham learned that there was no longer any reason to fear for his mother's life; eventually she recovered without undergoing surgery.[12]

The manner in which the circle of petitioners to the Rebbe was broadened to include a newly religious ex-pilot, a nonreligious skeptic, and a Muslim Bedouin demonstrates Chabad's characteristic practice of broad dissemination of its teachings and its breaking down of boundaries. The network of associations that connected the question to its answer in the last case offers a good opportunity to expand on the issue of the efficacy of the resort to *Igrot Kodesh*. That responses are fit to the question at hand should not be surprising given the rich system of interpretation and sophisticated maps of symbols for the construction of reality that Chabad religious-mystical teaching offers.[13] Messianic Chabad's reading of reality is a semiotic paradise. Everything that happens in the world is a sign or cipher; everything can be deciphered and interpreted. Furthermore, in Chabad's dialectic of paradoxes, with its a-cosmic and panentheistic features, the material world and the symbolic-spiritual world cannot be separated. In Chabad theosophy, the *sefirot* are not only symbols and transcendental resonances. They can actually be felt immanently, as physical experiences. Every limb and organ of the body is a divine command. Each day of the year and each historical event is an exemplification of the yearly ritual calendar and metahistorical events. The divine and corporeal souls dialectically constitute each other; language is neither a barrier to understanding the world nor a means of understanding it, but the world's true nature. The letters of the Torah are not simply the building blocks of the divine law; they are the names of God, they are God himself, the heavenly source of the physical world. Representation (the "supernal root") and the embodiment of the world of the senses (the "lower root") are necessarily integrated in complementary causal systems. All physical and all psychological phenomena have cosmological significance. Chabad's systems of meaning constitute such a strong amalgamation of the material and mundane on the one hand and their divine sources on the other that it is difficult to bring to mind any Hasidic behavior to which spiritual meaning cannot be immediately attributed. Since everything is symbolic, that is, since everything simultaneously represents and embodies everything else, there are, in fact, no symbols.[14] In other words, everything works. Everything that happens in the world has meaning and an explanation, and this symbolic structuring is the first step in extricating a person from his or her plight in therapeutic interventions.[15]

Beyond Chabad's tautological dynamic, which is itself fertile ground for miraculous revelation, divination, and healing, there is the fact that the heuristic compass of the Rebbe's letters is itself extremely broad. The texts' richness and ambiguity are part of the reason, as is the broad swath of mediation that lies between the text and the supplicant—among them exegesis, explanation, and often translation, all by a Chabad expert who is involved in the process. It should also be kept in mind that the volumes of *Igrot Kodesh* are much better suited than any other text for posing questions to the Rebbe precisely because they consist of his replies to appeals made to him during his years of leadership about a large range of problems. While a petitioner today must seek an answer to his dilemma in responses provided to other petitioners at other times, the fact is that human suffering is not infinitely variable and that it largely falls into a small number of broad categories. This makes it easier to find an appropriate response. While modern psychology stresses individuality and distinctiveness, most people face more or less similar problems during their lives. Taking as a sample the first one hundred petitions reported in *Sichat Hage'ulah*, more than a third have to do with health issues, more than half if fertility issues are added. The next most common problems are, unsurprisingly, economic (housing and jobs), family concerns (marriage, spousal relations), and religious issues. Considering that each set of facing pages in *Igrot Kodesh* contains between two and four letters, and that, for the most part, each letter addresses several issues, even a skeptic should not be surprised to find that that appropriate answers can be found by randomly choosing a page, especially given that the text is processed through the mediation of a very broad heuristic.

In the example cited above an impressive match was found—the names of the petitioner and his mother, Abraham and Sarah, both appeared in the answer. Keep in mind, however, that in the traditional Jewish world these two names are very common. Getting from Kiryat Arba to the four sons of the mother Sarah requires an interpretive move, and the parallel between liberation from Pharaoh's edicts to release from the need for an operation is a broader construal of the text. Since the nature of the fit between the question and the answer is not defined in advance, the intertextual field in which associations between the petition and the Rebbe's letters can be sought is virtually infinite. As can be seen in the example of Abraham and his sick mother, such a connection can be made through names, but even here resemblances can be expanded creatively. Take the example of a petitioner named Moshe who has inserted his question or request into a volume of *Igrot Kodesh*. It is found to lie next to letter number 345, indicated with the Hebrew letters Sh-M-H, which can be reordered to give the name Moshe. Another example is that of a man named Ben-Kish who inserted his request and found that it marked a letter from the Rebbe about the Purim holiday. Here the connection is that, according to the Book of Esther, Kish is one of the ancestors of Mordechai, the hero of the holiday.[16] Further markers, such as dates, places of residence, occupation, and other personal details can create or reinforce connections. On top of this, most of the Rebbe's responses are general enough to seem relevant to a broad spectrum of problems. In any case, he almost always offers his blessing, and that in and of itself is considered an effective remedy for any trouble the petitioner has.

The following example illustrates the creativity of the interpretive process involved in the exegesis of the Rebbe's letter. A concerned husband petitioned the Rebbe via a volume of *Igrot Kodesh* that he found at Jerusalem's Sha'arei Tzedek Hospital. He related that his wife was about to give birth, but that the fetus had not turned over ("his head is above") despite the interventions of the doctors. The Rebbe's reply included a blessing for an easy birth and a request to name the newborn, if it was a girl, after the Rebbe's grandmother, Rachel. The Rebbe also instructed the petitioner to check whether there was a flaw in his *tefillin* or in the *mezuzot* affixed to the doorways in his home. The husband recalled that in the past a Chabad woman had told him that "our *mezuzot* are placed a little higher than they should be and it would be better to 'lower' them a bit." Since the *mezuzot* were, as the halakhah requires, on the top third of the doorpost, even though they were not "at the beginning of the top third" as is considered best, he refused to move them. He asked another question of the Rebbe and received an unequivocal reply regarding the placement of *mezuzot*: "at the beginning of the top third of the lintel." The husband was shaken by the response. "I knew that I could not waste a moment, I called a cab and ran home, where I quickly and carefully began to lower the *mezuzot*, one by one." When he finished, he was informed by phone that "the baby now has its head down." The birth went well and the parents named their new daughter Rachel, after the Rebbe's grandmother, as the initial answer had indicated.[17]

The creativity of the interpretive process notwithstanding, in Chabad's messianic worldview, the starting assumption is that there is necessarily a connection between the believer's request and the Rebbe's response. In a reality in which the Rebbe is the mover of the world, every answer he provides must be meaningful. So, for example, when a woman asked the Rebbe whether it would be wise to build an extra room in her apartment in the winter, given the strong rains common in that season, the answer she found in the Rebbe's letter included the word "approve," and elsewhere the expression "he is helped beyond nature." While these replies may appear bland to readers, she was no less than "astounded" by the precision of the answer.[18]

The efficacy of the use of *Igrot Kodesh* is buttressed by the significant role played by mediators. Meshichists involved in this practice initiate contact with people in distress, instruct them in how to submit their request to the Rebbe, and help explicate the reply they receive. For the average petitioner, their activity brings the practice to life, personifying the text, which metonymically represents the authority of the absent Rebbe. Clarification of the answer is especially important when it is given in Yiddish.

A month and a half following the first report of the use of *Igrot Kodesh* as a means of contacting the Rebbe, there was already an effort to institutionalize the process by suggesting a standardized formula for addressing him.[19] Six months later, the use of *Igrot Kodesh* was the subject of a lead article in *Sichat Hage'ulah* under the headline "The *Urim* and *Tumim* [Oracle] of Our Era." The article proudly reports how the practice had spread all over the country and become "a phenomenon of astonishing potency and scope."[20] The ritual character of the practice quickly consolidated. The full ceremony begins, according to an instruction pamphlet for opening *Igrot Kodesh*, with the "ritual washing of the hands without making a blessing (three times on each hand, alternating)." The pamphlet gives the following instructions for what happens next:

> The request for a blessing is written on a clean sheet of paper, in any language. At the top the full Jewish name of the petitioner should be inscribed, and the name of his mother, preferably in Hebrew. . . . [The petitioner] makes a positive decision to take on more *mitzvot* and good deeds and places the letter in one of the volumes of *Igrot Kodesh* and declares "Long live our lord, teacher, and rabbi, the King Messiah, forever and ever." The answer appears where the letter was placed, and needs to be read with concentration.[21]

As interest in the practice grew, some questioned its legitimacy. The wife of a Chabad emissary in the northern town of Shlomi was asked whether the Rebbe had indeed granted his consent to the procedure. The issue itself was resolved, in a process that might be termed "meta-communicative," by an appeal via *Igrot Kodesh*. The Rebbe's reply was unequivocal: "It is known that *tzadikim* are like their Creator, and like the Holy One Blessed Be He in his writing and in his Torah . . . *so it is with regard to our presidents, the presidents of Chabad who wrote themselves into articles and talks from which one should draw.*"[22] The circle of petitioners grew, including completely nonobservant Jews, people outside Israel, and children. One of the youngest petitioners left a handwritten note in a volume of *Igrot Kodesh*: "With the aid of heaven, to His Eminence the holy *admor shalita*, I wish to ask about my notebook that got lost. Should I continue to look for it or start a new notebook?" Before recording his and his mother's name the boy inscribed the word *fast* and underlined it twice.

Children's appeals to the Rebbe via *Igrot Kodesh* do not happen on their own. The Meshichists make every effort to educate children to write to the Rebbe as part of their effort to make his presence felt in their lives. For example, a teacher told the boys in his class in Nazareth Illit about the importance of the *Igrot Kodesh* Oracle, promising to write the request privately with each one of the students. He explained that the children had internalized the importance of the activity and were highly moved by it. The teacher photocopied the answers received and gave them to the boys to take home to their parents.[23]

The use of *Igrot Kodesh* as a way of making the Rebbe's presence felt also intensified over the years because interaction with him became more complex. Writing to the Rebbe sometimes turns into an ongoing dialogue. Meshichist publications offer many accounts of petitions to the Rebbe that go beyond requests for blessings, help, or advice. Such dialogues may include responses to comments made by the Rebbe or reports sent to him on a regular basis. The following example shows how the interaction between a believer and the Rebbe can stretch out into a long continuous exchange conducted via *Igrot Kodesh*.

A Hasid named Yosef Avraham, who had just moved into a new apartment, reported this to the Rebbe and received as a response a traditional maxim: "A change of place brings a change of luck." The Hasid also wrote to the Rebbe about his wife's difficulty in getting pregnant, asking his help in this regard. The response linked the couple's move into their new apartment with their fertility issue. And indeed, after they moved, the wife became pregnant. The Hasid wrote to the Rebbe for a third time, asking what name to give the baby. When he opened *Igrot Kodesh* the name Yosef Yitzhak appeared. He saw the appearance of his own first name as a sign of divine providence in his own life, but wrote to the Rebbe a fourth time asking permission to give his son only the name Yitzhak (the tradition in most Jewish communities is not to give a child the same name as either parent). The Rebbe's reply this time referred to the worshippers at a synagogue named Bnei Yitzhak, which the Hasid saw as consent to his request. His wife entered the delivery room at the hospital at the same time that a family member was getting married, and the Hasid was not sure where he ought to be. He wrote to the Rebbe a fifth time and received a clear answer: "He who wants his work to be done by others should not shirk it. And with regard to a trip, in my opinion he should stay where he is until the matter is over in good time and with success." In fact, his decision to remain with his wife turned out to be a fateful one. Complications began and her condition quickly began to worsen when no medical personnel were in the room. The husband was the only one to hear her cries and called out urgently for help. The birth ended successfully, and the baby was named Yitzhak.[24]

Given such complex exchanges, in which answers are sometimes given rapidly and the promises they carry are realized immediately, it is hardly surprising that the Meshichists call petitions to the Rebbe "online conversations." One impressive example of an ongoing dialogue with the Rebbe via *Igrot Kodesh* can be found in the book *Attachment [to the Rebbe] as a Personal Experience.*[25] The author, a widow who became religious and a Meshichist, describes how she has been assisted by *Igrot Kodesh* in every important event in her life.[26]

The easy accessibility of this channel of communication with the Rebbe and the speed with which replies are received has added to its popularity. When a rabbi from Nahariya had to abandon his car on a roadside because of a malfunction and no one stopped to give him a ride, he called his wife and asked her to place "an urgent request for a blessing in *Igrot Kodesh*." Five minutes later she called back with "a fantastic response: . . . *that the King Messiah said . . . on a paved and clear road.*"

Two minutes later a rabbinic colleague stopped and offered him a ride. The narrator exulted: "You came to me *mamash* out of *Igrot Kodesh*."[27]

Maintaining an ongoing dialogue with the Rebbe via *Igrot Kodesh* is particularly noted in stories which involve his miraculous assistance in the birth of healthy babies despite complications. A typical example involved a woman in her third month of pregnancy who was told that the fetus had Down syndrome. She asked the Rebbe for his blessing via *Igrot Kodesh*. The Rebbe gave his blessing and also said that her husband's *tefillin* should be inspected. When this was done, it turned out that a word, meaning "the males," on the parchments inside the *tefillin* had faded. The doctors recommended an abortion, but the Rebbe categorically opposed it. The woman, armed with the Rebbe's blessing, refused to follow medical advice. In the seventh month the doctors discovered that the fetus was in distress and again pressured the woman to have an abortion, but the Rebbe again opposed it. Medical tests grew more frequent as the situation worsened. The wife's principal caregiver suggested "an injection straight into the fetus's heart to finish off the story." But, in response to a letter, the Rebbe again promised the birth of a healthy boy and a circumcision ceremony to follow. In the eighth month the doctors notified the woman that she would have to undergo a Caesarian section because of the fetus's "monstrous head," but the Rebbe promised "good tidings for the newborn" and suggested that he be named after the Rebbe's father, Levi Yitzhak. The operation was scheduled for the seventh day of the Hebrew month of Kislev, but the previous midnight the woman felt that birth was approaching. The family opened *Igrot Kodesh* and received confirmation that the time had come for the birth. The next day the woman was rushed into the operating room; she was equipped with a dollar bill that the Rebbe had blessed and a vial of "living water" from the Rebbe's *mikveh* (ritual bath). Despite the doctors' dire warnings, she gave birth to a healthy baby. The circumcision ceremony (*brit milah*) was held eight days later, on the fourteenth day of Kislev, the Rebbe's wedding anniversary. The Rebbe had overseen the pregnancy, as the story's title put it, "The Whole Way." He had been petitioned and had answered no less than six times.[28]

In emergencies, when there is no time at all to compose a letter to the Rebbe, a volume of *Igrot Kodesh* may be used as a healing amulet. A rabbi from Tel Mond came to the help of a woman who was seriously wounded in an automobile accident, lying unconscious by the side of the road. He remembered that he had a volume of *Igrot Kodesh* in his car, but realized that "these were critical seconds and I would have no time to write." He sprinted to his car, took out the book, and placed it close to her head, called out "Yechi Adoneinu," and inwardly asked for the King Messiah's blessing "to come in an instant." The wounded woman's eyes began to blink; he put the book even closer to her face. "Now a real miracle happened. The wounded woman, who had been unconscious, raised her right hand . . . gripped the book as she opened her eyes . . . and brought the book close to her to kiss it." She was evacuated by ambulance to the hospital, where she enjoyed a rapid recovery. Such use of *Igrot Kodesh* as a cure is reminiscent of similar uses of the dollar bills that the Rebbe used to distribute, and of the water from his *mikveh* (see Chapter 4). In all three cases, the therapeutic value of the object lies in its metonymic connection to the Rebbe.[29]

The institutionalization and routinization of the use of *Igrot Kodesh* as a channel of communication with the Rebbe were made explicit in a lead article that appeared in *Sichat Hage'ulah* about three years after his withdrawal. The article provides the rationale for the use of *Igrot Kodesh* as a sensible way of making decisions. "The process of making a decision," it explains, "requires deep and thorough analysis, taking into account all the factors that seem relevant to us, in an attempt to examine their interlocking effects, connections, and implications, and simulation of the outcomes." Yet because of "our limited capacities for understanding, analysis, and data-gathering, and lack of objectivity," especially when the question is not purely one of halakhah but rather affects everyday life and matters in which people can make choices, "all [authorities] agree that we are permitted, able, and need to use the channel of *Igrot Kodesh* [provided by] the Rebbe *shalita* the King Messiah." The combination of scientific and rational language with that of mystical messianism, so characteristic of Chabad, is clearly apparent here.[30]

While the article portrays the scale of the use of *Igrot Kodesh* in the superlative language characteristic of the Meshichists, it does seem to be the case that large numbers of people petition the Rebbe in this way, among them many Hasidim from the Chabad mainstream and members of a much broader public. The Meshichists work to expand the use of the oracle by manning *Igrot Kodesh* stands at major public events, among them the annual pilgrimages to the tombs of Rabbi Shimon bar Yochai and the Baba Sali, but also the New Age Boombamela festival.[31] They also make the use of *Igrot Kodesh* accessible by phone, fax, internet, and live radio broadcasts. For example, Rabbi Ilan Hayun, director of the Chabad Center at the Hazahav Mall in Rishon Letzion, operates a twenty-four-hour hotline which petitioners can call. The service is advertised on the radio, billboards, posters, and with business cards. Hayun describes the activity in *Sichat Hage'ulah*: "Upon simply dialing 050-8080-770, callers hear the opening jingle 'Messiah makes us miracles.' Afterward the announcer refers them to the different departments: 'To request a blessing from the Rebbe . . . press 1. For stories of actual miracles (which happened to different people via *Igrot Kodesh*), press 2.'" Upon choosing the first option, [the caller] receives immediate recorded instructions regarding the sequence of activities necessary for completing the bibliomantic ritual. "The huge numbers of callers, throughout the day, require us to employ several receptionists who personally receive each request, record the request on forms, and place them in a volume of *Igrot Kodesh*. After receiving the answer, the caller receives the response in a systematic and comprehensible way, with explanations of all the details in the letter he received. . . . With us, miracles do not happen every day but every few minutes."

Similar instructions can be found on the website igrot.com.[32] As the Meshichists see it, the use of *Igrot Kodesh* is a "broad channel of divine revelation" because of its popularity and the miracles it brings about, "which cannot be defined in terms other than the time of redemption"; thus the "critical importance of publicizing these miracles and wonders."[33]

The use of *Igrot Kodesh* is so widespread that it is even evoked in advertising campaigns, for example, one for "bioenergetic orthotics" for the Haredi public. The rabbis whose endorsements appear in the ads include "the *admor* of Gur *shalita*" and the "*admor* of Vizhnitz *shalita*," along with the "Lubavitcher Rebbe, *tzadik* of blessed memory." To the last-named, the Chabad Rebbe, a note is appended: "via *Igrot Kodesh*." The use of the term "*tzadik* of blessed memory," traditionally used when mentioning the name of a late rabbi, clearly shows that the advertiser is not a Meshichist. People petition the Rebbe regarding life-and-death questions and other matters of great importance, but they also ask him about quotidian matters such as lawsuits and driving tests, and even basketball games (the Rebbe's response in the latter case was "the Hasidim have the upper hand") or Lotto, one of Israel's national lottery games. True, a woman who placed in a volume of *Igrot Kodesh* a Lotto form she had filled out in the hopes of winning a prize received a reprimand: "When a person seeks *ploys in material matters* and is keen about luxuries not only will this not help, but it will even harm him."[34] But direct appeals to the Rebbe on matters of little consequence, such as obtaining donuts distribution on Hanukah or hitchhiking, are not rejected as improper.

The Chabad imperative to disseminate the tidings of the redemption throughout the world can be seen in the wide range of groups that use the *Igrot Kodesh* channel. Within a very short time the oracle propagated among a widening circle of petitioners, reaching even non-Jews. Messianism, even in a manifestly national religion such as Judaism, is directed at all of humanity, and the most notable manifestation of this is Chabad's campaign to urge the observance of the seven Noachide laws among Palestinian Arabs in Israel and in the territories. Rabbi Boaz Kali, director of the operation, proposed to the editor of the Israeli Arabic newspaper *Al-Sinarah*, Lutfi Mashour, and his wife Vida, that they publish an Arabic translation of the seven laws. Vida asked if she could request a blessing from the Rebbe in Arabic and was answered in the affirmative. She asked for a blessing for a good livelihood and life for her and the rest of her family, and made a "good decision" to disseminate the seven laws in the newspaper. She received the blessing, along with condolences that moved her deeply because her father had died just a month before.[35]

Even lawbreakers can benefit from the Rebbe's blessing via *Igrot Kodesh*. Reports of criminals who have had their sentences reduced after petitioning the Rebbe in this manner are devoid of moral judgment. In one case, a Jewish suspect was extradited by Germany to the United States. He wrote to the Rebbe with the assistance of a Chabad rabbi who cares for Jewish prisoners. The question was a plea bargain involving a two-year prison sentence and a fine of $500,000 that the defendant's lawyer was urging him to accept. But the Rebbe's answer ended with the words "In my opinion, don't pay." The man rejected the deal, to his lawyer's displeasure, but in the end he was sentenced to two years in prison without a fine, and he had already been in prison for nearly that long.[36]

While sometimes the replies the Rebbe provides via *Igrot Kodesh* seem to be precise and effective, they can seem even more dramatic when the answer received appears at first glance to be irrelevant but nevertheless sets a process in motion after which it turns out to be entirely on the mark. Such cases reveal the full depth of the gap between the shortsightedness of human petitioners and the Rebbe's comprehensive vision and perfect foresight. For example, a man who wrote the Rebbe seeking an appropriate wife for his son received a demand that he have his *tefillin* examined. The scribe who checked the *tefillin* found no flaw in them but, in the course of their conversation, mentioned that he had a daughter who had reached marriageable age. The son and daughter met and then got married.[37] Another such case involved a woman who had lost an expensive piece of jewelry. Her son, who had written to the Rebbe about a different matter, received the reply that he should start learning *Chitat* (a Chabad book combining the Five Books of Moses, the Psalms, and passages from *Tanya*). When the son took his *Chitat* book off the shelf he found the lost item behind it.[38]

The Rebbe's supernatural powers stand out in particular when an answer is provided even before the petition via *Igrot Kodesh* has begun, as the prophet Isaiah promises (Isaiah 65:24): "Before they pray, I will respond." A couple from Kiryat Arba turned to the Rebbe when all their attempts to rent out their apartment failed. As soon as they began composing their letter, the phone rang—the caller became their tenant.[39] The Or Moshiach Center in Jerusalem had searched in vain for a Torah scroll for the synagogue on its premises. The staff resolved to petition the Rebbe, but even before they did a donor appeared.[40]

Since the Messianic ecology is replete with signs and traces of the Rebbe, the miracle stories involving the *Igrot Kodesh* Oracle are often interwoven with other means by which the Rebbe's presence is made felt. Some of the most prominent of these are pictures of him, which are often integrated into the *Igrot Kodesh* ritual. Along with ritually washing their hands, making a decision to observe additional *mitzvot*, and making the declaration "Yechi Adoneinu," some petitioners gaze at the Rebbe's picture before inserting their request into the chosen volume. When no picture of the Rebbe is available, some imagine his countenance. The dollars that the Rebbe distributed on Sundays, to be given to charity, are also another type of trace he left in the world. The dollars, which the Hasidim carefully guard, also play a role in the *Igrot Kodesh* Oracle. Such a connection can be seen in the story of a man who was unsure whether he had been correct to divorce his wife. The Rebbe's answer, "It is good for a man to live with his wife," helped the couple to decide to remarry. After several delays and much doubt they set the wedding date for the first day of the month of Elul. The bridegroom told a woman of his acquaintance that he was about to remarry his ex-wife thanks to the blessing of the Rebbe. The woman was moved to grant him a dollar she had received from the Rebbe with his blessing. The man was astounded to discover that a note on the bill said that it had been "received on the first of Elul."[41]

Igrot Kodesh joins forces not only with such traces that the Rebbe left in the world, but also with encounters with the Rebbe that take place in special states of consciousness, such as dreams and dissociation, as well as ones that take place in normal waking states. The integration of the textual channel involving *Igrot Kodesh* and the visual channel of a dream or other such revelation creates a powerful ensemble of ways in which the Rebbe's presence is felt in the lives of his Hasidim. The next story illustrates this.

A woman had a dream in which a disembodied voice permitted her to ask three questions. Since she was not married at the time, her first question was, "How will I find a husband?" The answer came from a book she saw in her dream: "I then saw an open book resting on a cloud. The pages of the book began to turn over in the wind and stopped when I saw before me a page with these words emphasized: '*Allow me to bring this to fruition*' [lit. 'to bless what has already been finished']." Her second question was: "Should I sell my apartment and move to Jerusalem?" Again she saw the pages turning over and they stopped when the words that stood out were "*May there be success spiritually and materially.*" While the account does not relate what her third question was, it gives the answer: "*Trust the Holy One Blessed Be He and He will help.*" Even though she had already posed her three questions, she asked the name of the miraculous book that had revealed these answers in her dream. The answer came "in an authoritative, quiet, and soothing voice: '*Igrot Kodesh*, Volume Six.'" The woman went to a Chabad House near her home, where she inquired about purchasing *Igrot Kodesh*. The saleslady, in an act of "personal providence," gave her Volume 6 to use in her petition to the Rebbe. The answers she received in her dream came true—she got married, sold her apartment, and moved to a new home in Jerusalem, the address of which was number six. She later continued to consult with the Rebbe via the volume of *Igrot Kodesh* that she had purchased. The woman first saw the book from which she received her answers in a dream, but at the end of the story there is a real transfer—from revelation in a dream (oneiromancy) to revelation by means of a book (bibliomancy).[42]

In the following example, the movement is in the opposite direction—from the text to a special state of consciousness that combines a near-death experience with an out-of-body experience. Neither is a picture of the Rebbe absent from the story.

A Chabad woman from Safed, who taught Torah classes for women, went to a hospital in Haifa for a medical examination. Her husband, who remained at home, suddenly felt an overwhelming urge to make a contribution to charity. He put eighteen shekels (Israeli currency) into a charity box that displayed a picture of the Rebbe. (The number eighteen, written in Hebrew letters, spells the word *chai*, life, and it is thus traditional to make charitable donations in a multiple of this number.) At the very moment he did this his wife had a severe asthma attack and the husband was urgently summoned to the hospital. He quickly opened *Igrot Kodesh*, but the response focused on a Torah class for women. According to the account in *Sichat Hage'ulah*, the husband "read it again, trying to find [in the Rebbe's letter] words of blessing for his wife, but he did not succeed." In the meantime, his wife collapsed, suffering from an allergic reaction to the medication she had been given. She sensed that her soul was leaving her body and hovering above it. She suddenly saw the Rebbe surrounded by her five children, who danced and leapt around him, singing "Yechi Adoneinu." She addressed the Rebbe: "What about my Torah class?" The Rebbe smiled at her, and then she miraculously woke up and gradually recovered. The dissociative experience in this story—a woman on the verge of death, outside her body—is in dialogue with the text: the direct encounter with the Rebbe elucidated the apparently obscure reply given by the *Igrot Kodesh*—it was the Torah class that the woman taught that saved her life.[43]

At times, a petition to the Rebbe via *Igrot Kodesh* is accompanied by a waking experience of seeing the Rebbe. The Rebbe's response via *Igrot Kodesh* may impel the person who experienced such a vision to share it with others. This was the case with a Hasidic preacher, Rabbi Shlomo Zalman Landa, who frequently had experiences of seeing the Rebbe. But when a group of children he met in a synagogue asked to hear more about these experiences, he refused to talk about it. A few days later, however, upon returning to the synagogue, he had regrets about his reticence. He randomly opened a volume of *Igrot Kodesh* and found, on the page the book opened at, "the Rebbe *shalita* the King Messiah writing about the importance of miracle stories, especially for Jewish children, among whom it is accepted most naturally!" The Rebbe's reply rid him of his reluctance. He gathered the children and told them that he had indeed had the privilege of seeing the Rebbe with his own eyes. He quickly received his reward: "As I spoke to them, I suddenly sensed something special. I raised my eyes and I saw the Rebbe . . . standing and looking at me. The Rebbe . . . nodded, as if he were saying: 'Well done!' And then he vanished." The preacher immediately told the children about the revelation he had just received.[44]

Another person who saw the Rebbe faced a dilemma after realizing that he was the only person to have seen him in the crowded synagogue at 770 during the Pesach holiday. "Maybe I was tired and imagined it," he wondered. When he asked for advice via *Igrot Kodesh*, the answer was: "It is, after all, no coincidence that our first meeting—and it is my hope that it will be continued in a good way—took place on the eve of the seventh day of Pesach, the day of the parting of the Red Sea." When the petitioner turned to the previous page to read the beginning of the letter in which that sentence appeared, "I was astounded to read the clearest possible statement: 'I wish to express my pleasure at your visit and this opportunity to become acquainted with you face to face!'"[45] The text in the last two cases validates the revelation and, along with other signs, grants an objective dimension to the subjective experience of seeing the Rebbe.

It is not just dream visions of the Rebbe that may end with receiving a message from him via *Igrot Kodesh*. The same can happen in the case of a waking experience. For example, Rabbi Shlomo Zalman Landa, mentioned above, was debating whether he should cancel a trip to Europe, where he was to raise funds for the yeshiva where he serves as preacher, because of difficulties at home. The Rebbe appeared to him one day at the Chabad House in the Shikun Heh neighborhood of Bnei Brak. The Rebbe pointed toward the bookcase, at a volume of the *Igrot Kodesh* of Chabad's first three leaders. He opened the volume at random and found a letter written by the first *admor*, Rabbi Shneur Zalman, to a Hasid named Shlomo Zalman who had made a fundraising trip for a yeshiva in the Holy Land. Landa reported: "The answer could not be clearer. . . . I now knew that I would make the trip no matter what."[46]

In another case, the transition from opening *Igrot Kodesh* to revelation took place interpersonally. A child went with his mother and other children to a mass convocation at Bloomfield Stadium in Jaffa on 11 Nisan 2007, commemorating the Rebbe's birthday. He had to go to the bathroom but did not know where to find it. He used his cell phone to call his mother, who was sitting in a section set apart for women. She inquired by means of a pocket-sized volume of *Igrot Kodesh*. A short time later an adult "who looked like the Rebbe" appeared and led the boy and his friends to the bathroom. He vanished after returning them to their seats.[47]

To sum up, since the Event of Gimel Tammuz in 1994, the *Igrot Kodesh* Oracle has taken its place as an effective, accessible, and popular means of contact with the Rebbe, a way of receiving his blessing and advice on life issues, large and small. The fact that the praxis grows out of a long tradition of consultation of sacred writings, one accepted in Judaism as a whole and in Chabad specifically, seems to have encouraged people to use this method. Indeed, the use of *Igrot Kodesh* is common even among the Meshichists' opponents in Chabad. The Meshichists emphasize the apparent paradox that it is much easier to communicate

FIGURE 5. Pocket-sized volume of the Holy Letters. Photographer: Ran Bartov.

with the virtual Rebbe today than it was before his withdrawal. The new practice now gives everyone access to the Rebbe directly, or via local mediation available to all. Every imaginable question gets answered on the spot. Furthermore, the request can easily expand into an ongoing dialogue about a widening range of subjects, and can be augmented by communications technology—telephone, fax, radio, and computer. It is no coincidence that the Meshichists refer to this practice as "*Igrot Kodesh* by fax" or "the online Rebbe."[48] Some believers carry a pocket-sized version of one of the volumes of *Igrot Kodesh* in their purses, briefcases, or backpacks so that they can consult with the Rebbe at any time and about any subject. The Rebbe has thus become more accessible and closer to his followers than he was in his lifetime. He is "with us more than ever," as the Hasidim say.[49] This is especially important given that practices of making the Rebbe present are more widespread on Chabad's periphery, among new Hasidim, Mizrachim, and women, beyond the Chabad elite. A direct consequence of the Rebbe's growing accessibility and availability is that he has become radically decentralized—everyone can approach him. Having fundamentally democratized Chabad, *Igrot Kodesh* is liable to become a way of circumventing authority, and thus presents a threat to the movement's cohesion and its traditional leadership.

The threat that *Igrot Kodesh* presents to the authority of Chabad's rabbis is evident in a warning issued by the chief rabbi of Kfar Chabad, Mordechai Ashkenazi. People should not blindly trust the oracle, he cautions, especially in cases in which the answer, when deciphered for the petitioner, runs counter to the Torah's precepts or the halakhah. The democratic, if not downright subversive, aspect of the egalitarian practice of consulting *Igrot Kodesh* can be seen in the strident disputes that arose between the Meshichists and their opponents after the Rebbe's departure. When a Chabad millionaire from Australia, Joseph Isaac Gutnick, accused the Meshichists in Safed of being insane, a member of the Association for the True and Complete Redemption wrote to the Rebbe, who told them "to continue the systematic labor of publishing the tidings of Redemption and the Redeemer."[50]

The subversive potential of the radical Meshichists could be seen in a ferocious debate over the minor fasts (four days each year on which Jews are enjoined to fast from sunrise to sunset, three of which commemorate stages in the fall of Jerusalem and the exile of the Jews). Some Meshichists argue that, on the verge of the final redemption, these should no longer be observed. Rabbi Zimroni Tzik, the editor of *Sichat Hage'ulah*, who was accused of issuing such a ruling, was condemned by Rabbi Gedalia Axelrod, who heads the Chabad community in Haifa and chairs its religious court.[51] He compared Tzik and his followers to the cult of Shabbetai Zvi and threatened to ostracize him if he did not withdraw his ruling. He claimed to have the Rebbe's support—which he received via *Igrot Kodesh*. In reply to his letter of complaint against the Meshichist, the Rebbe stated that "the outcry must come from the rabbis."[52]

Rabbi Tzik did not take that lying down. He also addressed the Rebbe via *Igrot Kodesh* and also got his support: "The rabbis pressured me to say something about the fasts. From that time to the present I did not speak out publicly about the fasts, but the Rebbe asked me to several times and unfortunately I did not do so . . . and that is why this whole ruckus started."[53]

One more indication of the threat to rabbinic authority posed by communication with the Rebbe via *Igrot Kodesh* comes from a dispute over the management of Chabad's institutions in Haifa's northern suburbs. Rabbi Moshe Oirechman, representing the Chabad establishment, sparred a zealous Meshichist group led by Rabbi Yigal Pizam. An anti-Meshichist publication attributed the deterioration of the relationship between the two groups, which reached the point of blows and stone-throwing, to the new means of contacting the Rebbe. "When Rabbi . . . Pizam was asked why he lent his hand to trespass [control of the institutions], *he replied that he has an instruction from the* Igrot Kodesh *that permits him to do so. Can we, in the name of* Igrot Kodesh, *let lawlessness reign against God and against his Torah and his Messiah!!!*"[54] Rabbi Moshe Landa, head of the Chabad religious court in Bnei Brak, no doubt had the *Igrot Kodesh* Oracle in mind when he wrote about "*a method in which everyone does as he wishes and hangs himself on an invisible tree.*"[55]

An enlightening example of how the new practice decentralizes authority in Chabad is provided by a case in which Rabbi Levi Yitzchak Ginsburgh, a famous preacher from Kfar Chabad who belongs to the Meshichist camp, refused to heed the pleas of Rabbi Motti Grolnik of the Chabad House in Petah Tikva to hold a Shabbat convocation with counselors of the Ezra youth movement, on the ground that he had invited guests for the Sabbath. Two yeshiva students, fervent Meshichists, refused to accept his demurral and petitioned the Rebbe via *Igrot Kodesh*. The answer they received was: "And I send this letter quickly and it is still possible for the said person to make a full repair." Furthermore, the original letter by the Rebbe was addressed "To Rabbi, the Hasid Yitzchak Ginsburgh who is required to take every opportunity to infuse the love of God in his students." They called the preacher and read him the reply; he changed his plans and accepted the invitation, influenced in particular by the fact that the original letter had been addressed to his uncle.[56]

Rabbi Ginzburgh himself describes the *Igrot Kodesh* Oracle as the culmination of a multistage process through which the acceptance of the Rebbe's authority became swifter and more effective. At first, petitioners had to write letters and mail them to the Rebbe. It took them a long time to make up their mind and then to find the time for writing. Sending the petitions by airmail would take time too, and written replies, if received at all, arrived after weeks or even months of waiting. Sometimes the replies were not understood by the petitioners who had to look for an expert in a nearby Chabad House for explanation. And when this lengthy process was completed, "the person was not always in the same state of [spiritual] awakening that he had been when he wrote the letter."

The epistolary exchange became quicker when petitioners could fax their letters instead of mailing them; and when the Rebbe began handing out dollars, a more direct way of contacting him was established. Together with the dollar for charity, the supplicants received on the spot the Rebbe's advice and blessing, "along with his pure gaze . . . the gaze of the Messiah." With the advent of *Igrot Kodesh*, the Rebbe's instructions and blessings could be accessed immediately by all.[57]

In his account, Rabbi Ginsburgh sees no fundamental difference between modern technology such as fax and mystical means such as the *Igrot Kodesh* Oracle as ways of communicating with the Rebbe. Chabad teaching sanctifies the technological devices produced by modern science and sees them as expressions of God's presence and benevolence. As such, all these media have a similar epistemological status. Another process that characterizes communication with the Rebbe is the increasing virtualization of the techniques as the digital age progresses—from landline telephones to cell phones, from letters to faxes to email. The virtualization and digitization of the communications media in the postmodern age fit in well with Chabad's dialectical mysticism, which moves between existence and nonexistence and imbues the virtual Rebbe with presence and actuality.

The *Igrot Kodesh* Oracle is not necessarily the final link in the decentralization and democratization of Chabad. Given the creativity and breaking down of borders that accompanies these processes, new paths of communication with the Rebbe that circumvent authority can appear spontaneously. For example, an advertisement proclaiming "Speak to the Lubavitcher Rebbe" offers "astonishing channeling with a huge capacity for solving all sorts of problems via telephone *mamash*, like speaking with the Rebbe (not with *Igrot Kodesh*)." In fact, in the field of Israeli New Age mysticism and spirituality, communication with the Rebbe, with or without *Igrot Kodesh*, is increasingly available.[58] Channeling the Rebbe, which ostensibly makes him even more present than the *Igrot Kodesh* ritual ("*mamash* like speaking"), might now sound like an esoteric practice that would constitute no threat to the familiar methods in use today. But it points to the fundamental problem of the widening Meshichist fringe, and also, perhaps, to the increasing difficulty of maintaining boundaries in a religious movement that has now spent many years in the shadow of a present-absent leader.

CHAPTER 4

SENSING THE REBBE

Traces and Practices of Embodiment

Messianic ideology brims with signs of the Rebbe, traces he left behind him in the world. Many of these traces are to be found in arenas in which the Meshichists conduct ritual practices with the Rebbe's active participation. Together, the traces and practices constitute an environment in which Hasidim can truly and ingenuously sense that the Rebbe is present in their lives. For the purposes of this discussion, I will address the traces and practices separately.

Traces

The Rebbe's home, known simply as "770"; his chair, upholstered in red velvet; his Torah scroll; the dollar bills he distributed for charity on Sundays; his lectern at his *beit midrash* (study hall); the water from his *mikveh*, in which he immersed himself; the *sukkah* built for his personal use during the Sukkot holiday—all these objects, and many others, maintain a connection to the Rebbe by virtue of proximity, contiguity, or synecdoche. In semiotic terms, these objects signify the Rebbe indexically or metonymically. These types of signifiers or traces are particularly effective ways of making the absent Rebbe close and sensible, because they "participate, in one way or another, in the thing that they signify. They have a 'real connection' to their object."[1]

Devotees of all religions establish connections to exemplary figures with metaphysical standing by means of signifiers. Examples are splinters of the cross on which Jesus was crucified and the relics of martyred saints in Catholic churches, hairs from Muhammad's beard in mosques, and footprints of the Buddha on rocks in southeast Asia, all of which have a "real connection" with the revered figure. These objects bolster the sense of closeness to holy figures and reinforce the belief that they have the spiritual ability to intervene in favor of believers in real and concrete ways, even if the believers do not deny that their holy men and women have died. Still, while the mechanisms and practices to be described in this chapter are not unique to Meshichist Chabad, the Rebbe's presence in the Meshichist ecology is singular, certainly in Judaism. It stands out both ideologically, given the claim that the Rebbe is alive and among his believers, and technologically, given the broad use of advanced techniques for making the Rebbe present.

The Rebbe's residence and belongings have been left untouched, just as they were prior to his occlusion. They have also been reproduced, in an effort to make them common and accessible. For example, exact replicas of 770 have been built all over the world, including in Israel.[2] A number of Hasidim have even designed the facades of their homes and libraries to resemble the Rebbe's house. Images of 770 are embroidered on the bags in which Meshichists keep their *tallitot* (prayer shawls) and, in some of their synagogues, the ark where the Torah scrolls are kept is also built in the shape of the Rebbe's home. Invitations to weddings and bar mitzvahs include a picture of the house. Many Hasidim use *mezuzot*, charity boxes, and packages of candles that are designed as miniatures of 770; their children put together puzzles depicting the building.

The extent to which Hasidim are devoted to the Rebbe's traces can be seen in an advertisement in a Hasidic newspaper that extols a particular strain of citron (the *etrog*, a fruit used ritually on the Sukkot holiday) imported from Calabria, Italy. According to the ad, these *etrogim* (pl.) are "descendants of the *etrog* used by the Lubavitcher Rebbe," that is, they are taken from trees grown from seeds from an *etrog* used by the Rebbe. Another advertisement commends *etrog* marmalade originating from the Rebbe's fruit.[3]

The examples of the *etrog* and 770 both display a move from singularity to multiplicity, characteristic of many of the Rebbe's traces. The house can be replicated over and over again, and *etrogim* descended from the single fruit used by the Rebbe can be cultivated and harvested year by year. This move stands in stark contrast to the Rebbe's conduct during his lifetime. Not only did he spend most of his days concealed in his

FIGURE 6. Replica of "770": In Kfar Chabad (above); the original building in Crown Heights (below).

FIGURE 7. Replica of "770": Facade of a private house. Courtesy of the Association for the True and Complete Religion.

study, with his Hasidim getting to see him only at restricted opportunities; as his tenure progressed, he became less and less accessible. In 1982 he stopped receiving Hasidim individually and met only with groups; these audiences grew less and less frequent as he aged. Beyond his frequent visits to the grave of his father-in-law and predecessor, he rarely left 770. Yet today his traces are reproduced and replicated in a process that in some cases seems to have no limit. This is the case with photographs of the Rebbe, for example, as well as with water taken from his *mikveh*, which is constantly replenished by mixing it with ordinary water.

Hasidim are exposed to a rich collection of traces simultaneously, especially when they make pilgrimages to "be with the Rebbe" at 770. But similar exposure happens at home as well. Photographs of the Rebbe hang on the walls of every room and appear on the covers of books in Meshichist homes. Such images also appear on a large variety of other items, from *kiddush* cups used on the Sabbath and holidays to clocks. A framed dollar bill that was given by the Rebbe customarily hangs on the living room wall.[4] Bottles filled with *mikveh* water, believed to have healing power, are also displayed in living rooms. Some homes include a replica of the Rebbe's chair—an initiative of Rabbi Yigal Hoshiar, who has called on "every family to set aside a suitable chair in the living room, and all members of the family will know that no one sits in this special chair, which is reserved for the King Messiah alone." Hoshiar stresses that "it was clear to us that it was necessary to adhere to the original design of the Rebbe's chair . . . at his *beit midrash* at 770 in New York, including the velvet upholstery." He adds with satisfaction that the initial chairs he had made were bought up immediately.[5] The fact that the chair is "reserved for the King Messiah alone" underlines the expectation that the Rebbe will visit the Hasid's home, making the relationship an intimate one. Rabbi Reuven Danin placed such a chair in his home in Haifa in the full belief that "the Rebbe will sit here on the chair."[6]

This high level of indexicality typifies not just the Meshichist landscape but also the Meshichist body. It is easy to identify Meshichist men because they wear *kipot* (skullcaps) embroidered with the "Yechi Adoneinu" mantra and sport Messiah flag lapel pins. There are many other signs as well. They carry a small card with a blessing and the Rebbe's

FIGURE 8. Replica of "770": Torah ark. Courtesy of the Association for the True and Complete Religion.

FIGURE 9. Replica of "770": Clock. Courtesy of Miriam Feldman.

photograph in their pockets or wallets; their *tallit* bags are embroidered with an image of the Rebbe's home; many incorporate the sequence 7-7-0 into their telephone numbers, email addresses, and the passwords they use to access their bank accounts online. At their wedding ceremonies, many Meshichist bridegrooms don the Rebbe's shirt, *sirtuk* (frock coat), and *gertel* (cloth belt). In many cases, the veil which the groom lowers over the face of his bride is the one used by the Rebbe's wife. All these items are available on loan. In other words, beyond the fact that the virtual Rebbe has become all-seen thanks to his ubiquitous photographic image, he is also borne on the bodies of his Hasidim. They feel a close and intimate connection with him[7] and term themselves the Rebbe's emissaries and children.[8] Many of them name one of their children Menachem Mendel, Mendy for short, after the Rebbe. They also see him as an exemplar of Hasidic behavior whom they seek to emulate. They try with all their might not just "to be with the Rebbe" but also "to live the Rebbe." They quote his best-known sayings, imitate his movements and gestures, and seek to follow his instructions to the fullest extent possible. In this sense they become walking icons of the Rebbe.[9]

I will focus on three of the myriad traces left by the Rebbe that are especially prominent in the Meshichist ecology: water from his *mikveh*; the dollar bills he distributed; and *Chitat*, a book comprising daily readings from the Five Books of Moses, Psalms, and *Tanya* (the book's name is an acronym of the Hebrew names for these three parts—Chumash, Tehilim, *Tanya*). The Rebbe called on his followers to bear a copy of this book on their persons at all time. His image appears on many of the book's editions. These signifiers continue to be circulated and to affect their recipients, and thus contribute to making the Rebbe's presence felt. I will turn first to the Rebbe's *mikveh* water, which has become a healing potion in a process that can be mapped systematically, as I have already done with the use of *Igrot Kodesh* by tracking miracle stories that have appeared in *Sichat Hage'ulah*.

The Rebbe's Mikveh *Water*

Holy water possessing healing powers appears in many religions, Judaism among them.[10] At the beginning of February 1996, a year and eight months after the Rebbe's occlusion, the readers of *Sichat Hage'ulah* were first presented with the foundation myth of "living water" from the Rebbe's ritual bath. "There is indeed such a thing," the pamphlet's editor declared enthusiastically: "Rabbi Israel Halperin, director of the Chabad institutions in Herzliya, has a bottle of water from the *mikveh*, taken after the immersion of the Rebbe the King Messiah, may he live forever and ever, and its special powers for deliverance and healing for all have become clear."[11] Rabbi Halperin, a confirmed Meshichist, came up with the idea of using the water for healing back in 1987, after he heard that the Rebbe himself had suggested to someone to "seize the opportunity" to immerse in his *mikveh* immediately after him. Rabbi Halperin waited for the Rebbe outside the bathhouse, made his way in immediately after the Rebbe left, and filled a bottle with the blessed water. The emphasis on the immediacy of the action highlights the metonymic connection between the Rebbe and the water. It is also significant that Halperin entirely forgot that he possessed this "living water"; he remembered it only after the Rebbe's occlusion, when the niece of a friend was hospitalized "in very serious condition." The friend was not reassured by a blessing he received from the Rebbe via *Igrot Kodesh*; he kept weeping, leading Rabbi Halperin to make use of the forgotten water. The pioneering nature of the deed is evident in what he told his friend: "Look, I'll give you something that up until now I haven't given and have never thought of giving from it to anyone." He poured a small amount into a small plastic container, and the friend took it off to the hospital. According to the report, a few days later the girl recovered.

Following this success, the friend hastened to pass the water on to the wife of a friend who had suffered paralysis in both hands. This time the precious water was economical in the extreme: "He added a single drop of the 'living water' to a glass of regular water, the woman said the blessing [over water] and drank it." The liquid proved effective despite the parsimonious consumption.

During the years that followed, *Sichat Hage'ulah* published dozens more stories of cures caused by drinking the holy water or rubbing it on painful limbs, in most cases accompanied by a petition to the Rebbe via *Igrot Kodesh*. The miracles were given prominent placement and presented as signs that the redemption was beginning. As in the founding story, many of the users passed their water on to others who needed it, enlarging the circles of users. The magical logic, following homeopathic practice, turned the *mikveh* water contained in a single bottle into an inexhaustible resource, because a drop of the holy water could pass on healing powers to any larger quantity of ordinary water with which it was mixed. The Rebbe's *mikveh* water remains in use today, although the number of miracle stories has declined compared to those of the period following the innovation. Between February and April 1996 *Sichat Hage'ulah* ran ten stories, some of which, like the founding story, included more than one case of healing.

The use of the *mikveh* water as a medicine or ointment did not escape criticism, as the editor of *Sichat Hage'ulah* noted already at the time he published the first story. "The story has already made headlines, the media are in a frenzy about it, and as is their wont there are some who advocate it and others who are searching for ways to disprove it."[12] An echo of such criticism can be heard in the story of a woman who was suffering from bad sores and pain: "After all, the water is from the *mikveh*, and has been sitting with Rabbi Halperin for thirteen years [early reports said seven years]. True, it was the Rebbe himself who immersed himself in that water, but it is still just water from the *mikveh*. . . . " With many qualms, the woman decided to rub a bit of the water on her sores; the next day she discovered that they had vanished, "despite her feelings." The change in her attitude began at a gathering of women where each participant received a bottle of "the Rebbe's water" and drank it together after together making a "good decision" and recited the mantra "Long live our lord. . . . " The grateful woman immediately sent word to Rabbi Halperin: "I am still in shock, but I have learned one thing: You don't play games with the Rebbe. . . . "[13]

From this point onward the stories evince not even a shadow of doubt about the possible hygiene problem of using the water. The medical logic displayed by the practice of rubbing the water on the body to cure surface ailments (such as sores) and imbibing it to cure internal infirmities is retained in the subsequent stories.

An examination of twenty stories published over the course of the first two years following the first appearance of the "living water" shows that, with one exception, the water served solely as a treatment for physical problems and serious illnesses. The rhetoric of the miracle stresses the dire nature of the diseases, the helplessness of the doctors involved, and the failure of competing practices from the religious milieu, such as pilgrimages to the graves of saints and even to the Western Wall.[14] In general, however, as with other means of making the absent Rebbe present, the use of the water is part of a ritual in which the patient plays a central part. The ritual aspect was quite apparent in the initial weeks after "living water" was distributed at Messiah and Redemption Rallies. The participants drank the water together at the end of the rally as the anthem "Yechi Adoneinu" blared from the loudspeakers. When used individually, the application of the water is preceded by reciting this mantra three times, the recitation of the traditional blessing used before drinking water, and the request of a blessing from the Rebbe via *Igrot Kodesh*.

I will offer an example of this ceremonial structure by means of a specific instance involving an elderly woman suffering from acute renal failure, who required regular dialysis.[15] She had become bedridden because of intestinal necrosis that brought on a severe infection. A large portion of the intestine had to be removed in an emergency operation, after which the doctors informed the family "to expect the worst." At this point her son-in-law hastened to obtain a bottle of "living water," which she drank after proclaiming the mantra and making the blessing. Her daughter also rubbed the water on her body and her son-in-law placed a request for a blessing in a volume of *Igrot Kodesh*. The Rebbe replied that "regarding what he wrote regarding the matter of health—it is also understood that the light of the Torah, that is, the interiority and its matters touch on and have a special standing—a blessing for good tidings." The son-in-law understood the message immediately: "When you study Hasidic teachings [the inner Torah], it brings healing." He began to give classes in Hasidism in the home of his mother-in-law, who "remained in the intensive care unit for about two weeks, during which she continued to drink from the 'living water,' and we on our side continued to give classes in her home. Her condition slowly improved, to the astonishment of the medical staff, who acknowledged that her recovery was a great miracle."

In keeping with my decision to remain within the bounds of evaluating miracle stories but not the miracles they relate, I will not try to determine the extent to which this "medical miracle" has ontological validity, beyond its rhetorical and textual construction. But the narrative shows the multidimensional nature of the therapeutic intervention. This included suggestive physical treatments in the form of drinking the "living water" as a medicine and rubbing it on the body as an ointment, much like standard medical remedies; these are integrated into a religious ritual involving the recitation of the mantra and of the blessing; on top of which there is symbolic spiritual intervention in the form of teaching Hasidic lore, this action growing out of the interpretation of a text, the Rebbe's letter from *Igrot Kodesh*. Such a range of therapeutic intervention, reaching from the physiological to the symbolic pole, and anchored in a ritual framework that endows it with meaning and bolsters faith, seems to contribute to therapeutic efficacy.[16]

In recent years the therapeutic process has been further enhanced by sumptuous packaging offering a "miracle-working water kit," containing a bottle with a label that displays a large picture of the Rebbe.[17] The water from the Rebbe's *mikveh* has continued to perform medical miracles in the years since the Event of Gimel Tammuz. An anxious couple from Kfar Yonah, between Tel Aviv and Haifa, approached their local Chabad emissary because their daughter-in-law's water had broken in the sixth month of her pregnancy. The doctors told her that her pregnancy had to continue for another two months to ensure that the baby be born healthy, but could not guarantee that the medical interventions at their disposal could avert a premature birth. The emissary helped them query the Rebbe by means of *Igrot Kodesh*, and his answer, sealed with a blessing for a cure, was "to put off the medical treatment for two months for its success." But the couple remained apprehensive. "What should we actually do?" they asked. The emissary suggested that he give a bit of the Rebbe's water to the pregnant woman. "It will be water to replace that which has been lost," he said with a smile. The results were quick to come: "She was miraculously able to put off the birth, without any special medical interventions, until the desired date."[18]

Dollars for Charity

Late each Sunday morning the Rebbe used to hand out dollar bills to Hasidim and admirers who thronged at the entrance to 770; the dollars were then meant to be passed on to a charity. This special custom began on the Rebbe's birthday, on the eleventh of the month of Nissan in 1986. It offered his followers, including women, a rare opportunity to meet him face-to-face, even for a brief moment, and to receive his blessing. The event grew hugely popular, with people waiting in long lines to file through the foyer of 770 where the Rebbe stood. During his lifetime the dollar bills he handed out, which were specially marked in advance,[19] became valued as sacred objects that people struggled to obtain. Following the Event of Gimel Tammuz, these dollar bills continue to make their way around the world and perform miracles. Believers place a huge value on them. At a convocation that I attended at the Shalom veRe'ut Synagogue in Bat Yam on January 5, 2013, marking the second centennial of the first *admor*'s death, a framed dollar bill of the Rebbe's was auctioned off as a benefit for the Association for the True and Complete Redemption for a sum, in Israeli currency, equivalent to about $1,300. By comparison, a copy of the famous portrait of the first Chabad *admor*, in an opulent frame, sold for about $470. It is not only the dollar bills that are preserved but also the documentation of who received them. Film clips immortalizing the Sunday dollar handouts are preserved in Chabad's photographic archive. Anyone who has received one of the Rebbe's dollar bills can also purchase the photographic evidence of having received it.

The dollar bills, which retain the holiness of the Rebbe's touch, evince healing powers in many ways. They are placed under the pillows of the ill and injured in order to aid their recovery. This was done, for example, by the father of a soldier in Israel's Border Police who was shot in the chest at the beginning of the Second Intifada. He was hospitalized in serious condition and was unconscious for more than two weeks. After the dollar was placed under his pillow, he opened his eyes and began to move his arms and legs.[20] A Hasid who needed complex and painful root canal work owned one of the dollar bills, which he always bore together with his Israeli identity card. He placed the dollar on his cheek and chanted "Yechi Adoneinu" several times; his pain disappeared.[21] Both placing the dollar bill on an injured limb and placing it under the sick person's head are familiar practices, used also with the Rebbe's photograph. Both the dollar and the photograph are seen as protective and healing charms with a wide range of indications.

The dollars' prophylactic power extends beyond the medical field. A Chabad Hasid from Buenos Aires received three of them while on a visit to Brooklyn, in addition to the Rebbe's personal blessing for a long life. A few days later, on March 17, 1992, the Israeli embassy in the Argentinian capital was destroyed by a car bomb while the Hasid happened to be there. Miraculously, he emerged unscathed. According to *Sichat Hage'ulah*, "About a day later, when the names of the wounded and dead became known, it turned out that all the people who had asked him to mention their names to the Rebbe on his trip . . . had miraculously been saved, at worst came out with a few scratches, while others who had been standing right next to them had been hurt much more seriously."[22] In this case, the Rebbe's dollars saved people from a catastrophe. But people who own them do not hesitate to use them for more prosaic purposes. For example, one woman won the Israeli lottery after holding her lottery card and dollar together and proclaiming "Long live our lord . . . " three times.

A single dollar bill given by the Rebbe can help several people. It is customary to lend the Rebbe's bills to those in need, for a set period of time, especially when the recipients need it for a purpose for which the dollars have already been proven effective. During my research, I encountered specific dollar bills with specialized effects—one, for example, which had proven that it could save people who were undergoing operations, and another that was effective in helping women become pregnant. Beyond their curative effect, the miraculous power of these dollars, whether on loan or given as a gift, is connected to the time at which the Rebbe handed them out. An illustrative case is that of an Israeli woman who visited New York in 1987; she had planned to visit 770 on a Sunday morning to receive a dollar from the Rebbe, but in the end was too busy to get there. She finally visited 770 in the year 2000, six years after the Rebbe's occlusion. But she was upset that she had missed the opportunity to meet him in person. A Chabad friend, seeking to lift her spirits, gave her one of the Rebbe's dollars. When the woman examined the date on which the dollar had been given, she was astounded to discover that her friend had received it precisely at the time she had visited New York in 1987. She was absolutely certain what this meant: "On Sunday, 22 Tammuz 5747, the Rebbe deposited . . . this dollar bill [with my friend] for me."[23] A woman serving as an emissary of the Rebbe in Jerusalem's Talbiyeh neighborhood regularly brought meals to the protest tent maintained next to the nearby residence of the prime minister by the family of an Israeli soldier, Gilad Shalit, who was being held prisoner by Hamas in the Gaza Strip. She also gave the soldier's mother a dollar bill she had received from the Rebbe twenty years previously. Gilad was set free on 20 Tishrei; when the Chabad woman examined the dollar bill she was astonished to discover that she had received it on exactly that date.[24]

As is the case with other traces of the Rebbe, the number of "his" dollars has risen steadily since the Event of Gimel Tammuz. This proliferation is possible because the distribution of dollar bills has continued. Late on Sunday morning one can still visit the foyer of 770 to receive one. The details of the ritual have been carefully preserved, as is only appropriate for a mimetic practice intended to assert the Rebbe's continued presence. Now that the Rebbe is invisible, however, visitors take dollar bills from a pile placed on a table in the room. These "new dollars" also make their way around the world and perform miracles that are publicized in Meshichist publications, with stress on the fact that the dollars in question were given after the Event of Gimel Tammuz.

People's potent desire to own the Rebbe's dollar bills can be seen in stories about obtaining them in miraculous ways. One classic example comes from a rabbi from Bnei Brak, who desperately wanted one. One day he received repayment of a $100 loan. The borrower redeemed his debt in single dollar bills. The rabbi carefully examined all the bills to see if one of them had come from the Rebbe, but was disappointed to find that none had. His wife consoled him by saying "A person who deserves one will receive one." But he went to bed "feeling somewhat sad." That night he dreamed of the Rebbe, who repeated his wife's reassurance: "A person who deserves one will receive a dollar." The rabbi complained to the Rebbe: "And I don't deserve one?" The Rebbe smiled and responded: "Of course you deserve one." The Rebbe held out a dollar bill to him and blessed him, telling him that he would succeed and that his wishes would come true. His most important wish came true the next day. In the morning, the rabbi heard from his neighbor, a childless widow, that her husband had appeared to her in a dream to remind her that, thirty years previously, they had received three dollar bills from the Rebbe. The widow's husband told his widow to grant one of them to the rabbi. She did so, and also gave another one of the dollars to the rabbi's wife so that she too could enjoy the Rebbe's blessing.[25]

A pure expression of the passion for owning one of the Rebbe's dollars can be found in the report of an Israeli charity operative. While he was not a Chabad Hasid himself, he visited 770 each time he made a fundraising trip to the United States. He once arrived there just prior to the morning prayer service. As was customary before the Event of Gimel Tammuz when the Rebbe entered the room, a custom that continues today, the worshippers, packed into the synagogue, stepped back to open a path in the crowded room to allow the now-invisible Rebbe to walk down to reach his place. "Mesmerized," he gazed at the place designated for the Rebbe and addressed the invisible Rebbe: "I have arrived to receive a blessing from you and I understand that I have your blessing for raising money and success, but I want to see it. . . . It is especially difficult that this time I am not receiving a dollar from you." After his visit to 770 he went to raise money in Brooklyn's Borough Park neighborhood. At the first synagogue he visited to solicit donations from morning worshippers, one man searched his pockets and wallet but could find no money to offer. "Suddenly," the fundraiser related, "his eyes lit up [and he declared]: 'I don't have any money in the normal sense of the word. I have a dollar that is worth a bit more than one dollar.'" The man told him that, on the way to synagogue, he had found a dollar bill in a puddle. When he examined it, he saw that it was inscribed with the words: "Received from his Excellency the Lubavitcher *admor*, may he have a long and good life." He gave the dollar to the fundraiser and said, "Apparently heaven wanted you to ask and receive this special dollar from me."[26]

In this story the dollar bill clearly functions as a metonymic signifier of the Rebbe. As with the case of many of the apparition stories that take place at 770, there is a notable contrast in this story between the messianic ecology in which the Rebbe's presence is manifested (the morning prayer service) and his absence, in the form of the dollar that the fundraiser wants but does not receive from the Rebbe. In many apparition stories, it is this disparity that leads to seeing the Rebbe, as I will show below. In this case the disparity is the basis for receiving a dollar bill that partially embodies the absent Rebbe.

In keeping with the semiotic logic that enables an infinite concatenation of connections based on proximity or contiguity to the Rebbe, it turns out that not only the "new dollars," received since the Rebbe's occlusion, are effective. Photographic images of his dollars also perform miracles. As with the use of *Igrot Kodesh* and the Rebbe's *mikveh* water, the innovator of this practice is known. It is a Hasid from Kfar Chabad who provided a woman with a tumor with a photocopy of a "tried and tested" dollar bill that the Rebbe had once granted along with wishes for "a full recovery soon." A while later the woman reported to the Hasid that her tumor had disappeared, after which "he collected other dollars the Rebbe had provided as charms for various things and made copies of them for those in need of salvation." The wide range of specific uses of particular dollars shows that some of them have come to be seen as having special application for discrete problems. So, for example, there are dollar bills that grant a good livelihood, cure illnesses, find a marriage partner, enable fertility, and resolve marital tensions. In addition, there are others that prevent one's children from intermarrying, guarantee a safe flight, provide a blessing for little boys at the time of their first haircut at the age of three, and even bring luck in the national lottery (the rule in this case is that 5 percent of the proceeds are to be paid to the owner of the original dollar).

The indications of each individual dollar bill derive from the blessing the Rebbe made when he granted it ("full recovery," "great success," "long life"); from its serial number (the digits 9494 in the serial number give good luck because the numerical values of the Hebrew letters that spell out *mazal tov*, meaning "good luck," add up to 94); and from the date on which it was given. For example, a dollar bill given by the Rebbe on 10 Shevat, the eve of the day he became *admor*, can strengthen the connection with him; one granted on 18 Elul, the birthday of the Ba'al

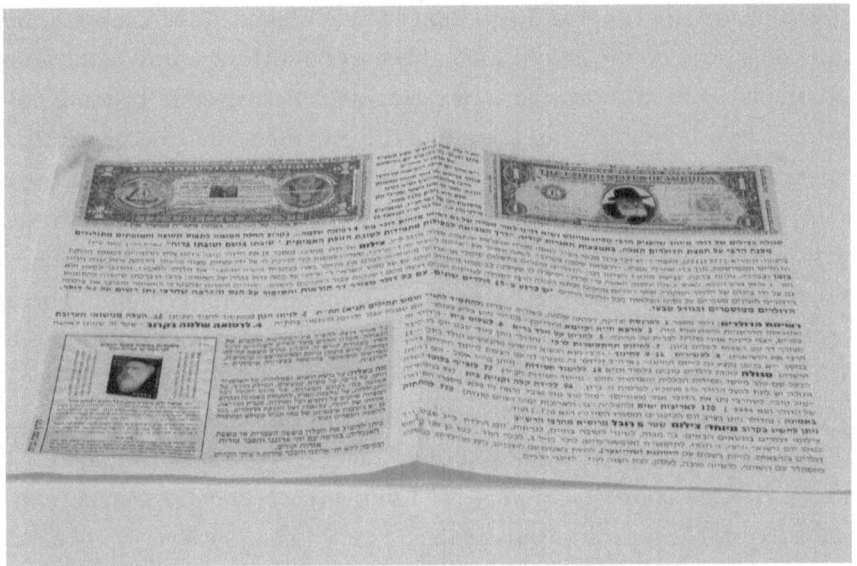

FIGURE 10. The advertisement for the photocopied dollars. Photographer: Ran Bartov.

Shem Tov, the founder of Hasidism, and of the first Chabad *admor* can help a person in his studies of Hasidic teachings. The dollars come with explicit instructions about how to use them and the Rebbe's suggestions for good behavior (especially in the matter of spousal relations and the education of children). The Hasid who first had the idea of using a photocopy of a dollar did not hesitate to publicize the success of the new method. He announced that he was conducting a search for other dollars that had been proven effective in specific kinds of cases, for example, good relations with one's mother-in-law, or with one's neighbors, or one's children, or business partner. He also sought dollars that had brought success in legal matters, in business, for a bat mitzvah ceremony, and those that had remedied poor eyesight.[27]

Chitat

Chabad calls this volume, which, as noted, contains daily readings from the Five Books of Moses, Psalms, and *Tanya*, a "safety kit." The characterization grows out of a statement of the Rebbe according to which "holding these books [*Chitat*] together with a charity box in one's car is a special charm for keeping the passengers safe."[28] And indeed, most of the miracle stories connected to *Chitat* have to do with surviving bad traffic accidents. Even in cases where cars are totally destroyed in head-on collisions or by falling into an abyss, the drivers ostensibly emerge without injury thanks to the *Chitat* and charity box in the car.[29] According to one such story, a car equipped with this "personal safety kit" skidded in the first rain of the season and almost crashed into a traffic light, but then "a huge power stopped the car just a few millimeters from the light." Three other cars that also skidded there, but which were not so equipped, were left "crushed and overturned" on the road.[30]

This contrast between the vulnerability of cars without *Chitat* books in them and the invulnerability of those that carry the books is magnified when the case is not just one of road safety but also defense against attacks by Israel's enemies. During the Second Lebanon War, in 2006, an IDF convoy in southern Lebanon was hit by rocket fire; Ofer Danino was driving one of the vehicles that was attacked. The driver of the vehicle behind him was killed by a direct hit; the driver of the vehicle in front of him was badly wounded, and the vehicle Danino was in was perforated by hundreds of pieces of shrapnel. He was unhurt, however, thanks to a copy of *Chitat* in the vehicle.[31]

The safety kit does not save only motor vehicles. A baby carriage containing the daughter of a Chabad woman from the town of Emanuel slipped out of the hands of the baby's brother and plummeted down the stairs of their apartment building. The carriage flipped over, "flying down with the baby inside . . . until it came to a halt with a huge crash at the bottom of the stairs, with the baby thrown out of it on her face on the floor." The neighbors, who heard the horrible racket, were sure that "the worst had happened," but they found the baby "smiling and without a scratch." The parents attributed the miracle to the copy of *Chitat* that the mother had placed in the carriage, and immediately reported it to the Rebbe via *Igrot Kodesh*. He responded: "I had the pleasure of receiving your letter . . . in which you express your thanks to God for the rescue of your daughter."[32]

In addition to its "specialization" of saving people from automobile accidents, *Chitat* serves as a personal safety kit. During the Second Lebanon War the editor of *Sichat Hage'ulah* proudly reported: "Thousands of soldiers have over the last few days equipped themselves with a *Chitat* kit for protection, safety, and rescue and the picture of the Rebbe *shalita* the King Messiah." The article was accompanied by a photograph of a soldier wearing camouflage face paint, holding up his safety kit.[33]

Three years earlier the kit saved the life of a soldier named Yossi Vaknin during a combat operation in Lebanon. Before the operation, Vaknin related, "I removed several combat materials from the pocket close to my heart and replaced them with a *Chitat* kit," complete with a small pocket-sized charity pouch. A bullet fired at him during the battle penetrated the kit and halted at the charity pouch, a few centimeters away from his heart.[34] In keeping with Chabad's best military tradition, the kit was described in this case as a bulletproof vest much more effective than the materials it had replaced. In other cases, involving bad traffic accidents, it is stressed that, even though the car was totaled, the kit "remained whole and unscathed," much like pictures of the Rebbe at disaster sites.[35]

Practices of Making the Rebbe Present

In addition to the traces of the Rebbe that pervade the messianic environment, and to pictures of the Rebbe, to which I will devote the next chapter, the Meshichists also employ a complex set of ritual practices through which the Rebbe's presence is actualized. The practices are mimetic, inasmuch as they make the Rebbe an active participant and seek to recreate the past precisely.[36] These take place for the most part at 770, as part of the daily routine in the Rebbe's home. Hasidim who visit the house in order to enjoy the Rebbe's presence are drawn into a special ecology in which the Rebbe is the moving force.[37]

The practices of making the Rebbe an active participant and focal point in the ritual daily schedule at 770 began shortly after the Event of Gimel Tammuz, in 1994. Five years later, Rabbi Tuvia Doron offered "Impressions from the Holiday Month with the Rebbe *shalita* the King Messiah." Even though we cannot see the Rebbe with our eyes, he claims, the Rebbe is the only one who directs the affairs at 770. All the prayer groups conducting services in the hall

> do their best to finish before the prayers with the Rebbe . . . they remove the cover from his chair and lectern and begin to sing "Long live our

lord...." At the end of each of the daily prayers they declare "Yechi Adoneinu" three times, and the same after each reading from the Torah, and on every Sabbath eve at the end of "Lechah Dodi" [liturgical hymn]. On Simchat Torah the arrangement is that the purchasers of the *Atah hareta* verses [which are auctioned off to raise money for charity] give the honor to the Rebbe . . . and the *gabbai* announces in a voice hoarse from shouting: "So-and-so has purchased an *Atah hareta* verse and honors his Holy Excellency, our lord, teacher, and rabbi, the King Messiah, *shalita*." The huge crowd is silent for a moment—now the Rebbe . . . is saying it— and then everyone repeats [the verse]. . . . During the rounds of Simchat Torah dancing, the familiar Simchat Torah melodies quickly turn into the singing of "Long live our lord. . . . " At the foot of the platform of the Rebbe . . . a *gabbai* holds the Rebbe's "little" Torah scroll . . . and between each round hundreds of people file by it to kiss its cover.[38]

FIGURE 11. Soldier with a *Chitat* safety kit on the front page of *Sichat Hage'ulah*. Courtesy of the Association for the True and Complete Redemption.

The manifestation of the Rebbe's presence in rituals observed at 770 is so concrete that an outside reader of the personal diaries written by Hasidim during visits to 770 will find it hard to believe that they do not see the Rebbe with their own eyes. The following passage is from a diary that I obtained, relating to the celebration of Hoshanah Rabbah, the last of the intermediate days of Sukkot. Each year on this day, the Rebbe handed out pieces of cake to Hasidim who filed through his personal *sukkah*. The account offers a "live" version of the event, in both senses of the word:

> About ten minutes later [the Rebbe] came out to distribute pieces of his cake at the gate of the lower Eden; that is, the foyer of his office in 770. . . . After the morning service his Holy Excellency the *admor* King Messiah *shalita* again presented his *lulav* [the collective name for the four species used in the Sukkot services] to the congregation (as he did each day), this time blessing the children and then, in a separate place, the women as well.

These accounts show that the three daily prayer services are particularly important in bolstering the feeling that the Rebbe is among his devotees. Prior to each service, after the cover is removed from his chair and lectern, the Hasidim direct their gaze at the staircase leading to the occluded Rebbe's study on the second floor. They welcome him by singing "Long live our lord . . . ," while opening up a "path" in the middle of the room to allow him to reach the platform where his seat is located. At the end of the prayer the crowd again splits, singing and dancing as the Rebbe makes his way out. On the nights following Sabbaths and holidays, audiences with the Rebbe are held in the study hall, just as in the past. The furnishings are the same ones that were always used—a white tablecloth covers the Rebbe's table, and loaves of *challah* and *kiddush* wine are placed on it. The Rebbe's chair stands by the table and the Hasidim sit facing him. A talk by the Rebbe is projected onto a screen or is read out loud by one of the rabbis. At the end of the audience, one of the elder Hasidim approaches and breaks the *challah* into tiny pieces that are distributed among the Hasidim. Slices of the Rebbe's cake (*lekah*) are handed out twice a year, on the eve of Yom Kippur and on Hoshanah Rabbah. A glass of wine is passed around three times a year—at the end of the audience on the second day of Rosh Hashanah, the night after Simchat Torah, and the night after the holiday on the seventh day of Pesach.

Special practices of making the Rebbe present are reserved for the holidays of the Jewish month of Tishrei—Rosh Hashanah, Yom Kippur, Sukkot, and Simchat Torah. When the Yom Kippur prayers are concluded, a portable set of steps is brought into the room for the occluded Rebbe to stand on so that he can view his Hasidim and hear their singing, as he did in the past. On Sukkot a personal *sukkah*, the temporary booth that Jews are commanded to reside in on this holiday, is built for him, and the four species of the holiday are placed there for him to use. Hasidim and other devotees file through the *sukkah*. Some of them extend their hands, whether in joy or in confusion, pretending to receive a piece of cake from the Rebbe. When he is called up to the Torah and expected to read a section of the weekly Torah portion, the entire room falls silent, with all eyes on his chair. After he makes the opening declaration of the blessing for reading the Torah, inaudible to the human ear, the entire congregation calls out the traditional response in perfect synchronization. Dollar bills continue to be distributed on Sundays, in the Rebbe's name, and the Hasidim stand on line as in the past, even if they cannot see the Rebbe with their own eyes. When the Hasidim stand beside the Rebbe's platform, their gaze is fixed on his chair, and they ask for his blessing, many of them no doubt conjure up his image in their minds. It seems likely that the experience of seeing the Rebbe at 770, to be discussed in detail below, is mediated, at least in some cases, by such visual imaging, as part of a process of sensory override in which summoning up the Rebbe's image turns into an actual experience of seeing him.[39]

But the Rebbe is not only made present at 770. Hasidim routinely invite the Rebbe to life-cycle events—circumcisions, bar mitzvahs, and weddings—and also to audiences, rallies, and celebrations in which a new Torah is brought into a synagogue. And just as the Rebbe is invited to ceremonial events held by his Hasidim, so they are invited to be with the Rebbe at 770 on holidays and other events, especially during the holidays of Tishrei.

The practices of making the Rebbe present demand a playful mindset of those who participate in them, as well as willingness to enter an imaginary world of "as if." This is obvious to outsiders who observe 770, but many Hasidim are also aware of it. They need to overcome inhibitions and discomfiture—should they stretch out their hand to receive a piece of cake that the unseen Rebbe is passing out in his *sukkah* on Hoshanah Rabbah? Should they ask him out loud for a blessing when they receive dollar bills on Sundays? Some people hold out their hands with great enthusiasm, others do so hesitantly and bashfully, and still others entirely refrain. Some Hasidim address the Rebbe out loud, others quickly whisper something, and still others find that they cannot say a word. The Meshichist test of faith requires being totally swept up in the subjective experience of "living with the Rebbe," and the suspension of any clearheaded belief in sensory input. The Meshichists must display uncompromising faith even when that seems to contradict their senses. They are even supposed to act as "holy fools," as the Rebbe himself suggested, by subordinating every idea or fact to the concept of redemption. The following story, from the era before the Rebbe, was trumpeted at a Hasidic convocation. It offers a model of behavior that combines uncompromising belief with free imagination and playfulness, a combination that repeatedly appears in Meshichist discourse.

A Jew who had come from Russia related that after the previous *admor*, Rabbi Yosef Yitzchak, had been exiled from the Soviet Union, his Hasidim, who felt orphaned, sought a way to be in connection with their absent leader. The face of one of them lit up. "Friends," he proposed, "we are going to visit the Rebbe." He set up several chairs in a line, sat in the front one, which he turned into a locomotive engine, made the sound of a train whistle, and announced: "This is the train to the Rebbe. Whoever wants to can join." Some of the Hasidim boarded the "train," chanting, like children, "We're going to see the Rebbe" and waving goodbye to those who remained behind. The laggards gazed at their friends as if they had lost their minds. The Jew who told this story said that, in the end, those who had boarded the "faith train" later managed to get out of the Soviet Union covertly, while the so-called "sane" ones who had hesitated remained behind "and are hardly [living] like Jews."[40]

Most of the Hasidim enter the absent-present Rebbe's virtual world with relative ease thanks to the "horizontal" factor of group solidarity and social conformity that is fostered by the messianic ecology, together with the "vertical" factor of massive socialization into life with the Rebbe that children of Meshichist families undergo from birth. Children from these communities are exposed continuously, almost on a daily basis, to film clips of the Rebbe, photographs of him, and other traces; they witness others addressing him directly.[41] Furthermore, these children receive large doses of the Rebbe's presence at ceremonial events, which open with the public reading of the twelve verses that the Rebbe enjoined all children to learn, along with the proclamation "Long live our lord...." This, for example, is the practice at Camp Oro shel Mashiach, where the camp grounds are designed as a miniature Crown Heights with 770 at its center. Huge pictures of the Rebbe adorn the public spaces, and the program is replete with rituals in which the Rebbe is an active participant.[42]

Traces of the Rebbe, the still photographs, and the film clips, as well as the practices of making him present, in which he participates, allow his Hasidim to sense him as close and concrete. This feeling is especially strong at rallies and ceremonial events to which the Rebbe is invited, in which he "participates" in various ways. I learned just how all-pervasive, involving all the senses, the Rebbe's presence can be when I attended a wedding at Kfar Chabad.[43]

The Rebbe's participation in the wedding had a clear spatial component. On the Sabbath preceding the wedding, the bridegroom, who lived in New York, was called up to read from the Torah in 770, the Rebbe's home. From there the groom flew to Israel for the wedding. The reception was held at 770 in Kfar Chabad, which is an exact copy of the Rebbe's home, while the ceremony was held in the wedding hall adjacent to the Beit Menachem Synagogue, named after the Rebbe. The Rebbe was also personally embodied in the bridegroom himself; while everyone called him Mendy, his full name was the Rebbe's, Menachem Mendel, and the bride's name was none other than Chaya Mushka, the name of the Rebbe's wife. Since many Chabad families give their children these two names, such a match is not uncommon. A marriage between a young man and a young woman bearing these names reproduces the Rebbe's traces in the world in another way as well—the bride and groom, as young Hasidim, not only bear the names of the Rebbe and his wife but also see them as inspirations and exemplars. All Chabad children are in some sense the Rebbe's children, and bearing these names makes that symbolic connection more concrete.

The connection between the groom and the Rebbe was also reinforced in a physical and tactile way. After the couple's parents signed the traditional agreement laying out their commitments to the young couple, the groom donned, in keeping with tradition, the Rebbe's shirt and *sirtuk*, enabling him, as it were, to "wear" the Rebbe. The groom then proceeded to the women's section of the hall to perform the first act of the wedding ceremony itself, by lowering a veil over the face of his bride. The veil was that used by the Rebbe's wife at her wedding. After this ritual, the groom proceeded to take his place under the wedding canopy, where the bride soon joined him. There a textual link to the Rebbe was also made—a letter the Rebbe had sent to the groom's parents, offering his blessing to them at their wedding, was read out loud. Furthermore, at the end of the wedding every guest received a copy of the Hebrew edition of the book *Letters from the Rebbe*, a collection of ninety-seven of his letters. The Rebbe was also present visually and sonically; at the end of the ceremony his image and voice appeared in a film clip that was screened in front of the wedding canopy, in which he offered a blessing for brides and grooms. The Rebbe on the screen directed his gaze at the guests, who watched him breathlessly. When the Rebbe completed his blessing, the groom emotionally proclaimed three times "Long live our lord, teacher, and rabbi, the King Messiah, forever and ever," with the crowd roaring its response, repeating the mantra after him each time. Following the ceremony, the guests assembled in the foyer of the hall to pray the evening service with the Rebbe, who could be seen on a screen over the entrance to the hall on which films of convocations led by him were projected continuously. The festive meal that followed also took place under his watchful gaze—huge portraits of him hung on either side of the hall, on both the men's and women's side. Would it be farfetched to say that the Rebbe indeed attended the wedding *mamash*?[44]

CHAPTER 5

SEEING THE REBBE I

Chabad's Visual Culture

Rebbe Menachem Mendel Schneerson's impressive countenance, with his penetrating blue eyes and his white beard, is ubiquitous in Israel, both in public spaces and private homes and institutions. The face of no other rabbinic figure of our time is better known around the world. Its pervasiveness accords with the centrality of popular images in today's global culture, with its increasing stress on visual literacy. In the past, Judaism looked askance at such images, but that taboo is a thing of the past. The Second Commandment, "You shall not make for yourself a sculptured image, or any likeness," once taken to forbid all images of any sort, gradually came to be interpreted more leniently, especially after the spread of photographic technology at the end of the nineteenth and in the early twentieth centuries. Photographs and prints depicting rabbis and saints, living, dead, and ancient, spread widely through the Jewish world. The upheavals of the twentieth century, which fragmented Jewish communities, left many Jews without access to the spiritual leaders to whom they and their family had looked; images served as a way of conveying the charisma of absent, distant, and inaccessible rabbis, ensuring that these men (and in rare cases, women) remained a vivid presence in the lives of the devout.[1] But Chabad has taken this much farther than any other Jewish Orthodox group, creating a comprehensive visual culture based on the image of the Rebbe, during and after his tenure as *admor*.

Maya Balakirsky Katz has elucidated the history of Chabad's use of such images.[2] Chabad's visual culture did not start with the Rebbe. Images of five of the movement's seven spiritual leaders are in use, beginning with a famous painting of the first *admor*, Shneur Zalman, and continuing through the myriad images of the last, Rebbe Menachem Mendel Schneerson. The phenomenon is unprecedented in Hasidism. The sixth *admor*, Yosef Yitzchak Schneerson, the Rebbe's father-in-law, was the first Hasidic leader to use photographs of himself as a key instrument of his leadership. His photographs became all the more essential after Yosef Yitzchak was cut off from most of his followers in the Soviet Union. In 1927 he was forced into exile in Riga, then moving on to Otwock near Warsaw and finally to New York. As an absent leader, he encouraged those Hasidim who remained in the Soviet Union to send him photographs of themselves and to keep a photograph of him, as a way of remaining in contact. In essence, he maintained a virtual court based on the photographs of his extended family.[3]

Chabad has its roots in Czarist Russia, but from the mid-twentieth century it was reshaped with great energy by Menachem Mendel Schneerson in Crown Heights, Brooklyn, within the bounds of the largest metropolitan area in the United States, a country he called "a benevolent polity." The impact of American culture on Chabad is clearly evident in its organizational structure and its means of communication, its public relations operations, its ties with other Jewish and non-Jewish communities, and its extensive use of modern technology. The cultural and literary critic Harold Bloom counted Chabad an "American religion" in his book of that name.[4] We may presume that Chabad's extensive use of visual images was bolstered by the general American culture, which is based—so some scholars maintain—more than any other culture in human history on visual evidence and images.[5] It should be noted that, in 1994, the American Congress ordered a medal struck with the Rebbe's image, in recognition of his educational and moral labors.

At a variety of opportunities, the Rebbe recommended Hasidim setting out to serve as Chabad emissaries that they bear on their persons and frequently contemplate a pocket-sized photograph of his predecessor, Rabbi Yosef Yitzchak. Such contemplation, he said, would help bolster the feeling of connection with him. It would also avert a variety of ills, such as weakness of will, gluttony, fear of the night, and sleep disorders.[6] Initially he refrained from distributing pictures of himself, but later reversed himself. During his leadership, the Rebbe enhanced the role of court photographers in Chabad, with the result that thousands of photographs of him were distributed among his Hasidim and the public at large. These were supplemented by film clips made at the convocations he held on the nights after Sabbaths and holidays, and during his Sunday distributions of dollar bills. The still photographs and films provided detailed documentation of his daily routine as a religious and political leader. They show him at prayer, granting blessings, and preaching Hasidism and the redemption, providing a corpus of images for use in practices that invoke the occluded Rebbe's presence. Even before the Event of Gimel Tammuz, pictures of the Rebbe were displayed in Chabad houses, on Mitzvah Tanks, and in the homes of Chabad emissaries around the world. Hasidim were able to maintain a connection with the Rebbe not only by means of his pictures but also by watching footage of the convocations, first transmitted by satellite and afterward available on the internet. Following his occlusion, this focus on his visual image intensified. The photographs, originally intended to bolster the connection between the Rebbe and his followers, became to a large extent a replacement for that connection.[7] This is especially true in the case of the many Hasidim who never had the privilege of meeting the Rebbe during his lifetime. Chabad's young members, and Hasidim who have joined the movement in recent years, know no Rebbe but the virtual one. They and others benefit from a seemingly inexhaustible store of images, available on any number of websites, some of which offer a spiritual-mystical ambience integrated with aggressive marketing techniques to persuade viewers to purchase copies of the photographs from them.

This combination is best exemplified by the website www.pneimelech.com, which offers a catalogue in which "you can find our extraordinary and wide range of pictures. The pictures can reach you in any size, on a poster [printed] on the highest-quality paper, on Belgian canvas with a twenty-year guarantee against fading (!!!) or on any other material you can think of." The pictures are categorized by subject, under headings such as "Close-up," "770," "Convocations," "Prayer," and "Holidays." They replace the living Rebbe; as the website says, "the pictures of the Rebbe will give you a shot in the arm and confidence right when you need it. You will never be alone under the Rebbe's smiling gaze!" The website suggests giving pictures of the Rebbe as gifts to guests, "something that will adorn the home, refrigerator, or office—an eternal souvenir"; and it advertises bargains "from amazing stained-glass that depicts the Rebbe, for doors or windows, to a wall built from small stones that create an amazing mosaic of a breathtaking picture of the Rebbe."[8]

Given this creative marketing, it would not be an overstatement to say that the Rebbe's image has been instrumental in enhancing his and his movement's popularity, constructing Chabad identity after his occlusion, and turning this Hasidic *tzadik* into a universal messiah. In Meshichist circles, viewing portraits of the Rebbe and films of his convocations seems to be of no less importance than the study of Hasidic texts. Consider this account of a gathering at 770 on the anniversary of the Event of Gimel Tammuz in 2009, reported on Chabad.info on June 25, 2009: "Some sat around a [text of a] talk given by the Rebbe, the King Messiah, *shalita*; some listened to a fascinating lesson on the teachings of the Messiah, and some contemplated holy pictures [of the Rebbe]."

The Rebbe's images so saturate the lives of believers that it would no exaggeration to say that Chabad messianism is characterized by a kind of iconophilia. This concept, and others that accompany it, such as "religious vision," "visual piety," and "sacred gaze," come from the research literature on Christianity, a religion with prominent visual and iconic elements. But they would seem to apply to the Meshichists as well. The scholars who coined these concepts sought to divert the focus of discussion from the images themselves to the entire visual field, and to the practices of contemplating the images.[9] This analytic emphasis is consistent with what is occurring in Chabad. The Meshichist press proudly proclaims the use of pictures: "The picture of the Rebbe, the King Messiah, has become one of the images in greatest demand by all strata of the people. A picture of this sort hangs in many homes, and a special survey recently conducted showed that the Rebbe's picture . . . is the one found most commonly in the wallets of the Jewish people."[10] As far as the commandment against making images goes, the Meshichist literature grounds the visual cult in precedents from Jewish sources, some of which are based on the prophetic verse "your eyes will watch your Guide."[11] Indeed, the rabbis of the Talmud discuss the premise that a student's view of his master and teacher in the same room while studying can be an asset to the learning process.[12] Hasidic writings expand this, claiming that contemplating the *tzadik* itself benefits the contemplator.[13] The practice of calling up the *tzadik*'s face in one's mind (visualization) is mentioned in the works of Kabbalists, among them Rabbi Yitzhak Luria, Rabbi Avraham Azulai, and his grandson Chaim Yosef David Azulai (known as the Hida), as effectual in rectifying the human soul. This practice spread among Hasidim, especially during prayer.[14] Rabbi Sholom Dovber Wolpe, a leading Meshichist, stresses the importance of bearing a picture of the Rebbe on one's person and bases his position on the sources cited above and similar teachings by the Rebbe in his letters.[15]

In one case, the Rebbe sent a petitioner a photograph of his father-in-law, Rabbi Yosef Yitzchak, noting that "seeing a holy man gives strength to walk in the path of the Torah and commandments." He cited a tradition that Joseph, tempted by Potiphar's wife in Egypt, was saved from sin when the image of his father, Jacob, appeared before him.[16] Replying to a letter from a man who suffered from anxiety, he wrote: "You should place close to you a picture of his Holy Excellency, my teacher and father-in-law the *admor* . . . and even a quick glance will rid you of all fear."[17] The Rebbe also declared that Rabbi Yosef Yitzchak would turn his benevolent gaze on anyone who contemplated an image of him.[18] During the Rebbe's lifetime, much stress was placed on this direct and reciprocal contemplation—without the mediation of a picture—between a Hasid and his *tzadik*. When a Hasid cited the purpose of a pilgrimage to the Rebbe on holidays, he would say that he was going "to see and be seen."[19] The Rebbe, however, expanded this reciprocity to include the encounter between the Hasid and a *picture* of the Rebbe. To the best of my knowledge, this is quite exceptional in Judaism, and it is characteristic of some of the visual rituals that took hold after the Event of Gimel Tammuz. The Meshichists implement the Rebbe's directive, but replace the picture of Rabbi Yosef Yitzchak with one of the Rebbe himself.

The most famous image of the Rebbe, among the countless ones available, is one in which he is shown waving his hand in encouragement. The circumstances under which this image was produced and distributed show that it has taken on a life on its own.

FIGURE 12. The Rebbe's iconic image: On a poster in Tel Aviv. Photographer: Menahem Rosenberg.

The story behind the famous picture was first told in *Sichat Hage'ulah* about half a year after the Rebbe's occlusion, under the headline "A Picture Is Worth a Thousand Words."[20] The photograph was taken by Shimon Roumani, one of Chabad's elite court photographers, in 1987, as the Rebbe surveyed Chabad children who were participating in a Lag

FIGURE 13. The Rebbe's iconic image: On stickers. Photographer: Ran Bartov.

FIGURE 14. The Rebbe's iconic image: On the Partition Wall between Israel and the Palestinian Authority (the caption in Arabic urges Palestinians to do good). Courtesy of the Association for the True and Complete Religion.

B'Omer parade. The picture underwent a process of mythification as believers began to see in the raised hand of the Rebbe the face of a cute baby.[21] Following the discovery, many stories began to appear regarding the picture's power to help childless women conceive. In 1988, while the Rebbe was still alive, the picture became hugely popular in Israel, when thousands of copies of it were printed on Rosh Hashanah cards that were distributed for free and used by Israelis for the holiday. Hundreds of thousands of copies were subsequently handed out during the elections held later that same year, elections in which the Rebbe endorsed and actively campaigned for the Agudat Israel ultra-Orthodox party.

Since his occlusion, this photograph has become even more pervasive in public spaces and on the walls of people's homes. From time to time it is included as an insert in Israel's leading daily newspapers. It is the common element shared by all the "Redemption Products" distributed by Meshichist groups, displayed prominently at the Messiah and Redemption Fair, on handouts advertising the Rebbe's Ten-Point Mitzvah Campaign, and on other publicity items such as keychains, cards listing emergency telephone numbers and others bearing the Wayfarer's Prayer, pendants to hang on rearview mirrors, and personal charity boxes.[22] In many cases the item comes with instructions on the importance of contemplating the picture.[23] The Redemption Products listed above are only a small portion of the available sacred and secular items bearing the image. These include wall clocks, wristwatches, night-lights, children's games, boxes of Sabbath candles, and *kiddush* cups.[24] The goal of this "holy industry" is, of course, to spread word of the imminent Redemption:

> The general idea is to employ items that we all use, to the point that we are unable to imagine our lives without them. That means landline and cell phones, telephone books, refrigerator doors, napkin holders, bookmarks, pencil cases, and so on. When adorned with a colorful and well-designed sticker bearing the picture of the Rebbe . . . together with appropriate captions, such technical accessories get upgraded to being accessories of the time of the Messiah. The content and value of the items are appropriate for all ages.[25]

The iconic image of the Rebbe is included in all Meshichist publications, including *Sichat Hage'ulah* itself. Since issue 296, which came out on

FIGURE 15. Calendar displaying the Rebbe's iconic image. Courtesy of the Association for the True and Complete Redemption.

May 19, 2000, six years following the Event of Gimel Tammuz, the photograph of the Rebbe with his raised arm has appeared in the upper left corner on the pamphlet's front page, under the masthead. Just two weeks later a photograph of 770 was added, occupying a permanent place at the bottom right corner. A year and a half earlier, beginning with issue 225 (December 11, 1998), a Messiah flag, displaying a crown, was given a fixed place in the upper right-hand border of the front page. These visual representations—the Rebbe's countenance, his home/temple, and the flag—constitute a trinity of images that embody the idea of the Messiah and the redemption. *Beis Moshiach* magazine, the most important weekly put out by Meshichist circles, also displays the Rebbe's picture on its cover. But here the image changes; each issue displays a different photograph from the huge number available. Each issue cover displays one such photograph, and an image of 770 appears in the upper right corner. One inviolable rule is that a picture of the Rebbe appears on the covers of all Meshichist books, and sometimes additional photographs appear within the book.[26]

The lengths to which such visual representations can be taken can be seen in Chaim Sasson's book *Now I Knew*,[27] which includes "a treasury of sources, glosses, proofs, and clues about the revelation reality of the King Messiah." In addition to a photograph of the Rebbe on the cover and others on many other pages of the book, his image appears on the upper left corner of each set of facing pages in the 675-page work. This visual alliteration seems to be aimed at ensuring that readers will be unable to avoid the Rebbe's gaze as they read.

FIGURE 16. Keychains, card, and candle box displaying the Rebbe's image and his abode. Photographer: Ran Bartov.

FIGURE 17. Clock with the Rebbe's image. The caption reads: "We want Messiah now." Courtesy of Miriam Feldman.

FIGURE 18. Car-window shade with the Rebbe's image. Photographer: Ran Bartov.

The placement of a photograph of the Rebbe on the front page of *Ezrachim Bimdinat Hamashiach* (Citizens in the Messiah State), a periodical aimed at young people and New Age spiritual seekers, is particularly intriguing. The magazine offered material on messianism and redemption, as well as on spirituality, nature, healing, and self-fulfillment. The cover of each issue depicted a picture of the Rebbe gazing out over a panoramic landscape of mountains and wilderness, or even over the entire universe, using satellite photographs. These images create an impression that the Rebbe exists on some higher plane, from which his gaze encompasses all of creation. The process of exalting the image of the Rebbe as the Final Redeemer has led some extreme Meshichist groups to employ language that explicitly ascribes divine status to him. This subversive ascription has met fierce resistance both inside and outside Chabad. It may well be that such images express ideas that cannot easily be given textual expression, or even spoken of. Viewers can accept the Rebbe's heavenly status more easily by contemplating such images than by an explicit verbal statement about his divinity.

The Meshichists are fully conscious of the important role that pictures play in making the Rebbe present. According to *Sichat Hage'ulah*, "Even his picture gazing on us from almost every corner . . . and the immediate connection made in the minds of all of us between it and the Messiah, illustrates another aspect of his mounting presence in our lives."[28] It is not only the quantity of pictures that is important—their size is also a significant factor. Meshichists take pride in hanging huge images of the Rebbe. Some of these are fixtures, such as the portrait that gazes down from a high billboard, unmissable by drivers on Tel Aviv's Netivei Ayalon freeway, and similar ones at major intersections in New York. Others are one-off images displayed at rallies, convocations, and celebrations. The hundreds of thousands who attend the annual pilgrimage of Rabbi Shimon bar Yochai on Lag B'Omer, at his tomb on Mount Meron, have in recent years been greeted by a huge picture of the Rebbe, twelve by seven and a half meters, held high by a crane mounted on a heavy truck. When the organizers of the Redemption Assembly in Bat Yam on 3 Tammuz 2004 succeeded, "against all odds," in raising a picture of that size, they remarked with satisfaction that "one of the attractive elements at the Redemption Assembly . . . was undoubtedly the

FIGURE 19. Typical cover of *Citizens in the Messiah's State* magazine. Courtesy of the Association for the True and Complete Redemption.

huge picture of the Rebbe . . . *a picture with which the unaided eye could be imbued with his sensible presence.*"[29] It is worth noting that at this same rally, in the shadow of that huge picture hanging over the amphitheater where it was held, the Rebbe also looked out over the crowd from two video screens and three billboards, in addition to myriad pictures of him on the walls. These visual representations underline and confirm the Rebbe's vitality and eternity. In addition, the Rebbe's pictures are a fixture of the photographs taken at such rallies and convocations, thus creating what might be called meta-iconization of his image. At such events, the speakers are generally photographed beside one of the iconic images of the Rebbe, and are thus commemorated in an intimate encounter with him by means of a picture within a picture.

Meta-iconization also takes place cinematographically. Some of the clips produced by Chabad contain segments showing an audience at a convocation watching one of the Rebbe's talks on screen, creating a screen-within-a-screen effect.

Pictures of the Rebbe are ubiquitous in Meshichist homes. In some homes I visited I saw pictures of him, in various sizes, hanging on the walls of every room and hallway. The home, not just the holy center at 770 and its avatars, becomes a messianic arena, replete with the Rebbe's presence.[30] The home is, of course, an important place of socialization: the children in Meshichist families grow up with the Rebbe concretely present in their lives, watching them from the sides of their cradles and beds and the walls of their rooms. Huge pictures of the Rebbe are also positioned prominently in other sites of socialization, such as the messianic summer camp Oro shel Mashiach, where children take part in activities that imbue them with a sense of mission and the desire to spread the word of the Messiah and the redemption.

Some Meshichists seek to expose babies, even newborns, to pictures of the Rebbe so that his shining countenance can penetrate their souls and shape them at the start of life. Under the title "The Youngest Pointer in the World," *Sichat Hage'ulah* offers the story of a newborn who ceases crying when a picture of the Rebbe is placed before him. When a professor in the maternity ward dismisses this by saying that newborns cannot see or understand, the baby responds by pointing at the picture.[31]

The Rebbe's followers also bear the Rebbe's picture on their persons, on a pocket-sized card with the text of the traditional wayfarer's prayer, or sometimes on their watches. There are other accessories that also enable Hasidim to turn their bodies into a sanctuary for the Messiah—for example, lapel pins and *kipot* inscribed with the "Yechi Adoneinu" mantra.

The power of the visual image is even greater in videos, especially when they were filmed in the house in which the Rebbe supposedly still remains, and where his absence is felt most painfully.[32] As one visitor put it: "You connect what you have seen all the time in videos and say to yourself, 'Here the Rebbe stands, here he strides, here he meets with Hasidim, this is the *parochet* [curtain on the ark in which Torah scrolls are kept] that he touched,' and the whole puzzle falls into place."[33] It should be kept in mind that film clips of the Rebbe giving talks or meeting with his followers are continually screened at 770. Chabad makes

FIGURE 20. Meta-iconization 1. Photographer: Sagiv Elbaz.

extensive use of the full extent of visual technology, adopting all the latest innovations almost as quickly as they become available. By these means, the Rebbe's presence becomes ever more dynamic for visitors to his home. "All those close to Chabad who enter [the building] are granted a special and fascinating tour, using a tablet [computer] that shows the Rebbe *shalita* the King Messiah at each point along the tour."[34] Chabad Hasidim who are not Meshichists also regard photographs, and film footage in particular, as vital for preserving a sense that the Rebbe is part of their lives.[35]

FIGURE 21. Meta-iconization 2. Photographer: Sagiv Elbaz.

Beyond the stronger sense of a living presence that films offer, much more so than still-portrait photographs,[36] the Chabad organization also makes a point of screening films of the Rebbe's convocations and assemblies on the same date on which the event was filmed. For example, at 770, on the night following Simchat Torah, films of the Rebbe among his Hasidim at this same event are shown—in other words, they are shown both in the place and at the time when they were filmed. The result is a tangible, sometimes jarring interweaving of two audiences, that on the screen and that which watches the film.[37] The faces of the celebrants,

FIGURE 22. At Oro shel Mashiach (Light of the Messiah) summer camp. Courtesy of Sagiv Elbaz.

both on the screen and off, are turned toward the Rebbe; all of them listen attentively to his words, and they all answer "Amen" or call out "Long live our lord" with a single, inseparable voice. These screenings have become an important part of the daily routine at Meshichist yeshivot. When I visited the Chabad yeshiva in Safed on the morning of November 12, 2008, I found a flier on the students' desks informing them that, following the afternoon prayer service, a film clip of the Rebbe's last convocation would be screened. It had been filmed precisely on this date, fifteen years previously. The Rebbe who appears on the screen was at that time unable to speak as a result of the stroke he had suffered, and simply waved his hand to encourage the ardent Hasidim before him. The students all gathered to see him on the screen, becoming so excited as they watched that, when it was over, they broke out in ecstatic dancing and Messiah songs, along with shouts of "Long live our lord," lasting for no less than twenty minutes. When I visited 770 in Crown Heights on July 8, 2012, I attended the afternoon prayer service, to which the Rebbe is invited as a matter of course. After the service, a conversation with the Rebbe was shown on a huge screen. Many of the Hasidim listened attentively, fixing their gaze on the Rebbe. Rabbi Shlomo Dobnik, an emissary of the Tomchei Temimim yeshiva in Be'er Sheva, explained the films' power to evoke the Rebbe's presence, remarking that the Rebbe on the screen sometimes fixes his gaze on specific members of the audience. If, as Dobnik watched such a film, the Rebbe gazed at him and cleared his throat, it meant, so Dobnik told me, that he could expect problems and difficulties that day. But when the Rebbe on the screen directed a greeting or smile at him, it was a clear sign that the day would be a success. The Hasidim seek messages from the Rebbe in the films in a practice that might best be called "videomancy," the visual equivalent of the bibliomancy of the *Igrot Kodesh* Oracle.[38]

As a concrete means for making the Rebbe present, the Rebbe's visual image is more than just a "true representation" that pervades the present and makes it possible to preserve the past faithfully and "revive" it.[39] The transformation from image to icon means a move from representation to re-presentation: the icon is taken by believers to be an aspect of the thing that it symbolizes, and as such it has a stimulating and interactive power that places it at the center of a larger visual ritual.[40] A woman in distress who found herself drawn to Chabad related: "I felt that, when I looked at the picture, it was as if he were actually with me, encouraging me and protecting me."[41] The tension between "as if" and "actually" in her words reappears time and time again in Meshichist discourse and requires clarification.[42] There can be no doubt that, for most believers, the pictures are more than representations of the Rebbe. Even if they are reluctant to claim that "the pictures are the Rebbe," they do consider the images to partake of something of him. They provide a partial presence. In the life space of all Chabad Hasidim, both radical and moderate, pictures of the Rebbe at the very least preserve his visage in the Hasid's consciousness, and thus maintain him in their lives. Chabad's iconophilia also creates a dynamic of self-amplification: the Rebbe's face radiates power in the Meshichist living space because his pictures pervade the home and his image appears on many household items—clocks, calendars, cards bearing emergency telephone numbers and the wayfarer's prayer, and books. This power constantly increases because the Rebbe's visual presence creates many opportunities to encounter and interact with him.

Many apparitions of the Rebbe occur in the wake of an encounter with a picture of him.

In the connection between the Hasid and the *tzadik*, the importance of mutual contemplation recalls the visual interaction between the believer and the god or guru in Hinduism, which is called *darshan*.[43] The Rebbe put great emphasis on this connection, and repeatedly recommended contemplation of a picture of his predecessor in times of distress. As evident from his reply to a woman suffering from bad thoughts, this contemplation is reciprocal: "*And remember that he, too, being a true shepherd of Israel, gazes at you at this moment, and will help you.*"[44] In the messianic tide that swept over Chabad after the Rebbe's occlusion, contemplation of his image took on added significance as it became connected to his manifestation to his followers: "As Hasidim focus more on the Rebbe . . . and look in his direction, he will reveal himself to them more quickly."[45]

To back up my claim that pictures of the Rebbe serve as focal points for a wide-ranging visual cult, I now present the wide range of ways in which pictures of the Rebbe are used by Meshichists. They fall into the following six categories:

1. The Picture as a Catalyst

Beyond making the Rebbe's presence felt in public and private spaces, pictures of him stimulate and catalyze a variety of actions and experiences that contribute to the Rebbe's miraculous intervention in the lives of his believers and to channels of communication with him. Encounters with the Rebbe's picture inspire people in need to address him via *Igrot Kodesh*. Thus, a childless man embraces the idea of contacting the Rebbe via his letters "as a result of the huge picture of the Rebbe . . . that catches the eye of anyone who enters our home."[46]

There are cases in which the picture enables a believer to identify the Rebbe in a dream or simply induces a person to remember him. Dreamers say that, even though they never met the Rebbe in person, they were able to recognize him without hesitation in a dream thanks to the pervasive pictures of him. Sometimes they make the connection only after the dream ends, when encountering a picture of the Rebbe. In all these cases, a picture enables a dreamer to identify a character in a dream as the Rebbe, and thus connects the private dream experience with external reality, which in turn validates the dream. For example, a teenage girl told her family that the Rebbe had appeared to her, distributing dollars. They asked her to describe how he looked, and she pointed to a picture of him from 1993 as the one that looked most like the image she had seen in her dream. Such a connection can be found not only in dreams but also in other kinds of apparitions of the Rebbe.

2. The Picture as an Amulet: Deliverance and Healing

The Rebbe's disciples believe that his picture has the power to change facts in the world in a dramatic way, even in the absence of any complex ritual or ceremony, simply by means of its presence or proximity to the body of the believer. There are many stories of such a picture being used magically to protect the believer and save him from tribulations or even death. The picture's magical powers were demonstrated, by means of what believers present as a scientific experiment, during a wave of terror that took place in Israel's Gush Katif settlements in the Gaza Strip in 2002. In the month of Tevet in that year, following a spate of attacks at the settlement bloc's major intersection, a large picture of the Rebbe was installed there. "Two quiet months ensued," *Sichat Hage'ulah* reported; "but one day the picture fell down. Amazingly, just two days later a soldier was killed by a bomb placed on the road," and other soldiers and civilians (who are named in the article) were killed soon thereafter. "The stinging and notable resumption of the attacks confirmed our hypothesis: the holy picture of the Rebbe *shalita*, the King Messiah, at the intersection had played a major role in keeping the entire road safe." When the picture's importance became clear, it was immediately put up again, and the road was then quiet for more than three months.[47] The person responsible for erecting the picture of the Rebbe at the intersection, the Chabad emissary to Neveh Dekalim, one of the settlements, found himself and his family under attack by Palestinians while driving in the area. "Little Mendy, who held the picture of the Rebbe *shalita*, the King Messiah, in his hands the whole time, was miraculously saved," *Sichat Hage'ulah* recounted.[48] During Israel's Operation Cast Lead in the Gaza Strip, in the winter of 2008–2009, "thousands of soldiers [equipped themselves] with defensive, guarding, and saving kits [containing] a copy of *Chitat* and a picture of the Rebbe *shalita* the King Messiah."[49]

Pictures of the Rebbe averted attempted attacks in other parts of Israel as well. In one such attack, in Afula, the perpetrators did not get into the city's central bus station, where they planned to stage an attack, by virtue of a Chabad stand where Hasidim encouraged passersby to put on *tefillin*, and the videos of the Rebbe continuously screened there.[50] Jerusalem's Machaneh Yehuda *shuk* (open-air market) was the target of several attacks. Prior to one of them, in April 2002, one shopper passed by an Israeli national-lottery booth and saw a picture of the Rebbe hanging inside. The shopper began singing "Yechi Adoneinu" to himself and then there was an explosion; even though he was very close to the attack, he suffered no harm. "I had a feeling that someone was enveloping me in a kind of protective wall and not allowing any piece of the powerful bomb to harm me," he related.[51]

The Rebbe's picture also saved lives in Itamar, a settlement in the northern West Bank where, in March 2011, Palestinians murdered the Fogel couple and three of their children. According to an account in *Sichat Hage'ulah*, the assailants also approached the home of the next house over, where Vicky and David Schneerson and their five children lived. When the perpetrators were apprehended, so the Meshichist publication reported, it transpired that "the kitchen window had been open on that horrible night and they saw the Rebbe's picture . . . which prevented them from entering." Another reason they were deterred from attacking the Schneerson home was that one of the children was just then reading the Rebbe's twelve verses out loud.[52]

Terrorist attacks and military operations are but a small part of the many tribulations in which the lifesaving power of the Rebbe's picture has been demonstrated. When a light aircraft carrying Israeli and British trekkers had to make an emergency landing in the Bolivian jungle, one of the passengers handed out "Messiah cards" to his companions, which displayed the Rebbe's image on one side and the Wayfarer's Prayer on the other. This passenger later related that he shouted to them in English: "The Rebbe, the King Messiah, will save us. You'll see." Despite the difficult conditions, the landing was successful. At the hospital where the passengers were taken to be examined afterward, he encountered the same British tourists, who were holding the picture of the Rebbe *shalita*, and kept praising him.⁵³ A yeshiva student participating in a study group at 770 was attacked in the middle of the night by a thief at a subway station. As the thief emptied his victim's wallet, he also took out the picture of the Rebbe that resided in it permanently. At the sight of the picture, the assailant grew agitated and asked who the man in the picture was. "It's my father," the student said, without thinking twice. The robber immediately gave him back all his money. The student told his story to everyone he knew and saw to it that each one of them would carry the Rebbe's picture in his wallet.⁵⁴

In the cases presented above, the picture served as an amulet that repels threats and dangers. But it can also be used actively as medical intervention, as in the following story, which relates explicitly to the magical powers of the iconic picture of the Rebbe. This picture is called "the picture with the baby" because "from a certain aspect, when looking at the [Rebbe's] open hand, you can make out the face of a sweet baby with black eyes, a cute upturned nose, and round cheeks."⁵⁵ A man from Hatzor HaGelilit, who was informed that his newborn's right hand was paralyzed, recalled the baby hidden in the Rebbe's picture and began to act: "I began to wave the picture back and forth over the paralyzed hand, accompanying the action with a silent prayer and supplication for the complete healing of our son." He continued doing this for hours to the chagrin of the nurses, who complained that "it's not sterile, and not effective." To augment the therapy, he attached the picture to the baby's hand with an adhesive bandage "so that it continued to 'radiate' on the hand for the entire Sabbath." In the wake of this treatment, the baby began to move its hand, to the astonishment of the medical staff.⁵⁶ The magic action in this case had a clearly sympathetic form, since it was the Rebbe's right hand in the picture, with its embedded profile of a baby, which took part in curing the paralyzed right hand of the baby in the hospital.

The Rebbe's picture also protects non-Jews. An Indian rickshaw driver in Dharamsala, two of whose children died suddenly, received a picture of the Rebbe from the local Chabad emissary along with some of the Rebbe's *mikveh* water. Thanks to these, he believed, and his promise to observe the seven Noachide laws, his four-year-old son remained healthy. Out of gratitude to his new patron ("I believe only in him"), he discarded the small idol of a Hindu god that had hung as a charm in his rickshaw and began to bear a picture of the Rebbe in his pocket.[57]

3. The Picture as a Survivor: Miraculous Preservation

The deadly terror attack on the Chabad House in Mumbai on November 26–27, 2008, perpetrated by Pakistanis, did not seem to offer much in the way of miracle stories. Nevertheless, a few days after the massacre, in which six people died, the Chabad.info website posted a photograph taken from a report on Israel's Channel 10 News, with a huge picture of the Rebbe at its center. The photograph was accompanied by the television reporter's statement: "Only the picture of the Rebbe remained whole, surveying the ruins." According to the Meshichists, even if the picture is not always able to save people in distress, it can at least save itself.[58] Another example comes from a couple in Hadera whose house burned town. While their home was completely destroyed, they found in a crumbling dresser a pristine picture of the Rebbe, who was wrapped in a *tallit* and wearing *tefillin*. When the husband, perhaps spurred by the sight of the Rebbe, proceeded to search for his own *tefillin*, he found, to his relief, that they, too, had suffered no damage.[59] Another home, this one in Haifa, was destroyed by the explosion of a gas balloon. *Sichat Hage'ulah* reported that "it was an unbelievable sight: among the ruins of the charred home, a picture of the Rebbe *shalita*, the King Messiah, hung on the wall, smiling and surveying the astounded [people] who came to see the result of the miracle with their own eyes."[60] In the last two cases the distinction between saving and being saved is not sharp, as the principal miracle is that, despite total destruction, no one was hurt. Nevertheless, the picture's survival is explicitly presented as a miracle in and of itself. Note also that in the accounts from Mumbai and Haifa, the Rebbe's picture is not an object of contemplation; rather, it observes the scene and people around it. The gaze, extending out of the picture, again stresses the vitality and dynamic nature of the Rebbe's image.[61]

As it happens, unfortunately, Chabad emissaries in India have been the victims of a number of attacks by Muslim extremists. In addition to

Gabi and Rivka Holtzberg, the couple murdered in Mumbai, Mira Ruth Sharf, the wife of the Chabad emissary in New Delhi's Grand Bazaar, was killed during a visit to Israel, along with two others. On October 15, 2012, a rocket fired from the Gaza Strip hit her home in Kiryat Malachi's Nahalat Kfar Chabad neighborhood during Operation Pillar of Defense. The author of an article on the event preferred to stress the visible miracles that occurred then—thousands of rockets were fired on Israeli communities during the operation, but almost no one was hurt:[62] The writer called on his readers to publicize the miracles, as the Rebbe insisted, but could not help adding: "Precisely in this light the death of the three martyrs is so upsetting. . . . " In the following issue, an article headlined "He is Troubled by All Their Troubles" informed *Sichat Hage'ulah*'s readers that the image of the Rebbe was discovered in the wall of the apartment in which the emissary was killed. In this case, it was not a picture that survived the destruction intact, but rather the damaged wall took the form of a silhouette of the Rebbe. The article was illustrated with a real picture of the Rebbe alongside the silhouette so that readers could note the similarity between the two. The discovery of the portrait in the wall recalls the discovery, mostly by Christians, of images of saints in any of a variety of objects.[63]

4. The Picture as a Magnet: The Power of the Gaze

Accounts by Hasidim of the power of the Rebbe's gaze are noteworthy against the background of the mystical aura that envelops the *tzadik* in all Hasidic movements, and the efforts of Hasidim to document every single movement made by their spiritual leader,[64] to gaze at his face, and to be the object of his holy gaze.[65] The forcefulness of the Rebbe's blue eyes contributed to the charismatic aura that surrounded him during his years of leadership. Many stories told of his ability to see into souls and hearts. Even the entry devoted to the Rebbe in the *Encyclopedia Britannica* describes him as "a mesmeric figure with piercing blue eyes."[66] Meshichist literature stresses the strong impression that the Rebbe's gaze made on famous public figures, among them Yitzhak Rabin and Ariel Sharon.[67] Ge'ulah Cohen, a former member of the Knesset and leader of the Greater Israel movement, who met the Rebbe in 1964, was par-

FIGURE 23. The Rebbe's image in the wall. Courtesy of the Association for the True and Complete Redemption.

ticularly impressed by the "pair of eyes gazing at you, not to see but to discover."[68] Elie Wiesel received much the same impression, according to a Meshichist source: "I had never seen such a powerfully expressive face or eyes. There is a fearsome and calming spirit in them, one that arouses and comforts. And they contain a will of steel. His gaze looks as if it could bring the End of Days. . . . During the days that followed my return from there I felt as if his eyes were following every step I took and reading every one of my thoughts."[69]

In addition to his ability to plumb hearts and souls, the Rebbe's gaze was said to have immense healing powers, as the two following stories show. The first centers on a student at the Chabad yeshiva in Safed who, at the age of seven, began to suffer from sharp eye pains brought on by severe inflammation. He had difficulty opening his eyes in the light. Despite being, in his words, a guinea pig for his doctors, his condition worsened to the point that there was concern that he would go blind. During a visit to New York he was taken to the Rebbe and asked for his blessing. The student related: "The Rebbe . . . looked at me for a moment that seemed to go on for an eternity—I felt as if an electrical current were going through me, *mamash*." After the encounter the inflammation subsided, and his eyesight gradually returned to normal.[70] The second story has to do with a dramatic event during a convocation led by the elderly Rebbe during the Sukkot holiday in 1992, a time when he was ill and unable to speak and seldom appeared in public. When the Rebbe finally appeared, his followers went into a frenzy and one Hasid was trampled by the crowd and lost consciousness. A medical crew tried to revive him but without success. The victim's cousin roared in the direction of the platform where the Rebbe stood: "Rebbe, he is dead!" The victim later related that, following this cry, "the Rebbe . . . leaned forward, cast his gaze down in the direction where I lay on the ground, and the moment his gaze 'landed' on me I began to convulse. . . . " Backed by the doctors' acknowledgement that this was a miraculous cure, the protagonist described it as "a resurrection of the dead in the literal sense, *mamash*."[71]

The healing power of the Rebbe's gaze is explicitly described in the first story as an electrical current. While this is not stated explicitly in the second story, it is implicit, with its picture of energy transmitted by the Rebbe's gaze that agitates and shakes the Hasid and restores him to life.

The Rebbe's penetrating gaze did not disappear from the world following his occlusion. It continues to function, even more powerfully, through his pictures. "What exactly does the Rebbe want from me, he is *mamash* pursuing me," a man from Kfar Saba protested just a few months after the Event of Gimel Tammuz. He said this following a dream in which he saw a figure he did not recognize, but whom he later realized was the Rebbe. The identification came when he encountered pictures of the Rebbe time and again and felt his gaze from them. As a result, he began to lead an observant life and to come under Chabad's influence.[72]

Another story on the force of the Rebbe's gaze was published two years later on the front page of *Sichat Hage'ulah* under the headline "The Picture of the King Messiah." It told of a Jew who had been lured into a non-Jewish cult. At the last minute he felt a pair of eyes gazing at him from a picture in a newspaper.

> The eyes seemed to seek him out and, mesmerized, he continued to look at them. . . . The Rebbe's eyes did not leave him. . . . The Rebbe seemed to speak to him from the picture. "Do not do this, you are a Jew . . . !" At first he tried to evade [the gaze], but the eyes did not let him go, they seemed to force him to look at them, as if they were saying, "I will not let you escape, you will look at me until you decide to revoke your decision."[73]

Being trapped by the Rebbe's spellbinding gaze, which forces one to look back, and the expressive power of that gaze, transmitting a clear message analogous to speech, are common motifs in stories I heard about the Rebbe. The magnetic power of the Rebbe's eyes guides, helps, and heals those who are caught in his gaze. Rabbi Zimroni Tzik, editor of *Sichat Hage'ulah*, told me that he can make out changes in the gaze of the photograph of the Rebbe hanging on the wall of his office, and that these changes guide him in making difficult decisions.

Such vitality transforms the photograph from a representation into a partial embodiment of the Rebbe. A woman from Herzliya made this explicit when she told the editor of *Sichat Hage'ulah* how she felt each time she walked by the Rebbe's picture in her apartment: "It is amazing but everyone can confirm it personally, how the gaze of the Rebbe, our Righteous Messiah, pierces the depths of the soul, even if it is a gaze from a photograph. It is a living gaze that makes a demand: 'You must be better.'" The woman's connection to the Rebbe's picture began as her eyes passed over the picture in walking by it, but after a while she felt "that something was stopping her. It was like an invisible hand that planted her eyes on the picture. She had a real feeling that the Rebbe . . . was saying to her: 'Ask for a blessing now.'"[74]

In the last two stories, the protagonists feel as if the Rebbe captures their gaze and transmits a message that can be heard, at least in the believer's mind. In the following story, too, the narrator relates that he "encountered the Rebbe's picture" while waiting fearfully at the bedside of his wife, who had been hospitalized for an operation. In this case as well it was the Rebbe's gaze that set the process in motion: "His piercing eyes gave me a feeling that he was looking at me at that moment. I suddenly felt a huge inner urge to let out my emotions. I looked at the picture and I began to shout 'Rebbe!!!'"[75]

The hypnotic power of the Rebbe's eyes gazing out from pictures of him stands out in many stories. A customs agent at the Moscow airport found a picture of the Rebbe in the bag of a Hasid and saw "special spiritual forces" in it. The Hasid gave him the picture, "and here, how wonderful it was to see this gentile standing there and continuing to look with devotion at the picture of the Rebbe, the King Messiah, cut off from everything surrounding him."[76] The same magnetic force affected an immigration official at a New York airport, who had treated a Hasid whose visa had expired with "terrible coldness." The Hasid related that, when she saw the Rebbe's picture between the pages of his passport, "a miracle occurred. Her expression changed suddenly and completely, her eyes seemed to be glued to the picture for a few seconds, at the end of which she handed him back his passport, indicating that it was approved."[77]

5. The Picture as an Icon: Ritual Encounter

The Rebbe's mesmerizing gaze is not one-way. A person captured by the picture returns its gaze, and in many cases directs requests or asks something of the Rebbe such that the encounter becomes interactive.[78] The distinction between this heading and the previous one is not sharp, but in the cases I will present in this section, believers take the initiative in turning their gaze to the Rebbe, generally in situations of crisis and distress. One dramatic example of such an appeal appears in the story of a young Israeli who was working in a coal mine in Australia and was trapped when a tunnel collapsed. He was rescued after pulling a picture of the Rebbe out of his pocket and shouting at it: "Rebbe, save me. Rebbe! Rebbe!"[79] A Chabad woman from Lod found herself alone at a large intersection at night. She was very frightened but suddenly remembered that "it is a great succor to a person, especially if he is a tense situation, to look into the eyes of his rabbi. . . . " She took out a picture of the Rebbe, gazed at his face, and after telling the Rebbe of her troubles, she was offered a ride by a religious driver who took her safely home.[80]

Another example is the story of a young Israeli man who tried to illegally cross the border from Mexico into the United States and found himself abandoned by his guide. *Sichat Hage'ulah* offered the story: "He soon finished the water in his bottle as he trudged through the desert toward the unknown. The sun beating down on him and the parchedness had their effect; the landscape began to dance before his eyes. Black birds circled above him. He realized that these were his last moments." But then he remembered that he had, in his backpack, a copy of the book *A Prophet among You*, which he had purchased in Israel before flying out. "He took out the book and gazed at the picture of the Rebbe [that appeared on the book's cover], and he cried out with the last of his strength: 'Rebbe, save me, I promise that I will become religious.'" Suddenly his cell phone, which had not been working up until then because there was no reception, came to life. The young man called the police and was rescued at the last minute by a helicopter.[81]

Most of the appeals to the Rebbe by means of his image have to do with medical problems. Sometimes the situation is a full-scale emergency. A man from Ashdod suffered from severe stomach pains, but the tests the doctors ordered discovered no cause. "At a certain stage, when the pain became unbearable, he stood next to the Rebbe's picture . . . with the words coming out of their own volition, accompanied by hot tears: 'Rebbe, I don't have the strength to suffer any more. You must help me, help me.'" Just as he was appealing to the Rebbe his brother-in-law appeared and took the sick man to the emergency room. This time the doctors found the cause of the pain and treated it. They explained that, thanks to the immediate care that he received, he was spared medical complications.[82] Another dramatic medical story begins at a class in *Tanya* at a Chabad House. One of the participants suddenly collapsed, unconscious. His pulse stopped and resuscitation efforts, massages, and respiration could not restore it. The rabbi from Kfar Chabad who taught the class related: "When I saw what was happening, I put on my sash (as is customary when appealing to the Rebbe) and stood facing the Rebbe's picture . . . with all the participants in the class watching me with bated breath." He called for the Rebbe's help, enumerating the merits of the Hasid lying before him, and asked that the Rebbe restore him to life. Electric-shock treatment brought the Hasid back to consciousness, just as, in the story related above, the Rebbe's electrifying gaze in his lifetime revived the Hasid who lost consciousness after being trampled by a crowd at 770. It is hardly surprising that the rabbi who told the story said that "the concrete miracle electrified all of us."[83]

A young woman whose baby daughter faced an eye operation for blocked tear ducts sat down with the baby on her lap facing the Rebbe's picture. With tears in her eyes, she asked for his blessing. Beforehand she had given charity in the amount of the letter *'ayin* (which also means "eye"; the letter's numerical value is seventy), and made a decision to try to look at everyone kindly (lit. "with a good eye"). Aside from calling out for the Rebbe's help, she also dripped "the Rebbe's water," from his *mikveh,* on the affected eye. Three days later the baby had recovered completely.[84] The ritual the woman conducted facing the picture was clearly based, as we have seen in other cases, on principles of sympathetic magic—to cure the affected eye, the mother sheds tears like water, gives a sum of charity represented by the numerical value of the Hebrew letter whose name means "eye," and promises to try to see people "with a good eye." It should be kept in mind, however, that this repeated focus on the eye, growing out of a concrete problem, is also grounded in the larger context of the Rebbe's gaze, as this young mother and her baby girl gaze at the Rebbe's picture and are exposed to his benevolent gaze. Furthermore, this ritual encounter also takes place in the larger messianic context, which calls on people to open their eyes in order to see the redeemer, who is at present invisible to physical eyes. On top of that, the numerical value of the letter with the same name as the word for "eye" is 70, an element of 770, Chabad's holy site.

Another young woman implored the Rebbe to heal her daughter who needed an operation on her hand following a severe injury. The mother, standing by her daughter's bed in the room where the anesthesia was being administered, noticed a picture of the Rebbe hanging on the wall, together with a prayer for doctors; it had been donated by a previous patient. The woman related: "I looked at him and found myself murmuring tearfully, 'Rebbe, you must help me! I have heard that when people say "Long live [our lord . . .]" you help them, so here I am saying [it].'" This story resembles the previous one in highlighting the therapeutic role played by the Rebbe's picture in times of medical crisis. It also shows how the ritual was constructed, with the appeal to the picture being supplemented by the recitation of the "Yechi Adoneinu" mantra.[85] Notably, despite the fact that these cases center on a miraculous intervention that saves a life or cures an illness, the picture serves not as an amulet, as it does in one of the previous categories, but rather as an icon that embodies the Rebbe and makes it possible to appeal to him.

Another story centering on a medical problem, in this case a possible heart defect in a fetus, offers a way of tracking the institutionalization and dissemination of the ritual involving the Rebbe's picture. The sister of the pregnant woman suggested that she ask the Rebbe for his blessing in the following way: "Stand close to the holy picture of the Rebbe . . . and recite a chapter from the Psalms with great intention, and afterward declare your acceptance of his kingship ('Long live our lord . . . ') and make your request."[86]

As the use of the Rebbe's picture has become standardized and widespread, it also has come to be used in the preparations prior to opening *Igrot Kodesh*. When a woman who was facing an economic crisis went to a Chabad rabbi in Nahariya to get help via *Igrot Kodesh*, he instructed her to wash her hands ritually and write a letter to the Rebbe. But before she was to insert the letter into one of the volumes, he requested: "Now gaze at his holy picture and take upon yourself a good decision and declare the holy declaration 'Long live our Lord.'"[87] Gazing at the Rebbe's portrait as part of the ritual conducted prior to making a request by means of *Igrot Kodesh* is known to children as well. For example, seven-and-a-half-year-old Rivka Chaya wished to stand in for her father, who was suffering from a high fever, in asking for a blessing from the Rebbe via *Igrot Kodesh*. Before conducting the bibliomantic ritual she gazed at the Rebbe's picture. "She had been taught from a young age about the Rebbe *shalita*, the King Messiah's instruction saying that before appealing to him one should look at his picture and by this means he comes to the aid of the supplicant, because he is connected to every Jew and wants the best for him."[88]

In the final story in this section, the visual interaction is explicitly based on the Rebbe's instructions. The emissary in the Chabad House in La Paz, Bolivia, worked hard to prepare a Shabbat repast for all the trekkers who generally showed up, but none arrived. Saddened by this, he recalled "that the Rebbe . . . says that when you look at the picture of the prince of the generation, he, as a true shepherd, looks at you from the picture and thinks about you." Having recalled this, he put it into practice. "I approached the Rebbe's picture . . . and told him in simple words how hard we had worked to prepare food for Shabbat . . . and I asked him to send us travelers." In the end seven guests arrived, and as they enjoyed the Sabbath meal they told their host that they had not originally intended to come to the Chabad House that evening. But one of their number had, starting at seven in the evening—precisely the time when the emissary was pouring out his troubles to the Rebbe's picture—launched a campaign to persuade his companions to change their plans and go to the Chabad House for dinner.[89] Note the dominance of the number seven in the story—seven in the evening, seven travelers, and the seventh day, the Sabbath. In addition to the sanctity of the Sabbath and the central role that the number seven plays in Jewish tradition, it also figures in Chabad numerology, since the Chabad holy site, 770, is the *axis mundi* and the Rebbe, the King Messiah, is the seventh and last *admor* of Chabad, in the seventh generation that marks the dawn of redemption.

6. The Speaking Picture

The piercing gaze of the Rebbe in the picture, which captivates the observers as if they had been hypnotized, in many cases conveys an explicit message. Some of the people whose stories were presented here felt that they heard the Rebbe speaking to them, but their way of saying so stresses the subjective nature of that feeling—it is "as if" he spoke. But this qualification grows increasingly hazy in other stories, up to the point of the subjects claiming to have actually heard the Rebbe's voice. In the following three stories the Rebbe actually speaks from within his picture; they exemplify what psychiatrists call in clinical context an auditory hallucination. It is a type of revelation that parallels the more common visual apparitions of the Rebbe, and in some measure overlaps with them (since in some cases in which people report seeing the Rebbe, he also speaks).

In the first case, a young man was pondering whether to leave his non-Jewish girlfriend. He encountered a picture of the Rebbe at a Messiah and Redemption Fair held at the International Convention Center in Jerusalem. As he faced "the famous picture from the early days of his leadership, with a gaze that penetrates everything," he had the familiar experience of being cut off from the real world. "He stood as if nailed to the floor, entirely still, I saw that he quite simply wasn't here," the account relates. But the interaction with the picture does not end there: "Suddenly, he bowed his head in front of the picture, as if to say that he agreed with something he had heard. He was overwhelmed." The rabbi who had accompanied the young man to the fair and who relates his story does not state explicitly that the message was conveyed by speech, but his account indicates that the young man actually heard the Rebbe's voice. His decision to leave his non-Jewish girlfriend bolsters the sense that he did so after being berated by the Rebbe.[90]

In the following two stories, speech explicitly emerges from the picture. The first involves a destitute man who had reached a dead-end in his life. In despair, he resolved to kill himself. But "at the last minute, something incomprehensible drew him to stand before the picture of the Rebbe . . . and to explain what he intended to do. . . . Then, without understanding how it happened, he heard, sensed, that the Rebbe . . . was speaking with him, in a clear voice, *mamash* from the picture: 'Don't do it! Call my sons.' And he heard it again: 'Don't do it! Call my sons.'"

He noticed, at the bottom of the picture, the telephone number of the Association for the True and Complete Redemption. After calling and telling the person who answered of his woes, he changed his decision. "You see, this picture saved me," he told the Meshichist who wrote down his story."[91]

The combination of the spellbinding gaze and the verbal message appears even more explicitly in the confession of a thief who returned a briefcase he had stolen from a resident of Haifa. According to the thief, when he opened the briefcase he found a pocket-sized picture of the Rebbe. The thief relates: "Suddenly his gaze from the picture fell on me.

I could not tear my eyes away. Then something astonishing happened. He began to speak to me from the picture, 'Stop! Give the briefcase back.' I was in shock and thought that maybe I was imagining it, but then I saw and heard it again: 'Stop! Give the briefcase back.'"[92] The repetition of the verbal message in the last two stories strengthens the conviction of the narrator and his audience that the Rebbe's voice was real.

This chapter has been devoted to the visual culture that has come to play an increasing role in Chabad. The detailed account of its ritual manifestations raises intriguing questions about the place of visual representations in general, and of the images of the Rebbe in particular, in the Meshichist discourse. That discourse identifies the beginning of the era of redemption with "the revelation of his Holy Excellency the *admor* the King Messiah *shalita* before the eyes of all." At the beginning of the chapter I remarked that the opposition to visual images that long held sway in mainstream Judaism gradually eroded over a long period, and reached its nadir at the time of the photographic revolution. Furthermore, the sense of sight takes precedence over the other senses as a means of validating reality and establishing the truth, as evidenced by classic Jewish sources long before the precipitous rise in this sense's importance in the modern age.[93] Vision's superiority is evident, for example, in the interpretation of the demand made by the Israelites at Mount Sinai, where they tell Moses, according to a midrash, "We want to see our king!" The object of the request is God and it serves as a model for the era of redemption, and specifically for the repeated calls that the Meshichists make for the Rebbe to reveal himself.[94] Visual images have also played an important role in Jewish mysticism in some eras, including in Hasidism,[95] even though Hasidic culture also stresses vocal and aural aspects of the connection with the divine.[96]

Seeing the world in a new way, and the demand that people should open their eyes to see it that way, is a feature of messianic prophecies in many religions. The Rebbe voiced this demand over and over again in his talks, and in particular during the final part of his tenure. He worded it in many different ways, and as was his custom, he ascribed it to his predecessor: "All the loose ends have been tied, the Children of Israel have repented and finished everything . . . and all that is required is for the

FIGURE 24. The Rebbe's photograph from 27 Adar 5752 (2 March 1992). Photographer: Friedrich Vishinsky. Courtesy of the RebbeDrive.

Holy One, Blessed Be He, *to open the eyes of the Children of Israel so that they will see that the true and complete redemption is already here.*"⁹⁷

The opening of eyes is of critical importance given the claim that we are truly on the threshold of the redemption. The extent to which the Rebbe took the connection between seeing and redemption can be learned from one of the qualms regarding the question of why the redemption did not come to fruition despite the fact that the necessary preparations had already been accomplished. In a talk he gave on the first day of the month of Av, 5751 (1991), the Rebbe suggested that it might well be that the final obstacle remaining was that blind people could not read *Tanya*. He thus ordered that this sacred text be issued in Braille so that "the eyes of the blind will be opened," as is prophesied to happen in the era of the redemption.⁹⁸

In the end, the Rebbe vanished and could no longer be seen by eyes of flesh and blood, leaving behind him an unredeemed world. The many pictures remaining from his tenure as leader of Chabad, which immortalize him in all his splendor, help his followers and admirers to make him present, close, and concrete in their lives—but they also underline his absence. This complexity comes up again and again in Meshichist publications, which are replete with pictures of the Rebbe. For example, Chabadinfo.com posted this: "On the occasion of 27 Adar, twenty years (!!!) since the terrible and horrible absence and concealment began in the year 5754 [1994] as well as the Event of 27 Adar 5752 [1992, the day of the Rebbe's stroke], [we offer] a special photograph depicting His Holy Excellency the *admor* the King Messiah after the morning prayer service on the morning of 27 Adar, prior to his trip to the holy sanctuary [his father-in-law's grave]. With intense longing to see the Rebbe with eyes of flesh, and in complete faith and certainty that . . . we will have the merit of the true and complete Redemption immediately *mamash*."⁹⁹

It is indeed an impressive image. The Rebbe, wearing his *tallit* and *tefillin*, directs his eyes at the camera and waves his hand in encouragement. As in the film clips screened at 770 and in Chabad Houses, on the same day of the year on which they were filmed, this picture is disseminated on the anniversary of the day it was taken—the day the Rebbe collapsed on the grave of his father-in-law, after which he never regained his health.

Several questions emerge from this: Does the unity of place and time embodied in the image help his Hasidim cope with their "intense longing to see the Rebbe with eyes of flesh," inasmuch as it moves time backward and places their energetic and active Rebbe before them? Can Chabad carry on by preserving a virtual Rebbe who is above and beyond time, one who exists in pictures and other signs? It is difficult to offer unambiguous answers to these questions, but I will do my best to grapple with them in Part III, in which I discuss the cosmological aspects of the Meshichist religion. But before I do that I need to examine other ways in which the Rebbe is made visually present to his followers, and through which he becomes a close entity in the landscape in which his Hasidim live.

CHAPTER 6

SEEING THE REBBE II

Dream and Waking Apparitions

The figure of the Rebbe frequently appears in the minds of his Hasidim, whether spontaneously and uncontrollably or as a result of a deliberate process of evoking his image in thought (visualization). The Hasidim report that they hasten to visualize the Rebbe in times of need, particularly in states of emergency. The frequency and ease with which the Rebbe's image appears in the inner worlds of those who follow him clearly testifies to the central place he occupies in their waking lives. It is reasonable to presume that the intensity and accessibility of the mental image of the Rebbe in the minds of his Hasidim are reinforced by the prominence of the still photographs and film clips in which he appears in public and private spaces. And if the mental image of the Rebbe's countenance appears so frequently in their minds while awake, by way of deliberate visualization, it is almost certain that it also appears in special states of consciousness, among them dreams and dissociative states of various kinds. Like evoking the Rebbe's image in thought, the appearance of the Rebbe in special states of consciousness involves "inner pictures." But in dreams and dissociative states the experience slips "outside" and is usually perceived, in real time, as an actual event. This also holds true for the most dramatic set of experiences of seeing the Rebbe: watching him "out there" in wakeful states. These experiences, designated visual hallucinations in psychiatric context, will be discussed in the second part of the chapter, following a brief presentation of dream apparitions.

Dream Apparitions

Chabad Hasidim function within a traditional exegetical framework of religious-mystical character, according to which dreams may serve as a primary medium of communication between humans and the higher worlds. Dreams of the Rebbe, in their view, are objective and authoritative sources of significant information and are of a sacred nature.[1] As far as they are concerned, the Rebbe's appearance in a dream is one more aspect of his very real presence among his followers.

Since the Event of Gimel Tammuz, the Rebbe has frequently appeared in the dreams of believers and nonbelievers, men and women, adults and children. An examination of more than sixty dreams reported in *Sichat Hage'ulah* shows that in about a quarter of the reports, the dreamers make an explicit connection between their dream and a picture of the Rebbe. Often an encounter with the picture, before dreaming or following it, helps them to identify the dream protagonist as the Rebbe. Sometimes the picture, aside from stimulating the memory of the dream, itself plays a role in the plot. In the following account, the dreamer was unable to remember his dream when he woke up in the morning, but while making coffee his gaze fell on a picture of the Rebbe in his kitchen, "and suddenly, like lightning, the dream rose to the surface and appeared before my eyes. In my dream, I sat in the living room, with a mirror on the wall facing me, and I said to myself, why a mirror? A picture of the Rebbe should be there. . . . !" In his dream, the narrator took the photograph of the Rebbe from the kitchen and put it in place of the mirror in the living room, "and then suddenly, from the picture, the Rebbe . . . gave me a big smile."[2] That the picture of the Rebbe is transferred from the kitchen to the living room intimates a characteristic of the Meshichist ecology, in which the Rebbe's pictures hang on multiple walls in the homes of believers (and, while the account does not say so, perhaps the dream induced the dreamer to actually move the picture to a more central place in his home). The Rebbe's smile, emerging from the photograph, blurs the distinction between image and living figure, although in a dream (which was experienced as reality). In dream and waking apparitions both, the picture provides a way of clearly identifying the Rebbe, and in so doing makes a connection between private experience and external reality. In the dream at hand, the dreamer's desire to replace the mirror has symbolic significance; instead of looking at his own image in the mirror, he ought to be contemplating the Rebbe via his photograph.³ This may refer to the imperative to internalize the Rebbe, to identify with him, to abnegate oneself before him, and perhaps even to look like him.

The most concrete connection between the picture and a dream appears in the story of a municipal worker in Kiryat Malachi. In his dream he sees himself walking down one of the city's main streets, appalled and angry at the rubbish and junk lining the street. He suddenly makes out a stretch of street that glows with cleanliness, at the center of which is a table covered with a white tablecloth. Behind the table sits the Rebbe, gazing at the awestruck dreamer "with good and welcoming eyes." The Rebbe asks what he can do for him, and the man asks him for a blessing. The Rebbe draws a photograph of himself from his pocket and offers it to the dreamer, promising that with the picture he will have a blessing. The dreamer woke up elated, feeling that "the dream had been so concrete . . . that it was not just a dream." The day after the dream a Chabad Hasid gave him a picture of the Rebbe. He was so moved by "the dream that came true" that the very next day he decided to become more religious, apparently wishing to leave behind the filth he saw at the beginning of his dream (his previous life?) and become part of the radiance exuded by the Rebbe and his table. Today, "a large picture of the Rebbe is displayed on the wall of our home's living room."⁴ The sequence here is from the dream to the picture, more specifically from the picture in the dream to the picture in reality—first a small picture drawn out of a pocket, then a large picture on the living room wall. The connection between the picture in the dream and the picture in reality again contributes to the objectification of the dream.

Some visual representations of the Rebbe are so popular that they may serve as materials that propel a dream's plot. The connection between dream and reality, between dream and waking apparition, and between reality and its visual representation in still photographs and film clips all come to the fore in the dream of a student at a yeshiva in Safed. In the dream, the student was in a crowd of worshippers who were in the act of inviting the Rebbe to take part in the prayer service at the study hall in 770. Equipped with a camera, the student waited along the famous "path" that opens up in the room to enable the Rebbe to make his way to the *bimah,* the dais on which he customarily sits. When he saw the Rebbe passing within the path, he quickly positioned himself to take a picture. Suddenly, the Rebbe turned and looked at him. The student raised his head from the camera and asked the Rebbe for a blessing for his brother to find a bride. The Rebbe responded, "Blessing and success."[5]

This dream echoes the famous revelation that took place on October 14, 2006, when a telephone taking a video of the path in 770's study hall during one of the daily prayer services recorded a blurred image that was identified as the Rebbe. This brief video clip caused a major stir (and a major dispute) in Chabad. Many Meshichists viewed it as an objectification of the experience of revelation and a significant milestone on the road to the redemption that the camera ostensibly made possible. The epistemological tension between the apparition as a private subjective experience and the possibility of verifying it with a camera is prominent in the student's story. The Rebbe's appearance in the dream joins many other reports of his appearance in the study hall in 770 during prayers, but the wish that emerges from the dream is to once again record the Rebbe's appearance with a camera and thus to establish it as a public event. The fulfillment of the wish encounters a barrier in the dream story when the revealed Rebbe turns toward the dreamer, distracting him from taking a picture. This diversion may well reflect the problematic nature of the event on the epistemological level: the picture recorded by the camera in the dream is merely a reflection of a reflection of an ephemeral dream-world of images. The dreamer was compensated for his frustration in not having his original wish fulfilled by obtaining the Rebbe's blessing for his brother. The blessing received verification in the real world—a week later, the dreamer's brother found a bride. Furthermore, the wave of the Rebbe's hand as he granted the blessing recalls the famous "picture with the baby" such that the Rebbe's appearance in the dream has an objective and public representation outside the dream.[6] The story in *Sichat Hage'ulah* is illustrated with a large reprint of the Rebbe's "picture with the baby" in which the image of the dreamer has been inserted at the bottom, thus offering another echo of the same effort to document and objectify the dream.

The synergy that can take place between an image in a photograph and an apparition in a dream is demonstrated in the account of a dream that drew its inspiration from a famous photograph that had been taken earlier, when a boy from Jerusalem traveled with his family to Crown Heights "to be with the Rebbe" in the month of Tishrei 2004. In that earlier case, on one of the family's visits to 770 he had his picture taken in front of the *bimah* in the study hall. When the picture was developed, the family was astounded to see that it contained the image of a figure resembling the Rebbe, with his back to the camera. The photograph was received tumultuously wherever it reached, one place being a Chabad school for girls in Jerusalem where it aroused a range of reactions—from sharp condemnation to enthusiastic accolades. The day after the photograph was distributed in the school, one of the students had a dream in which she saw the Rebbe in front of her, "standing with his back to me, just like he appears in the picture. I wasn't sure if it really was the Rebbe . . . and suddenly he turned around and I saw that it really was him!" The Rebbe went out into the corridor, and the protagonist, overcome with awe and fear, ran after him and asked him explicitly if it was he in the picture. The Rebbe replied: "It's not only me, but also all the other Rebbes are there!" And he named all the other leaders of Chabad, while holding the picture in his hand. "Suddenly," she reports, "I saw the picture move, and within it our other forefathers the *nesi'im* passed by the Rebbe *shalita*, the King Messiah!"[7]

Here, the dream transparently functions as wish fulfillment. The objective but static picture does not permit a determination of whether the man with his back to the viewer is in fact the Rebbe, while the subjective but dynamic dream narrative can do so, as the Rebbe turns around twice to face the dreamer, allowing her to see his face. To remove all doubt, the Rebbe also offers verbal confirmation of his presence in the photograph, and on top of that adds that all of Chabad's spiritual leaders also appear there. The tension between dream and reality, and the visual representation of reality, is evident in this case. The picture the Rebbe holds in his hand may refer to the popular collage of portraits and photographs of the Rebbe and the four of his predecessors of whom images survive.[8] The model for the scene in which the dreamer saw the picture move and all the rest of the presidents passing by the Rebbe sounds more like one of the widely distributed film clips of the Rebbe than a still picture. Here, too, the fact that the picture in the dream imitates a popular picture in real life can mitigate the epistemological dissonance created by the fact that the picture in the dream is merely a reflection of a reflection in a fading world of images.

Dreams that relate to the appearance of the Rebbe stress the splendor of his countenance, focusing in particular on his white beard and piercing eyes. In one dream he appears with a royal crown on his head, in two of them he sits on a cloud, and in four he is surrounded by a halo of light.[9] All these indicate his messianic role. Most of the dream accounts highlight the Rebbe's positive facial expression, notably his smile and look of satisfaction. Nevertheless, the same face can become antagonistic and angry in dreams in which he demands that the dreamer observe the Sabbath, rid his house of the "Torah scroll of the missionaries," and even, in the dream of a thief, to return the money he had stolen.

Most of the dreams reported contain an easily discernible aspect of wish fulfillment. This is seen in particular in the validation they offer regarding the Rebbe's ontological status, as well as to his message of messianism and redemption. In these dreams the Rebbe appears lively, "in his full majesty and splendor" according to one report in *Sichat Hage'ulah*, and he assures the dreamers that he will come soon. The air of majesty that imbues these dreams of the Rebbe's revelation of himself as the Messiah and the huge enthusiasm that this arouses are spectacularly on display in the dream of a woman from Kiryat Motzkin who first opposed the publicity campaign proclaiming the Rebbe as the Messiah. She saw herself walking together with her family and many other people in the streets in a star-filled evening.

> Then suddenly there was a strong light from above, like lightning. *The skies were illuminated with a huge light. And from all four directions, from everywhere* mamash, *the figure of the Rebbe descending from the sky was visible.* I was looking when a divine voice declared that . . . "The Lubavitcher Rebbe is the King Messiah! The Lubavitcher Rebbe is the King Messiah!" And then I suddenly saw that the day was fading . . . but suddenly the skies were lit up

again with a huge light and again I saw the Rebbe's image everywhere, and again I heard a declaration: "Very soon, *mamash*, everyone will acknowledge this, even those who did not believe that the Lubavitcher Rebbe *shalita* is the King Messiah." The atmosphere was very festive, but I could not bear the excitement and I fainted in my dream and then I woke up.

The high point of this stunning dream is the Rebbe's double apparition.[10]

The claim that the Rebbe is alive receives explicit confirmation in these dreams. A woman enrolled at a Chabad women's institute in Safed struggled with whether the Meshichist stream in Chabad was correct. She received an answer in a dream in which she saw the Rebbe smiling at her. He assured the skeptical dreamer: "I live among you." She asked him whether he was not bothered by the declaration "Long live the King," and he answered serenely: "The public knows what it is saying!" Finally, she asked him why he did not reveal himself; he answered that he still did not have permission to do so.

This dream explicitly brings up the doubts and disputes surrounding the Rebbe's status as the Messiah, only to resolve them all in favor of that tenet.[11] The question regarding the declaration "Long live . . . " in this dream also appears in another, dreamed by a craftsman who had been asked to carve this declaration on a synagogue wall in Haifa but kept making excuses for putting off the job. When he finally showed up to do the work, he explained, "this time I could not refuse, simply because of the Rebbe! He hasn't let me sleep recently. He appears to me in a dream and says that I have to come and do this inscription."[12] The Rebbe's injunction leads to the carving of the words "Yechi Adoneinu" on the wall of a synagogue, thus fixing and propagating them. In contrast, when they are proclaimed or sung, whether in a dream or in reality, they are fleeting and leave no trace.

Most of the wishes the dreams fulfill are connected to personal troubles of various kinds, most notably medical matters. The Rebbe cures illnesses and treats childlessness and pregnancy complications by means of a blessing or explicit promise, often accompanied by offering a drink or a dollar bill for a blessing, as he did during his lifetime. In some cases, the promise comes with a forceful injunction: to affix *mezuzot* to the doorways of the dreamers' homes, to consult *Igrot Kodesh*, or even, in the case of acute problems, more urgent measures—such as, in one particular instance, to rush a sick woman to the hospital.

Several dreams involving the sensitive issue of complications in pregnancy tie the promise of a cure to a command not to terminate the pregnancy. One such case involves a woman who decides to have an abortion after being informed by her doctors that the fetus has a heart defect. In the dream, she sees herself in a clinic's waiting room, which is furnished with red chairs. Pictures hang on the walls, and a couple also waits there for their turn. Suddenly she sees the Rebbe, wearing his *tallit* and *tefillin*, sitting on one of the chairs. His face radiates intense light. While he remains silent, the dreamer senses that he is addressing her wordlessly: "I have come for you, don't do it." Disregarding the dream, she goes to have her abortion. But she is astounded to discover that the clinic she arrives at looks much like the one she saw in the dream, including a waiting couple closely resembling those she had dreamed of. She changes her mind and decides to escape before the Rebbe arrives, as he did in her dream. A few months later she gives birth to a healthy child, despite the doctors' warnings. Since that time, the mother "remembers and knows that he [her son] is the Rebbe's child."[13] The red color of the chairs in this highly charged dream could possibly refer to the blood shed at the clinic, but there is another association as well—the Rebbe's chair at 770 is upholstered in red velvet, and in the dream the Rebbe sits on a red chair in the clinic. There is an intriguing historical association between the clinic and 770, which the dreamer may have known of. Before the house in Crown Heights became the home of Rabbi Yosef Yitzchak Schneerson, the Rebbe's father-in-law and predecessor, it housed an abortion clinic.[14]

A wide variety of problems are solved in dreams, aside from health issues. Even the predicament of a yeshiva student, who did not know whether he had been born on the twenty-ninth or thirtieth day of the month of Nisan, was resolved by the Rebbe in a dream. The student saw him discussing a religious issue with an unidentified man. At the end of the conversation, the Rebbe said (in Yiddish): "You are referring to a passage in Tractate Ketubot, page 94b." The dreamer woke up and excitedly looked up the reference in the Babylonian Talmud. On the page specified by the Rebbe he found a passage involving a legal discussion about the validity of bills of sale for fields, containing the date 29 Nisan.

Chabad emissaries connected to the Rebbe and in need of his guidance and advice frequently have their needs answered in dreams. Rabbi Ya'akov Shmulevitz, director of the Chabad House in Beit She'an, classifies the kinds of dreams described by Chabad's emissaries as "Hasidic dreams," and suggests that when Chabad Hasidim wish each other good night they also bless each other by saying "May you have Hasidic dreams." This blessing can foster "the wonderful experience of a dream about the Rebbe, receiving a blessing from the Rebbe, or a teaching or simple encouragement from the Rebbe's pleasant gaze. There are no words to describe the sense of happiness of getting up in the morning and remembering that I saw the Rebbe in a dream."[15] This good-night blessing for dreams of the Rebbe (which is presumably aided by visualizing the Rebbe's face) vaguely echoes the practice, recorded in the Talmud, of seeking a dream.[16] This attempt to invite the Rebbe explicitly into one's dreams is another element in the developing visual cult of Meshichist Chabad.

In keeping with the vision that guided him during his entire period of leadership, in dreams the Rebbe also makes a great effort to bring Jews back into the Jewish fold of family, identification, and observance. He does his best to separate them from non-Jewish spouses and to get them to keep the Sabbath, eat only kosher food, and obey all the other rules laid down by the Torah and rabbis. Some dreamers state explicitly that they became more strictly observant in the wake of messages they received from the Rebbe in their dreams. I offer one account typical of this genre of recurring dreams about Sabbath observance. A woman from Bat Yam was surprised when the Rebbe came to her in a dream, "telling me firmly, *Shabbes* [Sabbath, in Yiddish], banging on a table with his hand to emphasize the word." Since the woman already observed the Sabbath, she disregarded the dream. But the Rebbe would not leave her alone. A few days later he appeared again, saying "*Shabbes, Shabbes!*" to her, and then he appeared again, repeating the word three times: "*Shabbes, Shabbes, Shabbes!*" All the woman's efforts to understand why the Rebbe was addressing her so insistently led her nowhere, until she realized that the Rebbe was not reproaching her for a transgression but rather warning her in advance about a future situation. A nonreligious relative who came to visit from France asked the woman and her husband to drive her to Netanya on the Sabbath. In the end, after long pleas, the couple relented and drove her. On the way they were involved in a traffic accident and slightly injured, enough to require that they be taken to the hospital. This incident provided the woman with the meaning of her three dreams.[17] The repetition of the dreams underscores the sense that, even if the Rebbe is not present, he is operating behind the scenes—he is close, attentive, able to respond immediately, and to appear at any time that there is a need.

One direct consequence of the Rebbe's nearby presence and the unlimited capacity for intervention that is attributed to him is that he at times appears in the dreams of disparate people as a way of bringing them together to help a Jew in distress.[18] Such a dream dialogue comes from an American man from the Satmar Hasidic community, who was serving a prison sentence. On the last day of the eight-day Pesach holiday he was perturbed because he had no wine and *matzah* left to observe the Hasidic custom of the "Messiah's Meal" on the night after the last day of the holiday. Anxious and depressed, he fell asleep and saw himself at an audience with the Rebbe. The Rebbe turned to him and commanded him to say "*Lechayim*," "To life," as Jews customarily say when they drink. He said that he could not say it because the prison authorities had refused to supply him with wine. The Rebbe said: "You must be happy, you have nothing to worry about, the *matzot* and wine are on their way to you." When the Hasid woke up, a prison guard came into his cell and, to the man's astonishment, gave him wine and *matzot*. She explained that a "rabbi" had come to her in a dream and told her that "there is a Jew here who needs *matzot* and wine." She wondered how she would obtain the items, and the Rebbe responded: "The *matzot* are in the prison pantry and the wine in the refrigerator nearby." After the holiday the Hasid showed the guard pictures of Chabad's spiritual leaders, and she identified, without any hesitation, the Rebbe as being the one who had appeared to her in her dream.[19] Presumably it is no coincidence that the Hasid's wish, fulfilled by the Rebbe, had to do with the Messiah's Meal.

The Rebbe's ability to stage-manage people and instigate events throughout the universe—in keeping with his messianic status—can be seen in the next two dreams. Dreamed by the same person, they involve four characters and a single story-line that stretches from New Zealand to New York. The narrator is a young Israeli cab driver living in New York. One of his regular passengers was a Chabad emissary in New Zealand who came to the United States from time to time to raise money. One night, after taking the emissary to the airport to catch a flight to Chicago, the cab driver heard the Rebbe speaking to him in a dream: "Get up and help the woman, get up and help the woman." Just as he was pondering this strange dream the telephone rang and he jumped out of bed to answer it. The caller was the emissary, who said that he had apparently left the bag containing his *tefillin* in the airport. He pleaded with the cab driver to do what he could to recover them. "I have to have those *tefillin* at any price," the emissary insisted. But a blizzard was raging outside and the cab driver decided to go back to bed. After falling asleep, he again heard the Rebbe ordering him to "Get up and help the woman." After hearing the Rebbe's injunction twice, the driver set out toward the airport, where he indeed found the *tefillin*. The next day, when he encountered the emissary, who had returned to New York, he learned why the emissary had come back to New York with such urgency rather than simply purchasing a new set of *tefillin* in Chicago. For years the emissary had been laboring to obtain a writ of divorce for a woman in New Zealand whose husband lived in New York. (According to Jewish religious law, divorce is contingent on the husband's consent.) Her husband angrily and loutishly rejected every request she made for a divorce. But on this visit the husband had finally relented and had granted the divorce. The emissary had placed the writ of divorce in his *tefillin* bag for safekeeping, but forgot the bag at the airport. The driver now understood the Rebbe's cryptic command: "Get up and help the woman."[20]

These nocturnal encounters with the Rebbe are not only important for the remedies they offer but also because of the mimetic nature of their narratives. In some cases, the interactions with the Rebbe take place as he engages in one of the activities with which he was identified in his lifetime, such as handing out dollar bills or cups of wine with his blessing, or dancing with his Hasidim. As I have already noted, these activities are held at 770 to this day, which is why I have termed them mimetic practices of manifesting the Rebbe's presence. I have collected testimonies from no less than six people who have dreamed of themselves taking part in the Rebbe's distribution of dollars or in the Rebbe's distribution of cups of wine; still others saw themselves dancing with him on the Simchat Torah holiday. In some cases dreamers see the Rebbe sitting at the head of a long table, as he did in audiences with his followers, and in others on the *bimah* during prayers. Important as the mimetic activity is for bolstering the belief that the Rebbe is alive, the dream landscape makes it possible to enhance it in various ways, perhaps growing out of the wishes of the dreamers. For example, women report dreaming that they saw Chaya Mushka, the Rebbe's wife, at his side, even though they never appeared in public together throughout his presidency and up until her death in 1988. Dreams, then, became a central means of manifesting the Rebbe's presence after the Event of Gimel Tammuz. Like the channels of visualization and of apparitions of the Rebbe in dissociative and waking states, there is a close relationship between the widely disseminated portraits of the Rebbe and such dreams. As I will show below, dreams have qualitative characteristics similar to those of apparitions of the Rebbe in waking states. In contrast with visualization, which is a deliberate practice, generally of a ritual nature, dreams and apparitions are spontaneous, although the Rebbe's appearance in a dream or waking state is preceded in a few cases by an explicit request that he reveal himself.

Apparitions in Waking States

While Chabad Hasidim see the Rebbe in special states of consciousness such as dreams, he also often appears to them while they are wide awake, in the normal course of their daily activities. Although apparitions of this type are rare in Jewish tradition,[21] I have assembled about eighty reports of apparitions in which the Rebbe reveals himself to his followers in this way. Most of them come from *Sichat Hage'ulah*; fifty-seven are found in the anthology *Lifko'ach et ha'Einayim* (Open Your Eyes). The rest come from interviews with Meshichist activists, several of whom experienced such apparitions themselves.

More than any of the other means of making the Rebbe present that the Meshichist imagination has produced, such waking apparitions seem to be acts of defiance against the painful vacuum left by the Rebbe's occlusion. In these, he appears to the human eye in what is, at least ostensibly, a fully and normatively conscious mental state, even if such appearances are fleeting and experienced on an individual basis. The messianic ecology fostered by Chabad's radicals offers fertile ground for investigating the processes that constitute the experience of seeing the Rebbe in reality. I will elucidate them by considering the components of the cultural toolbox that "invite" Hasidim to see the Rebbe. Furthermore, I will compare these apparitions to the wealth of ethnographic and historical material on similar phenomena in Christianity.[22] The many reports of waking apparitions of the Rebbe, their wide variety, and their wealth of detail offer an exceptional opportunity for analyzing the phenomenon.

Apparitions of the Rebbe: Principal Features

Reports of apparitions of the Rebbe have appeared in Meshichist publications in a slow but steady stream since the Rebbe's occlusion. My interviews show, however, that the phenomenon is much broader than the textual evidence would indicate. The backgrounds of the reporters of such experiences are heterogeneous, but men predominate. Women and children, who occupy a prominent place in Catholic visions of this sort,[23] are a minority among those who see the Rebbe—about a third of the reports come from women and a sixth from children. Although most of the testimonies involve ordinary Hasidim, some come from rabbis and educators who are well-known figures in the movement. Almost all of the reports emanating from Chabad come from the Meshichist faction. More than two-thirds of the reporters are Israelis, largely established and new Hasidim. A small number of completely nonobservant Jews, as well as two non-Jews, say they have seen the Rebbe. Among the latter, he was often identified after the experience, when the reporters encountered a picture of the Rebbe.

Most of the witnesses experienced a single encounter with the Rebbe, but some report seeing him more than once, generally twice, on different occasions. But there are also serial seers of the type common among Catholic believers in the modern age.[24] Rabbi Shlomo Zalman Landa, a Hasidic spiritual mentor from Bnei Brak, is the most well-known among them. When I interviewed him, I learned that his six encounters with the Rebbe reported in print are but the tip of the iceberg—such apparitions are common occurrences in his life. Along with such serial apparitions, there are simultaneous ones in which more than one person sees the Rebbe at the same time. Most often it is two people, but in one case no fewer than seven women saw the Rebbe at the same place (770) and at the same time (Shemini Atzeret following Sukkot, 2005).

With regard to location, two-thirds of the apparitions occur in places I call "ritual." About half of them occur in 770, and the rest in satellite locations, mostly Chabad Houses. Meshichists are awed by Rabbi Landa's experience of seeing the Rebbe not only in 770 but also in other places around the world. Their excitement shows that 770 is the accepted and expected place to have such an experience. Indeed, the Rebbe makes appearances in his home in Crown Heights more often than he does throughout Israel. In only about a third of the cases does the Rebbe appear in a mundane context, but these locations are highly varied and reinforce the claim that he can reveal himself to his believers anywhere: at home (sometimes in the kitchen, "between the refrigerator and the sink"), at school, in hospitals and courthouses, on the bus, in open fields, and even in the depths of the sea and the heart of forests. From a global point of view, the Rebbe appears mostly in the United States (almost always at 770) and somewhat less in Israel (where he appears in many different places). There are only a few reports of seeing him in other places in the word: Australia, France, India, Vietnam, and Egypt's Sinai Peninsula.

Similarly, the Rebbe tends to be seen on some days more than on others. About half the apparitions occur on Jewish holidays; about three-quarters of those that take place at 770 occur on such days. No less than a third of the appearances at 770 take place during the holidays of the month of Tishrei, most of them during Sukkot, and especially on the holiday that concludes that week, Simchat Torah. As is the case with other Hasidic groups, Chabad counts Tishrei as the preferred month to visit the *admor*. Chabad Meshichists did not stop making the pilgrimage to 770 in Tishrei after the Event of Gimel Tammuz, and may even go in greater numbers.[25] Previous Chabad leaders viewed the last two days of Sukkot, Shemini Atzeret and Simchat Torah (celebrated on consecutive days in the Diaspora but on the same day in Israel) as being of special spiritual significance, days on which the fruits of the sacred labors and prayers of the Days of Awe, Rosh Hashanah and Yom Kippur, could be harvested, and days on which one may draw joy and divine abundance for the entire year. The Rebbe himself said that Simchat Torah has a special place in bringing the Messiah. During his tenure, Simchat Torah was celebrated at 770 with huge crowds and with the Rebbe's active participation. It is thus not surprising that these days "are especially apt for seeing the face of the Rebbe *shalita*, the King Messiah."[26] Sabbaths, Purim, Pesach, the Rebbe's birthday (11 Nisan), and the day of his occlusion (3 Tammuz) are also significant days for apparitions. In contrast with the large numbers of apparitions experienced at 770 on holidays, most of the Rebbe's appearances on weekdays take place in secular locations.

Most of the Rebbe's appearances are fairly brief, ranging from a flash of a few seconds to several minutes. In general, the viewer and the Rebbe do not interact verbally. Rather, the Rebbe fixes his penetrating gaze on the viewer, makes a gesture of encouragement, or nods in affirmation. In eight cases, however, the Rebbe conveyed a clear message in his own voice.[27] In most of these cases the utterance was quite succinct: he said "*Lechayim*" to a woman who raised a cup of wine in the direction of the *bimah* in the synagogue at 770; "Strangle it" to a girl who encountered a snake; "You need faith" to a nonobservant young man who expressed skepticism about apparition stories he had heard; "My girl, everything will be fine" to a woman suffering from cancer. The Rebbe may speak in Hebrew, Yiddish, or French, in accordance with the language used by the person who experiences the apparition.

Explaining Apparitions

While there are many similarities between waking apparitions and what psychiatry calls visual hallucinations, classifying the experience of an encounter with the Rebbe as pathological is problematic. I say so based on a wide range of ethnographic material relating to the normative cultural uses of hallucinations in ritual contexts,[28] as well as on persistent evidence of hallucinations in normal populations.[29] No less than a third to one-half of all widows and widowers report hallucinations involving the departed spouse.[30] Obviously, it would be an overstatement to claim that no one who reports seeing the Rebbe suffers from mental issues. Nevertheless, given the heterogeneity of the reports and the fact that most of the testimonies come from people who function normatively in their communities, an explanation based on an assumption of psychopathology misses the mark. Furthermore, in sharp contrast to psychotic hallucinations, apparitions of the Rebbe are pleasant, rare, and brief.[31]

I will therefore not limit myself only to rejecting the claim that apparitions of the Rebbe are a type of mental disturbance. I rather seek to see them as a type of accomplishment[32] that Chabad's dense messianic ecology enables. This approach is fairly close to that of the Hasidim themselves, even if the explanation I will offer is cast in concepts that they do not use. My starting point is a claim derived from signal-detection theory, according to which hallucinations are the products of misattributions that happen when stimuli coming from external and internal sources are not correctly distinguished from each other.[33] The probability of a misattribution grows when a disturbance occurs in the cognitive processes responsible for this discernment. Richard Bentall has identified three categories of impediments: beliefs and expectations, stress (emotional arousal), and environmental noise. I will use this threefold framework, which offers a nonpathological explanation for hallucinations, to explain the Rebbe's apparitions. However, the misattribution model is too schematic and tenuous to comprehend all the dialectical complexity of the messianic world from which the experiences of encounters with the Rebbe come. I thus want to flesh out and elaborate the cognitive model's three sets of factors through the use of ethnographic material.

In the model's terms, Chabad's mystical teachings inform the Hasidim's beliefs and expectations. The emotional distress experienced by Hasidim following the Rebbe's occlusion falls into the category of stress that causes emotional arousal. Beyond those factors, we need to take into account the myriad objects and practices that play a decisive role in shaping the nature and timing of the apparitions, especially those that occur at 770 and its correlative sites. What the cognitive model terms "noise" or ambiguous stimulation, the ethnographic perspective, closer to lived experience, prefers to see as context, that is, the cultural framework and social conditions that constitute and are constituted by the messianic ecology. In the spirit of the mediation paradigm that I presented in my introduction, the emphasis is on the concrete practices and material means that pave the way to the sublime experience of the Rebbe as present, by seeing him. I will now fill in the model's categories.

The Chabad doctrine is a central element in the category of beliefs and expectations. Chabad's mystical theosophy fosters a "hermeneutics of suspicion" toward the world as perceived by the senses. I have noted that a number of scholars stress the a-cosmic aspects of Chabad theosophy, which denies all reality to the visible world and ascribes vitality and essence to the invisible God. Others argue, however, that Chabad theology includes both a-cosmic and panentheistic aspects, and that it does not seek to resolve the tension between them. The extent to which the average Chabad Hasid knows about the fine points that scholars dispute remains an open question. Whatever the case, both believers and scholars agree that Chabad's theosophy blurs the distinction between what is and is not, the physical and the spiritual, and the revealed and hidden. This haziness can reinforce a noncritical acceptance of sensory experiences that have no material basis.

The refusal to accept the painful vacuum left by the Rebbe's departure fits the model's category of stress and emotional arousal. Since the Event of Gimel Tammuz, Chabad Hasidim have been shouting: "We want to see our king!" The Meshichist discourse is characterized by ambivalence: while most Hasidim belonging to this camp evince full confidence in their belief that the Rebbe's occlusion is simply the last test to be faced before the redemption, they also lament his absence (as in the cry " 'Ad matai?," "How long?") and demand of him that he reveal himself immediately.[34] Beyond the general distress produced by the Rebbe's occlusion, some of the encounters with him evince more acute and specific distress. I will address these experiences in greater detail when I compare apparitions in ritual and mundane spaces.

Cognitive expectations and emotional arousal thus provide the mood and the motivation that sustain the possibility of seeing the Rebbe. But, more than anything else, what makes such apparitions possible is the "noise" created by the messianic environment—by which I mean the dense system of concrete signs connected to the Rebbe and the practices in which these signs are set. This system, with its three components—pictures, traces, and practices of making the Rebbe present—creates the perceptual field in which the Rebbe may sometimes be seen. These three components have been discussed in previous chapters, so I will focus here on their direct or indirect links to apparitions.

The impressive visage of the Rebbe is displayed prominently in private and public spaces, in a way that is unprecedented in the Jewish world. The visual culture that Chabad produced in the second half of the twentieth century was amplified after the Event of Gimel Tammuz, and preserved the unmediated connection between the Rebbe and young and new Hasidim who had never met him in person during his lifetime. In addition to the dissemination of photographs of him, the repeated screening of films showing the Rebbe at audiences and handing out dollar bills also plays an important role. This footage offers an especially strong sense that life with the Rebbe continues. Chabad makes a point of screening the clips precisely on the same calendar date on which they were filmed. This coordination of time (and space as well, when the films are screened at 770) bolsters the sense of the Rebbe's real presence. This sense may not entirely erase the gap between the actual and the virtual, but it nevertheless enables all Chabad Hasidim, both extremist and moderate, to keep the Rebbe's image alive. The prominence of the still photographs and films does not mean that they are a necessary or sufficient condition for apparitions of the Rebbe. Concrete encounters with beings from other worlds clearly preceded not only the invention of photography but also the first traces of iconography in ancient religions. But there is plenty of support for the claim that icons facilitate apparitions. Photographs, as precise representations of the photographed person— "a certificate of presence"[35]—are all the more useful.

The connection between Chabad's visual culture and waking apparitions of the Rebbe is no doubt mediated by the strong cognitive schema that intensive exposure to photographs of the Rebbe creates in the consciousness of Hasidim. Presumably the practice of visualization that is extremely widespread in Chabad plays a key role in the processing of portraits of the Rebbe into stable and accessible mental images. The Rebbe himself suggested to his followers that they envisage the countenance of his father-in-law and predecessor when addressing him in writing while visiting his grave, and he presumably did the same during his frequent visits to that site. In many of his talks, he advises envisioning Rabbi Yosef Yitzchak not only when a problem arises but every morning prior to or following recitation of the dawn blessings, as well as when studying an essay, article, or letter that he wrote. The Rebbe also told his Hasidim to imagine the figure of the Messiah on various occasions, especially at the time of the "Messiah's Dance" on the last day of Pesach. His followers seem to have followed this injunction by viewing the Messiah in the guise of the Rebbe who was dancing with them. Notably, a number of those who experienced apparitions of the Rebbe saw him dancing with his Hasidim.

The Hasidim enthusiastically adopted this practice of visualization, as may be seen in the large number of items in Meshichist publications about or by people who mentally conjured the Rebbe's image when coping with difficulties or problems. In most cases, visualization is based on a conscious, deliberate, and controlled practice—the Rebbe's image may be "pulled up" as needed. It is done flexibly and autonomously, thanks to the strong imprint of the visual image in the memory and consciousness of Hasidim. The picture "outside" becomes a picture "inside." While none of the people I interviewed explicitly reported a process of deliberately visualizing the Rebbe's face that segued into a sense of seeing him in reality, the boundaries between the two are permeable, and the possibility of such a process seems to me to be quite reasonable.

In any case, the iconophilia of Meshichist Chabad casts light on the importance of pictures in paving the road to apparition, even in the absence of explicit reports of using visualization as a way of seeing the Rebbe. The visual cult involves a ritual interaction that includes mutual contemplation between the petitioner and the Rebbe, a sense of being caught by the Rebbe's piercing eyes, and receiving a message of encouragement and support from him. It should be noted that the connection between pictures and apparitions becomes explicit in cases of auditory experiences; recall that there are several reports of hearing the Rebbe's voice come out of a photograph of him.

The fact that the physical posture and gestures made by the Rebbe in many of the reports of apparitions precisely match his appearance in the most familiar photographs of him corroborates the hypothesis that the latter play a significant role in shaping the apparitions. This correspondence stands out in *Lifko'ach et ha'Einayim*, where no less than twenty-nine photographs of the Rebbe are interspersed within the text. The pictures accompanying the reports precisely depict the Rebbe's posture and gestures as conveyed in the book's testimonies. For example: "He looked at me with a penetrating gaze and waved his holy hand in a gesture of encouragement"; "wrapped in a *tallit* with his face to the wall"; "holding the back of the chair." All these are taken word for word from reports of apparitions. The possibility that photographs served as stimuli that guided the apparitions cannot be dismissed.

Testimony of this move from photograph to apparition comes from the report of a woman who was preparing to have her pregnancy terminated in the wake of complications. During preparations for an ultrasound scan prior to the operation, she experienced an apparition: "*On the wall facing my bed* I suddenly see the Rebbe . . . with his hat and blue eyes, as he says to me with a broad smile: 'Don't worry, everything will be fine.'" The scan showed that everything was normal, and the astonished woman was sent home.[36] The fact that the Rebbe revealed himself on the wall hints at the possibility that what took place was a subjective process in which the two-dimensional Rebbe in the photograph turned into a three-dimensional one in an apparition. This possibility is bolstered by the unique experience related to me by a woman who had become observant and joined Chabad. When she addressed a huge photograph of the Rebbe hanging in her living room to ask for help, she was astonished to see the Rebbe emerge from the picture and stand before her for a short time. The Rebbe stepping out of the photograph is a dramatic culmination of the iconic process of making the Rebbe present, leading from picture to apparition.

The still photographs and film clips of the Rebbe can thus help a person see him in an apparition. However, even the Meshichists find it difficult to disregard the problematic status of these experiences as private and subjective events. Such apparitions are generally perceived as being true in the eyes of the witnesses, but they cannot be given public validity. Indeed, some of the witnesses state explicitly that they initially refrained

FIGURE 25. A photograph from *Open Your Eyes*. It appears with the following caption: "She saw the Rebbe . . . walking in the path (*shvil*) that was opened up for him." Courtesy of the RebbeDrive.

from sharing their experience, out of concern that their experiences will be dismissed and ridiculed in their communities as imagined or dreamed, or even as a symptom of madness. Pictures of the Rebbe taken *after* his occlusion helped believers cope with this difficulty. Much like the role played by miraculous photographs at sites of pilgrimage where the Virgin Mary has appeared,[37] here too the pictures help substantiate and objectivize the experiences.

This is eminently clear in two public events that caused an uproar among Meshichists. The first involves a boy from Jerusalem who had gone to 770 with his family in Tishrei 2004 "to be with the Rebbe." His parents took his picture in front of the *bimah* at the synagogue that is part of the building. To their astonishment, when the photograph was processed, it showed an elderly Hasid standing near the boy with his back to the camera; they and others identified the man as the Rebbe. The parents insisted that no one but the boy stood there when they took the

התמונה. מימין עומד הלל כהן, כשמשמאל נראה הרבי שליט״א מלך המשיח

FIGURE 26. The boy with the Rebbe in 2004. Source: *Lifko'ach et ha'Einayim*, Reshet Chabad Lubavitch, 2007, p. 177. Courtesy of the RebbeDrive.

photograph. While the identification set off a controversy in Chabad, many Meshichists maintain that the photograph provides the missing link that validates the Rebbe's eternal presence.[38]

The second event took place on October 14, 2006. A visitor to the synagogue at 770 took a video with his cell phone of the "path" that Hasidim open to make way for the Rebbe prior to a prayer service. Many visitors to 770 take such videos and pictures to document their experience, but this time the camera caught a low figure with a white beard striding energetically toward the Holy Ark between the dancing and singing Hasidim on each side. Even though the image appears for only a split second and the footage is of low quality, the Meshichists have stated with certainty that the figure is the Rebbe, and that the Revelation began on that day. The huge excitement set off by the event was described by one Hasid: "For years since the occlusion on Gimel Tammuz, the Rebbe the King Messiah *shalita* has revealed himself many times to individuals, especially at 770 . . . what was new this time was that he was seen by hundreds of thousands."[39] The film clip was seen over and over again on Meshichist websites, and still pictures taken from it are used by some activists as screen savers.

The Messianic ecology is also replete with signs that are not photographs, which I call traces. These signs include, for example, the Rebbe's house (770), his sacred possessions, the dollar bills he handed out to the public, and water from his *mikveh*. All these take part, by means of physical contact, proximity, or synecdoche, in the Rebbe, which they signify. In doing so, the absent Rebbe becomes close and sensuous. These traces, along with the photographs of the Rebbe, construct the perceptual field that forms the backdrop for the apparitions described here. Like the photographs, the traces for the most part lend themselves to duplication and reproduction, sometimes indefinitely, making them accessible through wide dissemination. The abundance and huge range of such traces amplify the Rebbe's presence in ritual and domestic spaces and grant the Hasidic wish of "being with the Rebbe." The abundance overflows from the landscape onto the bodies of the Meshichists, who make massive use of signs of the Rebbe, such as lapel pins bearing the messianic emblem, skullcaps emblazoned with the mantra "Yechi Adoneinu," and dollars distributed by the Rebbe and photographs of him kept in the wallet. By bearing these objects on his person, the Hasid who never saw the Rebbe and who cannot see him now partakes of that physical contact or proximity with him. Through these objects, the devotee touches the Rebbe and becomes a walking icon of him.[40]

These traces are also integrated into a complex set of ritual practices centered on the Rebbe; they are part of the daily routine at 770. As I have already noted, half of the apparitions of the Rebbe take place in his home, most of them during rituals that include the three daily prayer services, the distribution of dollars on Sundays, and the audiences held with the Rebbe on the nights following holidays and special occasions, in which the Rebbe participates actively (by means of these very traces). But the Rebbe also appears in secular places that are not replete with these signs. What distinguishes the apparitions in "his royal sanctuary" from those that take place "in all parts of his dominion"?

Ritual versus Mundane Apparitions

Two out of three apparitions take place at sites belonging to or closely associated with Chabad, places imbued with a rich fabric of photographs, traces, and practices that evoke the Rebbe and make him present. Dialectically, however, this same fabric accentuates the fact that the Rebbe himself cannot be seen. Given the profusion and intensity of the messianic ecology, which serves as a framework that summons the seeing of the Rebbe, it should hardly be surprising that most apparitions occur in the "right place," the Rebbe's residence at 770, and at the "right time," on holidays and ritual occasions, in which the Rebbe is meant to be front and center. Even in this environment, which invites seeing the Rebbe, and in which the wish to see him is sometimes stated explicitly (while, presumably, the supplicant visualizes the Rebbe's face in his or her mind), apparitions are not common and should be deemed a contextual accomplishment, not easy to achieve; but when they do happen they are hugely moving. Such experiences, however, are entirely different from apparitions in which the Rebbe appears unexpectedly, far from the suggestive environments of 770 and its correlates. Here I will look closely at the differences between the two.

The appearances of the Rebbe at 770 seem to be influenced by the unbearable disparity between the rich messianic ecology that the site offers and his very notable absence. This dynamic is clearly dialectical: the signs and practices meant to fill the painful void left by the Rebbe's occlusion are liable to intensify rather than alleviate the pain. This is especially true in the case of longtime Hasidim who have clear memories of the golden age in which they enjoyed close contact with the Rebbe at 770.[41] But the same messianic environment that is liable to deepen the abyss is that which constitutes the perceptual field in which the wish to see the Rebbe "now and immediately *mamash*" is sometimes granted. I offer two cases that demonstrate this dynamic.

An Israeli Hasid on a trip to the United States went to 770 "to worship at the morning prayer service with the Rebbe *shalita*, the King Messiah" one last time before returning to Israel. He related that, after the reading of the Torah and the declaration "Yechi Adoneinu," he sensed "how from inside me the cry of 'How long?' broke out three times [and after that another Chabad mantra, in English], 'Rebbe, we want Moshiach [Messiah, in Ashkenazi pronunciation] now!'" Following his cry, "something astonishing took place before my eyes. I suddenly saw the Rebbe *shalita*, the King Messiah, standing on the *bimah* in front of me, adorned in his *tallit* and *tefillin*. He stood to the right of his lectern, leaning on it with his holy elbow, with his back to the white wall and his face toward the congregation."[42] Despite the witness's emotional response, the Rebbe's appearance was not entirely unexpected. He had called on the Rebbe to reveal himself, and this is just what the Rebbe did, in the place where he was supposed to be.

In several cases people have explicitly called on the Rebbe to appear. After the evening service on the night of Yom Kippur at 770, "when the Rebbe . . . remained to recite psalms with the congregation," a student from a yeshiva in Safed recalled the years in which he had been privileged to participate in this same event "and to see the Rebbe . . . dressed in white like an angel of God, and I was overcome with a powerful desire to see the Rebbe's face . . . as of old." This wish became an explicit request: "Rebbe . . . I know with absolute certainty that you are here, alive and well, and unchanged! Please, enable me to see you with my physical eyes!" At first the request was not answered: "When I continued to look in the direction of his holy place, I still could see nothing but the red chair and lectern covered with a white cloth." But the Hasid then enlisted the merit of his eminent grandfather, "one of the great Hasidim of Russia, of huge devotion," and when he turned his gaze again to the *bimah*, his heart "missed a beat": "I saw the Rebbe . . . standing in his place, dressed in the *kitel* [white robe] of Yom Kippur and wrapped in [his] *tallit*."[43]

The tension between the rich messianic environment and the painful void at its center can be seen in both stories. The traces of the Rebbe—the *bimah*, his red chair, and his lectern—as well as the ritual practices in which he is meant to be participating (the morning prayer service in the first case and the public recitation of psalms on Yom Kippur night in the second) intensified the sense of absence of these devotees and impelled them to demand the Rebbe's appearance. At the same time, this backdrop served as a sensory catalyst for an apparition. The practices during which the Rebbe appears include daily prayers, the distribution of dollars on Sundays, the fervent dancing with Torah scrolls on Simchat Torah, and audiences with the Rebbe on the nights following the Sabbath and holidays. The Rebbe is generally seen on the *bimah* in the same postures that were characteristic of him during his tenure (and which became well-known by means of photographs)—he leans on his lectern, touches the curtain on the Holy Ark when going up to and descending from the *bimah*, and waves his hands in encouragement. In three cases the Rebbe was seen along the path that his Hasidim open up in his honor as he enters and leaves the synagogue for prayer services. That, of course, was the place where the film clip mentioned above recorded his presence in October 2006.

The Rebbe's dress and appearance in these accounts are appropriate for the events at which the apparition took place. During the prayer service he appeared wrapped in his *tallit*, and on Yom Kippur dressed in a *kitel*. On Sundays he is seen handing out dollar bills, on Sukkot reciting the blessing over the *lulav* and *etrog*, and at audiences handing out small cups of wine and slices of cake. It should be noted that the dollars, *lulav* and *etrog*, and wine and cake are also elements in practices of making the Rebbe present that are observed at 770. Apparitions at Chabad Houses, "satellite branches of 770,"[44] are paler variations of the Rebbe's appearance at 770, because they appear in an environment that is less packed with traces of the Rebbe and practices involving him as a participant.

The apparitions in manifestly secular surroundings make up about a third of the reported episodes. Most of them are triggered by severe distress and sometimes life-or-death situations. None of these apparitions were rooted in the painful absence of the Rebbe itself. The opposite is also true—none of the apparitions at 770 or its subsidiary locations grew out of any distress other than the Rebbe's absence. The rich messianic ecology that provides the cognitive-perceptual substrate for ritual apparitions is almost completely absent in secular ones, in particular those that take place outside the home. It seems that in these cases the distress is acute enough to summon up the apparition even in the absence of the many dominant cognitive clues that are found in the ritual apparitions. I will present a number of apparition stories that grow out of trauma.

A girl attacked in a field by a snake screamed in panic: "Rebbe, save me!" The Rebbe appeared before her, urged her to strangle the snake, and she, her spirits raised by his proximity, found the strength to do so.[45] In another case, a bus on its way from Jerusalem to Beitar Illit was shot at by Palestinians. During the incident, a passenger saw the Rebbe standing in front of her "pulling her down to the bottom of the bus." This saved her, while the girl sitting next to her was killed by the assailants.[46] In another case, a diver suffering from nitrogen narcosis was saved by a fellow-diver. After recovering, he vaguely recalled two figures bringing him up to the surface, but his friend insisted that he had acted alone. A few days later, when the survivor encountered a photograph of the Rebbe, he recognized him as the mysterious "third man."[47] These three cases can be placed on a continuum, beginning with an explicit call for help; continuing through a sudden manifestation of the Rebbe, recognized by the viewer; and ending with the appearance of an enigmatic figure who is identified as the Rebbe only after the fact, by the rescued diver. In the great majority of secular cases, the Rebbe appears by surprise, without being deliberately or ritually evoked. Even the calling out of his name in the first case was spontaneous and sudden, as the result of a traumatic event. It should hardly be surprising, given the sequence I have proposed, that the girls in the first two stories were affiliated with Chabad, while the diver in the third story was not.

Other stressful situations that catalyzed apparitions have been serious health problems, loss of a loved one, and severe economic crisis. Differences in the place in which the apparition took place and in the experience of it also display a gendered dimension. In cases of apparitions that occur in the public ritual spaces of 770 and its correlates, men report such experiences three times as often as women. But in secular places apparitions are reported by both sexes more or less equally. Most of the reports from the Rebbe's residence come from Hasidim, whereas a far more heterogeneous group testifies to having had such experiences in secular places, including people who are not affiliated with Chabad and some who are not observant Jews. Some of the latter identify the Rebbe only after the fact, generally after by chance encountering a photograph of him, as in the case of the diver.

The Rebbe's miraculous powers are demonstrated with particular force in mundane places, because only in these locations is he called on to save people facing crises. In most ritual arenas, the experiential climax is the vision of the Rebbe. Most of the Rebbe's apparitions in secular surroundings are classic examples of *deus ex machina* (divine intervention), even if preceded by deliberate visualization, which is a common phenomenon in states of emergency. At 770 most of the Rebbe's apparitions are also sudden and brief, but they seem to be more the tip of the iceberg of a much larger phenomenon of ongoing presence that generally remains submerged, even as it is felt in a concrete way. Intimations of the Rebbe's hidden presence at 770 can be seen in the following accounts.

The first example is that of a Hasid who went to 770 to attend the evening service "in the congregation of the Rebbe *shalita*, the King Messiah" on the first night of Sukkot. As soon as he entered the room he made out the movement of a hand "motioning me (from the Rebbe's holy *bimah*) to come closer." The Hasid tried to approach the Rebbe's place but was unable to make his way there through the packed room. When the service ended and some of the Hasidim began dancing in celebration of the holiday, he and others approached the lectern from which the Rebbe customarily gave a talk about the holiday on each of its seven nights so as to hear his talk. They waited quietly, as if listening. The Hasid was unsure whether he should stand there as if listening to the talk or join the dancing. His indecision reflects the difficulty posed by the Rebbe's absent-present status: "On the one hand it was not possible to disregard the faith of the Hasidim who were certain . . . that the Rebbe was here physically *mamash* and giving his customary talk. On the other hand, we heard nothing, and perhaps it was the Rebbe's desire . . . that we celebrate the holiday with joy!" The Hasid remained where he was, just below the lectern, debating the two possibilities. Then, when he raised his head, he saw "the Rebbe . . . standing there, leaning on the lectern from which he gave his talks! He smiled broadly and pointed with his holy finger at the Hasidim who stood there attentively and said: 'Do you see them? *They* are my devotees!'" The hesitant Hasid needed no more explicit indication.

"I thought to myself: I also want to be one of the Hasidim who 'belong' to the Rebbe. . . . " He thus remained standing with them. Later, when he told the man standing next to him about the Rebbe's apparition, he made out, in the corner of his eye, "a movement of somebody leaving the lectern from which the talks were given to the other lectern, where the Rebbe customarily . . . prayed." When he raised his eyes, he saw the Rebbe again, standing by the lectern he used in prayer. "I immediately lowered my head for a few seconds and when I looked up again I still saw the Rebbe . . . smiling at me and motioning with his holy hand 'Go!' as if saying 'I am done, go dance!'"[48] It should be noted that the Hasid saw the Rebbe (or his hand) in three different postures that perfectly match those of the Rebbe on the Sukkot holiday during his tenure. These short episodes of seeing the Rebbe look like surfacings or flashes during which the virtual Rebbe moves, as it were, from potential to actuality.[49] Such flashes during the course of a single apparition are familiar from reports coming from 770, but are almost unheard of in apparitions in secular contexts.

The Rebbe's ceaseless but covert presence at 770 is felt the most by children. On the whole, children rarely report apparitions, but those they do report last longer than the apparitions of adults, and among children there are more cases of recurring episodes of seeing the Rebbe (as in the previous example). People generally attribute this to the innocence and purity that typify them.[50] The epitome of such childhood innocence can be found in the story of one of the youngest "seers" to report a vision of the Rebbe—a three-and-a-half-year-old boy named Shalom-Ber who traveled from Jerusalem with his family to spend Pesach "with the Rebbe." The boy's father made every effort to instill the messianic experience in his children. "In our house . . . " the father reports, "our children are brought up [knowing that] the Rebbe is alive and well in the simple sense *mamash*, without any change. Even the smallest children grow up with that simple belief and [on the principle of] unmediated interaction with the prince of this generation. I frequently show my children film clips of the Rebbe . . . or give them pictures for them to keep with them." In light of this education, it is not surprising that when the father took his young son to an "audience with the Rebbe" on the Sabbath preceding Pesach, the boy insisted that he wanted to see the Rebbe. The father pointed at the Rebbe's red chair, but Shalom-Ber complained that he could not see anything because he was too short. The father and son went up the steps leading to the elevated platform on the east side of the room; when they reached the top step the boy chortled: "Here's the Rebbe, I see him!" He insisted on staying there so that he could see the Rebbe without interruption, and he continued to see the Rebbe each time the family went to 770 during the holiday week. A casual remark made by the boy after attending a prayer service at 770 shows how closely his visions were connected to the photographs of the Rebbe with which he was familiar: "Dad! The Rebbe waved at me! Just like in the video!" For the father, his son's repeated visions of the Rebbe were nothing less than a realization of the messianic idea. "As I understood it," he writes, "for Shalom-Ber, nothing was hidden."[51] This unique case, in which a boy saw the concealed Rebbe directly on multiple occasions, whenever he looked at the Rebbe's platform, stands at the opposite end of the spectrum from the onetime, sudden, and unexpected apparitions that are characteristic of apparitions that occur in mundane surroundings.

Reservations about Apparitions in Chabad

Apparitions of the Rebbe provide the Meshichist faction with corroboration for three of their claims: that the Rebbe is the Messiah; that his life did not end at the time of the Event of Gimel Tammuz; and that the world stands on the verge of the final redemption. As in many other apocalyptic movements, which impel their members to adopt new ways of seeing, the Rebbe himself made frequent use of visual idioms and metaphors (for example, "to open one's eyes") when speaking of the world-change from the mundane to the messianic era. If the prime goal of Chabad Hasidim is indeed to bring about that magic moment when the Rebbe-Messiah will reveal himself to the world, apparitions of the Rebbe offer a glimpse of that hoped-for event. As the Hasidim put it, they offer a "taste" of the redemption. Yet, despite the excitement that reports of such visions engender in Meshichist circles, many Hasidim have reacted to them with considerable qualms, misgivings, and reservations.

What is the source of this ambivalence? One obvious explanation is the undeniably subjective and private nature of these apparitions. Seers can tell others about their experience, but cannot easily offer proof that the apparition happened for real. The Meshichists use a wide range of means to validate and objectivize these private experiences.[52] The most important of these are images and traces of the Rebbe that document apparitions, like the photographs and film footage discussed above, in which the Rebbe appears out of nowhere. No less important are coins or dollar bills that the Rebbe grants during an apparition and which remain in the possession of those who saw him after the vision is over.[53] Other evidence includes testimony about the Rebbe's posture and gestures during apparitions that closely match his comportment prior to the Event of Gimel Tammuz. Such reports are especially convincing when they come from people who claim that they never met or saw images of the Rebbe. Also, a perfect correspondence between events "within the apparition" and "outside" it serves to objectify it.[54] Apparitions that occur simultaneously to more than one person break down the walls of private experience and enter the realm of intersubjective phenomena that can be shared. Finally come the confessions of nonbelievers who ridiculed the belief in the Rebbe's eternal life and were astounded to see him standing before them. Yet this repertoire of confirmations of the possibility of seeing the Rebbe as a physical, living presence is not enough to assuage an implicit sense of discomfort in Chabad discourse about such apparitions.

A second and perhaps more significant explanation for this ambivalence has its roots in Chabad's dialectic of presence and absence. The experiences of those who have been rewarded with apparitions of the Rebbe have been too few and too random to assuage the ache of his invisibility and to fill the void it has left. Arguably, the apparitions lead the Rebbe's Hasidim to the threshold of the Rebbe's public appearance as the Messiah. But these sporadic flashes of his eternal presence are not sufficient to slake the thirst for the ultimate redemption. Dialectically, the presence of absence can highlight the absence of his presence.[55] Uneasiness about the small number of apparitions is clearly evident in reports about seeing the Rebbe at 770. When Hasidim expressed puzzlement about a case in which the Rebbe appeared to a boy who lacked any special merit or pedigree, the editors of *Lifko'ach et ha'Einayim* explained that "the Rebbe's . . . manifestation is itself the normal state that should prevail all the time, and no reason need be sought for it. What should be sought, but is impossible to find, is the reason for the fact of which the Rebbe says . . . that it is completely incomprehensible, which is—why do all of us still not merit [his] complete and ongoing manifestation."[56]

A man who had become observant and was getting closer to Chabad saw the Rebbe on his first visit to 770. "For me it was the most natural thing," he said, "that in 770, the Rebbe's home . . . I would see him."[57] Yet, while these experiences are represented as "normal" and "natural," they remain infrequent.

If, for many Meshichists, apparitions are too rare, for Hasidim of a more spiritual orientation who adhere to the principles of wisdom, understanding, and knowledge (the words from which the acronym ChaBaD is composed), they are too frequent. These Hasidim view the unceasing quest for concrete proofs of the Rebbe's eternal nature as entirely superfluous. In their view, it constitutes a moral failing of the test the Rebbe set his disciples with his occlusion.[58]

A more moderate version of this critique is voiced within the Meshichist faction itself. According to Michal Kravel-Tovi,[59] the Hasidim submit to two inconsistent logical systems in constituting the messianic world in which they live. The first is pragmatic and subject to the evidence of their senses; there stress is placed on seeing as establishing the "true." The second is a mystical and dialectical system of an a-cosmic cast, with a hermeneutics of suspicion about the real world. These two systems contradict each other. Thus, the same Meshichist publications that extol apparitions of the Rebbe and trumpet them as proof that the Rebbe "is with us more than ever" also underscore, in other cases, the superiority of internal and spiritual vision. This latter view accords with the stress that Hasidic Judaism places on the "interiority of the Torah." One Meshichist activist put it this way: "Opening one's eyes may sound pretty easy . . . but it turns out that raising one's eyelids does not constitute opening one's eyes. The opening of eyes that the Rebbe taught . . . means opening the eyes of the mind, consciousness, and knowledge."[60] A similar inconsistency can be seen in the introduction to *Lifko'ach et ha'Einayim*. The editors apologetically inform their readers that "the purpose of this anthology is not to *prove* that the Rebbe . . . is alive and well in the simple sense *mamash* in his home—770; this belief is a reality stated by his holy Torah."[61] Just as pilots experiencing vertigo learn to trust only the objective evidence they see on their instruments, even if it contradicts their intuitions, so Hasidim learn to adhere to the Torah even against the evidence of their senses, this being the single source of guidance that enables them to overcome confusion and lack of knowledge when they are put to the test. But immediately following this the same writers declare: "We believe in perfect faith that the reality is that the Rebbe . . . is alive and well without any change, but clear vision is provided only by the evidence of one's eyes."[62]

Apparitions: Typology and Comparative Views

What insights can be gained from the waking apparitions reported by the Meshichists? The first one, from the psychological-anthropological perspective, is that the reports provide concrete evidence of the power wielded by culture in setting cognitive processes in motion in consciousness that make the unseen seen. While the recognition that cultural factors can affect fundamental mental experiences is not new, the detailed reports I have cited enable a clear evaluation of the extent to which the perceptual field of Chabad Hasidim is shaped by the dense messianic ecology in which they live. Given that this ecology is replete with explicit and concrete signs of the invisible Rebbe, apparitions of his presence in ritual arenas seem to be "apposite," just as a figure in a puzzle can be clearly seen even when central parts of the image are missing. This is due to the universal human perceptual capacity for constructing a complete image (*gestalt*) out of fragmentary stimuli.

The massive structuring of the messianic Chabad environment in fact poses the opposite question: Why are apparitions of the Rebbe not more common among Meshichists? This question is especially relevant with regard to 770, which, thanks to cultural expectations, deliberate intimations, and practices of making the Rebbe present, constitutes a highly suggestive environment that invites his manifestation. There are two answers to the question. First, it may well be that the reported apparitions are but the tip of an iceberg, and that the phenomenon is much more widespread. The second is that the capacity for seeing the Rebbe may well be differential, because it depends on mental traits or skills that are not equally distributed among believers. Absorption, "the capacity to treat what the mind imagines as more real than . . . what the eyes and ears perceive,"[63] may be the critical factor distinguishing between those who are able to see the Rebbe in special situations and those who are not. This ability may be improved with practice, but it cannot entirely overcome individual differences with regard to absorption.

A second insight: the clear differences between apparitions that occur in ritual and mundane spaces point to two distinct paths for perceiving visual stimuli that have no material source. The principal stimulation that invites such experiences along the first path is a rich cultural ecology that structures the perceptual field in which seeing the Rebbe becomes possible. Apparitions at ritual sites throughout the world—from visions of the Virgin Mary at pilgrimage sites sacred to her to sightings of Elvis Presley at Graceland Mansion—belong to this category, in which the place, expectations, rehearsal, and ritual practices come together to create an exceptional visual experience.[64]

A similar set of inviting factors could apparently be found in churches and monasteries in the late medieval period. The change that occurred then in the understanding of the Eucharist led to a transition from "receiving" Christ in communion to "seeing" him in the host at the moment of consecration. At the same time new practices of meditation and visualization appeared and spread widely, leading to a profusion of lay visions.[65] "It should not be surprising," Barbara Newman notes, "that a gaze fixed lovingly and habitually on the host, understood as the visible, edible body of God in the world, should sometime see it transformed into the infant Christ."[66] The blossoming of religious faith of all kinds at the end of the Middle Ages made "holy vision" more accessible to ordinary people. In retrospect, carved or painted icons and religious performances seem to be nothing but pale and unsophisticated precursors of today's visual technologies, but presumably they played a similar role in catalyzing apparitions. "A nun who daily wept before the Pieta or kissed the foot of the crucified Jesus would find it increasingly easy to visualize these figures in her prayer, and the line between 'visualization' and 'vision' is a fine one," Newman writes.[67]

The principal factor that invites visions on the second path is significant distress and the emotional instability that results. The threat to the individual in most cases is serious enough to catalyze a visionary experience under special circumstances, even in spaces that lie far from the suggestive scenery that serves as the background to ritual apparitions.[68] The two paths are far from mutually exclusive. Many of the people who have experienced visions at the pilgrimage shrines of various religions traveled to these sites because of some sort of life crisis. Furthermore, environmental prompts appear in mundane spaces as well. The frequent reports of seeing a lost loved one among the mourners grow out of grief-induced stress. Nevertheless, recently departed individuals are generally seen in the home in which they lived, which preserves their memory in the form of photographs and many other objects. Still, the disparity between these two types of experience is sufficiently clear to mandate further examination of the typology I propose, for comparison in a broader set of contexts.

My third insight is that comparing accounts of seeing the Rebbe, in contrast with those of Christian apparitions, shows that there is a notable epistemological difference between them. Christian visions of the medieval and early modern period are experienced as "*unusual* sensory experiences,"[69] detached, by definition, from everyday reality. Their manifestly spiritual nature is evident in the fact that what is seen is not a thing in itself but an image of it. Visions required that "the pathways of normal perception . . . are blocked in such a way that the eye does not focus on physical reality but instead turns inward toward images that exist within the mind."[70] Visionary mystics, such as Saint Teresa of Ávila[71] and Saint Hildegard of Bingen,[72] believed that true visions emerge from the soul and sought to distinguish their mystical experiences from the physical act of seeing. In light of the emphasis on alternative ways of seeing, it is hardly surprising that "altered states of consciousness have been the *sine qua non* of visions."[73]

Accounts of people who have had visions at Marian pilgrimage sites do not reflect a systematic religious doctrine, but their otherworldly character is evident. In many cases the Virgin floats above them, and the visionaries turn their gazes skyward to see her. She also appears in different forms: "like a cloud" or "like a big ray of light coming from the sky very slowly."[74] Like Chabad Hasidim, today's Evangelical Christians long for their Messiah to be close and accessible.[75] They differ from the Hasidim, however, just as they do from Catholics, in that their preferred sensory modality for mystical communion is aural rather than visual. Despite this difference, however, the spiritual character of the visions familiar from earlier Christian eras is evident. God's voice "normally sounds like a flow of spontaneous thoughts rather than an audible voice," writes Tanya Luhrmann.[76] New converts to the church learn to discern God's thoughts from their own. Despite the manifestly mentalist nature of the visions reported by modern Christians, they too make a clear distinction between hearing God and normal hearing.

The apparitions at 770 and its satellite sites are of an entirely different nature: they are hyper-realistic. The denial of the Rebbe's death is a bold ontological statement that challenges and constrains the Meshichists' epistemological horizons, and consequently the soteriological implications of their experiences. Radical Chabad Hasidim are committed to the belief that the Rebbe lives "in body and in soul" at 770; they continue to see him there "just as before." He looks the same and his posture and gestures are in perfect accord with the way he appeared and acted before his occlusion. In visual encounters with the Rebbe, the basic dimensions of reality are not violated. The Rebbe appears in the right place at the right time, and the experiences of those who encounter him obey the normal rules of sensory perception. I suggest that the discontent inherent in the apparitions is amplified by the disconcerting gap between, on the one hand, the future-oriented picture of the hyper-enchanted world-on-the-verge-of-redemption that the Rebbe promoted, and on the other the past-oriented and hyper-real nature of the experiences of seeing him. In such incidents, the viewers' state of consciousness does not undergo any dramatic change. The Rebbe appears with his feet on the ground; the gaze is horizontal, not vertical; the scenery terrestrial, not celestial; and the physical environment remains unchanged. In the end, the apparitions, like other reproductions of the Rabbi's icons and traces, are but replicas through which a lost past is temporarily restored.

The distinction between the two types of apparitions can be placed in greater contrast by looking at the historical (or metahistorical) location of these phenomena in the Christian context. When Jesus appears to his disciples following his crucifixion and resurrection, his physical, bodily presence is palpable—for example, they touch his wounds. Following his ascension to heaven, encounters with him become less concrete and more spiritual.[77] The spiritual nature of the visions that follow the ascension creatively broadens the horizons of religious imagination. Concepts such as mythopoeic function[78] and autonomous imagination,[79] used in the discourse of anthropologists and scholars of religion, seek to denote this creativity. The epistemological openness inherent in the processes so conceptualized establishes experiences that, according to Lurhmann, are "light, fanciful, not-real-but-more-than-real."[80] Michelle Stephen argues that, while such experiences do not look like external reality, "they become more than external reality" in that they facilitate freedom of thought and a rich life of imagination and invention.[81] In comparison with Christianity, the Meshichists seem to be stuck in a preascension phase, as they anxiously wait for "this generation's Moses" to appear and reveal himself to the world "now and immediately *mamash.*"[82]

PART III

MESHICHIST COSMOLOGY

CHAPTER 7

SCHNEERSONCENTRISM

The Rebbe Steers the World

The Rebbe's preeminent status in the Meshichist camp, as evidenced both by the writings of its key rabbis and the ritual practices of its lay members, is reflected in a range of beliefs and perceptions that the Rebbe is an omnipotent actor in the world. It goes without saying that this cannot be separated from the wealth of midrashic and kabbalistic traditions about the supernatural capacities of *tzadikim* (pl.), and certainly not from the miracle-working powers that Hasidism attributes to the *tzadik* or *admor* of a Hasidic community, the leaders of Chabad among them.[1] Nor do the Meshichists relate to the Rebbe's role in the world in isolation from that of his predecessors in Chabad, especially the two who preceded him. But the idea that the Rebbe controls the world and shapes history by virtue of his mission as the Final Redeemer has reached new heights in Meshichist discourse. The broad range of the Rebbe's actions is a prominent feature; he intervenes in the daily affairs of individuals and changes the course of decisive political events that affect the lives of millions. The Rebbe's power to help his Hasidim when they are in trouble or distress has been discussed extensively in previous chapters. This one will focus on the Rebbe's control of the forces of nature and his involvement in the international and geopolitical arenas.

The Rebbe demonstrated during his lifetime his ability to halt and divert storms and to change the weather suddenly. At the end of August 1992, Hurricane Andrew threatened southern Florida after sowing destruction in the Bahamas. Many of Miami's inhabitants fled northward, and there was special concern about the safety of the city's Chabad Hasidim, because "the Chabad institutions in Miami lay exactly on the storm's path." At that time the elderly Rebbe was already partly paralyzed and speechless. Nevertheless, when he was asked whether the Hasidim should evacuate the city, he shook his head and hand in the negative over and over again. The Hasidim, of course, obeyed. Given the forecast that "the largest winter storm known in American history . . . was liable to flatten everything that had been built in southern Florida over hundreds of years," the local press declared that "the people of Chabad are committing suicide, and anyone who stays should first write their wills." Chabad publications, and a short film *In the Eye of the Storm* directed by a Meshichist activist,[2] recount the hurricane's approach in apocalyptic language reminiscent of the account of Noah's flood. As *Sichat Hage'ulah* describes the episode: "The water was supposed to rise and cover the entire city, and the experts who were interviewed one after the other said that people should ready themselves for horrifying and shocking sights." But the great drama ended with a miracle: "The storm changed its direction and hit . . . an area that many had fled to, and in Miami there was hardly any property damage."[3] The film declares, with undisguised glee, that the followers of Maharishi Mahesh Yogi in Miami, who, in accordance with their spiritual leader's counsel, fled to a supposedly safe haven, were ravaged by the storm there.[4]

The Rebbe's control of the forces of nature has been demonstrated again and again since the Event of Gimel Tammuz. In Chapter 3 on "Writing to the Rebbe," I recounted that, in the first story to appear in print that documents the use of the *Igrot Kodesh* oracle, the petitioner asked the Rebbe to "fix the weather right now," that is, to stop the unrelenting rainstorm that threatened to inundate a rally of Chabad children in Givat Olga. The petition was answered almost immediately. The cessation of rain after a petition to the Rebbe is chronicled in relation to rallies, convocations, and other activities. For example, the rabbi of the Ohalei Keidar prison in Be'er Sheva wrote to the Rebbe, asking that he end a huge storm that had hit the area just when the rabbi was planning to celebrate, along with the inmates, the bringing of a new Torah scroll into the prison synagogue. The Rebbe immediately interceded, "as everyone stood in shock in the face of what seemed like a heavenly vision not of this world. All around the prison facility the skies were gray, heralding imminent rain, but in the center of the sky, precisely over the prison, the blue sky and sunrays could be seen. That's the way it was during the hour the event lasted, with everyone looking and seeing."[5]

Two decades after Hurricane Andrew came Hurricane Sandy, which hit New Jersey hard in October 2012. An electronics factory owned by a Chabad Hasid was in danger of being flooded. A convocation was organized in Crown Heights to help him: "Everyone broke out singing 'Yechi,' as they waved their hands as if they were pushing the storm away . . . making the same gesture the Rebbe *shalita*, the King Messiah, used to move the hurricane in 1992, exactly twenty years ago." The Rebbe's hand gesture in the "visible wonder" of Hurricane Andrew became an inspiration and a model to be imitated by his Hasidim. The results were much the same: "Only when the storm had passed did the huge miracle become apparent. The factory was the only one not to be flooded, remaining dry and without any damage. The storm simply skipped it, someone pushed it away."[6]

The Rebbe controls not only the forces of nature but also human history. As the King Messiah leading the world toward its redemption, he is perceived as determining the sequence of events in the geopolitical realm. The Rebbe declared, time and again, that the world was ready for the redemption, and that his generation, the seventh since the founding of Chabad, would have the privilege of seeing the arrival of the Messiah "immediately *mamash*." In this vein, key events during the second half of the twentieth century, among them the Six Day War, the collapse of the Soviet Union and the opening of its borders to Jewish emigration, the First Gulf War, international disarmament and cooperation treaties, and scientific and medical advances all became, in his eyes, manifest signs of the redemption. According to his followers, he even foresaw some of these events, reinforcing his status as a prophet. However, beyond the prophetic powers the Meshichists attribute to the Rebbe, they believe that he also shaped events and set them on the course of the redemption. A Meshichist publication on the Gulf War, for example, states explicitly: "Not only did the Rebbe, the prophet of our generation, know and declare in advance, advertising it broadly, the miraculous outcome of the war, *but he determined its results!!!*"[7] All

Chabad Hasidim believe that the movement's leaders, from the founding *admor* Shneur Zalman to the Rebbe, were the chosen successors of the founder of Hasidism, the Ba'al Shem Tov, and his student the Maggid of Mezeritch, in a line meant to disseminate the teachings of Hasidism as a condition for the arrival of the Messiah. The claim that *tzadikim* of this line possess unlimited powers is a direct corollary of that core belief. But the feeling of being on the verge of the final redemption that was fostered by the Rebbe, along with the identification of him as the Messiah, clearly magnified his powers and miracles beyond any attributed to his predecessors.

A Meshichist article headlined "An Invisible Hand Is Steering the World into a New Geopolitical Order" describes how the Rebbe controls the world:

> Despite the follies, fraud, and fatal errors perpetrated by [world] leaders, and their lack of openness, it seems as if everything is going in a new direction. The world is uniting and a new, egalitarian, and humanitarian world order is coming into being. It feels as if someone invisible has decisively taken the leadership out of the hands of the leaders and is finally piloting our tormented world toward a safe haven. Yes, he began working sixty years ago and changed course sixteen to twenty years ago. And now he is already in the air, progressing with greater speed than any Iranian missile. Long live the King.[8]

While the opening sentence remarks on the dark clouds casting their shadows on our world, they cannot withstand the new world order illuminated, according to the Meshichists, by the light of the redemption. When horrifying disasters take place anywhere in the world—floods in Pakistan, mudslides in China, fires in Russia—it is because "someone has apparently decided to shake up the system" in preparation for the new era. The results are immediate: "The prime minister of Japan apologizes to the Koreans for [Japan's] brutal occupation [of Korea]. No one could have compelled the Japanese government to do it, but it was done. *And it was done only because of the determination of one person, the Rebbe* . . . the prophet of our generation, who has proclaimed unambiguously that the world is ready for Redemption."[9]

In the political arena, the Rebbe grapples with the superpowers and imposes his will on their leaders. The changes in Russia and France, which the Rebbe interpreted as manifest signs of the redemption, have a special significance for the Meshichists. Chabad's historical accounting with these two countries, detailed below, is dramatically depicted in a mass performance, "The Franco-Russian War," staged every year at the end of the Oro shel Mashiach summer camp. The campers are divided into the armies of these two countries, and they battle by means of slogans and speeches meant to fire up their soldiers and convince their enemies to join them. The posters and costumes used in this extravaganza give an indication of its historical roots—Napoleon's invasion of Russia in 1812. The real war, however, is between the two great revolutions of the modern era, the French and the Bolshevik, and the paths of secular redemption that they offer. The central message conveyed by the pageant, the climax of the camp term, is the clear superiority over these competing secular ideologies of the spiritual revolution led by the Rebbe, which leads to the true and complete redemption.[10]

Chabad's special interest in Russia grows out of the fact that the movement emerged, and most of its early members lived, in Belarus and Ukraine, which were part of the Czarist empire. When Napoleon invaded Russia, Chabad's founder, Rabbi Shneur Zalman, supported Czar Alexander I, and Chabad Hasidim believe that it was the Alter Rebbe's spiritual intervention that brought about Napoleon's defeat.[11] The *admor*'s support was not, however, motivated by love of Alexander; rather, he abhorred Napoleon and the values of progress that he sought to spread. The difficult living conditions endured by the Hasidim in the Russian Pale of Settlement in the nineteenth century worsened even further in the twentieth century, under the antireligious and repressive Soviet regime, and many of them were persecuted and sent into exile. Rabbi Yosef Yitzchak, who ascended to Chabad's leadership in 1920, risked his life when he repeatedly clashed with Soviet officials in his efforts to defend traditional Jewish practices. He was arrested several times, and according to Chabad historiography was sentenced to death, but his sentence was miraculously commuted to deportation. In 1927 he was compelled to leave the Soviet Union, and was separated from most of his followers.

Unsurprisingly, Chabad views the disintegration of the Soviet empire as its historic victory over the communist regime, its sworn enemy.[12]

For the Rebbe, the high point of Chabad's campaign for the redemption in its "years of miracles" (1990–1992) is

> breaking through the borders of that country, which in its time advocated and declared war against the dissemination of the Torah and Judaism, to the point of a war against faith in the Creator of the world and his leadership (including the imprisonment of my teacher and father-in-law, his Holiness the *admor* and *nasi* of our generation, and afterward and as a result of that, his departure from the boundaries of that country).

As he saw it, "the fall of the previous regime and the establishment of a new regime that has declared [its support of] justice, integrity and peace, on the basis of belief in the Creator of the world and his leadership," was an important building block of the redemption.[13] To the metahistorical framework professed by the Rebbe, his Hasidim added the claim that the architect of that dramatic turn in history was the Rebbe himself: "In the year 5751 [1991] we are seeing how the Rebbe . . . is demolishing the oppressive power and dismantling communism, which bore the banner of atheism, and since then millions of people throughout the countries of the Commonwealth of Independent States are free to believe in the Creator of the world and his leadership."[14]

The Hasidim believe that even before the fall of the Soviet Union, the Rebbe was dealing blows to its leaders. When Stalin launched the Doctors' Plot show trials at the beginning of 1953, in which nine physicians, most of them Jews, were charged with an attempt to poison the Soviet leader, the Rebbe "took action to face the evil using the divine tools in his possession."[15] During a convocation held on the Purim holiday that year, he told a story about a Hasid in Czarist Russia who joined in the cheers of a crowd chanting "*Hura!*" in honor of the czar, but instead shouted "*Hu ra!*," Hebrew for "He is evil," without anyone else sensing the difference. In a state of devotion and with a fervent expression on his face, the Rebbe made a triangle out of his fingers and declared "*Hu ra! Hu ra! Hu ra!*" "Two days later it transpired that at the very moment in which this was sounded at the Rebbe's convocation, the tyrannical dictator Stalin died." This action saved three million Jews from death, the writer of the story relates, as following the Doctors' Plot the country's Jews were to be sent to camps in Siberia. On top of that, according to *Sichat Hage'ulah*, the Rebbe used his mystical power to promote the death of Brezhnev in 1982 and of his successor Andropov in 1983. "The way was prepared for the great revolution in the Soviet Union."[16]

In this story, which exhibits the "rule of three" in the form of a folktale, the Rebbe is depicted as an all-powerful *tzadik* who can smite the enemies of Judaism using mystical practices of a manifestly magical cast.

Chabad also has a long historical grievance against France. Rabbi Shneur Zalman supported Czar Alexander against Napoleon because of his fear that the values of liberty and equality proclaimed by the French Revolution would do harm to Judaism even if they were beneficial to Jews as individuals. He fled the invaders, and the difficulties he encountered in his flight hastened his death.[17] The *admor* predicted Napoleon's defeat, and in its wake appropriated "Napoleon's March" and made it into a sacred Chabad melody. In Hasidic-kabbalistic terms this was the beginning of the work of "refining" France, a labor that intensified when subsequent Chabad *admorim* (pl.) visited that country. As the cradle of revolution, France bestowed fundamental secular values on the world as a whole and thus became the sworn enemy of religion. France was thus seen, in kabbalistic terms, as "the empowerer of the shells [evil forces] and of the severe judgment," and needed to undergo special processes of refinement and purification. The Rebbe, as always, maintained that it was his father-in-law, Rabbi Yosef Yitzchak, who was accountable for this rectification process thanks to his visits to France, as well as the emissaries and sacred writings he sent there, and to the religious institutions he founded in that country. But the Hasidim linked France's final rectification to the Rebbe's residence there from 1933 to 1941, and to the dissemination of the wellsprings of Hasidism there afterward, through his emissaries.

The rectification that the first *admor* achieved by taking the secular "Napoleon's March" and imbuing it with holiness by making it into a Chabad anthem was completed by the Rebbe on Simchat Torah 1973 when he sacralized the "Marseillaise" by using it as a melody for a liturgical poem traditionally sung by Jews on Sabbaths and holidays, "Ha'aderet Veha'emunah." The Rebbe went into great detail about the rectification of France, using the complex messianic hermeneutics that he had formulated. He connected the concepts of exile and redemption in the French context using the last two verses of Obadiah, one of the minor prophetic books of the Bible ("And that exiled force of Israelites [shall possess] what belongs to the Phoenicians as far as Tzarfat [a place name used in modern Hebrew to designate France], while the Jerusalemite exile community of Sepharad [now used to designate Spain] shall possess the towns of the Negev. For liberators shall march up on Mount Zion to wreak judgment on Mount Esau; and dominion shall be the Lord's" [Obadiah 1:20–21]). The Rebbe etymologized the name Tzarfat, claiming that it came "from the same root as *tzeruf* [to refine or purify], and refining and purifying bring the redemption"; the numerical values of the letters, he noted, add up to 770, the home of the Messiah.[18] Furthermore, rearranging the letters of "Tzarfat" provides the word *paratzta*, "you broke through," a Chabad code word for spreading the wellsprings of Chabad teachings, which the Rebbe saw as a breaking through of all boundaries. The Rebbe compared this border-breaking to the messianic age by adducing two biblical verses. The first (Genesis 38:29) tells of the birth of Judah and Tamar's son Peretz, whose name means "breach," and who was the forefather of the royal line of King David and thus of the Messiah. Regarding the second, "One who makes a breach goes before them" (Micah 2:13), the seminal medieval biblical commentator Rashi says that the "one who makes a breach" is no other than the Messiah, the savior of Israel. The Rebbe enthusiastically noted the presence of Chabad Hasidim from France in the crowd when he gave this talk. He called on "Napoleon's March" to be played when he finished and told his audience to whistle along. All this demonstrated his sense that Chabad had won a historic battle—the cradle of the secularist revolution has become an important Hasidic center. In the Schneersoncentric scheme of things, Chabad, led by the Rebbe, is a spiritual superpower, contending with and defeating earthly powers.

In contrast with Russia and France, the United States, the leader of the free world, has been seen by the Rebbe and his followers as a "benevolent kingdom." This positive attitude is not surprising, given that the United States offered asylum to Rabbi Yosef Yitzchak and his son-in-law and future heir during World War II. Furthermore, the United States enabled the movement they headed to reorganize and recover from the twin disasters the sect had endured—Nazi occupation and Soviet oppression. American freedom of religion, and the close ties that senior Chabad figures established with politicians and top officials on the federal and state level, did much to help the movement flourish and gain popularity. The fact that Chabad reestablished itself in the New World is evident in the American style it adopted in many areas: it emphasized political involvement and public relations, became adept at using the media, attributed great importance to advertising and dissemination of its message, and established a wide-ranging visual culture.

From a Schneersoncentric point of view, however, Chabad's leaders helped the United States no less than they received help from it. The Rebbe, as was his habit, attributed this aid to Rabbi Yosef Yitzchak. He claimed that by virtue of the fact that the center of Chabad Hasidism moved to the New World with the previous *admor*, the "lower hemisphere" (as America was designated) was refined and purified, and the process of the giving of the Torah began there as well.[19] The establishment of the United Nations in New York was also a product of Rabbi Yosef Yitzchak's arrival in the city a short time previously. The construction of the UN building in 1951 was tied to the Rebbe's accession to the position of *admor* that year, "emphasizing that unity and peace among all nations is a result of the activity of the *nasi* of our generation in refining the world (by disseminating the Torah and Judaism and justice and uprightness throughout the world)." Similarly, the Meshichists attribute much of the UN's most successful endeavors to the Rebbe, among them great-power treaties of cooperation and for the limitation of weapons of mass destruction.[20] As they have it, the Rebbe elevated the lower hemisphere into holiness by turning the passion to get rich into a huge wave of charity, by using the great scientific-technological leap forward to disseminate the wellsprings of Hasidism, and by making the most of the modern crisis of values to preach adherence among the gentiles to the seven Noachide laws. Yet even a benevolent kingdom like the United

States was not exempt from punishment when it strayed from the right path. In Meshichist historiography, the United States was pummeled by Hurricane Katrina because of its support for Israel's disengagement from the Gaza Strip, and the value of the dollar collapsed because of the country's efforts to establish a Palestinian state.

The Rebbe intervenes in the most distant corners of the world—far beyond Russia, France, and the United States. In their efforts to identify events around the world as omens of the redemption that bear the Rebbe's signature, the Meshichists have gone as far as to attribute to him even the demolition of the huge Buddhas of Bamiyan by the Taliban in Afghanistan in 2001. The act, according to the Meshichists, was part of the project of ridding the world of idols, as God commanded. Despite the Bible's assertion that "All who worship images, who vaunt their idols, are dismayed" (Psalms 97:7), there is still "a shadowy and dark side of human society that worships false gods and bows down to and burns offerings to idols."[21] Without realizing it, the Taliban who shattered the idols were doing the Rebbe's bidding.

While the Rebbe's gaze encompasses the entire world, his primary interest is events in Israel. Chabad under Rabbi Yosef Yitzchak virulently opposed the establishment of the state of Israel,[22] but once the Jewish state had come into being the movement, under the Rebbe's leadership, took an active part in the country's political and religious discourse. It is thus unsurprising that Chabad Hasidim believe that key events in the country's history were shaped by the Rebbe. I have already mentioned a few of these, but here I offer two more, both connected to Iraq: the attack on the Iraqi nuclear reactor in 1981 and the First Gulf War of 1990–1991. Chabad Hasidim maintain that several miracles took place during the first of these. For example, the Jordanians and Saudis did not detect or go on alert when the Israeli bombers on their way to this mission flew through those countries' airspace, even though they were not camouflaged, and the Iraqis did not counter with antiaircraft fire or rockets and did not send their own air force to meet the Israeli planes. According to Chabad Hasidim, these were the product of "a number of extraordinary spiritual actions for the success of the initiative" (among them fasts, rallies, and sacred study) initiated by the Rebbe.[23]

Chabad Hasidim also recount in detail how the Rebbe's miraculous interventions in the First Gulf War (Operation Desert Storm) prevented the Iraqis from using their chemical and biological weapons. In these accounts, the Rebbe was the true commander of the campaign. For example, an article commemorating the twentieth anniversary of the war states that on Monday, July 23, 1990, the Rebbe paid a visit to the grave of Rabbi Yosef Yitzchak, "for the first time ever on the first day of the [Jewish] month, and remained there for more than ten hours. *Mamash on this date* the Central Intelligence Agency of the American Department of Defense [sic] declared a *high alert* for a war in the Gulf region."[24] The implication is that the Rebbe's prayers at the grave of his predecessor pulled the strings of the American war machine. Two of the people who attribute the outcome of the military engagement in Iraq to the Rebbe are Rabbi Gidi Sharon, a former combat pilot, and Rabbi Avishai Ifergan, who once commanded an elite IDF unit. Both men are *ba'alei teshuvah* who joined Chabad after completing their military service. They lend an authoritative cast to the claim that the Rebbe's spiritual powers were in evidence on the battlefield.

Chabad's potent messianic orientation has positioned it on the right end of the Israeli political spectrum. In this view, one of the consequences of the final and complete redemption will be the recognition by all the world's nations of the Jewish people's spiritual preeminence and the sacredness of the Promised Land as defined by the Bible and rabbinic tradition. The Rebbe consequently utterly rejected all territorial concessions by Israel and opposed any recognition of the national rights of the Palestinians and any negotiation with them. The Meshichists, following his lead, claim that any political leader who disobeys the Rebbe's commands in this regard will be punished. As proof of this, they point to the fact that in the ten years between 1992 and 2002, six different Israeli governments came and went and none of them completed its full term. The reason is that "the King Messiah dissolves governments" when they stray by declaring their willingness to enter into negotiations with and make concessions to the Arabs.[25] The heavy price paid by public figures who were involved in the disengagement from the Gaza Strip in 2005 is, according to the Rebbe's followers, further evidence of the long reach of his wrath.[26]

But the Rebbe's rebuke was meant solely to pave the way for the glorious future awaiting the Jewish people in its own land during the messianic era. The perfect faith that Chabad Hasidim have in the Rebbe's prophecies is especially notable when it comes to revealing the unknown treasures. These beliefs sometimes make their way from Meshichist publications into business journalism, as two articles from the economic newspaper *TheMarker* illustrate. One piece opens with a promise the Rebbe made to Haifa's mayor, Aryeh Gur'el, in 1988: "This is one of the characteristics of Haifa, that it has the sea, and in it there is a valley, and in that valley there are gems and pearls. The Holy One, Blessed Be He, has created a marvel: he secreted them deep in the land." The Rebbe drew this from Moses's blessing to the tribe of Zebulun, "For they draw from the riches of the sea, and the hidden hoards of the sand" (Deuteronomy 33:19). The Jewish sages and mystics interpreted this to mean that treasures would be discovered on the shores of the Holy Land. Inspired by the Rebbe's prophecy, an Israeli businessman and Chabad Hasid founded Shefa Yamim, a company dedicated to searching for gemstones in Haifa Bay. He announced that he had found a huge 5.72-carat diamond.[27] The second item is about Givot Olam, an oil-exploration firm drilling in the area of Rosh Ha'ayin, on the basis of the biblical verse "With the best from the ancient mountains, and the bounty of hills immemorial" (Deuteronomy 33:15). The company's founder, Tuvia Luskin, presented his results to the Rebbe in the early 1990s, and the Rebbe gave him his blessing and promised that he would succeed.[28]

The Rebbe rules the world because he is the Messiah, and it exalts him above all other sages and holy men of the Jewish tradition. Nevertheless, he is also attentive to the distress of individuals and everyday problems, and intercedes to remedy them. Moreover, the Hasidic doctrine that sees divine sparks everywhere in the mundane world has even greater potency in Chabad because of its intense involvement in the world outside its own sectoral boundaries and its messianic doctrine of dispersion and breaking down borders. As a result, in popular messianic religion, mundane and everyday matters also fall under the Rebbe's suzerainty. The King Messiah who calms storms, destroys great powers, and topples governments is also invoked to ensure the victory of a favorite basketball team or to help a follower win Israel's national lottery—all of which serves to spread the Rebbe's fame as the savior and to hurry the redemption.

The Rebbe's achievements on the playing field are too many to mention. Given the shortage of space, I will offer only one example. The Hapoel Galil Elyon basketball team won Israel's 1992/1993 basketball championship when fans from the Chabad neighborhood in Safed attended the decisive game with Maccabi Tel Aviv, which had almost always held the championship. They hoisted a sign emblazoned with the slogan "This will be a year of great wonders," the acronym of which was the current Hebrew year. They handed out Messiah flags, "Prepare for the coming of the Messiah" signs, and pictures of the Rebbe, and played the song "Moshiach, Moshiach," which thereafter became the team's anthem.[29] Beyond sports, Hasidim do not hesitate to appeal for the Rebbe's intercession in the smallest matters, such as obtaining jelly donuts for an event, getting picked up while hitchhiking, or winning the lottery. Such matters may seem less than momentous given the Rebbe's eminence, but what is significant is the full range of interventions, from the mundane to the earthshaking. Nothing in the world or in the individual lies outside the authority of the Rebbe, the King Messiah.

CHAPTER 8

THE APOTHEOSIS OF THE REBBE

The glorification of the Rebbe's supernatural powers and control of history seem to be unrivaled in contemporary Judaism. In fact, it seems to be an innovation within Chabad itself; recall that the movement's founder, Rabbi Schneur Zalman of Liadi, opposed the popular view of the Hasidic *tzadikim* which ascribed magic powers and miracles to these saintly spiritual figures.[1] Today, in contrast, since many Chabadniks believe that the Rebbe is the Messiah, in Chabad's radical wing the boundary between the Rebbe and God himself has grown increasingly fuzzy, to the point where some identify the Rebbe as God.[2] The Chabad mainstream lashes out at the movement's fringe groups that explicitly attribute godly status to the Rebbe, terming them "Elokists" (from Elohim, one of God's names, with the *h* replaced by a *k* to avoid pronouncing the sacred word).[3] But the Meshichist discourse as a whole provides fertile ground for such extreme phenomena. Furthermore, the link between the identities of *tzadikim* and God has a basis in familiar rabbinic teaching, and even more so in Kabbalah. This link is a cornerstone of Hasidism's institution of the *tzadik* or *admor*, especially in Chabad.[4] According to Shaul Magid, Hasidism's growth beyond "the Christian gaze" freed its thinkers to craft a Jewish theology bearing shades of a belief in God's incarnation in human form, in the *tzadik*, without the troublesome awareness of its proximity to Christianity.[5] A variant of this theology can be seen in today's Chabad.

The Rebbe himself spoke of his predecessor, Rabbi Yosef Yitzchak, as the physical embodiment of the highest essence of the Godhead, while at the same time greatly expanding the ideal of the *tzadik* who, by adhering to God, makes the divine accessible to the Hasidim of the generation of redemption.[6] These positions, which indicate that the attribution of divine status to the Rebbe did not come out of nowhere, help the Meshichists mitigate the radical implications of their claims. Nevertheless, the apotheosis of the Rebbe by the central Meshichist groups, not just by that faction's fringes, is exceptionally broad and forthright, as the following examples will show.

Rabbi Tuvia Doron, the director of the Messiah and Redemption Center in Jerusalem, maintains that a *tzadik* like the Rebbe "is sometimes called 'the emissary of the supernal man who is like him—to the point of being like him *mamash*,' and sometimes 'the essence of [God's] being,' godliness wearing the body of the *tzadik*. In any case, the existence of the *tzadik* is a foundation of the world; since he is the generation's *nasi*, he necessarily exists *and there is no reality without him*."[7] Rabbi Haim Levi Yitzchak Ginsburgh, a central figure in the Meshichist camp, argues that one may compare a flesh-and-blood human being to God because the Rebbe, "even though he is a soul within a body . . . is a 'vessel' imbued with the light of the infinite."[8] Elsewhere, Ginsburgh wrote that "there is a Rebbe among the Jews, and he does not fall under the constraints of nature, and everything happens at his will."[9] Rabbi Zimroni Tzik, editor of *Sichat Hage'ulah*, maintains that "we are indeed still witnesses, in these very seconds, to the occlusion of the revealed side of the King Messiah, the Rebbe *shalita* from Lubavitch, but precisely at these moments what is being revealed is his essence that is tied to God's essence to the point that they are one."[10] The Rebbe's connection to the divine world is a corollary to his status as the Messiah, meaning that he has a superior soul, the only and general soul that is identified with God's essence. According to Tzik, "The Messiah will be endowed with the highest soul . . . 'singular'. . . . When you say 'first' it is clear that a second follows . . . but when you say singular you negate the possibility of anything else. Such is the case with the 'singular' soul. Not only are the two bound together— the soul and its creator—but rather they are a single conglomerate, one unit *mamash*."[11]

Here is Tzik's depiction of the Rebbe on the third of Tammuz 5756/1996, the second anniversary of his occlusion:

> Since the Rebbe ... ascended to the leadership forty-five years ago, everyone saw that he could not be placed within the constraints of nature, neither within the bounds of matter nor the bounds of spirit. This was evident in his heavy and utterly precise schedule, his eating habits, and the minimal time set aside for sleep, in his saintliness and purity, his vision extending beyond time and place, his ability to go against the current of every person, his leadership and his utter devotion to others, individually and collectively, the astounding innovative teachings he revealed, the profusion of his talks, articles, and holy letters, his astonishing memory and, in fact, everything else. All these were just a few of the signs of the breaking down of the boundaries of bodily and spiritual nature that we were witness to in the Rebbe, the King Messiah, may he live forever and ever. ... The sparks of light slowly joined together into a single shining figure, entirely above nature in nature. The figure of the King Messiah, may he live forever and ever, began to take form and reveal itself to us.[12]

Despite the fact that some midrashic, kabbalistic, and Hasidic texts pave the way toward seeing the *tzadik* as divinity in human form,[13] the deification of the Rebbe has been roundly criticized within and outside Chabad.[14] Rabbi Elazar Menachem Shach (1899–2001), the spiritual leader of the Lithuanian (non-Hasidic) Haredi community, once famously remarked that Chabad is the sect closest to Judaism. That acerbic appraisal came in response to the Rebbe's invocation of his father-in-law, Rabbi Yosef Yitzchak, as the divine essence of God's being embodied in the human *tzadik*. Some Chabad Hasidim and leaders were shocked and shaken when, following the Event of Gimel Tammuz, new adherents to Chabad, on the movement's fringes, began to declare that the Rebbe was God. Furthermore, these adherents voiced their beliefs explicitly and radically, without making any effort to temper their views by invoking traditional texts linking the *tzadik* to God. One extreme example of this phenomenon is Meir Baranes, a *ba'al teshuvah* from Safed and self-proclaimed "spokesman for the Messiah." Baranes has published pamphlets and advertisements in the media in which he declares, casting off all restraint, that since "the Rebbe said that the King Messiah bears the name of the Holy One, Blessed Be He, we must piece the data together and add to the name of the Lubavitcher Rebbe, the King Messiah, the title

Our Righteous God." Elsewhere he wrote: "Here is our Righteous Messiah, here is the Lubavitcher Rebbe, *admor nasi* of our generation, here is our God. This is God, the Lubavitcher Rebbe, the King of Kings of Kings, the Holy One Blessed Be He *mamash*."[15]

In a series of newspaper advertisements, Baranes addressed God directly in a defiant tone. He insisted that God must repent for not redeeming his people "after two thousand years of exile and the killing of six million Jews in the Holocaust." He ended his plea in a threatening voice: "Keep your agreements! Do not force us to begin huge demonstrations against you." According to Baranes, he took this aggressive approach from the Rebbe himself, "who said many times that the only thing that is still delaying the redemption is that the Jewish people must demand redemption with real insolence. And that is what I am doing."[16]

The Chabad establishment quickly repudiated Baranes, depicting him as insane. In fact, Baranes incurred a severe head injury in an automobile accident during his military service. Furthermore, he has a record of violence (the most severe example of which was an attempt to run over Safed Chief Rabbi Levi Bistritsky, a member of Chabad, whom Baranes accused of persecuting him), has served time in prison, and has been confined to a psychiatric hospital. It may well be true, then, that the strangest of his positions grows out of mental distress and the circumstances of his admittedly exceptional life. Nevertheless, without diminishing the importance of these psychological factors, any assessment of his position on the Rebbe must take into account the social context and the ideological soil from which grow Baranes and like figures whom the Chabad mainstream terms "negative elements" and "weeds."

Two points need to be made in this social and ideological context. First, newly religious Hasidim constitute a high proportion of the radical Meshichist groups in Chabad. And many of them, like Baranes, are of Mizrachi origin. These new Hasidim are motivated by religious fervor. They intensively seek spiritual and mystical experiences and display a profound revulsion for institutionalized and routine religious life. It is hardly surprising, then, that Chabad's messianic-redemptive climate feeds these people's spiritual worlds and that it is fed by them. They sense a direct connection to the Rebbe even though (and perhaps precisely because) the great majority of them never encountered him during his lifetime. They tend to lionize him without being constrained by any of the inhibitions that the routine of normative religious life imposes. Even if Baranes is mentally unstable, the position he takes is not foreign to Chabad's fiery messianic climate. In my interviews with Meshichist activists I heard a surprising level of forbearance for his pronouncements, despite the fact that he has been denounced by spokesmen for the movement's mainstream. My interviewees contend that Baranes's provocative language is that of a holy fool; even if it is uninhibited and illogically phrased, and perhaps evidence of mental illness, it expresses the horizon-expanding nature of the Age of Redemption that has hitherto been hidden and repressed in Chabad because of its explosive nature. "You are in the service of the Rebbe even when you are mentally unstable," said one of my subjects. Other Hasidim who suffer from psychiatric problems also find a place for themselves in the Meshichist camp, where their lack of reserve enables them to bring up controversial issues that the religious establishment has a tendency to keep quiet.

Second, Baranes's road to Meshichist Chabad was paved with turbulent personal experiences in which the Rebbe appeared to him in a variety of ways, most commonly in states of crisis and distress. These experiences are not fundamentally different from those adduced in my previous chapters on how Hasidim make the Rebbe present in their lives. For example, Baranes began to advertise the Rebbe's divinity after an incident in which he lost consciousness in a cab in New York. As he flitted between life and death, he felt his soul separating from his body, rising heavenward, and standing on trial before the heavenly court. As in the reports of other Hasidim, the Rebbe burst into the courtroom to make an ardent defense for him. On Baranes's account, the Rebbe declared that "he will be a Hasid in Brooklyn."[17] As he does with other Hasidim, the Rebbe appeared in Baranes's dreams, and then while he was awake and praying in the *beit midrash* at 770. Baranes's report of this experience is no different in any way from the template of ritual apparitions discussed in Chapter 6. Given this correlation, it is hardly surprising that, in the wake of these experiences, Baranes added the name Menachem to his first name, becoming Meir Menachem. He was a sought-after speaker at Redemption and Messiah rallies until he went overboard with his provocative advertisements.

Meir Menachem Baranes is not the only Meshichist Chabad Hasid to voice an explicit Elokist position. A couple from Afula Illit, Efraim and Feige Kaminker, printed and distributed a series of leaflets in the 1990s under the title "Welcome King Messiah." In the leaflets, they repeatedly addressed the Rebbe using their own revised version of the "Yechi Adoneinu" mantra: "Long live our lord, teacher, and rabbi, the King Messiah, forever and ever the essence and being of our Creator and Maker and Redeemer." A title that refers to God, "*Kudsha brich hu*," meaning "The Holy, blessed is He," is used by radical Meshichists when they address the Rebbe.[18] Directly addressing the Rebbe as the creator of the universe is viewed by many in and outside Chabad as an ultimate desecration of God's name (and very much like following the path of the Christian messiah). But that is just what these extreme Meshichists do; they have no compunctions about changing "Long live our Lord, teacher, and rabbi the King Messiah forever and ever" to "Long live our Lord, teacher, and creator."[19] Some of them even posted billboards bearing the Rebbe's countenance and the legend "This is Our God for Whom we have waited."[20]

Perhaps these examples do not provide sufficient evidence for the existence of a significant Elokist camp in Chabad. Yet, in my opinion, these voices cannot be separated from the animated discourse in Meshichist circles about the Rebbe's divine status, as is intimated by the ambiguous approach taken by Meshichists toward Baranes and others like him. This contrasts with mainstream Chabad figures, who have no compunctions about referring to the Elokists as "mentally ill" and "crazy." A participant in a Chabad.info forum on February 10, 2008, had this to say about a woman who had become a *ba'alat teshuvah*:

> [She displays] signs of severe spiritual debility . . . and signs of very real mental illness (she receives heavenly messages directly broadcast [to her]). When this girl recited the blessing following a meal, my eyes went dark! It turned out that every place that [the text of the prayer has] the name of God, she says "the Rebbe," God have mercy! . . . perhaps I

should have rent my garments when I heard heresy that contradicts the thirteen principles of faith!. . . . What became clear is that the girl came under the influence of those madwomen called "Elokists."

The debate that ensued between the writer of the post and the website's editors is illuminating. According to the writer, he had termed the Elokist phenomenon a "cult," but the editors had amended this to "no more than lonely and crazy women." He complained: "I wish that were the case! Unfortunately, this is a phenomenon that has already gathered no little force." The editors defended themselves by claiming that the group that was the subject of the article was made up of a small number of mentally disturbed women who had been censured by all Chabad rabbis. This response typifies the Chabad establishment's attempt to minimize the dimensions and importance of the Elokists.

In the face of the sweeping assertion by the establishment that all the Elokists are mentally disturbed, Meshichists have been attempting to float the idea of the Rebbe's divinity in a gentler and vaguer way, so as to test the waters to see how it is accepted. According to a report in *Sichat Hage'ulah*, for example, Rabbi Shmuel Alkaslasi of Bat Yam made a familiar Meshichist declaration at the circumcision ceremony for his son: "Long live our lord, teacher, and rabbi, the King Messiah, for ever and ever," to the displeasure of his brother-in-law. The latter's young daughter, not yet three years old, took up the mantra and made it into "her song." A few weeks after the ceremony, the little girl came down with a severe food-poisoning condition which required urgent hospitalization. She lay for an entire day with high fever, her senses clouded, . . . "and [the doctors] warned against the worst possible case." But the next morning she opened her eyes, entirely recovered, and broke out singing the mantra, but with a difference: "Long live our lord, teacher, *and Creator*, the King Messiah, forever and ever." According to the report, "her father was in a total state of shock" following her rapid recovery (and perhaps also upon hearing what his daughter was saying).[21] Since both Rabbi Shmuel Alkaslasi and his twin brother Shaul, who live in Crown Heights, were condemned as Elokists in a mainstream internet forum,[22] it is hard to avoid the suspicion that Shmuel's original "Long live" declaration, which served as the girl's model, also included the word Creator, but that it was revised by *Sichat Hage'ulah* to make it less blunt. Terming the Rebbe "Creator" is easier to digest if the person saying it is a little girl who had just emerged from a high temperature and clouded consciousness. The intention of the editors may not have been only to soften the story but also to buttress the validity of the controversial Elokist claim by putting it in the mouth of a child whose artlessness and purity allow her to state profound truths simply.

Ideas latent in both earlier and later mystical literature about the divine status of the *tzadik* seem to be rising to the surface in what Chabad Hasidim believe to be the messianic age, and are galvanizing many in Chabad, not just outright Elokists. Well-known rabbis of the Meshichist school have referred to the Rebbe as "the essence of [God's] being." Beyond that, the extent to which this concept has had an impact and become accepted doctrine is evident in times of crisis, when Meshichist worshippers spontaneously appeal to God and the Rebbe without making any distinction between them. For example, a couple who found themselves in the midst of a violent demonstration in the Israeli Arab town of Um al-Fahm during the Second Intifada were rescued after crying out "Shema Yisra'el" and "Yechi Adoneinu." The coupling of the first, a statement of the most fundamental Jewish belief, that of God's unity, with the mantra that proclaims the Rebbe as the Messiah, says it all. Chabad.info, which is not by any means a Meshichist website, appealed to the Rebbe following the bloody attack on the Chabad House in Mumbai using language generally reserved for a petition to God: "Rebbe, act for your own sake if not for our sakes." This is not much different from a headline in a Meshichist publication that applied to the Rebbe a passage from the Jewish prayer book that speaks of God: "He is our father, he is our king, he is our savior."[23]

The deification of the Rebbe also finds expression in Chabad's visual culture. Arguably, the cult of the Rebbe's image in popular messianic culture is one manifestation of this phenomenon.[24] But it is much more explicit in places like a synagogue in Kiryat Bialik, in which "above the Holy Ark, facing the worshippers, hangs a huge picture of the Rebbe *shalita*, the King Messiah."[25] According to Dahan, "Many Hasidim have placed a picture of Rebbe Menachem Mendel Schneerson on the eastern wall [of their synagogues] and pray to it directly."[26]

In my discussion of Chabad's visual culture, I noted that on the cover of each issue of the Meshichist periodical *Citizens in the Messiah's State*, without exception, the Rebbe looks down from on high (at the top of the cover) over a panoramic satellite or aerial photograph of Israel or the world. I suggest that this placement of the Rebbe in "heaven," overlooking these landscapes, is the visual equivalent of the blunt statements of the Rebbe's divinity that I have cited in this chapter.[27] Dahan lends support to this hypothesis when he notes that billboards showing the Rebbe looking down from a blue sky were emblazoned with the verse "The Lord exists forever; your word stands firm in heaven" (Psalms 119:89).[28]

CHAPTER 9

"TO MAKE MANY MORE MENACHEM MENDELS"

Creation and Procreation in Messianic Chabad

Meshichists tell miracle stories that sing the praises of the Rebbe's procreative powers. Such stories offer one more way of inferring their beliefs and fantasies regarding his divine status.[1] Such stories relate that the blessing of the Rebbe, who was himself childless, enabled long-barren women to conceive after medical advice and fertility treatments had proven fruitless. This blessing, as I will show, is part and parcel of Chabad's visual cult. In many cases, it works immediately, leads to the birth of an exceptional number of twins and triplets, and sometimes even works for several women simultaneously. The genre of wondrous fertility stories is common to many Hasidic sects, and grows out of the *tzadik*'s central obligation to mediate between his followers and the divine and to see that they receive "living and enduring seed," first and foremost sons. But given the Rebbe's standing as a *tzadik* recognized as the Messiah, the fertility stories told about him exhibit the special quality of blurring the boundary between him and God. Some of the Hasidim I interviewed explicitly stated that such miracles were essential to leading the world into the messianic age. Before the Messiah can reveal himself, all Jewish souls created by God that had not yet inhabited Jewish bodies need to be born in this world. According to the Babylonian Talmud (Niddah 13b; Avodah Zarah 5a), "The [Messiah] son of David does not arrive until all souls in *guf* have been disposed of." Rashi glosses: "There is a room called *guf*, and from the beginning all the souls ever to be born were created and He put them there."[2] Furthermore, in the Rebbe's teachings, the redemption itself is viewed as a cosmic birth.[3]

The fertility stories show that contemplation of a picture of the King Messiah plays an important role in the cult of the Rebbe. The most important image in Chabad's visual culture is the iconic photograph, depicting the Rebbe raising his arm in encouragement in a Lag B'Omer children parade. The mythical halo surrounding this image was bolstered when people began to see "the face of a cute baby" in the picture. The most common interpretation of the image provided by those I interviewed was that the baby in the picture is the baby who was born or would be born to childless couples who requested the Rebbe's blessing to help them conceive. Indeed, some women have reported that the boy or girl born in the wake of the Rebbe's intervention looked much like the baby who appears in the Rebbe's hand in the photograph. Does this imply a fantasy that the Rebbe is the father of the child? Recall that Meshichist brides customarily contemplate an image of the Rebbe, held in their hands, during their wedding ceremonies. The possibility that this visual image accompanies such couples at their most intimate moments has a basis in a well-known Hasidic injunction.[4]

A story titled "The King Messiah's Baby" demonstrates the construction of the fantasy of the Rebbe as a bestower/begetter of children in the imaginations of believers. The story relates that a woman who had been barren for several years after her marriage received "a special dream in which the Rebbe *shalita*, the King Messiah, handed her a baby and informed her that she would give birth in the month of Tishrei." There are further examples of dreams in which the Rebbe hands a baby to barren women, but in this case the woman's husband also saw the Rebbe, in an apparition while he was awake, on the staircase leading up to their apartment: "The Rebbe . . . stood there, in the stairwell, looking at me with a penetrating gaze, examining my innermost thoughts and feelings. In his left hand the Rebbe . . . held a tiny baby with blond hair, blue eyes, and fair skin, who also looked at me. I was completely overcome with terror and fear. I do not know how long I stood there, but I quickly fled upstairs, entered my apartment, and shut the door behind me."

It was not long before the dream came true: "On Sunday, 23 Tishrei 5770 [1999], a healthy baby was born. When I went in to see my wife and

FIGURE 27. A bride holding the Rebbe's photo. Photographer: Gili Getz.

the baby, I was astonished to see that he looked just like the baby that the Rebbe . . . had held in his hand nine months before!" While he does not mention the iconic photograph here, it is possible that the narrator views the baby that the Rebbe granted to his wife as having been sired by the Rebbe. This is implied by the fact that the description of the baby matches the Rebbe's own appearance and is reaffirmed by the name the happy parents give him—Menachem Mendel. The baby bears the Rebbe's name and shares the Rebbe's blue eyes and the fairness of his hair and complexion, and like him fastens his gaze on the narrator. In short, the baby is portrayed as a miniature Rebbe.[5]

Further testimony that Hasidim can fantasize the Rebbe as the progenitor of a baby born after an appeal to him is provided by a woman in the advanced stages of a pregnancy. At a medical consultation following tests showing that the baby had Down Syndrome, her doctors advised terminating the pregnancy. The woman came home despondent, "with a prayer in her heart—from where will succor come?" She was plagued by horrible thoughts until she fell asleep and the Rebbe appeared to her in a dream.

In her dream she saw herself facing a huge table that had been set and was laden with all sorts of good food, and the Rebbe . . . sat at the head of the table. "While I had never seen him face-to-face, I recognized him immediately. After all, his picture is everywhere," she later related. He looked at me and said that I had nothing to fear and that everything was fine. *And then he held out his arms in front of him and spread out his hands from which, to my astonishment, broke a great light from which emerged . . . a baby.* I was electrified, and when I turned to go out, he again turned to me and said, "Wait, you have a healthy and whole son, you will have a normal birth."[6]

While the "picture with the baby" is not mentioned explicitly in this dream, it clearly is the inspiration for the baby's emergence from the Rebbe's hand. The promise made in the dream was kept two months later when the woman gave birth to a healthy boy. A short time after the birth, the Rebbe again appeared to her in a dream: "You see, the birth went well. You see that you have a healthy child and that he will be one of my Hasidim." The boy indeed displayed a special connection to the Rebbe: "In his carriage and bed there are pictures of a number of rabbis, but he shows no interest in any of them except that of the Rebbe *shalita*, the King Messiah, which he takes and kisses." The baby's special fondness for the Rebbe is hardly surprising given that in his mother's dream he emerged from the Rebbe's hand.

In such stories, reflecting special states of consciousness such as dreams and visions, the boundaries between birth and divine creation are blurred. Two parts of the Rebbe's body are mentioned as having a special connection to his generative intervention—his eyes and his arms and hands. The power of the Rebbe's blue eyes, which continue to radiate powerfully from photographs of him following the Event of Gimel Tammuz, was discussed in Chapter 5. A psychoanalytic reading of these stories might term the Rebbe's penetrating and intimidating gaze as sexual and phallic. The symbolic parallel between the eye and the penis is made by Freud in his classic analysis of the Oedipus myth, in which self-inflicted blindness is interpreted as castration.[7] The parallel can also be found in the Midrash[8] and in kabbalistic sources.[9] Note that the Rebbe's procreative blessing is directed at both men and women; this blurring of gender boundaries may be connected to his unique ontological status as the King Messiah.

The Rebbe's raised arm, the limb at the center of the fertility stories, would also seem to be a symbolic expression of phallic potential. The baby's identification with the Rebbe's hand in the iconic image of course reinforces the connection between the hand and fertility. The baby emerging from the Rebbe's hand is, as it were, coming from his loins. The intrusive male power of the King Messiah is prominent in Meshichist literature.[10] As for the arm as a symbol of male potency, while there are precedents in the midrashic literature,[11] they hardly exhaust the myriad symbolic meanings of the "picture with the baby." Keep in mind that the baby in question is located in the Rebbe's palm, and at least in the last of the stories presented above, it emerges—that is, it is born—from the hand. That would indicate that in the experience of believers, the Rebbe can appear both as impregnator and impregnated.

Taken together, these visual images, which have their source in the iconic picture of the Rebbe, and the ramifications they have in the mental lives of his believers, especially in the form of dreams and visions, create a theme that is endemic in myths and folklore—male parturition. The theme places the creative process of giving birth on the male side.[12] This theme is palpable in the stories related above. As opposed to midrashic and mystical sources, which stress the idea that teaching the Torah is like giving birth,[13] and to similar ideas of pseudo-procreation that appear in a variety of societies,[14] these stories depict a kind of parthenogenesis. It is not a metaphor in which male creation (cultural production) takes the place of "inferior" female creation (biological procreation). In the messianic imagination, a baby may be born from the Rebbe's palm just as Athena emerged from Zeus's head and Eve was created out of Adam's rib.[15]

The attribution, in popular imagination, of both male and female functions to the Rebbe is entirely consistent with his mystical identification as a representation of Malchut (Kingdom), the tenth and last element in the structure of God described by the Kabbalah's diagram of the *sefirot*, the divine emanations.[16] Malchut is understood to be manifestly female in nature, absorbing and containing the profusion of the *sefirot* above it. Yet its attribute with regard to the world below it, as its name implies, is that of the "male" qualities of kingship and dominion. These two faces of Malchut accord with the two opposing inclinations in the Rebbe's personality and mode of action: on the one hand, his utter self-abnegation with regard to his predecessor, his father-in-law Rabbi Yosef Yitzchak; on the other, his position as the leader of the entire Jewish people, with the mission of "imposing the rule of God and the Torah on the world and all that is in it, with full force."[17] According to Alon Dahan, after the death of Rabbi Yosef Yitzchak, the Rebbe appointed him to a second term as leader of the generation, this time as the ninth holder of that position. By making his predecessor not only the eighth but also the ninth *nasi* of Chabad, the Rebbe identified him with the male *sefirah* Yesod, the manifestly phallic component of the Kabbalah's anthropomorphic representation of the Godhead, and himself with Malchut and its dual male-female nature. This dual sexual nature was further emphasized by the fact that, since he would himself have been the ninth *nasi* (counting from the founder of Hasidism, the Ba'al Shem Tov) but for his predecessor's double term, the Rebbe and Rabbi Yosef Yitzchak were thus together as intertwined as Yesod and Malchut, male and female, as part of the process of redemption. More generally, the integration between the male and female in the higher spheres reflects the androgynous, two-faced model of God that the Zohar and the kabbalistic doctrine of redemption perceived as the ideal.[18] Indeed, the boundary-breaking that is so central to the Rebbe's own messianic teachings includes a bold move toward a type of androgyny that rises above the binary division between male and female.[19]

The combination, in the Rebbe's person, of the phallic quality of his penetrating gaze and raised arm and the feminine capacity for that hand to contain a baby and "give birth" to it in his own image, hints at a nebulous conception, in the stories cited above, of insemination and birth as a process of self-creation that is not far distant from the kabbalistic concept of the process of divine creation. Are the experiences, dreams, and visions of believers guided by fantasies of the Rebbe as the Creator? Recall that the Rebbe, childless himself, is perceived as the "head of the Children of Israel" (a title that, in Hebrew, is an expansion of the letters of "Rabbi"). He is the spiritual leader of all Jews, and his

Hasidim-emissaries are totally tied to him ("The *nasi* is all"). It is hardly surprising that his Hasidim have described the connection between them and him and between him and their children by invoking the relation of a father to his children.[20] Some of my interviewees marveled at how Chabad children develop an immediate connection with the Rebbe despite never having seen or spoken to him in person. The answer can be found in the repeated assertion of Meshichist fathers that they instill their children with the sense that they are the children of the Rebbe, "our father and king," no less than they are the children of their biological father.[21] It still needs to be asked, however, whether this feeling exists only on the linguistic level or goes deeper.

The fertility stories I have collected, especially those in which the Rebbe is visible in a photograph or is seen in dreams or apparitions, share several recurring themes: (1) a baby is born thanks to the power of the Rebbe's blessing; (2) the baby is sometimes contained within the Rebbe's palm, and in a few cases also emerges from within his hand; (3) the baby is conveyed to the father or mother by the Rebbe; (4) the baby looks like the Rebbe; (5) the baby is given the Rebbe's name. The dissemination of the Meshichist version of Chabad Hasidism seems to find expression, in part, in this trope of the Rebbe replicating himself in the world in what looks like a process of cloning more than sexual reproduction. The belief that the Rebbe is the Messiah fits in well with the fact that he was childless, as the Messiah enjoys eternal life and is forever present among his believers. But the Rebbe's occlusion in the Event of Gimel Tammuz left a painful vacuum that imperiled his identification with the Messiah. The many miracles related to fertility told in Meshichist Chabad groups contribute to speeding the redemption ("The [Messiah] son of David does not arrive until all souls in *guf* have been disposed of"). But beyond that, they offer concrete compensation for the fact that the Rebbe had no children of his own. Some of the babies born thanks to his intervention are seen, in the Meshichist imagination, as his progeny, in fact miniature copies of him.

Two widespread developments in Meshichist Chabad take this claim of the Rebbe's replication of himself beyond the realm of the merely speculative. The first is that the Rebbe is replicated today in uncounted ways outside the area of fertility. I have already written of Chabad's iconophilia and its use of the latest in visual technologies. The result is a virtual Rebbe who is present in the Meshichist ecology in a wide variety of portraits and representations. This profusion stands out not only in contrast with the period just prior to his occlusion, when the Rebbe was ill and unable to receive the public, but also with the prime of his life, when the opportunities for seeing and speaking with him were fairly limited. Paradoxically, these modern means of mediation between him and his believers and of making him present among them have turned a figure who, before the Event of Gimel Tammuz, was only available to his Hasidim in very limited ways into one who is now ubiquitous among them.

The second development grows out of the fact that Chabad Hasidim see the Rebbe as an exemplar of Hasidic behavior, and as such they seek to emulate him. A claim repeatedly made by my interviewees was that Hasidim strive to be like the Rebbe—not necessarily in the physical sense, although their uniform way of dressing helps in that regard—but also by means of identifying with him. They study his way of thinking and make supreme efforts to do his will and obey his instructions.[22] The Rebbe defined the role of the emissary, who carries out the most important work of preparing the ground for the redemption, by offering a maximalist version of the halakhic principle that "a person's emissary is like him" (that is, capable of performing legal acts in the name of that person): the emissary must identify himself totally with the person who sends him. As one writer on Chabad put it, "This identification is defined, in Hasidic terminology, as '[self-] abnegation.' In other words, the emissary erases his independent nature and becomes entirely identified with the goals of his sender, the *admor*."[23] In short, Hasidim who endeavor "to live the Rebbe" are the emissaries/representatives/children of the absent Rebbe, who, by their actions, make him present.[24] When the Rebbe's emissary in Shibolim, a village in southern Israel, the name of which means "ears of grain," was asked about his work, he first said that the sum of the numerical values of the three root letters of the village's name "is the same as that of the Rebbe *shalita*, the King Messiah."[25] He then added that this parallel between the two names paves the way for the supreme goal of his work as an emissary, which is, pure and simple, "*to make many more Menachem Mendels*, that is, *shibolim* in the plural, to make the sender happy."[26] Many Chabad Hasidim are named Menachem Mendel; in any family with boys, it is nearly certain that one of them will be named after him.[27] But even those with other names are perceived to be the Rebbe's progeny and his emissaries and representations in the world.

CHAPTER 10

HOLY PLACE AND HOLY TIME IN MESHICHIST CHABAD

Chabad now has two holy sites in the United States: the Rebbe's home, referred to simply as "770," from its address at 770 Eastern Parkway in Crown Heights, Brooklyn, and his grave, the shrine in the Old Montefiore Cemetery in Queens, next to that of his predecessor, Rabbi Yosef Yitzchak. While many Chabad Hasidim make pilgrimages to both these sites, there is a measure of dissonance between the two, a spatial representation of the discord within the movement regarding the Rebbe's ontological status. Avowed Meshichists, who deny that the Rebbe ever died—most of the Chabad Hasidim I interviewed among them—largely avoid the grave, and as such I will not discuss it in this book. Instead, I focus on 770. The Rebbe's home was built in Gothic Revival style in the 1930s and was purchased in 1940 for Rabbi Yosef Yitzchak when he arrived in the United States.[1] It is the movement's beating heart, the location of its international headquarters and the office of the Rebbe and his secretaries. More than anything else, however, it is known as the Rebbe's house. He moved in at the end of the 1980s, after the death of his wife, and over the years it became one of the symbols most identified with Chabad, a kind of "metonymy of the Rebbe."[2] The Meshichists control the central public space in the building, the huge *beit midrash* and synagogue, called the "large *zal*,"[3] where prayer services and convocations are held.

A huge level of holiness is ascribed to 770, "in a manner far beyond that of any other Jewish religious site established in recent centuries."[4] The house is also called "Beis Chayenu" ("House of Our Lives" in Ashkenazi-inflected Hebrew), "Beis Rabeinu shebeBavel" ("House of Our Rabbi in Babylon," that is, in the exile), and "Beis Moshiach" ("House of the Messiah"; the numerical values of the Hebrew letters in this name add up to 770). It is also called "Mikdash Me'at" ("Lesser Temple," a term traditionally also used to refer to synagogues) and "Beis haMikdash Shelanu" ("Our Temple"). The holiness of 770 extends to the entire neighborhood, with its name, Crown Heights, and the names of some of its streets, such as Kingstone Avenue and President Street (where the Rebbe lived before moving to 770) taking on symbolic value as parts of the abode of Chabad's *president* (*nasi*), adorned with the *crown* of the *King* Messiah. Meshichists sketch out a map of Chabad's sacred precinct by calling Lubavitch (formerly) and Crown Heights (today) "our Jerusalem," the Rebbe's synagogue "our Temple," and his office "our Holy of Holies." In this scheme, the Rebbe himself becomes "the Holy Ark containing the tablets of the Covenant."

These labels are not just metaphors. The Rebbe declared that the Third Temple would descend from heaven as a "completed edifice," and that it would first be revealed at a place "where the Temple journeyed and sat there during the exile," i.e. 770.[5] The Meshichists make a bold claim—that while "the divine presence never budged from the Western Wall . . . here [at 770] is the principal place where the divine presence resides." This home, "where he [the Messiah] sits . . . and impatiently waits to redeem Israel," is the cosmic center point from which the redemption will break forth and spread. Furthermore, even after the Temple is revealed, the "House of our Rabbi in Babylon" will not lose any of its glory or the divine presence, "as it will then become attached and adhere and unite entirely with the Third Temple." This united sanctuary will then be borne on "divine clouds" to the Holy Land, followed by all the Jewish people led by the Rebbe, "and they will together be established in Jerusalem." What this means is that already now, when Hasidim visit 770, they are "in the place that is the principal part of the Third Temple!"[6] The supremacy of the sanctuary in the exile over the Holy Land is stated explicitly and unapologetically, as may be learned from the lament of a preacher from the Kfar Chabad yeshiva in Israel on how quickly his time in the Rebbe's home passes: "And even before I managed to take in something of the endless bounty that they offer here, it was already time to return to the Land of Israel—and to be far physically, not to say spiritually, from the gushing spring that overflows with life."[7]

In my discussion above of the concept of the "rectification" of France in Chabad teachings, I mentioned that the numerical values of the letters of the Hebrew word for that country, Tzarfat, add up to 770. I also noted that when the letters of that same word are rearranged, it spells *paratzta*, meaning "you broke through," a term that in Chabad refers to the dissemination of its messianic doctrine. Furthermore, 770 highlights the holy number seven, representing the seven days of creation as well as Chabad's seventh generation, prophesied to be the generation of the redemption, which will be heralded by Chabad's seventh *nasi*. The redemption will bring the Jews from the "seven lands" (that is, from the whole world). Furthermore, Rabbi Yosef Yitzchak lived for seventy years (a number that indicates the completion of his rectification of the world). The charged meanings of all these intensified in 2010, the Hebrew year TaSH'A, the numerical values of which add up to 770 and the principal letters of which form the word *teshu'a*, salvation. This unification of time and place led one Meshichist rabbi to declare that "we are being redeemed today in the year 5770."[8]

I have already noted that replicas of 770, or sometimes just of its facade, have been built all around the world, including in São Paulo, Santiago, and Buenos Aires in South America; Los Angeles, Cleveland, and Tacoma in the United States; Milan in Italy; Manali and Dharamkot in India; and in Melbourne, Australia. In Israel, aside from the precise replica at Kfar Chabad, built in 1986, there are reproductions in Jerusalem's Ramat Shlomo neighborhood as well as in Migdal Ha'emek, Kiryat Ata, Zichron Ya'akov, Ofakim, Mitzpeh Ramon, and in the West Bank settlement of Itamar. The Carmon family of Gedera reproduced the facade of 770 on their home. David Sarig of Karnei Shomron builds bookcases designed to resemble 770. Holy arks of the same design can also be purchased, as can charity boxes and *mezuzot*. The image of 770 is also embroidered on *tallit* bags and on *parochot*, the curtains that hang in or on arks. Chabad children put together 770 puzzles. And it should hardly be surprising that when a snowstorm hit Israel's highlands in December

2013, members of Chabad's youth movement built a snow sculpture of 770.[9] Rabbi Ya'akov Waronker, a *ba'al teshuvah* who served as an intelligence officer in the U.S. army, received permission to change the number of the New York City elementary school where he serves as principal from P.S. 748 to P.S. 770. A kosher Chinese restaurant in Miami is called Pagoda 770; "at the end of their meal, diners receive fortune cookies [containing a fortune] on the subject of the redemption."[10]

The booklet *Tzurat haBayit* (Form of the Home/Temple), issued in the same format as *Dvar Malchut*, collections of the Rebbe's talks, is a regular part of the curriculum at Meshichist yeshivot. It is studied in particular during the three summer weeks that fall between the fasts of 17 Tammuz and 9 Av (Tisha B'Av), a time when the Rebbe called on students to study with *shturem* texts relating to the redemption and Messiah and the construction of the Third Temple.[11] "As you study it," he told them, "it is as if you are building it."[12] The booklet includes exact blueprints for 770 and all its parts, among them a "bricked-up window," "central air-conditioning system," "fuse box," and "bathrooms."[13] It comes with a detailed account of each part of the building and the renovations made there. The descriptions are concrete and material yet clothed in symbolism. For example, the house's three stories are paralleled to the three highest *sefirot*, Chochmah, Binah, and Da'at, the initials of which gave the Chabad movement its name. The three Gothic pediments on the facade symbolize the three pillars on which, according to the Talmudic sages, the world stands: the Torah, the sacrificial service in the Temple, and charity. The anteroom to the Rebbe's chamber is called the "Lower Eden" or the "Holy," whereas his office itself is called the "Upper Eden" or "Holy of Holies."[14]

Thanks to the many traces of the Rebbe in the building and the practices of making him present by continuing his participation in rituals and events, 770 preserves the routine of life with him. This routine is broadcast to the entire world by satellite. The 77olive website offers "a twenty-four-hour viewing experience . . . during prayers, convocations, and assemblies. Using your computer and software you can be in our Rebbe's house in Babylon in real time and even catch the moment of revelation that will come immediately *mamash*."[15] The fact that the Rebbe is not seen directly on this live broadcast is indeed a problem. "I was bothered by the thought of how to cope with this completely incomprehensible reality," one Meshichist related, "to be in 770 when physical eyes cannot see what they so much want to see." But the potency of the means of making his presence felt in many cases compensates for this: "Prayers with the Rebbe . . . the 'path' that opens in advance of each service, the convocations, dancing [with the Torah], Simchat Torah, I was in continual wonder at the sense of the Rebbe's presence."[16]

The Meshichists believe that the redemption will begin at 770, and in their view the auspicious time for it is one of two significant dates in the Rebbe's life—his birthday, 11 Nisan, and 3 Tammuz, the day of his occlusion. These days are prominent ones on the Chabad calendar, which also marks the birth and death days of the movement's earlier leaders and other key events in their lives. Among the most important of these are the Days of Redemption, the days on which the first *admor*, his son Rabbi Dovber Shneuri, and Rabbi Yosef Yitzchak, respectively, were released from prison, and Didan Natzach, 5 Tevet, commemorated, at the Rebbe's decree, on the day Chabad won a court ruling in a trial regarding books housed in the movement's library.[17]

With the approach of 11 Nisan, the expectations of an imminent redemption surge in the Meshichist camp:

> From [the beginning of] the month of Nisan, the month of the redemption, the manifest miraculous leadership begins, as we count the days to the Bright Day, 11 Nisan, the day of the Rebbe's birth . . . the day his sign reaches its apex, the revelation of the essence of his soul when he comes and redeems us in an eternal redemption: in Nisan they [the Children of Israel] were redeemed [from slavery in Egypt] and in Nisan they will be redeemed.[18]

The Hasidim cite various characteristics of the Rebbe that are connected to the number eleven. On 11 Shevat he ascended to be *nasi*, and Shevat is the eleventh month. On top of that, his first year as *nasi* was 5711 (1951). They also argue that "*the birth of the Jewish people on Pesach begins on* 11 *Nisan,* on which Israel's connection to and unification with the essence of God, for *ehad 'asar* [eleven] is *ant hu chad* ["He is one" in Aramaic], such that 'Israel and the Holy One, Blessed Be He, are all One.'"[19] Hence, the true and complete redemption in which the entire world will be rectified and in which all the world's nations will take part "is rooted in eleven!"[20] That being the case, "on this day and from this day on the Rebbe . . . showers and inundates a new abundance, in physicality and spirituality, an abundance of the time of the true and complete redemption, for all those connected to it and extending to all the people of the generation."[21]

Gimel (the third of) Tammuz is marked on a Chabad calendar for 2013 as World Redemption Day, apparently to distinguish it from Rabbi Yosef Yitzchak's Day of Redemption—the day he was released from a Soviet prison—which falls on the same date. On another calendar, the date is marked simply "Revelation Now." Even ardent Meshichists cannot deny that this is the date on which the Rebbe vanished and since when he cannot be seen by physical eyes. But, as they see it, exile is a necessary step toward redemption. They demonstrate this verbally by transforming the word *exile* (*golah*) into *redemption* (*ge'ulah*). In short, the Event of Gimel Tammuz is not a day when the prophecy of redemption failed but a step toward the ultimate Redemption, for on that day "the Rebbe turned to devote himself to his own matters so as to return to us in greatness."[22] They back this up by noting that the sum of the numerical values of the letters in "Gimel Tammuz" is equal to that in the declaration "The Messiah still lives."

This occasion brings to the fore the dissension between the Meshichists and their opponents in Chabad. The latter observe this day with a mass pilgrimage to the Rebbe's grave,[23] while the former largely avoid the cemetery and gather at 770. It is hardly surprising, then, that the headline of an editorial in a Gimel Tammuz edition of *Sichat Hage'ulah* proclaims that "*Once and For All—This Is Not a* Hilula *Day*" (a *hilula* is a public celebration held on the anniversary of a *tzadik*'s death).[24] The piece presents the command of the first *admor* "to live with the time," meaning "to live the weekly Torah portion, to internalize its substance and act in accordance with its teachings." This command mythically amplifies experienced time by integrating three metahistorical and historical events "of divine revelation" into current experience. The first event that took place on this date was Joshua's call during the war against the five Amorite kings for the "sun to stand still at Giv'on," which "symbolized the revelation of the Godhead in creation." The second event that testified to this date's special potential for redemption was the miraculous release of Rabbi Yosef Yitzchak from Soviet prison in 1927, after he had been sentenced to death by firing squad. "This day was revealed as the beginning of the redemption [of Rabbi Yosef Yitzchak], which was completed on the Festival of Redemption of 12–13 Tammuz," two days that mark Rabbi Yosef Yitzchak's birthday and the day he left the Soviet Union. The two events that occurred on 3 Tammuz "came to prepare us for the third time in which Israel and the world as a whole encountered this date." As the day of the beginning of the redemption, "there is no reason to try to cast Gimel Tammuz as a *hilula* day, God forbid. The *hilula* for a *tzadik* is a concept that, while it expresses a sublime state, refers solely to one who has died. Whereas the Rebbe . . . did not die! *The Rebbe is alive in body and soul, in the simplest sense of the word* mamash."²⁵

The last section of the editorial distills the temporal dimension of the Meshichist faith:

> Gimel Tammuz is the day on which the belief in the essence of God is revealed, as we have been taught that the King Messiah will be occluded but will again be revealed to Israel and redeem them. It is a day on which all unite around the pure faith in the prophecy of the Rebbe, the King Messiah, may he live forever and ever, that here the King Messiah is coming, the Messiah named Menachem, immediately *mamash, mamash, mamash.*

The day on which the barriers and limitations of nature were broken through three times has become the Festival of Faith and Redemption for the Meshichists. As they see it, the ability to withstand this test of faith is itself "*the huge and incomprehensible miracle of Gimel Tammuz.*"²⁶ As the most important date on the Meshichist calendar, Gimel Tammuz is a metonymy of an ongoing present, on the verge of the redemption, which demands Hasidim to continually withstand the test of its nonfulfillment. On that awful day in 1994 when the Rebbe vanished, an event that the Meshichists dialectically turned into "the beginning of the redemption," a moment began that has in the meantime been extended over twenty-five years. It is a type of test which the Meshichists compare to the forty days that Moses spent on Mount Sinai, out of sight of the Children of Israel whom he left at the foot of the mountain as he received the Torah.

The Meshichists' fierce faith, and their sense of superiority over those who are not willing to take the risk and to simply and truly brave the test of messianic faith, receives potent expression in a satirical piece by Rabbi Tzvi Ventura titled "Gentlemen! History Repeats Itself!" Using current journalistic language, the article depicts the doubt and lack of faith that spread among the Children of Israel at Mount Sinai on the thirty-ninth day of Moses's absence, in contrast with the firm faith of a small group of the tribe of Levi. While the Levites, connected to a satellite on Mount Sinai, are waiting for Moses to descend any moment with the tablets, the state radio and television stations are declaring conclusively that belief in Moses's promise that he will arrive following forty days is baseless. In the camp,

> Demonstrators from the Mixed Multitude Demands a Calf and the Mob against Eternal Life organizations . . . hold signs [saying] "Moses is Dead—Hooray for the Calf." One of them is even holding a stopwatch, and the moment the critical minute arrives and Moses has not come down . . . it will be crushing proof that the Mob is right and that an appeal should be made to . . . its Excellency the Calf. . . . The Levites in "Camp 770" keep studying an article that explains that the people, by virtue of their faith, give strength to Moses even in difficult times, when it is hard to believe. From time to time they break out in dancing that the media describes as "fanatical dancing with the goal of strengthening the believers psychologically."

A mobile intensive care unit, "along with several certified and uncertified psychiatrists," is waiting for whatever might happen. The stopwatch begins beeping loudly, and the newscaster declares: "Moses has not come and hasn't even called."[27] After five minutes Moses's death is announced. To back up the announcement,

> Satan presents a sound-and-light show (as described at length in the Midrash) of Moses's bier in heaven, being accompanied [in a funeral procession]

by a huge crowd. The members of the Doubt and Crying Ltd. Movement immediately break out in a huge roar and quickly paste-up death announcements on the streets. . . . The religious weekly *Hayweed* terms the Levite Camp 770 "a collection of irresponsible lunatics who are an embarrassment to all religious people." The Mob movement rushes to hand out fliers and stickers saying "Calf Now," and immediately begin Calf songs like "I Was Born to Be a Calf," "Sing a Song to the Calf," and more. . . . What is clear is that the tribe of Levi will not follow the calf.[28]

This Meshichist satire fires in all directions: it targets the national media and the sensationalist press; the left and secular Jews, among them members of Peace Now; religious doubters; and non-Meshichist Chabad Hasidim (who label the Meshichists mentally ill).[29] The sense of being under siege that is felt by radical Chabad Hasidim is expressed forcefully here, but at the same time they clearly feel the sense of superiority that comes out of serving a holy cause. They are the Levites of our day, the vanguard who face up to an ongoing test of their faith day by day, and who withstand it.

CHAPTER 11

THE OMNIPRESENCE OF ABSENCE

Messianism in the Technological Age

From the start of his leadership of Chabad, the Rebbe positioned the movement as "in the vanguard for yoking technology to the advancement of Judaism."¹ His enthusiastic adoption of technological innovations stood in sharp contrast to the distrustful and cool attitude displayed by many Haredi communities. This difference is grounded in Chabad's theosophy, which sees everything in the material world as testimony to the immanent presence of God. Consequently, Chabad demands of its adherents particular awareness of His presence in the ostensibly secular world. The positive attitude toward scientific discoveries that produced this approach was transformed, under the Rebbe, into an explicit theologization of new technologies.² The Rebbe applied to the modern world the adage of the Sages that "Everything the Holy One, Blessed Be He, created in his world, he created only to honor him."³ According to the Sages, he said, gold and cedars were created specifically so that they could be used in building the Temple, and thus "radio was created specifically for the Messiah." In keeping with this position, he unhesitatingly spoke of the radio and other technological advances in terms taken from divine spirituality.⁴

The theologization of science and technology is reinforced by placing them on the historical path that leads to the redemption. Chabad Hasidim frequently quote a prophecy from the Zohar according to which the gates of wisdom will open above and the springs of wisdom below in the year 600 of the sixth millennium (on the Jewish calendar), so as to rectify the world and prepare it for the redemption. According to

Chabad, that year, 1840 on the Western calendar, marks the beginning of the era in which the gates of heavenly wisdom opened and the inner meaning of the Torah—Hasidism—was revealed, and at the same time the springs of earthly wisdom burst forth and the great scientific revolution began. While this sanctification of modern science was consistent with the intellectual character of Chabad's philosophy from its inception, the Rebbe granted it an added dimension, given the fact that he became *nasi* in the cultural climate of the New World with its passion for scientific progress. Indeed, the Rebbe studied physics, electrical engineering, and mathematics in Berlin and Paris.[5] The adoption of new science does not mean that Chabad accepted the secular scientific ethos on which it was based. On the contrary, the movement attributes these advances not to the scientific method but to "the revelation and huge dissemination of the inner Torah."[6] This development plays a significant role in hastening the redemption.

On the practical level, the means of technology, especially mass communications technology, have been effective ways of "disseminating the wellsprings outside" of Chabad. As the movement's ambition is to use these means to reach every Jew in the world and spread its message throughout the world, it can hardly disregard them. The Rebbe taught his Hasidim how to enlist the "outside" in disseminating the wellsprings by using the best technology:

> Tape recorders and television cameras, which document the convocations and broadcast them throughout the United States. Satellite broadcasts for transmitting special gatherings to different places at the same time all over the globe. The use of telephones in the study of Torah in conference rooms. Virtual schools for the children of emissaries; virtual libraries. Twenty-four-hour live broadcasts from the House of Our Lives 770, which enables every Jew to live with the House of Our Rebbe in Babylon, in prayer services and convocations and all that is done there on weekdays.[7]

In other words, Chabad offers a textbook example of the media's importance in new and renewing religions, in accordance with the mediation paradigm presented in the introduction.

As these media are meant not just to spread Chabad teachings but also to make it possible "to simply live with the Rebbe *shalita*, the King Messiah," the instrumental and spiritual planes cannot be separated in Meshichist discourse. Science and technology pave the way for the redemption because they expose the material secrets that hold back the messianic revelation, at the same time that they uncover hidden divine treasures by means of Hasidic lore. "There are no more secrets, everything is being revealed," marveled the editor of *Sichat Hage'ulah*, citing together the miniaturization of photographic equipment, the documentation of public spaces by means of security cameras, the ability to view events on the planet earth by means of satellite systems, and the capacity for surveilling people by tracking their mobile phones. All these, he declared, are manifest signs of redemption.[8] At Science and Redemption Conferences organized by the Meshichists, the great achievements of the scientific revolution, among them robotics, computerization, the internet, genetic engineering, nuclear energy, and the conquest of outer space, are presented as contributing to global welfare, and as such they are part and parcel of the promise of the redemption. Theories such as relativity, quantum mechanics, and chaos, along with the scientific developments they have engendered, are perceived as versions of mystical concepts from Hasidic teachings, such as "the impossible nonexistent," "on the boundary and on what is beyond the boundary," and "creation *ex nihilo*" to explicate them.[9] The goal at such conferences is to integrate scientific theories into the principles of faith, while undergirding the superiority of the latter.[10]

During the Rebbe's lifetime, the sophisticated technology wielded by Chabad made it possible to imagine him as the Messiah by turning him into a figure with an international reputation. As Jeffrey Shandler puts it, "In some sense, the Rebbe was like the 'miracle of television'— able to be in more than one place at the same time, widely seen, and yet immortal."[11] This wonder, and the larger marvels of technology, only heightened following the Event of Gimel Tammuz. Not only was technology able to preserve the Rebbe's image and voice, as it had in the past, but the digital and internet age catalyzed procedures for communicating with him and making him accessible in an unprecedented way.

Terms such as "online Rebbe" and "*Igrot Kodesh* fax" indicate the ease and speed with which it is possible to make contact with the occluded Rebbe. Today people can receive the Rebbe's answers to questions they send him through *Igrot Kodesh* while on live broadcast on Haredi radio stations. Through Dialing for a Blessing, anyone can call to ask for the Rebbe's blessing and receive it by following the instruction of a computerized answering system that plays the "Yechi Adoneinu" song and records the request, which is then printed out on a special form. A photocopy of the response is sent to the caller with an explanatory letter and instructions for how to submit an additional request if that is necessary. The process is immeasurably faster than it was in the past, when people sent requests to the Rebbe by surface mail or fax.

In the age of computers, miracle stories are produced by the internet. One example involves Nili, who had been caught up for seven years in an inheritance dispute, the end of which was not in sight. She reached the conclusion that only a miracle could save her. Typing the word *miracle* into the search engine on her computer led her to igrot.com, a website full of tales of miracles experienced by people who petitioned the Rebbe by means of *Igrot Kodesh*. She wept and regretted that she had not petitioned the Rebbe earlier. She quickly wrote out her story and asked for the Rebbe's blessing. "I clicked on the 'send' button at the bottom of the page," she related, "and a few moments later the answer arrived." The Rebbe reminded her that, when she was sixteen, she had promised to set aside a small coin each day for charity. But a year later she had stopped doing so. Using a calculator, she computed the sum she had to make up and put it in a charity box at Elijah's Cave, a holy site on Mount Carmel. Two months later she won her court case. Nili was delighted: "The miracle I had hoped for came true" with the help of her computer and calculator.[12]

Since the Event of Gimel Tammuz, Chabad's sophisticated visual and digital technology has enabled it to maintain the virtual Rebbe as an active participant in the life of his Hasidim.[13] Smartphone technology has made the Rebbe's digital omnipresence even more pronounced, as it is not tethered to a home or laptop computer. This raises an obvious question: Does this maintenance system, a privilege enjoyed by believers in the late modern era, actually make them better off than believers in the ancient world? In connection with the many videos of the Rebbe, Shandler notes: "Since the Rebbe's death . . . the corpus of video documentation enables him to seem present for his followers, doing so in ways unlike any other means that Hasidim have had to connect with their dead *rebeyim*—whether through legends . . . printed collections of their teachings, gravesite shrines, or living descendants and disciples."[14]

In the ancient world, a similar function was filled by statues and paintings: they made venerated figures present. Their use in ritual brought the god close to his believers in ways reminiscent of the way the absent Rebbe is made accessible through Meshichist Chabad's practices that make the Rebbe present in his believers' lives. Nevertheless, the invention of the camera made it possible to place the past within the present in a vivid and actual way that, apparently, idols and icons could not.

Does the modern visual technology's advantage over traditional iconic representations pave the way for new forms of experience that expand the religious horizon? Clearly, visions and apparitions played an important part in the appearance and maintenance of archaic religious practices and in the changes they underwent, long before the appearance of the camera. But even if photographs and video clips of the Rebbe are neither sufficient nor necessary conditions for apparitions, they certainly can catalyze them. Furthermore, while apparitions of the Rebbe in waking states may be private, spontaneous, and rare even among his most zealous believers, "apparitions" on screen are public, deliberate, common, and accessible even to people with little or no association with Chabad. Today, for the first time in history, it is possible to "learn from the Rebbe himself" by means of videos of his talks and lessons.[15] Like photographs, film footage of the Rebbe is a conduit for conveying messages from him, no less than waking or dream apparitions. In terms of the mediation model, which sees religion and media as inseparably interwoven, the modern technology adopted so enthusiastically by Chabad enables re-mediations that shape the religious experience of its Hasidim in a way quite different from the nature of that experience prior to the appearance of such an advanced visual culture,[16] such that it contains the Rebbe's immediate presence.[17]

In my discussion of Chabad's visual culture, I note the complexity of the epistemological revolution that photography caused in the modern world in which it was invented. In the secularized modern linear conception of time, the intrusion of an absent figure into present experience intensifies the memory of that figure but is also liable to exacerbate the pain of absence. A number of thinkers, among them Roland Barthes and Susan Sontag, have maintained that photography is directed at the past; they have seen it as "flat death" or *memento mori*.[18] And, in fact, longstanding Hasidim who knew the Rebbe before his occlusion often sigh and shout "How long?" when they see a photograph or a video clip of one of his convocations. But the Meshichists' fervent faith that the Rebbe still walks among us, and the fact that most of them never knew any Rebbe but the virtual one, helps them suppress the morbid aspect of the image.

The magic that digital technology works in making the Rebbe present thus fits in with the miracle-filled world of the Meshichists. They live in a world of wonders, already illuminated by the Messiah's light, and are in a constant state of enchantment. Important geopolitical, socioeconomic, and scientific events are seen by the Meshichists as "signs of the redemption," milestones along the world's progress toward a new age of prosperity and harmony. These public events are supplemented by a cascade of personal miracle stories that offer proof of the Rebbe's benevolent intervention in the lives of his believers. The everyday lives of the new Hasidim and *ba'alei teshuvah* whom I interviewed are illuminated by the enchanted glow of the Rebbe-Messiah; in adhering to Chabad, they entered an age of marvels. The *nun* years, that is, the 1990s (the 5750s on the Hebrew calendar designated by the letter with the value 50, *nun*), in which Chabad messianic fervor rose to new heights, were referred to as the "years of miracles [*nisim*]" or the "years of wonders [*nifla'ot*]." But for the Meshichists, this magical era continued with heightened intensity after the Rebbe's occlusion in 1994. For them the entire world now broadcasts on a single frequency of Messiah and redemption, and having tuned into this station they pick it up everywhere and always.[19]

The virtual reality produced by new technologies helps make the Rebbe present and maintains the enchantment of life on the verge of the redemption.[20] This assistance grows out of the multiplicity of worlds that virtual reality allows one to live in, and breaks down the boundaries between internal and external experience. On the internet, people can place themselves in imaginary worlds with imaginary identities—imaginary but also profound and significant. The limitations of the body are surmounted in a two-way process: on the one hand, the human body includes more and more prostheses; on the other, virtual intelligence and computer literacy externalize physical and mental functions to the point of blurring the boundaries between the internal and the external.[21] When technology enables the replication of the organism (cloning) and makes it possible to upload mental contents onto the internet, it seems entirely possible to achieve a kind of eternal life. As I have shown, Chabad replicates the traces the Rebbe left in the world, as well as the Rebbe himself, with the goal of multiplying the number of "Menachem Mendels" in the world by means of the fact that his Hasidim-emissaries-spiritual descendants seek to emulate him and carry on his work. On top of this, the Rebbe's articles, talks, and letters are all preserved in libraries, some of them virtual, and many of the convocations and dollar-distributing events he starred in are preserved on film; some of them can be seen on the internet.

The technological infrastructure that maintains the virtual Rebbe thus bolsters the fundamental Meshichist belief that the Rebbe is alive and well.[22] The quality and sharpness of the visual field achieved by new visual communication technologies create a sense of enhanced reality and total involvement with the figure depicted. It offers a feeling of "being there"[23] despite the fact that the actual object is distant or absent. In terms of the mediation approach, the mediating technologies vanish or become transparent. When this sophisticated technological substrate is subordinated to Chabad's dialectical theosophy, with its a-cosmic and panentheistic tendencies, the potential for feeling the Rebbe's presence is heightened.[24] For the Meshichists, the virtualization of reality and the transformation of the virtual into the real open up creative and profound possibilities for the Rebbe's presence.

Jaron Lanier, who popularized the term *virtual reality*, claimed that it so radically integrates the internal and external, subject and object, self and the outside world that it can elicit mystical moods and states of consciousness.[25] Paul Virilio has stated that forms of distant communication (telecommunication) have a divine quality that is expressed in their total presence (everywhere and all the time), their all-encompassing scope, and their immediacy and urgency.[26] These qualities match, to an astounding extent, the Meshichist image of the Rebbe as omnipotent, omnipresent, and omniscient. Cyberspace seems to arouse latent Platonic sensibilities that have long since been shunted into the margins of the secularized and materialistic modern world. This sensibility lures the believer into seeing the virtual reality that constitutes it as being detached from the contours of place and time; it seems to be an eternal and transcendent world of ideas that relegates the reality perceived by the senses to merely a dim shadow of the true world.[27] In other words, the "spiritual" nature of the online world makes it possible to imagine traditional metaphysical concepts and to imbue them with renewed vitality.[28] This cultural climate abets the perception of the virtual Rebbe as bigger than life.

More than two decades after the Event of Gimel Tammuz, the Rebbe remains the unchallenged leader of Chabad, despite the disagreement between extremists and moderates regarding his ontological status. I have shown above how Meshichist Chabad has constructed a sophisticated system of methods and practices that makes the absent Rebbe present in the lives of believers. Even Chabad's radicals agree that the Rebbe cannot be seen by material eyes most of the time, and thus from outside Chabad we can speak of a virtual Rebbe. It is important to keep in mind, however, that "virtual" is not the opposite of the "real," but rather of the "actual." It is everything that enables us to immerse ourselves in another world and to be involved in it immediately and intimately, without feeling any barrier between it and ourselves. Cultural practices such as prayer, reading a novel, attending a play in a theater, or watching a movie also constitute virtual worlds and are constituted by those worlds. Gilles Deleuze, who made the virtual a key concept in his philosophy, sees it as a liminal zone of impending phenomena, of emergent potential.[29] Meshichists would have no trouble signing on to this abstract formulation as an apt description of their concept of redemption. In Chabad, the synergetic integration of, on the one hand, a mystic doctrine that blurs the distinction between what is and what is not, between the revealed and the concealed, between life and death, and on the other hand sophisticated visual and digital technology, makes it possible to intensify the presence of the virtual Rebbe and to make him more real than any truth. This presence has a number of dimensions.

In my discussion of how the Rebbe is made present visually, I showed that he is a *highly visible* figure thanks to the myriad still and filmed images of him that fill the private and public spaces of Meshichist life. The virtual Rebbe is also quite *accessible* and sensed as *close by*, even more so than was the case before the Event of Gimel Tammuz. This is due to the many images and traces of him in the actual and virtual reality in which the Meshichists live, most notably because of the way anyone can communicate with him and receive his blessing by means of the *Igrot Kodesh* oracle and images of him.

The Rebbe's intimate presence is not, however, limited to Hasidic territory. As befits the King Messiah, who steers the process of history, his presence is global. The Rebbe appears in the farthest corners of the earth—in the depths of the Red Sea, in a primeval forest in Vietnam, in a remote village in India. He also appears to non-Jews—to the principal of a school in France, to a prison guard in the southern United States, and to a Palestinian in Lebanon. He is also a *multiple* and *replicated* Rebbe because of his innumerable reproducible incarnations that can sometimes be reiterated infinitely. This stands in stark contrast to his singularity and childlessness during his lifetime, and to his diminishing accessibility as he aged. The virtual Rebbe is very close by because Hasidim *bear his image* on their bodies—for example, on the screens of their smartphones and tablets, on their credit cards, and on wallet-sized Wayfarer's Prayer cards. Even more importantly, his followers have no compunctions about appealing to him for help in the seemingly most trivial crises of everyday life. Yet, at the same time, he is *elevated and exalted*, steering worldwide events and changing the world with his Messianic powers, which bring him closer to God.

The combination of the Rebbe's exalted status and his myriad traces is hardly to be taken for granted. How can the Rebbe's image as the charismatic Messiah be preserved if he can be reproduced so extensively and indefinitely in the form of his photographs and the other signs he left behind him? According to Max Weber's classic definition, figures perceived as charismatic are seen as unique and endowed with exceptional personal characteristics.[30] If that is the case, reproduction may lead to contempt. For example, does not the mass production of photographs of the Rebbe, their commercial distribution, and their easy availability dissipate the mystery and enchantment inherent in him, inasmuch as they call his uniqueness and authenticity into question? The answer is in the eye of the beholder, or more precisely depends on the beholder's epistemological viewpoint. In my discussion of Chabad's visual culture, I noted that the transition from image to icon is tantamount to moving from representation to embodiment or to re-presentation (even if the embodiment is, for believers, only a partial presence of the supreme entity). According to iconographic logic that guides many of the Meshichists, "duplicating an original image would extend its power."[31]

In a study of portraits of the Dalai Lama, Clare Harris asserts that "importantly, it is the camera that captures the aura of an exceptional individual in a way that blatantly contradicts Walter Benjamin's famous complaint that mechanical reproduction would destroy the aura of the authentic and the original art work in the West."[32] In other words, whether the figure in the photograph is the incarnation of the Bodhisattva or of the Rebbe, the King Messiah, the picture can become a revered photo-icon. In this case, its multiplicity may be a virtue that in no way detracts from the charismatic aura of the figure portrayed; on the contrary, it may enhance it.

The combination of the exaltation and even divinization of the Rebbe and intimacy with him produces a *decentralized* Rebbe in which each Hasid shares. Anyone can write to the Rebbe today by means of *Igrot Kodesh* and receive a direct answer, usually without any need for intermediaries. Anyone can address him by means of his photographs, which gaze at supplicants from walls and screens in private homes and public spaces, and which can also be found on the persons of many Hasidim. Anyone can visit the Rebbe at his home in Crown Heights (or one of its replicas around the world) and sense that he is close by. Chabad is thus undergoing an accelerated process of decentralization and democratization, consistent, it would seem, with the Rebbe's vision of fostering the *tzadik* and messianic spark within each one of his disciples.[33] Yet this same process threatens the unity of the movement. The looming question is whether Chabad, "Judaism's first [monastic] order," can maintain its cohesion and unity despite the yawning fissures within it, or whether these forces will debilitate or split it.

PART IV

THE MESHICHISTS FROM A COMPARATIVE PERSPECTIVE

CHAPTER 12

MESHICHISTS, CHRISTIANS, SABBATEANS, AND POPULAR CULTURE HEROES

Critics of Chabad have made much of pointing out the similarities between the course Chabad has taken in recent decades and developments in the messianic movements that have arisen in other religions and at other times. These critics' inventive characterizations of Chabad include "halakhically observant Christians" and "neo-Sabbateans."[1] A systematic mapping of the similarities and differences between Chabad's messianic discourse and those of Christianity and Sabbateanism lies beyond the scope of this book's discussion; neither is it necessary, as there is already a corpus of research and polemic comparing Chabad's messianic teachings to those of Christianity.[2] As far as the comparison with Christianity goes, I need note only that the Meshichists incessantly cite sources from the Midrash, Kabbalah, and Hasidism that refer to the temporary occlusion of the Messiah as a possible stage in the process of redemption as laid out in Jewish tradition. One of the most cited of these comes from the medieval commentator Rashi, who wrote that "our Messiah will conceal himself after being revealed and will reveal himself again."[3] Traditional texts also offer the possibility that the Messiah will come from among the dead, a view more in line with the beliefs of the Chabad mainstream.[4] These sources support Chabad's claim that it is following a purely Jewish path, and thus counter the accusation that they are simply halachikally observant Christians.

A typical example of the way Chabad Hasidim handle the similarity between their and the Christian model of messianism is the "Emissary's Letter," written by a *mashpia'* (proctor) at the Kfar Chabad yeshiva in the year of the Rebbe's occlusion:

> A very strange claim ... in the framework of Satan's tireless actions that try to turn the hearts of Israel from the desire for the redemption—in the final moments before its arrival ... that the faith in the Messiah who suffers evil afflictions because of our sins ... and casts his life against this to the point that he ostensibly dies in order to atone for the generation's sins, and then returns to life and redeems Israel ... is the faith of the Christians—in that man [Jesus], may his name and memory be expunged, and how do we dare "copy" such a belief into the Holy of Holies [the Jewish religion]?!

His reply is categorical:

> And is it not clear to any rational person that the Christian faith and all its characteristics is an attempt to imitate Judaism, as a monkey imitates a man, and not the opposite, God forbid. According to that way of thinking we would also have to stop believing in God, God forbid, because that too is one of the foundations of the Christian and Muslim religions![5]

Nevertheless, this rhetoric, stressing the validity of the Jewish messianic model and claiming that it is more ancient, does not mean that the Meshichist discourse eschews manifestly Christological images. However, they are not necessarily the products of Christian influence but may derive from the dynamic that Chabad found itself in following the occlusion of the designated Messiah. An example of such "Christian residues" is the way a well-known Meshichist rabbi portrays the nature of the Hasidic connection to the Rebbe: "In practice, our relationship with God runs entirely through the generation's *nasi*, as we are 'the toenail in the foot of the son,' as the head of the *son* (the Rebbe) connects us with the *father*—to God."[6] The image of the *tzadik* as the beloved son of God can be found in the midrashic and kabbalistic literature, whence it was taken up by Hasidic writers (on whom Christian influence cannot be ruled out) as Moshe Idel has shown.[7] But Idel also remarks that this father-son axis is almost entirely absent from the messianic idea in Jewish mysticism.[8] In this case, in which the son-Rebbe is perceived as the Messiah, the similarity with Christianity cannot be disregarded.

A blunter example of Christological images in the Meshichist discourse comes from the Rebbe himself, in his explanation of the significance of the "Messiah's Meal" held at the end of the last day of Pesach. According to the Hasidic tradition, this custom was instituted by the founder of Hasidism, the Ba'al Shem Tov. During the meal, "the revealed light of the Messiah shines," he said. Chabad's fifth *admor*, Rabbi Shalom Dovber, enjoined his disciples to add to the traditional eating of *matzah* at this meal the consumption of four cups of wine, as at the Pesach Seder, to represent the "fourfold formulation of redemption" (the four wordings the Torah uses to refer to the Exodus from Egypt). It was the Rebbe, however, who declared explicitly that "*the revelation of the Messiah continues and penetrates action in practice, in physical eating that becomes His blood and flesh.*" The editor of *Sichat Hage'ulah* recounted this in a way that amplifies the parallel between the Messiah's Meal and the Eucharist:

> [For] a person who participates in the Messiah's Meal, his eating and drinking at the meal carries forward "the revealed light of the Messiah" into being part of His blood and flesh. In this the central matter of the feast—the Messiah and redemption—become part of our physical bodies *mamash*. You begin to live the Messiah.[9]

Here too there is a clear parallel between the Chabad practice and the Christian mass (which itself has its origin in the *matzah* eaten at the Pesach Seder). That does not necessarily mean, however, that the Hasidic practice came into being as an imitation of the Christian ritual. Arguably, the polemic the Jewish sages engaged in against the early Christians may have affected Jewish beliefs and practices (as can be seen in the shaping of the Seder and the content of the Haggadah).[10] It is certainly possible that Chabad has simply brought to the surface previously suppressed Jewish voices from this controversy. But over the generations these practices have become the heart and soul of Christian ritual, and it is hard to dissociate them from their Christological overtones.

The Sabbatean movement offers an illuminating precedent to which the Meshichist ethos can be compared. Gershom Scholem, in his monumental *Sabbatai Sevi: The Mystical Messiah*,[11] makes no mention of the book *When Prophecy Fails* by Leon Festinger, Henry Riecken, and Stanley Schachter,[12] but the phenomenological explanation he offers for the way the Sabbatean movement (like the early Christians) coped with messianic disappointment is quite similar to the theory of cognitive dissonance that Festinger and his coauthors offer: "Sabbateanism as a sectarian and . . . heretical movement grew out of the struggle between a sense of new life-feeling and the disappointment of the hopes that had originally given birth to it . . . when many sections of the people refused to accept the verdict of history, unwilling to admit that their faith had been a vain illusion fondly invented."[13]

Scholem's book can cast light on a number of aspects of the messianic dynamics that can be seen in Chabad, sometimes implicitly and at the movement's fringes. These can be juxtaposed to similar but more explicit and extreme phenomena that appeared among Shabbetai Zvi's followers. At the focal point of the tension that such a comparison points to are faith, Jewish observance, and antinomianism. The zeal, devotion, and dedication the Meshichists display both inside and outside the confines of Chabad grow out of their sense that they are the vanguard, the Rebbe's elite emissaries and frontline troops on the road to redemption. Resolute in their faith, they are not prepared to make any compromises regarding the exalted idea of the Messiah's arrival. Rather, they exert all their might to bring it to pass here and now, even if it runs against common sense and mundane reality. This willingness to strive against the current toward redemption proves, in their view, that they are the true Hasidim, those who pass the test of faith.

Shabbetai Zvi's followers felt much the same way. It was only after his conversion to Islam that he was tagged as a false messiah and his disciples as heretics. During the messianic fervor he aroused, however, it was his disciples who saw themselves as the true believers and his opponents as heretics. A rabbi in Rotterdam who, along with most of the members of his community, was a believer, described the "heretics" in this way: "a few quarrelsome individuals, or such as were affected by the leprosy of heresy, or such as had little faith and believed nothing but what their eyes could see and their hands touch."[14] Note the identification of some heretics as skeptics, who refuse to believe what their senses do not tell them. Shabbetai Zvi's disciples indeed put much stock in pure faith that is not based on signs and wonders, while at the same time being in awe of the miracles attributed to the Messiah. This dual approach can also be seen among the Meshichists, who place complete faith in the fact that the Rebbe is alive and is the Messiah over sensory experience that contradicts this belief. Yet, at the same time, they spread the word of the miracles performed by the Rebbe, the King Messiah, and disseminate testimonies of his revelation, because "clear knowledge can come only from what the eyes see."[15]

Following Shabbetai Zvi's conversion to Islam, his disciples began to claim that the conversion was merely a subterfuge (much the way some Gnostic cults viewed Jesus's crucifixion). Later, they claimed that his death was an illusion.[16] The Meshichists use similar arguments and formulations to deny the Rebbe's death. The Event of Gimel Tammuz only affected "our material eyes." Just as, according to the Midrash, Jacob the patriarch did not die, even though "they eulogized him and embalmed him and buried him" (Babylonian Talmud, Ta'anit 5b), the Rebbe's so-called death was simply "staged." The logic behind the two claims is identical: the true believer is the person who withstands the test and is not tempted by the testimony of his or her eyes.

The question of who is a believer and who a heretic is linked to the tension between strict observance of the halakhah (hypernomia) and outright transgression (antinomia). At first glance these are polar opposites, but both are contained within the internal logic of the process of redemption. The arrival of the Messiah will be hastened by preparing people's hearts for it, repentance, and the acceptance of the yoke of the Torah and commandments. The Rebbe, who fostered Chabad's network of emissaries so as to bring as many Jews as possible into the fold of Torah Judaism in general and Hasidism specifically, and thereby hasten the redemption, acted according to this logic.[17] Indeed, many Jews, in Israel and elsewhere, view Chabad as a major force for promoting Jewish heritage and values. Its emissaries' dedication to this task, at posts far distant from their home communities, along with their strict observance of Jewish law, the Hasidic ethos, and their Orthodox appearance, peg them in their own eyes and the eyes of others as representing the gold standard of Jewish commitment and religiosity.

But, while the road to redemption is paved with greater religious observance by all Jews, the age of redemption itself will be subject to a "new Torah."[18] Although the Babylonian Talmud (Nidah 61b) declares that "the commandments will be annulled in the coming future," halakhic authorities are divided on this issue. Maimonides and others claim that this does not refer to the messianic age. But the possibility that some of the commandments will be rescinded in the new age is consistent with the nature of that time and is accepted by many legal authorities. The disputes I presented previously regarding the Rebbe's divine status and the cancellation of the minor fasts shows that, despite Chabad's Orthodox facade, it is not immune to the antinomian inclinations of the messianic idea.

Unlike the messianic dynamic in Chabad, where the Rebbe promoted a vision of the redemption without declaring himself to be the Messiah, the messianic fervor of the Sabbatean movement was ignited when the charismatic Shabbetai Zvi declared his messianic vocation. It is not surprising, then, that the antinomianism that remains tacit in Chabad burst forth in full force among the Sabbateans, both regarding the divine status of the Messiah and the abrogation of the commandments. The earlier figure's self-identification as the Messiah led him to declare his own divinity explicitly. He signed letters to his followers as God's "eldest son," and even "I am the Lord your God Sabbatai Sevi."[19] A similar radicalization took place with regard to the observance of the commandments. Shabbetai Zvi annulled the Torah and its injunctions in the name of a new Torah and new commandments. He exhibited a particular interest in "changes in the liturgical calendar and the institution of new festivals."[20] Going much farther than abolishing the minor fast days, he also annulled the fast of the Ninth of Av. Without going into the "strange actions" he and his believers engaged in, suffice it to say that the antinomian tendency in Sabbateanism grew more acute after his conversion, when his followers began to view the observance of the commandments as a sin.[21]

Another aspect of the question of who is a believer and who a heretic that is on display in both these messianic movements is the debate over the association between faith and madness. What believers view as a manifestation of simple faith, or even spiritual elation, is merely insanity in the eyes of their opponents. In Chabad's institutional discourse, explicit references to the Rebbe as God are condemned and labeled as the symptoms of mental illness. The view of moderates that the extremists are mentally unstable is based on their view of themselves as sane. In contrast, the Meshichists argue that it is wrong to tar all unqualified declarations that the Rebbe is the Messiah and still alive, and even that he is God with the same brush of insanity. They themselves refer to bizarre and eccentric behavior as "holy folly," and see such fools as playing a role in paving the way for the Rebbe's redemption. Likewise, the Sabbatean movement also blurred the boundaries between prophecy and madness. Hundreds of believers, including many women and children, entered into frenzies and experienced prophetic visions about Shabbetai Zvi's messianism and the coming age of redemption. But nonbelievers claimed that they had been possessed by evil spirits.[22] Shabbetai Zvi, they claimed, was an epileptic charlatan.[23] As with the question of faith and heresy, the distinction between prophetic vision and hallucination, and between devotion and possession, is to a large extent in the eye of the beholder.[24]

The two movements also have sociological features in common. One of these is the presence of new believers in the inner core of zealous messianists. Scholem noted that the strongest support for Shabbetai Zvi's messianism came from communities that included Conversos who had returned to Judaism after fleeing the Iberian Peninsula.[25] Quite similar are Chabad's "immigrants," new Hasidim, including formerly nonreligious Jews and many Mizrachim, who fill the ranks of the Meshichists (although these latter groups are more peripheral socially and certainly economically than the Conversos were). Both Chabad's new adherents and the Conversos who returned to Judaism during the time of Shabbetai Zvi's ascendancy found in the messianic tide an experience of great spiritual significance, one that justified the metamorphosis of their lives and granted them a means of extricating themselves from the marginality forced on them by the rabbinic establishment. In both cases the messianic turbulence challenged traditional community hierarchies and turned the Sabbateans and the Meshichists, in their own esteem, into Judaism's true believers. The extent to which the logic of withstanding a test can be taken can be seen in the social climate among Shabbetai Zvi's followers after his conversion. The most committed of them, who were prepared to convert to Islam in the footsteps of their master, were called "masters of faith"![26] Here, too, the determination of who the believers were and who the heretics was a matter of perspective.

Finally, consider Scholem's comment that "the more the concrete figure of the messiah recedes and becomes blurred, the better the climate for the rank growth of a messianic legend which substituted for Sabbatai's actual deeds fantastic accounts far more marvelous. . . . Unencumbered by his actual presence, the movement developed rapidly by following the lines of apocalyptic tradition."[27] He was referring to the rise in Shabbetai Zvi's popularity after he was expelled from Jerusalem and disappeared for a time from the public eye; but it is an apt description of what happened to Chabad messianism following the Event of Gimel Tammuz, when the absent Rebbe became all the more present in the lives of his believers, "with us more than ever" as they put it.

In considering the practices of making the Rebbe present in the lives of his believers in the broader context of contemporary culture and against the background of the technological revolution that is so swiftly changing the boundaries of being and reality, it is tempting to extend the comparative framework beyond the familiar area of messianic movements. The speculative comparative remarks I will make here derive from my impression that the fashioning of the Rebbe as a culture hero fits well into the contemporary global culture of images based on an ever-increasing "visual literacy." The process of exalting the Rebbe is strangely reminiscent of the transformation of famous political and entertainment celebrities, such as Che Guevara,[28] Eva Peron,[29] Elvis Presley,[30] and James Dean,[31] into popular icons. Such a comparison might well be insulting to the Hasidim who are the subjects of this study, but even unbiased observers might have doubts about whether the comparison is appropriate, given the hugely different worlds of content in which these figures became larger than life. Nevertheless, as distant as these worlds are from one another, there are some surprising resemblances among them regarding the way that venerated figures are glorified in contemporary culture. Despite the huge differences between the Rebbe's religious-spiritual world

FIGURE 28. Portrait of Che Guevara as Jesus. In *Che Guevara: Revolutionary & Icon*, Trisha Ziff, ed., p. 87. Bus-shelter poster, UK. Collection of David Kunzle.

and the realms of politics, art, and popular entertainment, the experiences of devotees and fans can be quite similar. The enthusiasts of dead celebrities may endow their heroes with a halo of spirituality and holiness, and even see them as saviors. Such auras intensify and are disseminated by the pull exerted by striking visual representations. Che Guevara, a Marxist revolutionary who became the center of a para-religious cult practiced, for the most part, in Cuba, and Elvis Presley, the singer revered by the "Presleytarian" church in the United States,[32] are two good examples of such secular saints.

The visual image is the focal point of the comparison between the Rebbe and Che Guevara. The mythologization of the iconic photograph of the Rebbe ("the picture with the baby") is reminiscent of the metamorphosis of the famous portrait of Che,[33] which, as one commentator has noted, "accomplished more for his cause than the man himself accomplished in his lifetime."[34] The portrait, as it appears on posters and T-shirts, is often accompanied by the legend "Che lives," which is much like the epithets *shalita* ("may he have a long and good life") and *shilo* ("may he live forever and ever") among the Meshichists.[35] Portraits of Che, like those of the Rebbe, offer a broad spectrum ranging from religious images much like icons to commercial trademarks. For example, the Anglican Church issued a poster of Jesus bearing Che's face. The appropriation of the popular revolutionary's face by the church originated in the double connection between the two—first, Jesus could be seen as a social revolutionary, and second, Che, like Jesus, was seen by his followers as a martyr who sacrificed himself for the sake of humanity. From the Christian perspective, the red background of the original poster (preserved in the church's poster) symbolizes the pure blood of the martyr, not the red flag of communism.

Che Guevara's fame and the aura surrounding his martyrdom to the Marxist cause led to a wanton commercialization of his image in the global capitalist visual culture. In the years since his death, the iconic image of the tough revolutionary has appeared on the labels of Smirnoff vodka and other alcoholic beverages, T-shirts, purses, sunglasses, packs of cigarettes, musical instruments, and even contraceptives.

The Rebbe was also perceived as a revolutionary inasmuch as he sought to establish a new Jewish and world order by means of his messianic vision. But this revolutionary agenda, so different from Che's, is a flimsy basis for comparison. A more appropriate one would be the unflinching commercialization of the iconic images of both as a symptom of their ever-increasing popularity in today's global commercial culture. As I wrote in my discussion of Chabad's visual culture, the Rebbe's image appears on innumerable objects and products, some of which, such as wristwatches and sunscreens, are entirely secular in nature. These products are sold freely at Messiah fairs and can be ordered from Messiah and Redemption catalogues at Chabad centers and on the internet.

Comparing the King, as the rock star Elvis Presley is known, with the King Messiah might seem disrespectful and unacceptable. Yet Presley's

FIGURE 29. Cherry Guevara. Magnum ice cream, Australia. Collection of David Kunzle.

fans use religious idioms to describe him, calling him a saint and even a savior. Furthermore, his cult also makes use of flashy portrait photographs. But what is of special interest is that Presley's fans, much like the Meshichists, have stubbornly refused to accept that he died.[36] The "Che lives" slogan that accompanies Guevara's iconic image is a metaphor, but the claim that reordering the letters of "Elvis" produces the word "lives" is taken very literally by his believers, just the way Meshichists really mean it when they use the epithet *shalita* in mentioning the Rebbe. Both groups claim that their king still lives, in hiding. The Rebbe's presence is ubiquitous thanks to his pictures; the same sort of ubiquity is claimed for Elvis, although with humorist intent, in a book in which Elvis appears in unexpected places. The back cover states that the book "*Where's Elvis* offers photographic evidence that proves—if you look closely—that the rumors of the King's death are greatly exaggerated. Let's face it—photographs don't lie."[37] Given the prominence of the visual images and the denial of death in both cases, it should hardly be surprising that Americans report from time to time that they have sighted Elvis, much as Meshichists claim to have seen the Rebbe, and that in both cases the apparitions have a very realistic cast to them, as is appropriate in the case of a personage whose death is denied.

CHAPTER 13

FROM *TZADIK* TO MESSIAH

Comparing Chabad and Bratslav

Chabad and Bratslav, two of the most venerable of Hasidic sects, have been perceived, both by scholars and other Hasidim, as lying at two opposite ends of the larger movement's spectrum. Within the Hasidic orbit, Chabad is central and influential, with a hierarchical and authoritative structure and a stress on scholarship, the intellect, and reasoned introspection.[1] Bratslav, on the other hand, was for most of its history a small and marginal offshoot that had no institutions to unite its branches. Furthermore, its defining feature was simple faith and the sensory override of "casting the mind aside."[2] Yet, for all their differences, these two Hasidic movements have much in common, enough to make a comparison worthwhile. They are both marked by intensity and ardor, and both have been spreading in Israel and the rest of the world. But, more importantly, they share a feature that sets them apart from all other Hasidic sects. Chabad's Hasidim were orphaned with the Event of Gimel Tammuz, remaining without a leader and heir of their line of *admorim*. Bratslav Hasidim have been in the same situation for more than two centuries, since the death of the movement's founder, Rabbi Nachman (1772–1810). They are, together, a paradox that calls out for an explanation; they both lack the essential defining feature of a Hasidic community and its independent identity—the living *tzadik* who mediates between his flock and the higher spheres. Yet today they are the most dynamic and vital Hasidic movements in Israel and the Jewish world as a whole.[3] What explains the burgeoning popularity of these *admor*-less sects, which are utter anomalies in classic Hasidic life? Could it be that leaderlessness is actually a factor in their success?

Answering that question requires an examination of the principal lines of similarity between Chabad and Bratslav, with a focus on the propensity for border-crossing that they share. This boundary-breaking is closely tied to the messianic orientation of both sects, and most specifically to Chabad's attribution of messianic status to Rebbe Menachem Mendel Schneerson and Bratslav's less explicit designation of Rabbi Nachman as the Messiah. Identification of the *tzadik* as a messianic figure whose manifestation in the world shakes the historical order does not sit well with the routine of community and spiritual leadership being handed down a line of succession. For this reason, both Chabad and Bratslav lack an *admor*. This absence, which on the face of it should deprive a Hasidic community of the very essence of its existence, may well be an advantage and a success strategy inasmuch as it grants the average Hasid much greater room for initiative and autonomous action. Breaking down boundaries in a range of areas helps make the absent *tzadik*'s presence felt and turns him into a close and accessible figure in his believers' lives, free of the constraints of a hierarchical mediating structure.

The different time frames in which the two movements have been bereft of a *tzadik* might at first seem to make a comparison problematic. Bratslav Hasidim have been "orphans" for more than two hundred years, whereas Chabad Hasidim have been in that state now for twenty-five years. But recall that for most of that time Bratslav was a tiny movement struggling to survive; only in the last generation has it become popular. Chabad was from the start a dominant branch of Hasidism, but in opposition to the forecasts of some scholars, its growth accelerated at an even more rapid pace after the Rebbe's occlusion.[4] Furthermore, the refusal of the Hasidim in both camps to appoint heirs to their leaders was a product of those leaders' messianic status. The Hasidim belonging to Bratslav's several offshoots are much like the Chabad mainstream—they do not deny that Rabbi Nachman died, but stress his strong spiritual presence and expect him to reveal himself very soon as the herald of the redemption or as the Messiah's rabbi. They see his teachings as the key to the redemption of the entire world.[5]

Both Rabbi Nachman and the Rebbe were born with sterling Hasidic pedigrees. Rabbi Nachman was the great-grandson of Rabbi Israel

Ba'al Shem Tov, the founder of Hasidism, and he was the grandson and namesake of the Ba'al Shem Tov's student, the *tzadik* Rabbi Nachman of Horodenka. The Rebbe was the direct descendant and namesake of Rabbi Menachem Mendel, also known as the Tzemah Tzedek, Chabad's third *nasi*. In both cases this lineage was bolstered by a claim to be of the line of King David, from which the Messiah is destined to come. Furthermore, the names Nachman and Menachem also share a common Hebrew root meaning "comfort" or "consolation," with its obvious messianic connotations.[6] Also of huge importance in the messianic context is the fact that neither the Rebbe nor Rabbi Nachman had male issue at the time of their deaths; as Joseph Dan has noted, "the lack of an heir is an almost mandatory characteristic of a messianic figure."[7] Furthermore, the fact that the Rebbe was childless accorded with the Chabad myth that the movement would have seven *nesi'im*, ending with the arrival of the Messiah; some scholars even maintain that the Rebbe deliberately did not have children in order to fulfill this requirement.[8] Rabbi Nachman, who declared that the Messiah would be a descendant of his, had seven daughters; his two sons died at a young age, during his lifetime. Rabbi Nachman had held out messianic hopes for one of them, Shlomo Efraim, called the "holy child."[9]

Both Rabbi Nachman and the Rebbe enjoyed a much more exalted position among their Hasidim than the average Hasidic *tzadik* enjoys. Rabbi Nachman saw himself as a "*tzadik* for the ages" and the "true *tzadik*," and his followers adopted this view. The Rebbe was, in Chabad terminology, the *nasi*, a title that in ancient times referred to the president of the Sanhedrin, the high court and legislative body of the Jewish community in the Land of Israel. In Chabad parlance, "the *nasi* is all." He is the "head of the Children of Israel," the spiritual leader of all Jews. Both the Rebbe and Rabbi Nachman were compared to Moses, the "First Redeemer," and called the "Final Redeemer." In contrast with the theory of partial redemption, in which a *tzadik* belongs to a historical dynasty and redeems his community alone,[10] both Chabad and Bratslav preach universal redemption.

There are a number of areas in which Chabad and Bratslav Hasidim tend to cast off the constraints generally accepted in the Haredi-religious world. Their messianic visions are inevitably connected to boundary-breaking,[11] and this quite naturally arouses concern and opposition in the religious establishment. Messianic figures such as Jesus, Shabbetai Zvi, and Jacob Frank, as well as their heirs, formulated subversive and antinomian teachings that placed their communities at a far divide from normative Judaism. I briefly noted the "heretical" potential of Chabad's messianic vision in my discussion of the deification of the Rebbe and my comparison of Chabad and Sabbateanism. But even without this potential, the term *border* is a good tool for analyzing the characteristics that set Chabad and Bratslav apart from other Hasidic sects, and which contribute to their rapid growth. The breaking of borders fits in well in Hasidism with the idea of "disseminating the wellsprings," that is, spreading the teachings of the interiority of the Torah throughout the world as a condition for bringing the complete redemption, as the Messiah promised to Rabbi Israel Ba'al Shem Tov during his experience of his soul ascending to heaven.[12] But from the time Hasidism first appeared, it never had a leader who went so far in pursuit of this ideal as the Rebbe did. In his activist way, characterized by "breaking the structure of accepted Orthodoxy" and "breaking traditional examples," in accordance with Hasidism's slogan "and you will break forth (*ufaratzta*) to the west and the east, to the north and to the south" (Genesis 28:14) and using bellicose military imagery,[13] the Rebbe encouraged his Hasidim to use all the means that the modern world provides to bring the Jewish people back to the Torah and to speed the redemption.

Rabbi Nachman was drawn to physical and spiritual places that he himself called "the edge and end of [the people of] Israel, the place at which the boundary of Israel ends, because everything has an edge and an end."[14] His self-conscious messianism and sense of vocation led him to believe that not just his community and people, but also the entire human landscape beyond the Jewish people, were within the range of his influence.[15]

The most comprehensive border-crossing stems from the universal nature of the messianic vision. Messianic awareness seems to be what energizes the Hasidim of Chabad and Bratslav to take the Hasidic idea of "*ufaratzta*" to its limit. Chabad's messages of redemption are aimed at all of humanity while not in the least blurring the boundary between Jews and non-Jews. Chabad's appeal to the gentiles is secondary and restricted, aimed at convincing them to observe the seven Noachide laws.[16] But the fact that this appeal is explicitly part of the movement's agenda is surprising and exceptional. The "Hidden Scroll," a cryptic book that Rabbi Nachman wrote as his messianic credo, and which includes many of his messianic sermons, is of a notably universal character, and his vision of the redemption is directed at all of humanity and offers a picture of world peace.[17] Openness toward converts to Judaism and the importance of Jewish influence on other nations are values that Rabbi Nachman frequently addressed in his teachings. It should hardly be surprising, then, that the Bratslav website intended for the general public devotes a special section to the "Sons of Noah," the rest of humanity.

The universal compass of the messianic vision of redemption includes additional but less comprehensive types of border-crossing. First, Chabad and Bratslav view all Jews as targets for their missionizing. This inclusiveness is a product of the way the Rebbe and Rabbi Nachman perceived themselves as leaders with authority over the entire Jewish people, quite different from the sectoral and closed-off nature of the *tzadik* in other Hasidic sects. Chabad Hasidim have no hesitation about reaching out to secular Jews and trying to persuade them to observe the commandments and to bring them back into the fold of Jewish practice and belief. Chabad's outward-looking vision is exemplified in the emissaries it sends around the world, who work to promote religious and spiritual life wherever Jews live or travel.[18] Since most Haredi groups are insular and segregated from the rest of the world, the revolutionary nature of this project cannot be overstated. No other Jewish group does so much to light the divine spark in the soul of every Jew and to pave the way toward the redemption. It should hardly be surprising, then, that many Jews, and perhaps many non-Jews as well, see Chabad as representative of the Jewish people and the keeper of its flame. Bratslav Hasidim also exert huge energies to disseminate Rabbi Nachman's teachings in the broadest possible way.[19] Like Chabad, which publishes the Rebbe's teachings, all branches of Bratslav Hasidism print the writings of Rabbi

Nachman and his students. Both groups put out books, pamphlets, and other material aimed at a wide range of readers, far beyond their own communities.

Given that both groups address every Jew of every sort, it should hardly be surprising that they, and their radical wings in particular, take in large numbers of *ba'alei teshuvah* and Jews who are in the process of becoming more observant. These newcomers are themselves boundary-crossers and, when they join, they actually move the boundaries through their influence on their absorbing communities.[20] While I do not have quantitative data, the claim that most Israeli members of both these Hasidic groups were not born into them does not seem unlikely, especially with regard to Bratslav. In addition to bringing skills and modes of activity from the secular world into these Hasidic sects (for example, in the areas of technology and the media), such new Hasidim are inspired by religious fervor, intensive seeking of spiritual and mystical experiences, and opposition to routine and conformity. This augments the messianic climate in Chabad and Bratslav.[21] Such newly religious adherents, who grew up outside the protective and restrictive framework of a hierarchical religious community, view the Rebbe and Rabbi Nachman as sublime, larger-than-life objects of identification.[22] They engage these *tzadikim* directly in their search for maximal spirituality and religiosity.

As a direct result of the outward-oriented activity of Chabad and Bratslav, the border-crossing in both movements also has concrete geographical significance involving sharp cultural passages. In Israel, Chabad emissaries can be found carrying out "operational activities" in secular public spaces, seeking to persuade men to put on *tefillin* and women to light Sabbath candles. No less prominent, but quite different, are the Na-Nach Bratslavers, who dance and sing on street corners and in the middle of intersections in an effort to arouse the interest of passing crowds in the teachings of Rabbi Nachman. Chabad Houses established by the Rebbe's emissaries can be found all around the world, and many of them have become famous for the spiritual and material services that they provide to Israeli tourists and trekkers in far-flung lands. The Jewish Homes that Bratslav Hasidim run in India, Thailand, and South America are located in places that many young Israelis travel through. These operations by both movements are aimed at establishing a Jewish presence in places far distant, geographically and culturally, from Israel and other centers of Jewish life.

The central holy sites of both Chabad and Bratslav are located far away from Israel. The sanctity of Rabbi Nachman's grave in Uman, Ukraine—in the heart of territory that the Bratslavers view as impure and abhorrent—derives from the concrete and living presence of Rabbi Nachman's spirit there.[23] Similarly, the sanctity of 770 Eastern Parkway, in a small Jewish enclave in Crown Heights, Brooklyn, where most of the residents are black and Latino, derives from it being the place where the Rebbe lived and worked. In both cases, the exalted *tzadik* associated with the place imbues it with sanctity. This centrifugal trend, which draws believers to these distant places, runs counter to the idea of the sanctity of the Land of Israel. The Rebbe notably refrained from visiting Israel despite the fact that many pleaded with him to do so. Rabbi Nachman made a pilgrimage to the Holy Land, one replete with obstacles and disappointments, cut short before he reached Jerusalem.

The rise in the standing of such distant places is in part a result of the fact that, in this age of global tourism, it is possible to travel to them in comfort and at reasonable cost. On the ideological level, however, it is a concrete expression of the border-crossing messianic visions of Chabad and Bratslav. For Chabad Meshichists, 770 is a lesser Temple in which the Shechinah, the divine presence, resides. According to the Rebbe's vision of the redemption, the Third Temple will descend from heaven next to 770 and float with it to Jerusalem, with all the world's Jews in tow. The pilgrimage to Rabbi Nachman's grave is described as being like a visit to the Foundation Stone that lay under the Temple in Jerusalem, the place from which the creation of the world began and from which the divine abundance that maintains the world spreads. Some even claim that Rabbi Nachman's grave is holier than Jerusalem and the Temple's Holy of Holies.[24] According to Rabbi Yisroel Odesser, the founder of the Na-Nach branch of Bratslav, the redemption will begin when the child Messiah arrives at the grave in Uman, brings Rabbi Nachman back to life, leads him to the site of the Temple in Jerusalem, and places him to serve in the Holy of Holies.[25]

Gender is also an area in which both groups break down borders, or at least enlarge the territory they encompass. The Rebbe systematically empowered Chabad women, encouraging them to study Torah, the secrets of Kabbalah, and Hasidic philosophy, as well as to take an active role in the movement's institutions and as emissaries. He constructed an infrastructure for organized women's activism in the movement and assigned them a key role in bringing about the redemption.[26] The Rebbe argued that the hidden source of the ostensibly material and inferior world of women is in fact spiritual and sublime. When this spiritual feminine element is revealed in the generation of redemption, it will refine the lower spirituality of man. Furthermore, women's work to maintain and preserve the Jewish home in material reality makes the world fit to serve as a "lower dwelling" for God, which is the purpose of the creation in Chabad theosophy. That means there is an affinity between the redemption and Jewish women.[27] It is thus hardly surprising that women are well represented among Meshichist activists.

Rabbi Nachman constantly encouraged his followers to bring their wives closer to Hasidism. Bratslav women are prominent speakers at public events and notable presences on the movement's websites. They claim the right to engage on their own in one of Bratslav Hasidism's signature practices, *hitbodedut* (solo seclusion for mediation and prayer), just as men do, and to make pilgrimages to Rabbi Nachman's grave. Their demands have been controversial, but that does not prevent many women from taking action to approach God and the *tzadik* without the mediation of men. Like Chabad's famous women emissaries, such as Nechoma Greisman,[28] Bratslav boasts a number of prominent women, among them Tehilla Berland, wife of Rabbi Eliezer Berland, the head of the Shuvu Banim yeshiva. Her books, among them commentaries on Rabbi Nachman's sermons, are as prominent on the bookshelves of the group's Hasidim as are the books her husband has written.

Chabad and Bratslav also go much farther than any other Hasidic group in crossing ethnic boundaries. They are the only Hasidic sects to accept Mizrachim into their ranks without any reservations or restrictions. In fact, new Hasidim of Mizrachi origin constitute a majority in most branches of Bratslav, and make up an outsized proportion of the members of Chabad Meshichist groups.[29] In both groups the number of Mizrachi rabbis is continually rising. This should be no surprise: as these Hasidic movements reach out to all Jews, they fashion categories of identity that are less exclusive and more flexible and open than those known in any Hasidic group of the past. A person may be affiliated with Chabad even if he is not fully religiously observant "for now" (as Chabad Hasidim put it, in a positive light). Similarly, a person may venerate Rabbi Nachman, delve into his writings, and make the pilgrimage to Uman while maintaining another religious identity as well, through affiliation with, say, another Hasidic sect or the Mizrachi Haredi political and social movement Shas. Such people might be termed "part-time" Bratslavers. Such Chabad and Bratslav identities, which have a tendency to be broad and sweeping, reflect and reinforce the growing spectrum of religious life in Israeli society and the weakening of factional demarcation among religious Israelis. Tellingly, the first two letters of "Chabakuk," the acronym that designates the complex identity of Israeli neo-Hasidic New Age youth, stand for Chabad and Bratslav.[30] This nonfactional nature, so unlike that of the insular Haredi world, has contributed to the popularity of these two movements. Chabad and Bratslav are "Israeli," despite the way their Hasidim dress, and their draw is further bolstered by their universal and transnational vision.

Chabad and Bratslav are more willing than other Hasidic groups to adopt current secular innovations in both the areas of applied science and technology and the arts, and to harness them to their causes. They thus cross another social boundary that separates the traditional from the modern world. In Chabad, this openness derives directly from its theosophy, which teaches that all the medical, scientific, and communications innovations of the modern age are simply reflections of God's presence and will.[31] Chabad and Bratslav are far ahead of other Haredi groups in their use of film, video, the internet, and digital technology,[32] although of the two Chabad is much more sophisticated in its organizational ability and media savvy. The adoption of advanced technology does not mean the adoption of the modern ethos or of the scientific paradigms on which it is based. On the contrary, they recast science and technology in religious-mystical terms. This openness thus leads to a crossing of epistemological borders as well; in the late modern (or postmodern) world, the ostensibly intolerable absence of the *tzadik* can lead, paradoxically, to new horizons of religious daring and mystical experience.

At the heart of this very important boundary-crossing in both these Hasidic groups lie the efforts to turn the absent *tzadik* into a presence by constant movement and maneuvering between actual and virtual reality. The gravitational pull of religious belief systems as a whole grows out of their ability to illuminate persuasively hidden aspects of the universe and of existence; in Chabad and Bratslav that movement and maneuvering is especially prominent. As I have noted, Chabad's mystical teachings are based on a "hermeneutics of suspicion" toward the world as perceived by the senses. Chabad negates the world of the senses even as it displays a very high level of involvement in this reality, growing out of its assertion of the world's need for redemption. Bratslav Hasidim are committed to their rabbi's teaching, which urges them to abandon intellect and critical thinking in favor of a consciousness that is devoid of knowledge and guided instead by imagination, sensory awakening, and unqualified faith. Like Chabad, Bratslav doctrine is dialectical in nature—it seeks to turn situations of despair and helplessness into ones of joy and spiritual elation.

Against this background, each group has successfully made its virtual *tzadik* into an especially close and felt figure in public and private life. This effort to make the Rebbe present among the Chabad Meshichists has been discussed in previous chapters. As I have shown, the Meshichists' daily routine is conducted around the Rebbe; they may write to the Rebbe, be with the Rebbe, and even see him. As far as they are concerned, the Rebbe is more available and accessible now than he was before the Event of Gimel Tammuz in 1994. Of the two groups, Chabad is the more energized by the alchemical magic of transforming the invisible leader into something close and concrete through a wide-ranging system of signs (traces and images) and mimetic practices.

Rabbi Nachman is also exalted in the extreme by some of his followers. He, too, is the subject of a huge personality cult. Yet, despite their lofty and even divine status, their Hasidim feel the Rebbe and Rabbi Nachman to be approachable and close by. Today, both Chabad and Bratslav lack a Hasidic court of the classic type that mediates between Hasidim and their *tzadik* and which forms a barrier between them. In Chabad, the Rebbe's residence in Crown Heights is open to all, as is his grave in Queens; the same is true of Rabbi Nachman's grave in Uman. In Bratslav there is a tradition, dating back to Rabbi Nachman himself, of making confession before the *tzadik*, meaning, today, doing so at his grave.[33]

The comfortable combination of deification and intimacy found in the Na-Nach subgroup can be seen in questions posed on the internet to Rabbi Shalom Arush on the "Seclusion before God/Our Holy Rabbi" webpage.[34] This discussion and other Bratslav websites evince the ambivalence about addressing Rabbi Nachman during a Hasid's daily seclusion (*hitbodedut*). Some say this can only be done at the grave in Uman or at the Western Wall in Jerusalem. But the common wisdom is that a worshipper may speak with Rabbi Nachman as long as he does not pray to him, "but one may speak and make requests, just as one requests from a living person." The Hasidim participating in the forum are clearly eager to speak to their beloved rabbi and to pour out their hearts to him. Clearly, personal communication and intimate conversation with Rabbi Nachman are quite common, and reach their climax at his grave on Rosh Hashanah. Perhaps it is no coincidence that the Bratslav ethos that opposes institutionalization and authority has not produced an organized and structured channel of communication with Rabbi Nachman of the sort represented by Chabad's *Igrot Kodesh* oracle, but the search for guidance and advice in his writings is a central characteristic of Bratslav Hasidism.

Rabbi Natan, Rabbi Nachman's chosen student and disseminator of his teachings, knew that his master's image, so finely etched in his own consciousness, could not be seen by young Hasidim who had not met him face-to-face. He thus labored to make Rabbi Nachman present in their lives. Recall that Rabbi Nachman was active on the verge of the nineteenth century and the Rebbe in the second half of the twentieth, when photographs, with their ability to aid memory and memorialization, became available to all at a reasonable price. Photographs of the Rebbe can be found everywhere, but Bratslav, founded before the appearance of photography, was unable to preserve the visage of Rabbi Nachman himself. Rabbi Natan made a special effort to attach reasons and meanings to each and every observance, through which Rabbi

Nachman's Hasidim could sense their master's spiritual essence. Rituals were granted new interpretations that integrated them into the *tzadik*'s mythical life cycle. For example, the "*tzadik*'s descent" (to raise up the divine sparks trapped in the profane world) was made part of the ritual of the Days of Awe and the Ninth of Av. More important for this book are rituals that added another layer of meaning enabling the replacement of the lost visual memory with embodied memory, which is more resistant to attenuation. Thus, for example, Rabbi Natan proposed sensing the *tzadik*'s nearby presence by concentrated contemplation of the flames of the Hanukah candles.[35]

Over the course of the generations since Rabbi Nachman's death, he has been established as a figure who is close to his flock. They have access to him through his writings and evocative stories. Furthermore, the style of his teachings, and even more so his many talks, is manifestly personal. Rabbi Nachman placed his inner world, with all its vicissitudes, before his Hasidim, sharing with them not only the spiritual heights he scaled and his personal and national hopes, but also the religious crises brought on when those hopes were dashed. He maintained intimacy with his disciples, and his use of the second person, addressing his readers directly, gives them a sense of direct contact with him. The intimate nature of his writings enables readers to draw advice and personal lessons from them. In this way they serve, despite the difference in genre, much the same purpose that *Igrot Kodesh* does in Chabad. The intensive communication that Bratslav Hasidim maintain with their rabbi receives formal expression in a "pledge of allegiance" that they recite before every prayer service; some recite it also before the performance of each and every precept and observance. Another phenomenon unique to Bratslav is also aimed at establishing direct communication between Rabbi Nachman and his present-day disciples—the weekly Shabbat pamphlet distributed by one of its branches consists almost entirely of direct quotes from texts written by Rabbi Nachman himself, along with reports of his words and actions written by his disciple Rabbi Natan. There is no exegesis or retelling or interpretation of the meaning of these texts, as is common in pamphlets of this type put out by other groups, Chabad included.

In recent years another channel of communication with Rabbi Nachman has been established. It grows out of the testimony of Rabbi Yisroel Odesser, who claimed to have received letters from heaven that had been written by Rabbi Nachman. The most famous of these contained a mantra, "Na-Nach-Nachma-Nachman mi'Uman," the recitation of which would hasten the redemption. The mantra, based on the letters of Rabbi Nachman's name, became the textual equivalent of the iconic photograph of the Rebbe. It is emblazoned in huge letters on buildings and other prominent landscape features in Israel, and on thousands of automobiles. The Hasidim who follow Odesser's version of Bratslav bear the mantra as a charm, inscribed on a disc they wear around their necks. Chabad's Meshichists, of course, have their own mantra, "Yechi Adoneinu." Both groups wear *kipot* with their respective mantras printed on them, black ones for the Meshichists and large knitted white ones for the Bratslavers, serving as a visible mark of members of each. The Meshichists have also added "Yechi Adoneinu" to their liturgy; they open and conclude each prayer service with this declaration of allegiance to the King Messiah.

Lacking the possibility of devotion to a living *tzadik*, Chabad and Bratslav crafted alternative and original means of being in contact with their absent leaders. Especially salient is the direct and intimate contact with the Rebbe enjoyed by visitors to 770, and with Rabbi Nachman in Uman. Accounts of visits to each place speak not of a holy site but rather of an encounter with an individual who is present there. Chabad Meshichists, who deny that the Rebbe died, come to 770 "to see [the Rebbe] and be seen [by him]." When talking of Uman, Bratslavers say that "Rabbi Nachman welcomed me" (or "rejected me"). There too, pilgrims visit Rabbi Nachman himself, not his grave, and bid him farewell at the end of their stay.

The sublime messianic vision that beats in the hearts of Chabad and Bratslav Hasidim grants them a sense of mission and a purpose. These feelings of personal initiative and responsibility are reinforced by the sense that they act in the world as surrogates of their absent leaders. In Meshichist Chabad, the *tzadik*'s disappearance is seen as a supreme test of faith. Some of the Meshichists even interpret this withdrawal as deliberate, aimed at uncovering the latent messianic spark in each of his Hasidim.

In Chabad, this sense of vocation is expressed in national and communal terms and in explicitly military language, but its emissaries labor in isolation, far from the supportive framework of their community and extended families. It requires determination, personal initiative, independence, and unconditional commitment. Bratslav Hasidism has survived for two hundred years without a serving *admor*, which has given it an individualist and anti-institutional character (quite different from Chabad's strong institutional milieu) and notably noncombative language.

The pleasant demeanor characteristic of Hasidim from both groups is nurtured by their messianic visions and is something they deliberately cultivate. In contrast with the nostalgic orientation of most Haredi communities, which look to the past, the messianic messages of these two groups look to the future and provide these Hasidim with an optimistic and utopian view of the world. Unlike traditional apocalyptic views in which the messianic era emerges from catastrophe, these two groups maintain that redemption will occur as part of a "messianism of success."[36] Chabad sees historical and current events as omens of the age of redemption. In Bratslav, success follows success as they disseminate the name and teachings of Rabbi Nachman throughout the world and move their Hasidic sect and its master from the rejected fringes of Jewish society into the dominant center, accepted by broad swaths of the Jewish public.

At the core of the comparative analysis offered here is the claim that, for both these Hasidic sects, the lack of a *tzadik* does not keep the Hasidim from maintaining contact with him and internalizing his teachings. In fact, they are equipped with a range of tools that enable them to make the absent *tzadik* present, accessible, and available for conversation.[37] The painful vacuum left by the spiritual leader is filled, perhaps in a way superior to the period when he was alive, largely thanks to these tools, which are the products of modern technology. The huge distance between the living *tzadik* and the Hasid can be seen as yet another boundary that can be crossed more easily when the *admor* becomes virtual. He then becomes the birthright of all his Hasidim.

Both Chabad and Bratslav Hasidim feel a sense of personal responsibility and duty toward an all-encompassing system of meaning. In Chabad, it is the movement's a-cosmic and panentheistic mystical theosophy, which fully integrates the material and symbolic worlds such that the most sublime spiritual ideas are embodied in the world of the senses. In Bratslav, the system comprises the sum total of the homilies, stories, and fables authored by Rabbi Nachman, works replete with metaphors and allusions that provide a means for articulating a broad range of human experience.[38] There is also a series of books, *Likutei Halakhot*, based on the teachings of Rabbi Nachman, which imbues all the commandments and observances with a specifically Bratslavian meaning. The guiding principle is that all the commandments are connected to the *tzadik*, that is, to Rabbi Nachman. It is a commonplace that believers in every religion are equipped with an all-encompassing system of meaning. Yet no other Hasidic sect engages in the study of its own canon the way that Chabad and Bratslav do. Recall the sardonic comment attributed to Rabbi Elazar Menachem Shach, leader of the Lithuanian Haredi community, to the effect that "Chabad is the sect closest to Judaism." Given that Chabad has its own "Temple" at 770, scripture (first and foremost *Tanya*), ritual calendar (with days of observance connected to the lives of its seven leaders), symbols and emblems (images of the Rebbe and of 770, the crown of the Messiah, as well as its own straight-branched version of the Hanukah menorah and rectilinear image of the Tablets of the Covenant), melodies, and savior, the barb is more than just a joke. Yet the very distinct worlds of these two Hasidic sects are, in principle, open to all comers. The message of redemption that both movements preach is distinctly universal.

One price that both groups pay for being without a presiding *admor* is that they lack a unifying central authority, with the result that factionalism increases. Bratslav has been to a large extent divided throughout most of its existence, and it enjoys its current golden age divided into a large number of subgroups, some of which contend with each other. Chabad, which functioned as a centralized organization with an authoritative leadership, at least during the tenures of the last three *admorim*, had gradually transformed into a global federation of far-flung communities. The splits in Chabad raise the possibility that "Judaism's first [monastic] order" is undergoing a process of Bratslavization. The price would be high, but easier to pay, and might even have certain benefits, in the present era, as the center of gravity seems to be shifting from *admorim* and *tzadikim* to the Hasidim themselves. This tendency underlines the broad margins of autonomy and personal responsibility that the Hasidim enjoy. The Rebbe himself said that "every Jew in this generation, the final one of the exile and the first of the redemption, has been charged with a divine mission to prepare the ground for the redemption."[39] At one of his final convocations, he even said that every Hasid could attain the title of *admor*.[40] Elliot Wolfson argues that more than the Rebbe saw himself as the Messiah in the personal sense, he sought to bring about a collective messianic awakening among each and every one of his emissaries and all those he was connected with (and, in practice, every Jew). In this view, his aim was to rouse in each and every Jew the spark of the Messiah, creating an ambience that would pave the road to redemption.[41] According to Alon Dahan, the Rebbe's messianic teachings led to a "radical democratization of the highest rank—the *tzadik*."[42] A trend that has appeared in recent decades, in which Jews identify themselves as Hasidim in a general way without being affiliated to any particular court and without establishing a connection with a reigning *tzadik*, is part of the shift of the Hasidic center of gravity from the *tzadik* to the Hasidim. This certainly describes the way Chabad and Bratslav have become less binding categories of identity. Both of them gain from this openness as they reinforce it.

If there is any validity to the thesis connecting the messianic orientations of Chabad and Bratslav to their burgeoning popularity, it strengthens the argument that the messianic idea remains at the forefront of Jewish life and thinking today. The two central events that shaped Jewish history in the twentieth century—the Holocaust and the establishment of the state of Israel—can be conceptualized metahistorically as part of a messianic program, and have been presented as such by a number of religious groups.[43] The aura of the secular version of the pioneering-socialist Zionist vision of redemption during the prestate period, and the post-independence version of national rebirth, have dimmed considerably in recent years. The vacuum these have left is being filled by the national-religious hyper-Zionism of Gush Emunim and its heirs, as well as by the traditional practice of raising up admired messianic figures, among them the Rebbe and Rabbi Nachman. The optimistic hope for a future utopian messianic era that sustains Chabad and Bratslav is especially attractive given the grim scenarios of Israel's future broadcast by so many Israeli parties, pundits, and politicians.

Present-absent leadership is the factor that connects the messianic orientations of Chabad and Bratslav and the boom these two movements have enjoyed over the last few decades. The salient fact about them is that their leadership is virtual, granting it a presence that is adequate enough to provide a direction and spiritual milieu of meaning and purpose, and sufficiently absent to leave a wide degree of personal freedom. In a cultural-spiritual climate in which the pendulum is swinging away from the leadership and toward the Hasidim themselves, enabling individual initiative and marking out a space for autonomous action, the lack of a binding leadership can be an advantage. Every individual can receive inspiration and direction from the writings of Rabbi Nachman or find a response to his or her troubles in the Rebbe's letters in *Igrot Kodesh*. When the *admor* is absent, every Hasid can be an *admor*. The penchant for energetic activity and initiative displayed by individual Hasidim grows out of the work they do to make the Rebbe present and the vigorous imagination that this involves, from the "democratic" nature of the messianic project, and from the lack that creates autonomy and generates this "era of the Hasidim." The virtual nature of the *tzadik* in these two movements does not make him more distant or indistinct; the opposite is the case. A wide range of methods of making the *tzadik* present, among them sophisticated practices of manufacture, replication, and dissemination of representations and traces of the Rebbe and Rabbi Nachman— some of which modern technology has made available—help make the *tzadik* a living, close, accessible, and concrete presence for a large public. The model of absent-present leadership that these two Hasidic movements offer provides their members with inspiration and a framework to direct their lives, while at the same time encouraging the individual to take personal initiative. Offering relative freedom of thought and action, they turn out to be a recipe for success at this point in history.

CONCLUSION

The messianic tectonics of Chabad's recent generation, with its tremors powered by the need to sense the Rebbe close by, has carved channels into a landscape through which his presence can be felt. As interested as I am to understand Chabad messianism itself, I am no less concerned with what it can tell us more generally about religious experience and modes of action at large. As my book comes to an end, I want first to discuss how messianism offers an opportunity to investigate religious imagination. I will then turn to a number of issues connected to the messianic awakening itself.

The remarkable ambition of a fervid messianic movement lies in its replacement of history with the eternal redemption "immediately *mamash*." This messianism is rich with moments of reenchantment that give the world of believers experiences that are not a part of routine religious life. Chabad passionately seeks to transform the messianic idea from a potential into an actuality. But practices that aim to bridge the gap between the mundane and the sacred are an integral part of *every* religious system. The wide range of means that Chabad Meshichists use to experience their connection to their Rebbe can be seen in other faiths. Every religion, by definition, seeks to make seen the unseen;[1] the visual practices that allow Hasidim to "see the Rebbe" are simply particular means of achieving universal religious goals.

However, the Meshichist ecology may be more obvious in including a comprehensive and varied collection of mediating mechanisms because the Rebbe was once present, and no longer is present in the flesh. The explosion of modern technologies has also made these mediations particularly apparent. Thanks to the rapid development of print, communications, audiovisual, and digital technologies in recent decades, it has become easier to write to the Rebbe, to see him, and to sense him as proximate. Chabad's use of these new media greatly resembles the way that Evangelical Christians and fundamentalist Muslims use digital and contemporary media resources to reach congregants and possible converts.[2]

For believers, there are two important consequences to adopting such new technologies. The first is that, thanks to an all-encompassing system of religious meaning, they can coopt tools developed for the secular world into their own, and do so to the point that they are completely "theologized." For Chabad, the media revolution is part and parcel of its view of history and a sign of the approaching redemption ("Radio was created specifically for the Messiah"). Second, today's believers may have an epistemological advantage over their predecessors: these new media—film, in particular—provide direct, immediate sensory access to invisible entities that earlier believers did not have. Chabad's visual turn is thus reminiscent of the transition from sacred text to religious film among Christian Evangelicals in various places around the world.[3] Among many American Protestants this visual turn has remained subdued, although there are now Bible museums and as-if amusement parks that submerge the believer in a biblical world. Neither have Islamic communities taken a visual turn. Yet the testimony of the eye, fostered by photographs and film footage, may be more powerful than mere words in creating a convincing, persuasive experience that directly validates the metaphysical. Even though the Jewish prohibition against graven images has eroded over the years, it is hard to exaggerate the revolutionary significance of Chabad's visual culture. The cult of the Rebbe among Meshichists is an iconophilic phenomenon of unprecedented extent in Judaism.

In the subjective world of believers, mediating mechanisms themselves tend to dissipate and disappear thanks to what the mediation model calls "transparent immediacy." Believers experience the Rebbe directly and do not perceive the media that bears his image as standing between the Rebbe and themselves. The ethnographic writing of the anthropologist is a similar kind of mediator; he or she can also vanish from the reader's consciousness. I will not rehearse methodological issues again here, but it would seem that the huge number of signs left by the Rebbe in the world—the texts, traces, and pictures, many of which can be reproduced indefinitely—offer investigators possibilities for research that are particularly productive. Beyond the fact that the Rebbe's signs, from pictures and films to dollars and *mikveh* water, can be subsumed under what might be called material religion,[4] and are open to precise public inspection over a long period of time, spiritual experiences, such as visions of the Rebbe, which are manifestly private and subjective events, are written down, printed, reproduced, and disseminated through physical and virtual Meshichist communications channels. The minute that the miracles become miracle stories, that they are put into writing and widely disseminated, internal experiences of a mystical nature receive a material and concrete representation in text. In contrast, when traces of the Rebbe are presented virtually on the internet, it is easy and perhaps even crucial for believers to grant them a spiritual dimension, thereby annexing them to older metaphysical traditions. I describe the Meshichist social milieu as a "messianic ecology" in order to stress the fact that the plethora of the Rebbe's footprints constitute a varied, though structured and distinct, matrix in which it is relatively easy for him to be made present.

The signs of the Rebbe's presence, continuous and abundant, are thus available to the scholar who seeks to illuminate mystical or ecstatic experiences that derive from believers' inner worlds. I have chronicled the central role played by photographs of the Rebbe in the broad spectrum of subjective visual experiences. From the perspective of cognitive psychology, it is hardly a novel idea that photographs of the Rebbe will be internalized as mental schemes made up of vivid visual images. But the ecology is so saturated with such images, and the available reports of Hasidim on the role these images play in their experience are so detailed, that it is possible to follow this process minutely and with relative precision as it moves from "outside to inside." The extent to which the perceptual fields of Chabad Hasidim are shaped by this dense messianic ecology points to the powerful role culture plays in shaping fundamental cognitive processes, offering further confirmation of Clifford Geertz's classic claim about the public nature of culture as a whole, and of religion in particular.[5]

What can be learned about the characteristics of this messianism itself? My book shows how far the glorification of a revered *tzadik* can go when he is raised to the status of Messiah. Even if the sum of all the practices and beliefs of Chabad's radicals does not add up to a distinct Meshichist religion, there can be no doubt that it grants the Rebbe an exceptional and apparently unprecedented status in the Jewish Hasidic world. As presented in the chapters on the cosmological aspects of Meshichist Chabad, this status can be summed up by two diametrically opposed attitudes toward the Rebbe.

On the one hand, recognizing the Rebbe as the Messiah results in exalting and elevating him to a level unknown in the rabbinical world. For Meshichists, the Rebbe runs the world and shapes its history. The leaders of the earth's great powers and the forces of nature must bend to his will as the Final Redeemer. Among some Chabad Hasidim, this glorification of the Rebbe reaches the point of deification, stated with different levels of explicitness. The Elokists have no compunctions about terming him "Our Lord, Teacher, and Creator." They are but a tiny fraction of Chabad, but divinizing epithets such as "the essence of God's being in bodily form" are also used by central figures in the Meshichist movement. Chabad's visual culture displays evidence of the Rebbe's deification when his visage appears on the eastern wall of a synagogue, the wall worshippers face during prayer, or when a Meshichist publication depicts him looking down from heaven on a panoramic landscape. Visual elements emerging from the inner worlds of believers in special states of consciousness also testify to a fantasy or wish to see the Rebbe as divine. And as we saw, there are apparitions and dreams in which the Rebbe appears as a figure who grants a child to a childless woman in a manner reminiscent of the creation story.

On the other hand, despite his exalted status, the Rebbe is accessible and available for his Hasidim at every moment, much more so than he was during his tenure as *admor*. If we accept the claim that, in the eyes of his believers, the Rebbe's traces in the world are not mere representations but rather actual, if partial, embodiments, it is easy to see how the messianic ecology provides a plethora of opportunities for sensing his presence. Average Hasidim, and even people not affiliated with Chabad, may write to him (via *Igrot Kodesh*), petition him (by means of his photographs), and benefit from his benevolent intervention (through a dollar he has blessed or water from his *mikveh*). All this can be done directly, anywhere and anytime. Anthropologist Tanya Luhrmann shows that one explanation for the powerful appeal of the new Evangelical communities that have sprung up like mushrooms in the United States and elsewhere, outside the mainstream Protestant churches, is that they enable their members to speak to Jesus as a close friend, someone they can turn to for help in solving any problem they encounter in their daily lives, large or small.[6]

A similar process seems to be taking place in Chabad. The pocket version of *Igrot Kodesh* facilitates communication with the Rebbe at any moment. His acolytes can keep him close by carrying his image in their wallets and cell phones or by hanging it on the walls of their home. Hasidim who never met the Rebbe during their lifetimes are thus intimate with him in virtual form. Interaction between the two parties is not, of course, symmetrical, but it is mutual. The person who addresses the Rebbe through *Igrot Kodesh* receives an instantaneous reply; the follower who contemplates a photograph meets the Rebbe's gaze. Even during emotional moments when the Rebbe appears before a person who is awake, the encounter takes place at eye level. He may have divine status, but the Rebbe appears here on earth, among his Hasidim.

This close connection between the Rebbe and his believers is also evidenced by the broad range of the petitions he receives. The Rebbe, who is said to have used his divine powers to dismantle the Soviet Union, open its gates to Jewish emigration, mitigate the global arms race, and divert Hurricane Andrew from its path, attends to the most mundane problems of those who appeal to him. He can help a petitioner win a basketball game or pass a driving test. And his status as the King Messiah is universal—he responds to the pleas of Jews who are not Chabad Hasidim and to non-Jews as well. He is a decentralized messiah, one who acts in accordance with a democratic ethos: anyone can address him and nothing human is foreign to him. The belief that the Rebbe is active and accessible on all subjects, from the sublime to the profane, from the universal to the local, reflects his centrality in his believers' world and minds. After all, the Messiah soars beyond the boundaries of time and space.[7]

The aura surrounding the Rebbe King Messiah galvanizes his Hasidim. Chabad's recent history demonstrates just how rousing and compelling the attempt to actualize the messianic idea in the here and now can be. The faith and determination of the Meshichists is fed by the tremendous energy produced by the "hot" version of the messianic concept. They are confident that the world stands on the verge of ultimate redemption and that they, the emissaries-heirs-spiritual descendants of the Rebbe Messiah, are delegated to bring it about. This grants them a vocation, fills them with pride, and reinforces their sense of election and duty. In their view, the Rebbe's occlusion is a final test that they alone are successfully passing. Chabad in the wake of the Event of Gimel Tammuz is a good example of how believers cope with what seems ostensibly to be the disappointment of messianic expectations. Its ways of making the Rebbe present not only enable them to allay that disappointment but even to turn it into an engine of expansion and renewal. This flourishing emissary project, which has transformed Chabad into a global movement and allowed them to plant Judaism's flag in far-flung places, may be the most important means, in all of Chabad's wings, of maintaining a sense of mission and meaning since the Rebbe's 1994 occlusion.

One useful way of articulating the experiential orbit of boundless determination and commitment to the cause that the Meshichists display is Kevin Lewis O'Neill's concept of "messianic citizenship."[8] It is not incidental that *Citizens in the Messiah's Country* is the name of one the Meschichists' popular journals. The Meshichists' sense of moral responsibility with respect to the Jewish collectivity is genuine and deep, and it encompasses acts of citizenship that stretch far beyond the religious realm. Chabad Houses outside of Israel attract Jewish and Israeli visitors with a wide variety of civil concerns and life problems, and, in many respects, Chabad emissaries respond to these concerns and perform "consular functions" as if they were formal representatives of the state of Israel. Much like the mega-churches O'Neill describes, they engage in "transnational governmentability," expanding their involvement to areas where the state is barely present due to diminishing public resources and growing privatization. The array of problems the emissaries cope with span the mundane and the heroic; they go from providing information about insurance rates for rented vehicles to rescuing trapped vacationers following an earthquake or tsunami. And the military language Chabadniks employ in their outreach campaigns and other acts of duty resonates with the ethos of cognitive militarism that colors Israelis' sense of citizenship in a particular way.[9]

The famous explanation for the resilience of messianic movements in the face of disappointment emerged in the classic work by Leon Festinger, Henry Riecken, and Stanley Schacter, *When Prophecy Fails*,[10] and similar works. Festinger and his associates studied a small religious group in Chicago whose leader claimed to have received a message from another planet that the world would come to an end in a flood on December 21, 1954. Her followers had left their jobs, colleges, and spouses, and gave their money and possessions away in preparation for their departure on a flying saucer just prior to the catastrophe. Given this enormous investment, the researchers predicted that the refutation of the prophecy would be followed by enhanced commitment to the group and enthusiastic effort at proselytizing to seek social support. These responses, it was hypothesized, would reduce the state of mental discomfort—what Festinger termed *cognitive dissonance*—which was instigated by the refutation. The behavior of the believers after the critical date confirmed the researchers' hypothesis.

Given the way this explanation dominates the literature, it is hardly surprising that it has been used to account for the developments in Chabad at the turn of the last century.[11] I want to suggest that there is more to say. The Festinger approach suggests that there is a universal human drive to avoid the tension that cognitive contradictions and discrepancies cause. People confronted with such tension will invest in a return to cognitive equilibrium. In the case of a religious movement whose messianic expectations have not come to pass, believers will reduce dissonance by clinging more ardently to their faith, by disregarding facts that contradict it or by rationalizing it, and by committing all the more to their messianic calling.

On the face of it, the explanatory model of cognitive dissonance seems to fit Chabad, especially given that, since 1994, Chabad Hasidim, and Meshichists in particular, have displayed key responses to an unfulfilled prophecy that Festinger and his coauthors identified: enhanced commitment to the group and energetic enlistment of new members. But I want to suggest that the Festinger approach invites us to emphasize belief as central to religious action, as if the person who experiences dissonance simply tweaks a proposition. I would draw attention to the religious movements' elaborate cosmologies, inner logics, and broad systems of belief and conceptualization, all of which work to contain dissonance.[12] From the social constructionist perspective that I embrace, the social world of believers is always mediated by a rich collection of practices, principles, and claims that produce a near-total reality in which prophecy may become unfalsifiable. Chabad's theological and mystical doctrine, with its a-cosmic and panentheistic aspects, is fertile soil for the faith in the Rebbe's messianic vocation, and it provides ways to discount the inconvenient aspects of sensory experience that can be deemed deceptive. The messianic ecology establishes an epistemology that makes it possible to disregard contradictions and tensions or even embrace them as a religious ideal, thereby making it possible to live with dissonance indefinitely.[13]

I should emphasize that the ethnographic and textual analyses that this book offers are not meant to contradict the predictions of cognitive dissonance theory. Rather, I enrich that theory, endowing it with greater complexity through a conceptual system sensitive to the messianic ecology and in keeping with Meshichist discourse. This augmentation and enrichment also address the dichotomous, nondynamic element of the presumed mechanism of reducing dissonance. Life with a present-absent Rebbe is not achieved by a balancing cognitive reversal that is accomplished in one fell swoop. It requires constant maintenance. The ongoing success of turning the absent Rebbe into a presence thus takes on a variety of guises and produces unexpected results.

The Rebbe's prominence and availability has actually increased since he became a virtual messiah, and the dyadic connection between him and the individual Hasid has remained vital. Nevertheless, in recent years, with the loss of an authoritative leader who controlled every aspect of the movement, Chabad's social cohesion seems to have cracked. So has its rigid organizational structure. The breach between mainstream and Meshichist Hasidim will not easily be healed, even if it has not yet led to an actual split in the movement. The antinomian currents, even if currently restricted to the fringe of the Meshichist camp, are likely to enlarge the cracks because they are rooted in the logic of a messianic age and the "new Torah." Even the emissary operation, Chabad's most unifying institution, is actually two separate projects, one run by the mainstream and the other by the Meshichists. Given our lack of historical perspective, it would not be wise at this point for us to speculate on what changes lie in store for Chabad, but the phenomena I have documented in this book are certain to bring about change. That the virtual Rebbe is accessible "more than ever," to every one of his believers, is in keeping with his intention of instilling a collective messianic consciousness, but it also erodes Chabad's hierarchal authority structure, catalyzing autonomization, decentralization, and democratization of the movement. Already today, Chabad looks less like a religious order and more like a global federation that unites (albeit with impressive success) far-flung institutions, factions, and communities.[14]

The face of Chabad has changed, then, even if the practices and beliefs I have described do not constitute a "messianic religion" or new religious movement. Revolutionary change already began in the last century with the Rebbe's accession to leadership. Reconstructed in a manifestly American way as a transnational organization with a messianic mission, the movement now carries the banner of Judaism and markets its contents and values around the world. Its boundary-breaking has endowed the Rebbe's emissaries with a special neo-Hasidic identity that does not fit accepted religious categories. In this century, such changes, which accelerated after the Rebbe's apotheosis as a virtual messiah, will doubtless continue to accumulate thanks to the fertile soil of religious imagination and the innovative mediating technologies that render the absent Rebbe present in the life of all who seek him.

NOTES

Preface
1. *Admor* is a Hebrew acronym for "our master, teacher, and rabbi."
2. A Hasidic community without a reigning *tzadik* is rare but not unprecedented. The Bratslaver Hasidim have been in that situation for more than two hundred years since the death of the sect's founder, Rabbi Nachman of Bratslav, in 1810 (see Chapter 13).

Introduction
1. Marcus 1996, 2001.
2. Amir-Moezzi 2011; Sachedina 1981.
3. Scholem 1973.
4. Beit Halahmi 2001, p. 317.
5. Meyer 2014.
6. Ariel-Yoel et al. 2001; Ravitzky 1993.
7. The fear of the implications of the messianic idea for the Zionist movement and the state of Israel was clearly voiced by Gershom Scholem, the great scholar of Jewish mysticism: "Will or will it not be in the capacity of Jewish history to face this entry into concrete reality without destroying itself with the messianic demand that has been brought up from its depths? That is the question that a Jew of our generation poses for the present and the future, out of his great past, so full of dangers" (Scholem 1982: 262).
8. Aran 2013.
9. Outbursts of messianic fervor took place among Yemen's Jews in the second half of the nineteenth century, but they had little resonance outside that community (Eraqi Klorman 1993).
10. Scholem 1943, p. 129.
11. Sharot 1982.
12. Berger 2001; Heilman and Friedman 2010, p. 236; Schwartz 2011, pp. 386–399.
13. On Chabad's success on the world stage, see Biale et al. 2018, pp. 694–700.

14. On Chabad's classic era, see Elior 1993; Etkes 2014; Goldberg 2009; Halamish 1994; Loewenthal 1990; Schatz Uffenheimer 1968; Schwartz 2011. On the Rebbe's messianic teachings, see Dahan 2014b; Wolfson 2009.

15. Engelke 2010.

16. Meyer 2006, 2014; Meyer and Moors 2006; Stolow 2005. Moshe Idel has led a similar paradigmatic change in the study of Jewish mysticism, see Idel 1988, 2005a.

17. De Vries and Weber 2001.

18. De Vries and Weber 2001; Meyer 2005.

19. Derrida 2001; Derrida and Vattimo 1998.

20. Bolter and Grusin 1999.

21. Bolter and Grusin do not use the term *remediation*, as others have, in the sense of improving on or remedying prior technologies, but rather in the sense of re-mediation. They offer a few examples of remediation: as a medium, writing depends on speech, and the print medium depends on the written word; video and online media are based on the previous media of television and telephone.

22. Meyer 2005, p. 161.

23. According to this logic, similar to that of the simulacrum of Jean Baudrillard, there is no reality beyond the representations that constitute it, see Meyer 2005, p. 161.

24. Because of the centrality of sensory pathways in the mediation that produces the transcendental experience, Meyer refers to religious means of mediation as "sensational forms," see Meyer 2014.

25. For a critique of these approaches, see Casanova 1994; Castells 1996, 1997, 1998.

26. *Sichat Hage'ulah* 205, July 10, 1998, p. 1. All the quotations that follow are from this source.

27. Elior 1993.

28. Dan 1999, p. 196.

29. Kaplan 2006, p. 451.

30. *Sichat Hage'ulah* 1, July 8, 1994, p. 1.

31. *Beis Moshiach* 725, 22 Tevet 5770 (2010), p. 35.

32. Kantor 2013.

33. For these scholars' work on Chabad, see Dahan 2006; Dahan 2008a; Dahan 2010, 2014a; Gotlieb 2009; Halamish 1988; Kraus 2007; Schwartz 2011.

34. Kantor 2013, p. 59.

35. Bilu 2000.

36. *Beis Moshiach* 811, 28 Heshvan 5772 (2012). At the beginning of the article I described the encounters with Chabad emissaries that I related at the beginning of this book. One of the editors promised me that my piece would be printed in the form I submitted it, with the exception of one thing: he asked permission to cut the trekkers' response ("God exists!") to the emissary in the Peruvian city of Cusco following his promise to screen the final game of the Copa América soccer championship. I agreed.

37. Bilu 2000, p. 153; Marcus and Fisher 1986; Rosaldo 1989.

38. *Sichat Hage'ulah* 797, May 14, 2010, p. 4; *Sichat Hage'ulah* 884, Feb. 3, 2012, p. 4.

39. *Sichat Hage'ulah* 884, Feb. 3, 2012, p. 4.

40. Bilu 2013.

41. De Vries 2001; Singleton 2001.

42. Derrida, who takes miracle stories to be a genre of "testimony," blurs the distinction between a miracle and the account of one.

> Any testimony testifies in essence to the miraculous and the extraordinary from the moment it must, by definition, appeal to an act of faith beyond any proof. When one testifies, even on the subject of the most ordinary and the most "normal" event, one asks the other to believe one at one's word as if it were a matter of a miracle. Where it shares its condition with literary fiction, testimoniality belongs a priori to the order of the miraculous. . . . The miracle is the essential line of union between testimony and fiction. (quoted in De Vries and Weber 2001, p. 574, note 61).

43. Kravel-Tovi and Bilu 2008.

44. Beit-Hallahmi 2002; Katz and Popkin 1999; Robbins and Palmer 1997; Stone 2000.

45. Ravitzky 1993.

Chapter 1

1. Elior 1993, p. 12.
2. Dan 1999, pp. 118–177.
3. Idel 1992, pp. 84–89.
4. Green 1977; Poll 1995; Sharot 1982.
5. Dan 1999, pp. 150–177; Lenowitz 1998; Sagiv 2014. "The messianic idea, when it appears as a vital force in the Jewish world . . . is always closely linked to the apocalyptical" (Scholem 1975, p. 158), and thus to the end of history. While Judaism also offers a naturalistic model of messianism, Dov Schwartz shows that messianic naturalism, of which Maimonides is the classic champion, "came into being together with the need to suppress the messianic issue and prevent fruitless discussion of the subject" (Schwartz 1997, p. 246).
6. Etkes 2014; Rosman 1996.
7. Etkes 2014, p. 2.
8. Schatz Uffenheimer 1968; Scholem 1961.
9. Elior 1993; Ravitzky 1991.
10. Dan 1999, p. 200.
11. Schwartz 2011; Wolfson 2009. According to this approach, God and the human are reciprocally connected, constituting each other, such that God is in the world and the world in God (Culp 2009).
12. Joseph Weiss, Rivka Schatz Uffenheimer, and Rachel Elior are among those who attribute an a-cosmic view to Rabbi Schneur Zalman. Isaiah Tishbi,

Joseph Dan, Moshe Halamish, and Yoram Jacobson think otherwise (Etkes 2012, pp. 210–213). Wolfson refers to the paradox of integrating ostensibly contradictory orientations as "acosmic naturalism" and "apophatic panentheism" (Wolfson 2009, pp. 87–103).

13. Dan 1999, p. 190.
14. Etkes 2014, pp. 124–131; Pedaya 2011; Loewenthal 1990.
15. Loewenthal 1994, p. 382.
16. Friedman 2001.
17. Elior 1998; Friedman 2001; Heilman and Friedman 2010, p. 34, Rigg 2004.
18. Dahan 2008b; Heilman and Freidman 2010, pp. 29–58.
19. Rabbi Menachem Mendel regularly and frequently visited Rabbi Yosef Yitzchak's grave at the Old Montefiore Cemetery in Queens, and the time he spent praying and communing alone there with his predecessor lengthened by the year. It was there, on March 2, 1992, that the Rebbe suffered the stroke from which he never recovered (Heilman and Friedman 2010, pp. 237–239).
20. Fishkoff 1994; Friedman 2001; Heilman and Friedman 2010; Kraus 2007, pp. 92–131; Ravitzky 1993, 1999.
21. On Chabad's messianic fervor and its sources under Rabbi Menachem Mendel's leadership, see Elior 1998; Erlich 2000, 2004; Friedman 2001; Heilman and Friedman 2010, pp. 130–247; Kraus 2007; Ravitzky 1991, 1993, pp. 249–276; Shaffir 1993, 1994, 1995.
22. *Dvar Malkhut*, Vayera, 17 Marheshvan 1992.
23. Heilman and Friedman 2010, pp. 197–247; Yanover and Ish-Shalom 1994.
24. Dan 1999, p. 95. According to a more complex version of this tradition, the Rebbe's own tenure could be counted as the tenth and final term, parallel to the tenth and last of the *sefirot*, Malchut, which embodies the redemption (Dahan 2008a).
25. Dan 1999, pp. 194–196; Dahan 2008a; Gottleib 2009. In one of his last homilies, the Rebbe said: "God willing, the principal thing is that the true and complete redemption will come in practice *mamash* immediately *mamash*. . . . And [with] all the interpretations of *mamash*, and first of all in its simple meaning, *mamash*, *mamash*, *mamash*." It is hard to believe that he was not speaking of the way his followers interpreted the word *mamash*, either as representing the initials of his name, "Menachem Mendel Schneerson," or the initials of the phrase "Menachem is the Messiah's name." Alon Dahan (2008a) offers other persuasive indications that the Rebbe felt himself to be the Messiah, at least in the final years of his life. So too does Jacob Gotlieb (2009, pp. 173–203). Dahan (2008a) and Dan (1999) also suggest that the fact that the Rebbe was childless, a status tailor-made for the role of Messiah, was not the result of a biological problem but was rather mystically intended. This seems like a step too far to me, given that in his younger years Rabbi Menachem Mendel aspired to be an engineer, not a Hasidic

tzadik. More likely, the causal relationship was the reverse—the lack of children reinforced the older Rebbe's self-identification as the Messiah.

26. Dahan 2006, pp. 384–389; Heilman and Friedman 2010, pp. 230–235; Kraus 2007, pp. 86–91. During this talk the Rebbe expressed disappointment at the fact that his Hasidim were working to hasten the redemption because they were compelled to do so by his authority, "whereas if they were to . . . call out in truth the Messiah would certainly have come already!" This was the only time in any of his meetings with his followers that the Rebbe revealed any sense of desperation and personal failure. His conclusion, as he passes the torch of redemption from himself to his followers, reverberates even now: "I did my part, from here on out you must do everything in your power" (Dahan 2006, pp. 386–387; Heilman and Friedman 2010, pp. 231–232).

27. Dein 2011; Festinger, Riecken, and Schachter 1956; Stone 2000.

28. Leon Festinger's theory of cognitive dissonance (Festinger, Riecken, and Schachter 1956) was a central source of inspiration in the study of Chabad's messianic expectations (see Dein 2011; Dein and Dawson 2008; Shaffir 1993, 1994, 1995).

29. Yitzhak Kraus offers two measures of Chabad's growth following the Rebbe's death: the notable expansion in the number of emissaries around the world, and the multiplication of books published by Chabad concerning the Rebbe's teachings and person (Kraus 2007, p. 16). The Israeli news website Ynet, in an article ("The Rebbe Is Gone, Chabad Is Alive and Kicking" posted on July 7, 2008), offers further data. In 1994, when the Rebbe died, it reports, there were between six hundred and seven hundred emissaries around the world. In contrast, a convention of emissaries held in 2007 had 3,500 participants. This number does not include emissaries from the radical Meshichist groups, which have their own organization. *Ha'aretz* reported on Nov. 8, 2010, that the number of emissaries had risen to four thousand. See also Shandler 2009, pp. 255–256.

30. Friedman 2001, p. 175.

Chapter 2

1. Berger 2001, pp. 33, 41–61; Dahan 2014a.
2. Friedman 2001, pp. 174–229.
3. Kraus 2007, pp. 62–63, 71–73, 151–153, 206–223.
4. On the use of military images among students at Haredi yeshivot, see Stadler 2007.
5. Harari 2013, p. 179.
6. Compare: Gotlieb 2009, pp. 203–273.
7. Elbaz 2009.
8. There are four "battalions": Kaba (Kabalat ha'Ol, accepting the yoke of the commandments), Shemesh (Shelihut shel Mitzvot, the calling of the commandments), Matan (Mesirut Nefesh, willingness to give one's life for God), and Ahal (Ahvat Lohamim, the brotherhood of warriors).
9. Twelve verses from the Bible and the Sages that the Rebbe declared all Jewish children should know by heart.

10. The Meshichist slogan, meaning "Long live our lord, teacher, and rabbi, the King Messiah, forever and ever."

11. *Sichat Hage'ulah* 705, July 4, 2008, p. 4.

12. Elbaz 2009.

13. *Sichat Hage'ulah* 91, April 19, 1996, p. 1.

14. Tzarfati 1998, p. 20.

15. *Sichat Hage'ulah* 923, Nov. 23, 2012, p. 1.

16. Meshichists reorder the Hebrew letters of "Olga" to read *ge'ulah*, redemption; Goa in India, where a Chabad emissary teaches Torah, receives the same name by the addition of one letter.

17. Reinitz 2001.

18. Scholem 1973, p. 485.

19. Szubin 2000.

20. Baumgarten 2012, p. 171.

21. The huge number of children given the Rebbe's name, Menachem Mendel, recalls the same phenomenon among Shabbetai Zvi's followers, many of whom gave their messiah's name to one of their children (Scholem 1973, p. 479).

22. Dahan 2014b; Wolfson 2009.

Chapter 3

1. One-on-one *yehidut* was replaced by the oxymoronic "general *yehidut*," group audiences, and by fleeting face-to-face encounters on Sundays, when the Rebbe handed out dollar bills for his followers to donate to charity.

2. Thompson 1966; Trachtenberg 1970. Divination by means of books appears in a variety of contexts in Stith Thompson's index of folklore motifs, see Thompson 1966, M302.8, D1811.2.1, D1311.14. The ancient Greeks used Homer's *Iliad* in this way, the Romans the *Aeneid*, the Chinese the *I Ching*, and Christians the New Testament.

3. Reinitz 2001.

4. *Sichat Hage'ulah* 60, Sept. 8, 1995, p. 3.

5. *Beis Moshiach* 274, 11 Nissan 5760 (2000), pp. 48–50.

6. *Chabadinfo.com*, May 10, 2008.

7. In this paradigmatic story, the text used was not *Igrot Kodesh* but rather a collection of the Rebbe's talks, *Sichot Kodesh*. During the period that followed his withdrawal, a number of books containing texts of the Rebbe's had been used for this purpose if *Igrot Kodesh* was not available.

8. *Sichat Hage'ulah* 22, Dec. 9, 1994, p. 3.

9. Compare: Hirsch 2014.

10. *Sichat Hage'ulah* 23, Dec. 16, 1994, p. 3.

11. "'*Tracht gut vet zein gut.*' This is not psychological advice but rather a *practical teaching* by which it is possible to affect processes and developments" (*Sichat Hage'ulah* 71, Dec. 1, 1995, p. 1, emphasis in the original).

12. *Sichat Hage'ulah* 26, Jan. 6, 1995, p. 3.

13. Elior 1993; Schwartz 2011; Wolfson 2009.

14. Here are three examples of the ostensibly paradoxical connection between the material and the spiritual in Chabad teaching. The spiritual meaning of cancer is "the strengthening of the shell (*klipah*) of Amalek, insolence and existence without reason and the nonobservance of the love of Israel, and the remedy for it is the study of Hasidism and the love of Israel" (*Sichat Hage'ulah* 45, May 26, 1995, p. 3). Back problems are caused by "the burden of the long exile we have undergone," and reflexology treatment, which "by means of pressing on different points on the heel ends pain in the upper body, is connected to the fact that our generation is 'the heel of the Messiah,' that which will bring about the revelation of the head of the Children of Israel—the Rebbe . . . the King Messiah" (*Sichat Hage'ulah* 273, Nov. 26, 1999, p. 4). Finally, "Charity helps that there be a good heart," and thus, after a man who needed a bypass operation contributed to charity, medical tests showed that his problems had vanished (*Sichat Hage'ulah* 110, Aug. 29, 1996, p. 3).

15. Dein 1992; Dow 1986; Frank 1974; Lévi-Strauss 1967.

16. *Sichat Hage'ulah* 224, Dec. 4, 1998, p. 3.

17. *Sichat Hage'ulah* 433, Feb. 2, 2003, p. 3.

18. *Sichat Hage'ulah* 46, June 6, 1995, p. 3.

19. *Sichat Hage'ulah* 28, Jan. 20, 1995, p. 3.

20. *Sichat Hage'ulah* 32, Feb. 17, 1995, p. 1.

21. "Kotvim laMashiach beIgrot haKodesh veRo'im Nisim uNifla'ot" [no author, undated], p. 3.

22. *Sichat Hage'ulah* 34, March 3, 1995, p. 3 (emphasis in the original).

23. *Sichat Hage'ulah* 713, Aug. 29, 2008, p. 3.

24. *Sichat Hage'ulah* 195, May 1, 1998, p. 3.

25. Dobzhinsky 2001.

26. The book is a fascinating account of becoming religious following a painful loss that caused severe psychological distress. Frequent use of *Igrot Kodesh* provided the author with an intimate and ongoing relationship with the Rebbe, who served as a benevolent father-figure guiding her in every step in life. The Rebbe gave her a new name, Nechamah, from the same root as his own name and representing her turn from mourning to hope (Dobzhinsky 2001).

27. *Sichat Hage'ulah* 311, Sept. 1, 2000, p. 3 (emphasis in the original).

28. *Sichat Hage'ulah* 327, Dec. 29, 2000, p. 3.

29. *Sichat Hage'ulah* 578, Dec. 23, 2005, p. 3.

30. *Sichat Hage'ulah* 160, Aug. 15, 1997, p. 1.

31. *Sichat Hage'ulah* 902, June 15, 2012, p. 3. Rabbi Michael Karlburg is the director of the Festival Or organization, which seeks to bring the light of the redemption to New Age Festivals. Since "everything created by the Holy One Blessed Be He in his world was not created except to honor Him, . . . the goal of creating a festival is only that at this place the masses will be exposed to the light of Judaism."

32. On the burgeoning use of digital methods of revelation and prophecy, and their influence on religious imagination, see Ruah Midbar 2014.

33. *Sichat Hage'ulah* 569, Oct. 28, 2005, p. 1.
34. *Sichat Hage'ulah* 42, May 5, 1995, p. 3 (emphasis in the original).
35. *Sichat Hage'ulah* 385, Feb. 22, 2002, p. 3.
36. *Sichat Hage'ulah* 648, May 22, 2007, p. 3.
37. *Sichat Hage'ulah* 727, Dec. 9, 2008, p. 3.
38. *Sichat Hage'ulah* 808, July 30, 2010, p. 3.
39. *Sichat Hage'ulah* 134, Feb. 4, 1997, p. 3.
40. *Sichat Hage'ulah* 136, Feb. 28, 1997, p. 3.
41. *Sichat Hage'ulah* 813, Sept. 3, 2010, p. 3.
42. *Sichat Hage'ulah* 70, Nov. 24, 1995, p. 3 (emphasis in the original).
43. *Sichat Hage'ulah* 99, June 14, 1996, p. 3.
44. *Lifko'ach et ha'Einayim* 2007, pp. 142–143
45. Ibid., p. 97.
46. Ibid., pp. 140–141.
47. Note the parallel between the two types of communication—via cell phone between the boy and his mother and via *Igrot Kodesh* between the mother and the Rebbe. In the Meshichist world, rife with both wonders and technology, these two channels of communication have similar epistemological status. This event also exemplifies the iconic presence of the Rebbe, which may have abetted the revelation experience of the boy. At the beginning of the convocation the stadium was darkened and a film of one of the Rebbe's talks was shown on a huge screen.
48. Dein 2012.
49. "One aspect of the use of *Igrot Kodesh* is that more and more people conduct their daily lives under the Rebbe's guidance.... If in the past it was customary to ask a question 'from overseas' only in certain areas, with the reply coming only sometime later, the fact that it is now possible to receive an immediate answer via *Igrot Kodesh* brings about a positive change in the way we conduct our daily lives." (*Sichat Hage'ulah* 468, Oct. 17, 2003, p. 3).
50. *Sichat Hage'ulah* 223, Nov. 27, 1998, p. 3.
51. Prior to the Rebbe's departure, Rabbi Axelrod was an enthusiastic Meshichist. He numbered among the hundreds of rabbis who signed an official ruling identifying the Rebbe as the King Messiah and demanding that he reveal himself.
52. This text appeared on Chabad Online on Monday, 25 Iyar 5770 (1970).
53. *Zman Hage'ulah* 1, 29 Shevat 5771 (2011).
54. *Hashavua Shechalaf* 4, 27 Iyar 5751 (1991), p. 2 (emphasis in the original).
55. The letter was provided to me by Rabbi Yehoshua Mondshine (emphasis in the original).
56. *Sichat Hage'ulah* 489, March 12, 2004, p. 3.
57. *Sichat Hage'ulah* 639, March 16, 2007, p. 3.
58. See, for example, the website of Gila Buyum, http://www.oryada.com/eng.htm, a medium who works in the fields of numerology, astrology, Tarot cards,

and UFOs. She conducts "power clairvoyance evenings" with the Rebbe in cooperation with Rabbi Eliyahu Gabbai, a Chabad Hasid.

Chapter 4

1. Innis 2004, p. 201.
2. Balakirsky Katz 2010, pp. 144–173; Dein 2010, p. 89; Katz 2015; Weingrod 1993.
3. *Sichat Hage'ulah* 682, Jan. 25, 2012, p. 4.
4. Ehrlich 2004, pp. 63–64.
5. *Sichat Hage'ulah* 191, March 27, 1998, p. 4.
6. *Sichat Hage'ulah* 38, March 31, 1995, p. 4. Rabbi Danin draws his confidence that the Rebbe will visit his home from the Rebbe's promise that the "Messiah will tarry and visit every Jewish home."
7. Compare: Luhrmann 2004, 2012.
8. Fishhoff 2003; Heilman and Friedman 2010, pp. 248–278.
9. Berryman 2001, p. 603.
10. See, for example, Varner 2009; Weiss 2007. In contemporary Judaism, one notable example is the cult surrounding water blessed by the late Rabbi Israel Abuhatzeira, popularly known as the Baba Sali, which is believed to possess healing powers (Bilu and Ben-Ari 1992).
11. *Sichat Hage'ulah* 81, June 9, 1996, p. 3.
12. *Sichat Hage'ulah* 81, Feb. 9, 1996, p. 3.
13. *Sichat Hage'ulah* 82, Feb. 16, 1996, p. 3.
14. "R. Arieh began to go to the Kotel almost every day. From time to time he also went to visit the graves of saints. He received uncountable blessings, but the condition of the boy [who suffered from paralysis] worsened." Only a jar of "living water" sent from Jerusalem to Buenos Aires, where the boy lived, got him back on his feet (*Sichat Hage'ulah* 250, June 11, 1999, p. 3).
15. *Sichat Hage'ulah* 126, Dec. 20, 1996, p. 3.
16. Dow 1986; Frank 1974; Kleinman 1988; Turner 2004.
17. *Sichat Hage'ulah* 581, Jan. 20, 2006, p. 3.
18. *Sichat Hage'ulah* 873, Nov. 18, 2011, p. 3.
19. The dollars were inscribed with the legend: "Received from his Excellency the Lubavitcher *Admor shalita*" and the date on which they were distributed.
20. *Sichat Hage'ulah* 323, Dec. 1, 2000, p. 3.
21. *Sichat Hage'ulah* 312, Sept. 8, 2000, p. 3.
22. *Sichat Hage'ulah* 640, March 23, 2007, p. 3.
23. *Sichat Hage'ulah* 304, July 14, 2000, p. 3.
24. *Family Magazine*, Nov. 2011, p. 57.
25. *Sichat Hage'ulah* 811, Aug. 20, 2010, p. 3.
26. *Sichat Hage'ulah* 886, Feb. 17, 2012, p. 3.
27. These examples are taken from a notice, in my possession, published on 9 Shevat 5714 (2014), on the eve of the commemoration of Rabbi Yosef Yitzchak and the acceptance of the leadership of Chabad by the Rebbe, marked on 10–11

Shevat. The Hasid-innovator declared that the announcement was being made with the consent of the rabbi of Kfar Chabad.

28. *Sichat Hage'ulah* 608, Aug. 4, 2006, p. 3.
29. *Sichat Hage'ulah* 24, Dec. 23, 1994, p. 3.
30. *Sichat Hage'ulah* 80, Feb. 2, 1995, p. 3.
31. *Sichat Hage'ulah* 608, Aug. 4, 2006, p. 3.
32. *Sichat Hage'ulah* 193, April 10, 1998, p. 3.
33. *Sichat Hage'ulah* 732, Jan. 23, 2009, p. 1.
34. *Sichat Hage'ulah* 611, Aug. 25, 2006, p. 3.
35. The charity box that is generally included alongside *Chitat* is a protective device itself. The Rebbe proposed placing one on the walls of rooms in the home so that the walls "absorb" the precept of charity and become "reinforced." After Israel experienced a mild earthquake, the demand for charity boxes bearing the Rebbe's picture rose (*Sichat Hage'ulah* 71, Dec. 1, 1995, p. 1). There is also a portable model, "a small, beautifully designed, and compact plastic pouch, easy to carry in a shirt or coat pocket or IDF battle vest (the personal charity box is designed so that it does not jingle, making it appropriate for IDF operations)" (*Sichat Hage'ulah* 1032, Jan. 30, 2015, p. 4).
36. Kravel-Tovi and Bilu 2008, p. 69.
37. Dein 2010, pp. 87–100.
38. *Sichat Hage'ulah* 267, Oct. 15, 1999, p. 3.
39. Luhrmann 2011, 2012, pp. 230–232.
40. *Sichat Hage'ulah* 924, Nov. 30, 2012, p. 4.
41. Shandler 2009, p. 266.
42. Elbaz 2009.
43. The wedding was held at Kfar Chabad on Tuesday, Jan. 28, 2014.
44. In addition to the means of making the Rebbe present that are described here, some Meshichist brides hold a photograph of the Rebbe during the wedding ceremony. A guest in one such wedding commented: "The picture of the King Messiah was present everywhere. For example, in the hand of the bride, which she never relinquished. I wondered, of course, whether she would also enter her wedding bed with the King Messiah in her palm?" (Peled 2012, p. 126).

Chapter 5

1. Cohen 1998; Heilman 2004.
2. Balakirsky Katz 2007, 2010.
3. Balakirsky Katz 2007, p. 68.
4. Bloom 1992.
5. Dundes 1980; Meyert 1997.
6. *Kovetz Hitkashrut*, pp. 159–162.
7. Balakirsky Katz 2007, p. 72.
8. At the virtual store Chabad Shop, one can buy three-dimensional pictures of the Rebbe. Pictures of the Rebbe also play a central role on the Chabad.info website, where they appear under the heading "The King in His Splendor."

9. Morgan 1998, 2005; Plate 2002.
10. *Sichat Hage'ulah* 700, May 5, 2008, p. 4.
11. Isaiah 30:20.
12. Babylonian Talmud, Eruvin 13b.
13. Rapoport 2008, pp. 64–69.
14. Ibid., pp. 70–78. Rapoport stresses that the practice of contemplating the *tzadik* during prayer did not exist in Chabad and that the Rebbe even condemned it. His harsh execration of the practice indicates that it was quite widespread.
15. Wolpe 2002.
16. See Babylonian Talmud, Sotah 36b.
17. *Sichot Kodesh* 12, p. 266.
18. *Sichat Hage'ulah* 361, Aug. 31, 2001, p. 3.
19. It should be stressed, however, that two-way does not mean symmetrical when it comes to the mutual gaze of the Hasid and the Rebbe; the latter, categorically unlike the former, sees all that lies hidden in the soul of the Hasid who gazes at him.
20. *Sichat Hage'ulah* 26, Jan. 6, 1995, p. 4. All the quotes that follow are from this source.
21. On the claim in Christian visual culture to find hidden meanings in images of Jesus and Mary, see Morgan 1998, 2005.
22. *Sichat Hage'ulah* 31, Feb. 10, 1995, p. 1.
23. *Sichat Hage'ulah* 587, March 13, 2006, p. 1
24. Compare: Shandler 2009, pp. 235–236.
25. *Sichat Hage'ulah* 1032, Jan. 30, 2015, p. 4.
26. A cover image of the Rebbe does not necessarily mean that the book was published by a Meshichist group, but all books Meshichists publish include such an image.
27. Sasson 2000.
28. *Sichat Hage'ulah* 581, Jan. 20, 2006, p. 1.
29. *Sichat Hage'ulah* 503, June 18, 2004, p. 3 (my emphasis).
30. Compare: Dein 2010, pp. 91–92, 113–121.
31. *Sichat Hage'ulah* 1041, April 3, 2015, p. 3.
32. Shandler 2009, p. 252.
33. *Beis Moshiach* 683, 19 Shevat 5769 (2009), p. 47. Note that the Rebbe is described in present tense.
34. *Sichat Hage'ulah* 1025, Dec. 12, 2014, p. 1.
35. Shandler 2009, p. 268.
36. Comparing and contrasting Chabad's Messiah with messianic figures of previous generations, such as Jesus and Shabbetai Zvi, David Berger has noted that the Rebbe's followers, unlike those of these earlier figures, have the benefit of "the availability of a vast library of videotapes which can preserve a sense of the departed Messiah's physical presence" (Berger 2001, p. 29).
37. Shandler offers a description of this unsettling amalgamation: "Those

who watch this video can rise up from the profane life into another world, a spiritual world, and experience the numinous awakening in matters of divine worship and the holy illumination felt by those who participated in the *fabrengen* [convocation] itself" (Shandler 2009, p. 249).

38. Ibid., p. 266.

39. The uncanny revival of the past is the essence of the epistemological revolution brought on by photography, according to Roland Barthes (1981).

40. Morgan 1998.

41. *Sichat Hage'ulah* 859, Aug. 5, 2011, p. 3.

42. The conceptual framework proposed by W.J.T. Mitchell for looking at pictures at large illustrates the strong tension between representation and re-presentation. "The concept of image-as-organism is, of course, 'only' a metaphor, an analogy that must have some limits. The relevant questions, then, are what are the limits of this analogy? Where does it take us? What motivates its appearance? What do we mean by 'life' in the first place? Why does the link between images and living things seem so inevitable and necessary. . . . ?" (Mitchell 2005, pp. 10–11).

43. Babb 1981.

44. *Sichat Hage'ulah* 361, Aug. 31, 2001, p. 3 (my emphasis).

45. *Lifko'ah et ha'Einayim* 2007, p. 85.

46. *Sichat Hage'ulah* 402, June 28, 2002, p. 3.

47. *Sichat Hage'ulah* 402, June 28, 2002, p. 3.

48. *Sichat Hage'ulah* 470, Oct. 13, 2003, p. 3. Notably, the Rebbe was doubly present in this incident—in the picture that Mendy held and in Mendy's name itself; Mendy is a familiar form of the name Menachem Mendel, the Rebbe's name, which had been given to the boy.

49. *Sichat Hage'ulah* 732, Jan. 23, 2009, p. 1.

50. *Sichat Hage'ulah* 376, Dec. 21, 2001, p. 3.

51. *Sichat Hage'ulah* 393, April 26, 2002, p. 3.

52. *Sichat Hage'ulah* 905, July 6, 2012, p. 3.

53. *Sichat Hage'ulah* 596, May 13, 2006, p. 3.

54. *Sichat Hage'ulah* 600, June 9, 2006, p. 3.

55. *Sichat Hage'ulah* 476, Dec. 12, 2003, p. 3. The story is accompanied by the famous photograph, enhanced with a black circle around the Rebbe's hand, to aid readers in making out the baby's face. Meshichists have a variety of explanations of who the baby is, ranging from the Rebbe himself in his infancy to the possibility that it is a baby who was born to a childless woman thanks to his intervention.

56. *Sichat Hage'ulah* 596, May 13, 2006, p. 3.

57. *Sichat Hage'ulah* 587, March 3, 2006, p. 3.

58. Miracle stories on the preservation of pictures of the Rebbe were common during his lifetime as well. For example, during the Gulf War, in January 1991, an Iraqi rocket hit a gas station, shattering all its windows. A later account claimed that "only the picture of the King Messiah remained whole" (*Sichat*

Hage'ulah 762, Aug. 28, 2009, p. 4). Similar stories about the pictures of holy icons can be found in Christianity. The Black Madonna of Częstochowa, the national symbol of Catholic Poland, was unable to save its people from defeat and death in World War II, but stories of its own miraculous preservation and that of the Jasna Góra Monastery where it resided spread through the country (Niedzwiedz 2010, pp. 116–119).

59. *Sichat Hage'ulah* 494, April 16, 2004, p. 3.
60. *Sichat Hage'ulah* 711, Aug. 15, 2008, p. 3.
61. Mitchell 2005; compare: Appadurai 1986.
62. *Sichat Hage'ulah* 923, Nov. 23, 2012, p. 1.
63. *Sichat Hage'ulah* 924, Nov. 30, 2012, p. 1. The phenomenon of seeing the images of invisible personages on objects or in strange and unexpected materials extends beyond the religious and into the political world. At the end of October 2013, Venezuelan President Nicolás Maduro announced that the face of Hugo Chavez, Maduro's late predecessor, had been discovered etched into a stone unearthed during the excavation of a tunnel in Caracas (*Ha'aretz*, Nov. 7, 2013, p. 16).
64. This documentation appears in a unique genre, the diaries of Hasidim. Such accounts of the Rebbe's movements were widespread in Chabad prior to the Event of Gimel Tammuz, and Hasidim continue to write them today following visits to 770.
65. Rapoport 2008.
66. "Year in Review: Obituary," in *Encyclopedia Britannica Online* (1994).
67. Marcus 2001, p. 398, n. 77.
68. *Sichat Hage'ulah* 341, April 6, 2001, p. 4.
69. *Kit'ei Mekorot be'Inyanei Mashiach veGe'ulah*, Nisan 5757 (1997), p. 63.
70. *Sichat Hage'ulah* 383, Feb. 8, 2002, p. 3. The end of the story, in which the narrator thanks God "who enabled me through the Rebbe . . . to open my physical and spiritual eyes," underlines the connection between his flawed vision and the opening of his eyes as a condition for seeing the Rebbe. Only when everyone sees the Rebbe will the complete redemption occur.
71. *Sichat Hage'ulah* 380, Jan. 18, 2002, p. 3.
72. *Sichat Hage'ulah* 25, Dec. 30, 1994, p. 3.
73. *Sichat Hage'ulah* 90, April 12, 1996, p. 1.
74. *Sichat Hage'ulah* 115, Oct. 4, 1996, p. 3.
75. *Sichat Hage'ulah* 133, Feb. 7, 1997, p. 3.
76. *Sichat Hage'ulah* 162, Aug. 29, 1997, p. 4.
77. *Sichat Hage'ulah* 225, Dec. 11, 1998, p. 3.
78. Compare: Mirzoeff 1999; Mitchell 2005. Mirzoeff remarks that the visual event is not defined by the medium but rather by the interaction between the viewer and the viewed. Mitchell also stresses the visual bidirectionality between the viewer and the medium.
79. *Sichat Hage'ulah* 147, May 16, 1997, p. 3.
80. *Sichat Hage'ulah* 197, May 15, 1998, p. 3.

81. *Sichat Hage'ulah* 974, Dec. 6, 2013, p. 3.
82. Ibid.
83. *Sichat Hage'ulah* 630, Jan. 12, 2007, p. 3.
84. *Sichat Hage'ulah* 293, April 14, 2000, p. 3.
85. *Sichat Hage'ulah* 305, July 21, 2000, p. 3.
86. *Sichat Hage'ulah* 181, Jan. 16, 1998, p. 3.
87. *Sichat Hage'ulah* 379, Jan. 11, 2002, p. 3.
88. *Sichat Hage'ulah* 890, March 16, 2012, p. 3.
89. *Sichat Hage'ulah* 733, Jan. 30, 2009, p. 3.
90. *Sichat Hage'ulah* 573, Nov. 25, 2005, p. 3.
91. *Sichat Hage'ulah* 404, July 12, 2002, p. 3.
92. *Sichat Hage'ulah* 593, April 21, 2006, p. 3.
93. Schmidt 2000.
94. The Israelites' demand appears in *Mechilta deRabi Yishma'el*, Yitro 2. According to Rashi's commentary on the Torah, God's willingness to descend on the third day "in the sight of all the people, on Mount Sinai" (Exodus 19:11), which does not happen in the end, grows out of the people's refusal to accept only hearing the word of God through the voice of Moses as an intermediary.
95. Garb 2011; Wolfson 1994.
96. Idel 1995.
97. "Divrei Malchut," from talks on the Sabbath of the Exodus portion, 21 Tevet 1992, *Kovetz Shalshelet haOr*, Heichal 3, Part 3, p. 10 (my emphasis).
98. "Divrei Malchut," talks on the 'Ekev portion, 23 Menahem-Av, the Sabbath of the blessing of the month of Elul 5791 (1991), pp. 10–11.
99. Chabadinfo.com, 26 Adar 5772 (2012).

Chapter 6

1. Dodds 1951; Elior 2013; Grunbaum and Caillois 1966; O'Nell 1976; Tedlock 1987.
2. *Sichat Hage'ulah* 310, Aug. 25, p. 3.
3. The paralleling of mirror to picture can also be seen on a post that appeared on Chabad.org on June 16, 2013. In the question-and-answer section, a Chabad emissary is asked why Chabad Houses display the Rebbe's picture. He responds with a question of his own: "Do you have a mirror at home?" The inquirer replies that he has several mirrors, so that he can examine his appearance before he leaves home. The emissary explains that while a mirror helps us ensure that we look good in the present, contemplating the Rebbe's countenance is meant to ensure that we will look good in the future, as a result of the inspiration we derive from the picture.
4. *Beis Moshiach* 635, 2 Adar I 5768 (2008), p. 22.
5. *Sichat Hage'ulah* 803, June 25, 2010, p. 3.
6. An additional example of the epistemological problem and its solution by means of the objectification of the dream experience can be seen in another dream story, in which the dreamer awakened as the Rebbe offered him his pic-

ture, feeling troubled that he had been unable to bring the encounter to its completion. But his dejection turned to elation when he received a picture of the Rebbe the next day from a Chabad emissary (*Sichat Hage'ulah* 962, Sept. 4, 2013, p. 3). It could be argued that the frustration at having woken up prematurely underscores the general problem presented by any private revelation—even if the dreamer had woken only after receiving the picture from the Rebbe, the picture would not have remained in his hand once he was awake.

7. *Lifko'ach et ha'Einayim*, 2007, pp. 176–179.

8. Heilman 2001, 2004.

9. The light radiating from the Rebbe's face—for example, "his face shone with bright light" (*Beis Moshiach* 661, 5 Menachem-Av 5766 [2006], p. 18)—reinforces the analogy between him and the first redeemer, Moses; according to the Bible, when Moses descended from Mount Sinai with the Tablets of the Covenant, "his face was radiant."

10. *Peninei Hage'ulah* 46, Adar II 5957 (1997) (emphasis in the original).

11. *Sichat Hage'ulah* 398, May 31, 2002, p. 3.

12. *Sichat Hage'ulah* 642, April 13, 2007, p. 3.

13. *Beis Moshiach* 661, 5 Av 5768 (2008), p. 48.

14. Balakirsky Katz 2010, pp. 144–145.

15. *Beis Moshiach* 623, 6 Kislev 5768 (2008), pp. 26–27.

16. Anthropologists refer to dreams in which the Rebbe appears to a believer as "visitational dreams," see Bilu 2010; Crapanzano 1975.

17. *Sichat Hage'ulah* 741, March 27, 2009, p. 3.

18. Compare: Bilu 2010, pp. 139–166.

19. *Sichat Hage'ulah* 820, Oct. 29, 2010, p. 3.

20. *Sichat Hage'ulah* 970, Nov. 8, 2013, p. 3.

21. Visions and apparitions of various types are common in the Jewish mystical tradition (Garb 2011; Pedaya 2011; Wolfson 1994), but I here address the appearance, to people who are wide awake, of a figure whose death they deny. A closer analogue might be miraculous appearances, recorded in rabbinic and later works, of Elijah the Prophet, who ascended to heaven while still alive. There is an important difference, however—the Rebbe always appears as himself, whereas Elijah is a master of disguise, appearing in a wide variety of forms and avatars (Wiener 1978).

22. Tanya Luhrmann's comprehensive work on epiphanies among Evangelicals in the United States largely addresses experiences of hearing God's voice, reflecting the tendency of Protestants to have mystical experiences of an aural type (Luhrmann 2012). The visual modality dominates in apparitions of Jesus and the Virgin Mary among Catholics (Bynum 1987; Christian 1981, 1992, 1996; Newman 1985, 2005; Taves 2009; Wiebe 1997; Zimdars-Swartz 1989, 1991).

23. Christian 1981, 1996; Zimdars-Swartz 1991, p. 54.

24. Berryman 2001; Christian 1981, 1996; Zimdars-Swartz 1991.

25. Kravel-Tovi and Bilu 2008.

26. *Lifko'ach et ha'Einayim* 2007, p. 78.

27. The first such epiphanies reported only seeing the Rebbe. Testimonies about hearing the Rebbe's voice first appeared in 2003. In apparitions of the Virgin Mary reported in Spain during the twentieth century, Mary was first seen and only afterward heard (Christian 1996, p. 262).

28. Al-Issa 1996; Bourguignon 1970; Menezes and Moreira-Almeida 2010.

29. Boksa 2009; Luhrmann 2011; Sidgwick et al. 1894; Tien 1991.

30. Carlsson and Nilsson 2007; Grimby 1993.

31. I accept Tanya Luhrmann's suggestion to use the term *sensory overrides* to label such experiences, thus avoiding the clinical connotations of the term *hallucination*, see Luhrmann 2011, 2012, pp. 230–232.

32. Berryman 2001, p. 597.

33. Bentall 2000, 2003.

34. Kravel-Tovi and Bilu 2008, p. 74.

35. Barthes 1981, p. 80.

36. *Sichat Hage'ulah* 533, Feb. 4, 2005, p. 3 (my emphasis).

37. Berryman 2006; Bittel 2009; Davis and Boles 2003, pp. 381-382, 390; Matter 2001, p. 134; Wojcik 1996.

38. *Lifko'ach et ha'Einayim* 2007, pp. 170–176.

39. *Sichat Hage'ulah* 625, Dec. 8, 2006, p. 3.

40. Berryman 2001.

41. Kravel-Tovi and Bilu 2008. Kravel-Tovi has also described the emerging normative practice at 770 of seeing and sensing the Rebbe inside oneself, and the difficulties Hasidim face in doing so (Kravel-Tovi 2009).

42. *Lifko'ach et ha'Einayim* 2007, pp. 50–52.

43. Ibid., pp. 19–20.

44. Balakirsky Katz 2010, p. 152.

45. *Lifko'ach et ha'Einayim* 2007, pp. 170–172.

46. Ibid., p. 137.

47. Ibid., pp. 133–135. For apparitions of this type, see Geiger 2009.

48. Ibid., pp. 90–92.

49. Deleuze 2004, p. 260.

50. Bilu 1982, p. 275; Davis and Boles 2003, p. 386.

51. *Lifko'ach et ha'Einayim* 2007, pp. 39–41.

52. Compare: Davis and Boles 2003, pp. 394–398.

53. Compare: Bittel 2009; Christian 1996.

54. For example, the Rebbe appeared to a yeshiva student in Melbourne and promised him that his family's financial difficulties would soon end; he later discovered that at just this moment his parents were discussing how to cope with this problem, *Lifko'ach et ha'Einayim* 2007, pp. 109–110.

55. Handelman and Shamgar-Handelman 1997.

56. *Lifko'ach et ha'Einayim* 2007, p. 74.

57. Ibid., p. 97.

58. It is hard to see these Hasidim agreeing with Elliot Wolfson's claim that the Rebbe did not see himself as the Messiah but rather merely sought to instill

the Jewish people with a collective messianic consciousness, one in which existence and nonexistence, God and man, and the divine and mundane worlds are inseparably combined. But their ambivalence about apparitions of the Rebbe accords with Wolfson's critique of the Meshichists, who he says miss the point that "true vision consists of seeing the invisible in the visible, and not in seeing the nonvisible as visible." Wolfson, like some critics inside Chabad, maintains that "postmortem apparitions of the seventh Rebbe . . . are indicative of a profound spiritual blindness" (Wolfson 2009, p. 276).

59. Kravel-Tovi 2009.
60. *Sichat Hage'ulah* 206, July 17, 1998, p. 1.
61. *Lifko'ach et ha'Einayim* 2007, p. 3.
62. Ibid., p. 14.
63. Luhrmann 2012, p. 201.
64. The role played by expectations is tricky because "an apparition may be understood as the appearance within the physical environment to one or more individuals of a person they would not expect to be within the immediate perceptual range" (Zimdars-Swartz 1989, p. 125). Meshichists who visit 770 have to agree that the Rebbe is not in their "immediate perceptual range," but they still expect to see him. In this they resemble the pilgrims to the site sacred to Mary at Conyers, Georgia, who are told that "the rosary is at 12 and the Virgin Mary appears at 12:20" (Davis and Boles 2003, p. 385). These sorts of structured expectations are entirely absent from secular epiphanies.
65. Bynum 1987, pp. 53–56; Newman 2005.
66. Newman 2005, p. 16.
67. Ibid., p. 17.
68. Apparitions in life-threatening situations are reminiscent of the "third man factor," an uncanny sense of a mysterious presence who provides guidance and protection in difficult and dangerous physical conditions (Geiger 2009).
69. Taves 2009, p. 126 (emphasis in the original).
70. Newman 2005, p. 11.
71. San Juan 2008.
72. Newman 1985.
73. Newman 2005, p. 8.
74. Bitell 2009, p. 81.
75. Luhrmann 2012.
76. Ibid., p. 46.
77. Wiebe 1997, p. 142.
78. Price-Williams 1999.
79. Stephen 1989, pp. 41–44.
80. Luhrmann 2012, p. 83.
81. Stephen 1989, p. 56.
82. Chabad's realistic apparitions are reminiscent of reports of encounters with Elvis Presley in American popular culture (Doss 2005; Marcus 1991; Reece 2006). The comparison between Chabad and the "Presleyterian Church" might

seem forced, but it should be kept in mind that Chabad itself has been shaped in an American environment, which some scholars maintain is the most visually oriented culture in human history.

Chapter 7

1. Dan 1996.
2. *In the Eye of the Storm*, production: Community Ani Ma'amin, director: Yitzchak Ginsburgh, Brooklyn, New York (undated).
3. Another religious leader to divert a hurricane threatening the American south was the famous Evangelist Pat Robertson. In 1965 he repelled Hurricane Betsy from the shores of Virginia, and twenty years later, invoking Jesus, he redirected Hurricane Gloria (Katz and Popkin 1999, p. 236). I suspect that Chabad's story about repelling the hurricane that threatened Miami was influenced by the Christian story.
4. The account here is taken from *Sichat Hage'ulah* 261, Aug. 27, 1999, p. 3, and *Sichat Hage'ulah* 662, Aug. 31, 2007, p. 4.
5. *Sichat Hage'ulah* 892, March 30, 2012, p. 3.
6. *Sichat Hage'ulah* 924, Nov. 30, 2012, p. 3.
7. *Sichat Hage'ulah* 60, Sept. 8, 1995, p. 3 (emphasis in the original).
8. *Beis Moshiach* 651, 15 Elul 5768 (2008), p. 7.
9. *Sichat Hage'ulah* 811, Aug. 20, 2010, p. 1 (my emphasis).
10. Elbaz 2009.
11. Chabad Hasidim believe that Napoleon knew of Rabbi Shneur Zalman's magical preeminence and futilely searched for ways to counter it (Glitzenstein 1978).
12. After fleeing the Soviet Union, Rabbi Yosef Yitzchak resided for a time in Riga and then moved to Otwock near Warsaw. In 1940 he was rescued from the Warsaw Ghetto in an intricate operation and reached the United States (Rigg 2004). His survival of these two mortal dangers is viewed by Chabad Hasidim as the victory of Rabbi Yosef Yitzchak, "the Moses of his generation," over communism and Nazism.
13. *Divrei Hamelech*, talk on the Mishpatim Torah portion, 27 Shevat Adar A 5752 (1992), pp. 6–7.
14. *Sichat Hage'ulah* 358, March 16, 2001, p. 3.
15. *Beis Moshiach* 641, Purim, 5 Adar 5768 (2008), p. 41.
16. *Sichat Hage'ulah* 55, Aug. 4, 1995, p. 3.
17. Etkes 2014, pp. 259–280.
18. *Dvar Malchut*, Vayeshev Torah portion, 23 Kislev 5752 (1992), pp. 6–7.
19. Kraus 2007, pp. 49–53.
20. Rabbi Tuiva Doron maintains that the arms-reduction agreement signed by the two superpowers in 1992, marking a new age in international relations, grew out of the King Messiah's action of disseminating the seven Noachide laws. The meeting between the two powers took place at the UN building in New York, the city in which the *nasi* of the generation lived, rather than in the nation's

capital because New York is the Rebbe's capital (*Sichat Hage'ulah* 189, March 13, 1998, p. 3).

21. *Sichat Hage'ulah* 338, March 16, 2001, p. 3.

22. Heilman and Friedman 2010, pp. 197–200.

23. *Sichat Hage'ulah* 256, May 18, 2001, p. 1. The account there quotes the testimony from some of the pilots. See also *Beis Moshiach* 324, 3 Sivan 5701 (2001), pp. 38–46.

24. *Beis Moshiach* 705, 10 Menachem Av 5769 (2009), p. 53 (emphasis in the original); *Sichat Hage'ulah* 60, Sept. 8, 1995, p. 3.

25. *Sichat Hage'ulah* 338, March 16, 2001, p. 3.

26. The Meshichists frequently quote the Rebbe's execration of Moshe Katsav, then serving as minister of transportation, on January 15, 1992, following news reports that the government of Prime Minister Yitzhak Shamir was prepared to make territorial concessions to the Palestinians. (*"I, Menachem Mendel, will be the first to fight with full force and with all my might against Shamir, so that his government falls!"*) Among those who were punished for involvement in the Gaza disengagement were Prime Minister Ariel Sharon, who went into a coma following a stroke; Katsav himself, who was jailed after being convicted of rape; Finance Minister Avraham Hirschson, jailed after a corruption conviction; Prime Minister Ehud Olmert, forced out of office and then jailed for corruption; Chief of Staff Dan Halutz, who resigned under a cloud of charges regarding the misuse of his office; and Police Commissioner Moshe Karadi, who resigned his post after a commission of inquiry faulted him for the excessive use of force during the evacuation of Israeli settlements in the Gaza Strip.

27. *TheMarker*, Feb. 4, 2013, p. 38. The article states that "the Chabad Hasidim are furious that Shefa Yamim Exploration and Mining, which is searching for diamonds near Haifa, has been using the name of the Lubavitcher Rebbe to promote its business." The company responded that it would continue to act toward the realization of the Rebbe's vision, http://www.haaretz.com/israel-news/business/chabad-peeved-at-gems-explorer-exploiting-rebbe-s-name.premium-1.501304. On the discovery of gemstones in the area of Mount Carmel, see *TheMarker*, July 3, 2015, p. 26.

28. *TheMarker*, Feb. 11, 2014, p. 38. The company's Meged 5 drill struck oil, but its other attempts failed and the company was unable to raise more capital.

29. *Sichat Hage'ulah* 499, May 21, 2004, p. 3. Crediting the Rebbe with the victories of sports teams infuriates the Chabad mainstream. The second issue of an anti-Meshichist publication, *Hashavua Shechalaf/Seder baMachshavah*, from 13 Iyar 5755 (1995), lashes out at Betzalel Kupchik, a Meshichist who claims credit for the successes of the Hapoel Safed and Hapoel Galil Elyon basketball teams, while "no one reports that the [former] team lost several games despite Kupchik's promises (in the name of the Rebbe!). And that without going into the huge sacrilege caused by this." The same issue quotes from an article in *Yediot Aharonot* headlined "The Messiah Didn't Come, Doron Jamchi [star of the Mac-

cabi Tel Aviv basketball team] Came." According to the article, "The Rebbe was called in to help Hapoel, but with help like that who needs enemies?"

Chapter 8

1. Etkes 2014.

2. A similar, if much more blatant, process of deification of a Messiah took place in the Sabbatean movement. During states of religious ecstasy, Shabbetai Zvi, in sharp contrast with the Rebbe, said of himself that "I am your God, Shabbetai Zvi." Nathan of Gaza, the movement's prophet, maintained that Shabbetai Zvi's status as God was a corollary of his being the Messiah (Scholem 1973, p. 871).

3. High-echelon rabbinical figures in Chabad issued a "vigorous protest" against those who have called the Rebbe "our Creator, in essence and nature, God forbid." Such people, the rabbis declared, are heretics and apostates who should be avoided and whose religious services should not be used (a copy of the protest, dated Feb. 2, 1998, is in my possession).

4. Dahan 2010, p. 177; Garb 2009, pp. 67-68.

5. Magid 2014.

6. Dahan 2010.

7. *Sichat Hage'ulah* 15, Oct. 21, 1994, p. 3 (emphasis in the original).

8. *Sichat Hage'ulah* 1983, Jan. 30, 1998, p. 3.

9. *Sichat Hage'ulah* 639, March 16, 2007, p. 3.

10. *Sichat Hage'ulah* 236, Feb. 26, 1999, p. 1.

11. *Peninei Ge'ulah* 10, Torah Portion Emor.

12. *Sichat Hage'ulah* 99, June 14, 1996, p. 1.

13. "Kabbalists report experiences of unification with the Godhead and, in fact, Jewish mysticism is replete with accounts of the experience of integration into God, merging with him, and the Godly clothing the human, in different versions" (Afterman 2015, p. 229; see also Idel 1992).

14. Berger 2005.

15. The two advertisements quoted here are in my possession, but are not marked with a date or the publication in which they appeared.

16. Yair Sheleg, "Ultimatum to the Holy One," *Ha'aretz*, Sept. 3, 1999, p. B7. See Dahan 2006, p. 384.

17. *Yerushalayim*, Sept. 3, 1999, pp. 18–26.

18. Berger 2001, p. 92.

19. Berger cites further documentation of the deification of the Rebbe in Chabad. He claims that this "highly problematic theology [the doctrine of divinity] is deeply embedded among more than a few Lubavitch Hasidim in the mainstream of the movement" (Berger 2001, p. 98).

20. Dahan 2014b.

21. *Sichat Hage'ulah* 116, Oct. 11, 1996, p. 3 (my emphasis).

22. Chabad.info, Feb. 10, 2008

23. *Beis Moshiach* 330, 22 Tammuz 5761 (2001), p. 48.

24. Berger 2005.

25. Chabad Online website, March 4, 2008.

26. Dahan 2010, p. 149.

27. I do not have the space here to write at length about the antinomian forces in Chabad, a phenomenon of which the deification of the Rebbe is one significant aspect. Antinomianism has a foothold on the fringes of the Meshichist camp and has aroused much controversy. One prominent example is the abolishment of the minor fast days by some Meshichist leaders. The fasts of 17 Tammuz and 10 Tevet, observed from morning until evening, commemorate the destruction of Jerusalem and the First and Second Temples by the Babylonians and the Romans, respectively. According to tradition, they will become festive days in the messianic age. Some Meshichists have argued that, since the Messiah has arrived, the minor fasts should no longer be observed. For example, a YouTube clip shows Hasidim in Melbourne, Australia, feasting on 17 Tammuz, which they have turned into a holiday. Another clip shows Rabbi Yoel Kraus, a Chabad emissary on the island of Ibiza, doing the same; Kraus frequently appears at Messiah and Redemption Rallies. On January 21, 2010, the Chabad.info and Chabad Online websites published a ban issued by Rabbi Gedalia Axelrod, head of Haifa's Chabad community and president of the city's religious court, against Rabbi Zimroni Tzik on the grounds that he eats on the minor fast days. Axelrod compared Tzik and his followers to the cult of Shabbetai Zvi (who abolished traditional practices wholesale and instituted new and strange practices), and declared that they should be excommunicated if they did not desist from this practice. Tzik denied the charge, but the way he did so is telling. He claimed that the reports that he had eaten *in public* were false; but he also adduced passages from the Rebbe which could lead to the conclusion that the time has come to annul these fast days.

A group of mainstream Chabad rabbis also issued a sharp public rebuke to an organization, Jewish Women United for the Redemption of New York, which declared that the fasts had been abolished. The mainstream spiritual leaders charged these women, along with Rabbi Tzik and other Meshichist rabbis, with "desecrating the name Lubavitch" and being the agents of a "terrible destruction."

28. Dahan 2010.

Chapter 9

1. Bilu 2013.

2. At the height of the messianic fervor surrounding Shabbetai Zvi, many Jews married young in order to carry out this precondition for the Messiah's arrival (Scholem 1973, p. 474).

3. The connection between birth and redemption is evident in the rabbinic expression "the birth-pangs of the Messiah." In an issue of *Sichat Hage'ulah* relating to the Torah portion *Tazria'*, which addresses fertility, the Rebbe is quoted as saying: "It is known that birth hints at *redemption* (as is written 'Yet Zion travailed and at once bore her sons'), and the birth of a male hints *at the strength and force* of the true and complete redemption . . . by our Righteous Messiah; that is, that 'she gave

birth to a son' hints at the *birth* (revelation) *of the soul of the Messiah*, which is of the highest level . . . from the male world" (*Sichat Hage'ulah* 643, April 20, 2010, p. 1, emphasis in the original).

4. An important Hasidic text, *Ma'or vaShemesh* by Rabbi Kalonymus Kalman Halevi Epstein, states: "It is known that it is a very great omen for good sons that at the time of coition he imagine the form of the *tzadik* in his thoughts" (Epstein 1994, p. 46).

5. *Lifko'ach et ha'Einayim*, 2007, pp. 126–130.

6. *Sichat Hage'ulah* 432, Jan. 31, 2003, p. 3 (my emphasis).

7. "The blinding in the Oedipus legend and elsewhere is a substitute for castration" (Freud 2007 [1900], p. 378, note 86).

8. Blindness as a punishment for male sexual appetite appears in the Mishnah, which refers to the story of Samson: "Samson went after his eyes, and therefore the Philistines gouged out his eyes" (Mishnah Sotah 1:8). In one midrash, this symbolic equation appears in the context of self-denial. Rabbi Matia ben Harash saw a beautiful woman and feared that his evil instinct would overcome him, so he took a white-hot nail and "pierced his eyes" (*Midrash Tanchuma Menukad*, vol. 2, addition to the Chukat portion according to the Second Oxford Manuscript, p. 138).

9. Wolfson has noted the phallic nature of the gaze involved in the contemplation of the chariot and divine majesty among the "descenders of the chariot" in the *Heikhalot Rabati* (Wolfson 1994, p. 104). The parallel between the organs of vision and generation also appears, for example, in sixteenth-century sources, in which the repair for spilling semen is shedding tears, see Wolfson 2009, p. 366, note 143.

10. For example, the editor of *Sichat Hage'ulah* cites the Talmudic saying "It is the way of the male to conquer" (Babylonian Talmud, Mo'ed Katan 28a), and stresses that this is "a characteristic especially required by the Rebbe *shalita*, the King Messiah in carrying out his mission, conquering the entire world for the service of God." Likewise, he distinguishes between Rabbi Yosef Yitzchak's effort to keep the Jewish flame lit and the Rebbe's central interest that "is not a struggle for survival and what already exists but rather a forceful *penetration* by virtue of divine mission and *conquest* of the entire world" (*Sichat Hage'ulah* 643, April 20, 2007, p. 1, my emphasis).

11. The symbolic parallel between the hand and the phallus can be seen in a midrash that addresses Joseph's battle with his evil impulse in his encounter with Potiphar's wife: "He stuck his hands in the ground and a seminal emission emerged between the fingernails of his hands" (Babylonian Talmud, Sotah 36b). Joseph, traditionally called "the righteous," is identified with the phallic *sefirah* of Yesod, which occupies the place of the male member in the anthropomorphic description of the divine emanations.

12. Bilu 2000, pp. 16–46.

13. Goldberg 1987.

14. Hiatt 1971; Shapiro and Linke 1996.

15. For a psychoanalytic consideration of the creation of Eve, see Dundes 1976. Dundes proposed that the rib serves as a symbolic surrogate for the male sexual organ.

16. Dahan 2006, pp. 205–235, 2008; Kraus 2007, pp. 41–42; Weil 2009, pp. 61–85.

17. Dahan 2006, p. 227.

18. Idel 2005b.

19. Wolfson 2009, p. 220.

20. The Rebbe, for his part, termed the Chabad emissaries and yeshiva students "my sons" (*Sichat Hage'ulah* 803, June 25, 2010, p. 3). When the physician treating his wife, Chaya Mushka, called from the hospital to notify the Rebbe of her death, his first reaction was: "We have to tell the children, the *shluchim* [emissaries]" (Heilman and Friedman 2010, p. 222).

21. A dramatic example of the way Meshichist children's relationship with the Rebbe trumps what they have with their actual fathers comes from the pamphlet *Itanu Yoter miTamid* (New York, 1995, pp. 10–12). Rabbi Mishael R. tells of an eight-and-a-half-year-old boy who was in a coma in an intensive care unit following a severe head injury. A doctor was able to get him to open his eyes and asked him to identify his father. The boy did not respond. He showed no indication that he identified the man before him; he did not identify his mother either. But when the doctor held a picture of the Rebbe before his eyes, "A miracle happened! M nodded slightly, and suddenly his extinguished eyes lit up and he whispered: 'The Rebbe . . . ' He stretched out his hand, touched the Rebbe's picture and brought it to his lips, for a kiss . . . "

22. The effort to resemble the Rebbe physically is a familiar phenomenon in Chabad. Some of my interviewees interpreted the Talmud's dictum "It is incumbent on a man to go to pay his respects [*lehakbil*, literally to "receive" him, both in the sense of greeting him and of taking on his appearance and behavior] to his teacher on festivals" (Babylonian Talmud, Rosh Hashanah 16b) in concrete terms—to make themselves look like him. This interpretation can also be found in Bratslav Hasidism (*Likutei Moharan* 141, teaching 135).

23. Kraus 2007, p. 115.

24. Compare this with the claim that in the Tannaitic literature, the creation of man in God's image does not only mean that God and man resemble each other in some way but that God is actually made present in man, see Lorberbaum 2015, pp. 18–19.

25. The values of the letters Sh-B-L add up to 332, as do the letters of the name Menachem Mendel.

26. *Sichat Hage'ulah* 802, June 18, 2010, p. 4 (my emphasis).

27. Similarly, many Chabad girls are named after Chaya Mushka, the Rebbe's wife. Chabad children are also given the names of the movement's previous *admorim*, thus replicating part of the Chabad dynasty in their families.

Chapter 10

1. Balakirsky Katz 2010, pp. 144–173.

2. Shandler 2009, p. 249.
3. *Zal* is "hall" in Russian.
4. Katz 2015, p. 107.
5. *Kuntras Beit Rabeinu shebeBavel* (Brooklyn: Otzar haChasidim, 1992), p. 3.
6. *Sichat Hage'ulah* 763, Sept. 4, 2009, p. 3.
7. Rabbi Levi Yitzchak Ginsburgh, *Beis Moshiach* 669, 9 Marheshvan 5769 (2009), p. 12.
8. *Sichat Hage'ulah* 765, Sept. 18, 2009 (emphasis in the original). See also *Sichat Hage'ulah* 770 (Oct. 30, 2009), which represents the unity of time, place, and issue number.
9. *Sichat Hage'ulah* 976, Dec. 20, 2013, p. 1.
10. *Sichat Hage'ulah* 698, May 16, 2008, p. 1.
11. *Tzurat haBayit* (Va'ad Cha'yalei Beit David, 2006).
12. Ibid., p. 2.
13. Ibid., p. 4.
14. Garb 2009, p. 65.
15. *Sichat Hage'ulah* 394, May 3, 2002, p. 4.
16. *Sichat Hage'ulah* 664, Sept. 12, 2007, eve of Rosh Hashanah 5768, p. 3. See also Shandler 2009, p. 260.
17. In January 1987 a federal court in Brooklyn ruled in favor of the Chabad organization, headed by the Rebbe, and against Barry Gourari, the only grandson of Rabbi Yosef Yitzchak, who claimed ownership of the Chabad library. The judge ruled that the books belong to the organization, see Heilman and Friedman 2010, pp. 216–218.
18. *Sichat Hage'ulah* 591, March 31, 2006, p. 1.
19. *Sichat Hage'ulah* 388, March 15, 2002, p. 3 (my emphasis).
20. *Sichat Hage'ulah* 240, March 26, 1999, p. 1.
21. *Sichat Hage'ulah* 641, March 30, 2007, p. 2.
22. *Sichat Hage'ulah* 62, Sept. 22, 1995, p. 3.
23. Heilman and Friedman 2010, pp. 15–19.
24. *Sichat Hage'ulah* 99, June 14, 1996, p. 1 (emphasis in the original).
25. Ibid. (Emphasis in the original.)
26. *Sichat Hage'ulah* 681, Jan. 18, 2008, p. 1 (emphasis in the original).
27. The newscaster's words are a reference to a popular song by Israeli rocker Shalom Hanoch, "Waiting for the Messiah," which includes the repeated line: "The Messiah hasn't come, he hasn't called, either."
28. *Sichat Hage'ulah* 435, Feb. 21, 2003, p. 3.
29. The stickers paraphrase slogans of the Israeli peace movement (Peace Now; Sing a Song to Peace). *Hayweed, 'Esev-Shachat* in Hebrew, is apparently a jab at *Sichat Hashavua'*, a weekly Torah-portion sheet distributed to synagogues by the Chabad mainstream alongside *Sichat Hage'ulah*.

Chapter 11
1. Shandler 2009, p. 272.

2. Ravitzky 1999, pp. 254–257.

3. Mishnah Avot 6:11.

4. The Rebbe said that the radio "is of a nature that is above the measurement and constraint of time and place in our world" (quoted in Ravitzky 1999, p. 254).

5. Note that photography was invented in 1839–1840, an important date to note given the possibility that the highly developed visual culture of the United States influenced the widespread and creative use of photographs and films in Chabad, see Shandler 2009, p. 238.

6. *Sichat Hage'ulah* 394, May 3, 2002, p. 4.

7. *Sichat Hage'ulah* 924, Nov. 30, 2012, p. 4.

8. *Sichat Hage'ulah* 822, Nov. 12, 2010, p. 1.

9. *Sichat Hage'ulah* 149, May 30, 1997, p. 4.

10. Shandler 2009, p. 247.

11. Ibid., p. 264.

12. *Sichat Hage'ulah* 876, Dec. 9, 2011, p. 3.

13. The term *the virtual Rebbe* was coined by Shandler, who used it as the title of the chapter he devoted to Chabad in his book *Jews, God, and Videotape* (Shandler 2009, pp. 230–274).

14. Ibid., p. 252.

15. *Sichat Hage'ulah* 204, July 3, 1998, p. 1; while the Rebbe speaks in Yiddish, the clips are subtitled in Hebrew.

16. Meyer 2005.

17. Wolfson 2009, p. 5.

18. Barthes 1981; Sontag 1977.

19. Compare: Buber 1964. Here is a random example of the enchanted world inhabited by the Meshichists: A student at a Meshichist yeshiva whom I had previously interviewed asked to chat with me again just before he was to set off for a visit to 770. We met near my home and had a chat on a bench on a street corner. At the beginning of our talk, he pointed out a huge photograph of the Rebbe hanging on a fence nearby. At the end of the conversation we walked to the nearby bus stop, where he caught the bus back to his seminary. He then called me from the bus in great excitement to make sure I had noticed that he had boarded the 77 bus. Could I deny, he asked, that the Rebbe had been present during our meeting, via his photograph and his holy home (770)? Were I to reject that claim, would I not be deliberately disregarding the signs that the world was broadcasting to those prepared to attend to them?

20. De Vries and Weber 2001; Meyer 2005, 2006.

21. Taylor 1999.

22. Howard Rheingold aptly refers to advanced telecommunications research as "the science of presence" (Rheingold 1992).

23. Marc Taylor maintains that at the ineffable moment that Baudrillard

called "the ecstasy of communication," the screen and the viewer become one (Taylor 1999, p. 139).

24. Arjun Appadurai's distinction between "technoscape" and "ideoscape" is pertinent here. Chabad embraces modern technology while imposing on it its mystical doctrine (Appadurai 1996).

25. Lanier 2010.

26. Taylor 1999; Virilio 1994, p. 139. Such a divine quality is attributed, for example to Google. The Church of Google claims that Google is an omniscient entity that "can provide immediate answers to almost all questions, and this is much more than can be said about the popular gods of our time" (Ruah Midbar 2014, p. 647).

27. Nelson 2001.

28. Brasher 2001; Davis 1998; Noble 1997.

29. Deleuze 2004.

30. Weber 1978.

31. Belting 1994, p. 6, note 20.

32. Harris 2004, p. 142.

33. Garb 2009, p. 68; Dahan 2010; Wolfson 2009.

Chapter 12

1. Berger 2001, p. 28, 2005, p. 116.

2. Berger 2001; Marcus 1996; Marcus 2001.

3. Rashi on Daniel 12:12.

4. Dahan 2013. Cf. Kohl 2000.

5. Yoshevam Halevi Segal, *Igeret laShaliach* (Kfar Chabad, 1994), pp. 18–19. Note the formulation "casts his life against this to the point that he *ostensibly* dies," consistent with the Meshichist denial of the Rebbe's death.

6. *Sichat Hage'ulah* 231, Jan. 22, 1999, p. 3 (my emphasis).

7. Idel 2007, pp. 531–584.

8. Ibid., p. 568.

9. *Sichat Hage'ulah* 598, May 26, 2006, p. 1 (emphasis in the original). A no less explicit statement of this idea appears in *Sichat Hashavua'*, the weekly Torah-portion pamphlet of the Chabad mainstream: "When we eat the Messiah's Meal we absorb the messianic illumination into our bodies. The *matzah* that we eat and the wine that we drink become part of us" (quoted in Persico 2011).

10. Yuval 2008.

11. Scholem 1973.

12. Festinger, Riecken, and Schachter 1956.

13. Scholem 1973, pp. 689–690.

14. Quoted in Scholem 1973, p. 543.

15. *Lifko'ach et ha'Einayim*, 2007, p. 14.

16. Scholem cites the testimony of a contemporary, Rabbi Tuvia Harofeh, who "expressed his astonishment at the fact that many scholarly and eminent people were preserving their faith in spite of Sabbatai's death, explaining that

what had happened was 'mere illusion, for he was still alive, though hidden from the eyes of all living'" (Scholem 1973, pp. 923–924).

17. Kraus 2007.
18. "Said the Holy One, Blessed Be He, a new Torah will come out from me" (Leviticus Rabba 13:3). See also Jeremiah 31:31-33.
19. Scholem 1973, p. 235.
20. Ibid., p. 617.
21. Ibid., p. 818.
22. Ibid., p. 606.
23. Ibid., p. 629.
24. The ambiguity regarding what is prophecy and what madness can already be seen in the plaint of the prophet Hosea: "The days of punishment have come, for your heavy guilt; the days of requital have come—let Israel know it! The prophet was distraught, the inspired man driven mad by constant harassment" (Hosea 9:7). The *dybbuk* of Jewish lore, an evil spirit possessing a living person, has its origin in the charge that a Shabbetean prophet was "possessed by outside forces" (Liebes 1978–1979; Scholem 1973, p. 575).
25. Scholem 1973, p. 485.
26. Ibid., pp. 861–863.
27. Ibid., p. 252.
28. Ziff 2006.
29. Taylor 1979.
30. Doss 1999, 2005.
31. Hopgood 2005.
32. Plasketes 1997.
33. Passariello 2005, pp. 86–88.
34. Ziff 2006, p. 35.
35. Both these images are photographs taken during ceremonial gatherings. Che Guevara's photograph was taken by Alberto Korda, Fidel Castro's personal photographer, during the funeral of the victims of an attack at Havana's port on March 5, 1960; the Rebbe's picture was taken by one of his elite court photographers, Shimon Roumani, as the Rebbe watched Chabad children during a Lag B'Omer parade in 1987.
36. Doss 1999; Frow 1998.
37. Klein and Teensma 1997. The cover copy continues: "It is as if the King was liberated by the rumors of his death." This claim corresponds with the idea that the Rebbe is seen today more than in the past, thanks to the innumerable iconographic images of him.

Chapter 13

1. Etkes 2012.
2. Mark 2009.
3. Garb 2009, pp. 14-15.
4. Kraus 2007, p. 16; Shandler 2009, pp. 255–256.

5. Garb 2009, p. 70.
6. According to one Talmudic opinion, the Messiah's name is Menachem (Babylonian Talmud, Sanhedrin 98b). The correlation between a particular name and messianic consciousness appears in the cases of Jesus (Liebes 1984), Shabbetai Zvi (Idel 1997), Maimonides (Yuval 2007), and Rabbi Moshe Chaim Luzzatto (Dan 1999, p. 100).
7. Dan 1999, p. 195.
8. Dahan 2014b; Dan 1999.
9. The baby's name combined the names of the two messiahs mentioned in Jewish lore: the Messiah son of Joseph (or Efraim, son of Joseph) and the Messiah son of David (Shlomo, the Hebrew name of King Solomon).
10. Dan 1999, pp. 159–163.
11. Elliot Wolfson (2009) stresses that messianic consciousness involves liberation from all conceptual limits.
12. Dan 1999, p. 137; Etkes 2004, pp. 292–301.
13. Kraus 2007, pp. 62, 65.
14. *Chayei Moharan*, p. 219.
15. Weiss 1974, pp. 98–108.
16. Kraus 2007, pp. 80–83.
17. Mark 2010a.
18. Friedman and Heilman 2010, pp. 181–213, 267–297; Kraus 2007.
19. Garb 2009, p. 33.
20. Goodman 2004.
21. Mark 2010a; Szubin 2000, pp. 215–240.
22. Goodman 2004, pp. 144–148.
23. Garb 2009, pp. 67-68; Mark 2010b, pp. 112–146.
24. See Sternhartz 1984, Hilchot Shomrim, Halakhah 5; Horowitz 2000, p. 7.
25. Mark 2010a.
26. Morris 1998.
27. Dahan 2006, pp. 188–196; Weil 2009.
28. Weil 2009, pp. 76–85.
29. Compare: Shokeid 1988, pp. 139–160.
30. *ChaBaKuK*: Chabad, Bratslav, (Rabbi Avraham Yitzchak HaCohen) Kook, and (Rabbi Shlomo) Carlebach.
31. Kraus 2007, pp. 65–66; Ravitzky 1993, pp. 249–276.
32. Shandler 2009, pp. 230–274.
33. Rapoport-Albert 1973, pp. 65–96.
34. See Breslev.co.il, Jan. 18, 2008. Rabbi Arush sums up the discussion on the forum with the assertion that "if a person wants naturally to speak with our rabbi, he is able to do so."
35. Horn 2008, pp. 68–70.
36. Ravitzky 1993, pp. 249–276.

37. On a similar process, in Evangelical communities in the United States, of transforming a god into a close and intimate friend, see Luhrmann 2004, 2012.

38. An example: a workshop in "Spiritual Preparation for Birth according to the Teachings of Rabbi Nachman."

39. Kraus 2007, p. 39.

40. Ibid., p. 127.

41. Wolfson 2009.

42. Dahan 2010, p. 172.

43. Elior 1998; Freidman 1994; Rosen-Zvi 2002.

Conclusion

1. Orsi 2012.
2. De Vries and Weber 2001; Meyer and Moors 2006.
3. Meyer 2005; Meyer 2006.
4. Meyer 2014.
5. Geertz 1973.
6. Luhrmann 2012.
7. The Messiah links with the beginning of time—his name is numbered among the seven things created before the creation of the world (Babylonian Talmud, Pesachim 54a)—and with the end of days. In space, the Messiah's home (the numerical values of the Hebrew words add up to 770) will be included in the Third Temple.
8. O'Neill (2009) explored the ways in which neo-Pentecostals in Guatemala City perform their "Christian citizenship" through devotional acts propelled by a strong sense of moral responsibility for the city's social fabric and the nation's soul.
9. Kimmerling 1993.
10. Festinger, Riecken, and Schachter, 1956; Stone 2000.
11. Dein 2011; Dein and Dawson 2008; Shaffir 1993, 1994, 1995.
12. Melton 1985; Touminia 2005; Zygmunt 1972.
13. Kravel-Tovi and Bilu 2008.
14. Friedman and Heilman 2010, pp. 267–298.

BIBLIOGRAPHY

Afterman, Adam. 2015. "Paradigmah Chadashah beCheker haKabalah" (afterword). In Moshe Idel, *Shalshela'ot Kesumot: Technikot veRitu'alim baMistikah haYehudit*. Jerusalem: Shalom Hartman Institute, pp. 221–232.
Al-Issa, Ihsan. 1995. "The Illusion of the Reality of Illusion." *British Journal of Psychiatry* 166:3, pp. 368–373.
Amir-Moezzi, Mohammad Ali. 2011. *The Spirituality of Shi'i Islam*. London: I.B. Tauris.
Appadurai, Arjun. 1996. *Modernity at Large: Cultural Dimensions of Globalization*. Minneapolis: University of Minnesota Press.
Aran, Gideon. 2013. *Kukism: Shorshei Gush Emunim, Tarbut haMitnachalim, Te'ologiyah Tziyonit, Meshichiyut beZemanenu*. Jerusalem: Carmel.
Balakirsky Katz, Maya. 2007. "On the Master-Disciple Relationship in Hasidic Visual Culture: The Life and Afterlife of Rebbe Portraits in Habad, 1798-2006." *Images* 1, pp. 55–79.
Balakirsky Katz, Maya. 2010. *The Visual Culture of Chabad*. Cambridge, UK: Cambridge University Press.
Barthes, Roland. 1981. *Camera Lucida: Reflections on Photography*. New York: Hill & Wang.
Baumgarten, Eliezer. 2012. "Zehuyot Adatiyot beChasiduyot Bratslav." *Pe'amim* 131, pp. 147–178.
Beit-Hallahmi, Benjamin. 2002. "Rebirth and Death: The Violent Potential of Apocalyptic Dreams." In Chris Stout (ed.), *The Psychology of Terrorism*. Westport, CT: Greenwood, pp. 163–189.
Belting, Hans. 1994. *Likeness and Presence: A History of the Image before the Era of Art*, Chicago: University of Chicago Press.
Bentall, Richard P. 2000. "Hallucinatory Experiences." In E. Cardena, S. J. Lynn, and S. Krippner (eds.), *Varieties of Anomalous Experience*. Washington, DC: American Psychological Association, pp. 85–120.
Bentall, Richard P. 2003. *Madness Explained: Psychosis and Human Nature*. London: Penguin Adult.
Berger, David. 2001. *The Rebbe, the Messiah and the Scandal of Orthodox Indifference*. London: Littman Library of Jewish Civilization.

Berger, David. 2005. *HaRebbe Melekh haMashiach: Sha'aruriyat haAdishut vehaIyum 'al Emunat Yisra'el.* Jerusalem: Urim.

Berryman, Edward. 2001. "Medjugorje's Living Icons: Making Spirit Matter (for Sociology)." *Social Compass* 48, pp. 593–610.

Biale, David et al. 2018. *Hasidism: A New History.* Princeton, NJ: Princeton University Press.

Bilu, Yoram. 1982. "Pondering the 'Princes of Oil': A New Light on an Old Phenomenon." *Journal of Anthropological Research* 37:3, pp. 269–278.

Bilu, Yoram. 2000. *Without Bounds: The Life and Death of Rabbi Ya'aqov Wazana.* Detroit: Wayne State University Press.

Bilu, Yoram. 2009. "'Itanu Yoter miTamid': Hanchachat haRabbi miLubavitch baPeleg haMeshichi shel Chabad." In Kimmy Caplan and Nurit Stadler (eds.), *Manhigut veSamchut baChevrah haCharedit beYisra'el.* Jerusalem: Van Leer Institute, pp. 186–209.Bilu, Yoram. 2010. *The Saints' Impresarios.* Brighton, MA: Academic Studies Press.

Bilu, Yoram. 2012. "To Make Many More Menachem Mendels: Childlessness, Procreation, and Creation in Messianic Habad." *Contemporary Jewry* 32:2, pp. 111–134.

Bilu, Yoram. 2013. "We Want to See Our King: Apparitions in Messianic Habad." *Ethos* 41:1, pp. 98–126.

Bittel, Lisa. 2009. "Looking the Wrong Way: Authenticity and Proof of Religious Vision." *Visual Resources* 25:1–2, pp. 69–92.

Boksa, Patricia. 2008. "On the Neurobiology of Hallucinations." *Journal of Psychiatry and Neuroscience* 34:4, pp. 260–262.

Bolter, Jay David and Richard Grusin. 1999. *Remediation: Understanding New Media.* Cambridge, MA: MIT Press.

Bourguignon, Erika. 1970. "Hallucinations and Trance." In Wolfram Keup (ed.), *On the Origins and Mechanisms of Hallucinations.* New York: Springer, pp. 183–190.

Brasher, Brenda. 2001. *Give Me Back That Online Religion.* San Francisco: Wiley.

Buber, Martin. 1964. *BeSod Siach: 'Al haAdam ve'Amidato Nochach haHavayah* (published in English under the title *I and Thou*). Jerusalem: Bialik Institute.

Bynum, Caroline Walker. 1987. *Holy Feast and Holy Fast: The Symbolic Significance of Food to Medieval Women.* Berkeley: University of California Press.

Caplan, Kimmy. 2006. "'Alonei Parashat haShavua' baChevrah haYehudit haOrtodoksit beYisra'el." In Moshe Sluhovsky and Yosef Kaplan (eds.), *Sifriyot veOsafei Sefarim.* Jerusalem: Zalman Shazar Center, pp. 447–483.

Carlsson, Maria E. and Ingrid M. Nilsson. 2007. "Bereaved Spouses' Adjustment to the Patient's Death in Palliative Care." *Palliative and Supportive Care* 5:4, pp. 397–404.

Casanova, Jose. 1994. *Public Religions in the Modern World.* Chicago: University of Chicago Press.

Castells, Manuel. 1966–1968. *The Information Age.* Volumes 1–3. Oxford: Blackwell.

Christian, William A., Jr. 1981. *Apparitions in Late Medieval and Renaissance Spain.* Princeton, NJ: Princeton University Press.
Christian, William A., Jr. 1992. *Moving Crucifixes in Modern Spain.* Princeton, NJ: Princeton University Press.
Christian, William A., Jr. 1996. *Visionaries: The Spanish Republic and the Reign of Christ.* Berkeley: University of California Press.
Cohen, Richard I. 1998. *Jewish Icons: Art and Society in Modern Europe.* Berkeley: University of California Press.
Crapanzano, Vincent. 1975. "Saints, Jnun, and Dreams: An Essay in Moroccan Ethnopsychology." *Psychiatry* 38, pp. 145–159.
Culp, John. 2009. "Panentheism." *Stanford Encyclopedia of Philosophy.* Palo Alto, CA: Stanford University Press.
Dahan, Alon. 2006. *Dirah baTachtonim: Mishnato haMeshichit shel R' Menachem Mendel Schneerson (haRabbi miLubavitch).* PhD diss., Hebrew University of Jerusalem.
Dahan, Alon, 2008a. "Go'el Acharon lelo Yorshim: Ha'im R' Menachem Mendel Schneerson Bachar shelo Lehotir Acharav Yorshim, She'arei Basar, o Memunim miSibot Meshichiyot?" *Kabbalah* 17, pp. 289–309.
Dahan, Alon. 2008b. "Ma'avakei haYerushah beChasidut Chabad." *Kivunim Hadashim* 17, pp. 204–219.
Dahan, Alon. 2010. "Yechi Adoneinu Moreinu uVoreinu: HaAdam ha Elohi, Me'afyenei haMeshichiyut haChabadit vehaPulmus haMelaveh Otah." *Reshit: Studies in Judaism*, vol. 2, pp. 147–182. https://reshit.hartman.org.il/Article_View_Heb.asp?Article_Id=26.
Dahan, Alon. 2014a. "HaHofa'ah haSheniyah shel R' Menachem Mendel Schneerson: Shuvo shel haMashiach beMishnat Chabad ba'Idan haPost-Schneersoni." *Zehuyot* 4, pp. 73–90.
Dahan, Alon. 2014b. *Go'el Aharon.* Tel Aviv: Contento de Semrik.
Dan, Joseph. 1996. "The Contemporary Hasidic Zaddik: Charisma, Heredity, Magic and Miracle." In Dan Cohn-Sherbok (ed.), *Divine Intervention and Miracles in Jewish Theology.* Jewish Studies, vol. 16. Lewiston, NY: Edwin Mellen, pp. 195–214.
Dan, Joseph. 1999. *HaMeshichiyut haYehudit haModernit.* Tel Aviv: Ministry of Defense Press.
Davis, Erik. 1998. *Techgnosis.* New York: Harmony.
Davis, Phillip W. and Jacqueline Boles. 2003. "Pilgrim Apparition Work: Symbolization and Crowd Interaction when the Virgin Mary Appeared in Georgia." *Journal of Contemporary Ethnography* 32, pp. 371–402.
de Vries, Hent and Samuel Weber (eds.). 2001. *Religion and Media.* Palo Alto, CA: Stanford University Press.
Dein, Simon. 1992. "Letters to the Rebbe: Millennium, Messianism, and Medicine among the Lubavitch of Stamford Hill." *International Journal of Social Psychiatry* 38, pp. 262–272.
Dein, Simon. 2011. *Lubavitcher Messianism: What Really Happens When Prophecy Fails?* New York: A&C Black.

Dein, Simon. 2012. "Internet Mediated Miracles: The Lubavitcher Rebbe's Online Igros Kodesh." *Jewish Journal of Sociology* 54:1–2, pp. 24–45.

Dein, Simon and Lorne L. Dawson. 2008. "The 'Scandal' of the Lubavitch Rebbe: Messianism as a Response to Failed Prophecy." *Journal of Contemporary Religion* 23:2, pp. 163–180.

Dein, Simon and Roland Littlewood. 2007. "The Voice of God." *Anthropology & Medicine* 14:2, pp. 213–228.

Deleuze, Gilles. 2004. *Difference and Repetition.* London: Continuum.

Derrida, Jacques. 2001. "Above All, No Journalists." In Hent de Vries and Samuel Weber (eds.), *Religion and Media.* Palo Alto, CA: Stanford University Press, pp. 56–93.

Derrida, Jacques and Gianni Vatimo (eds.). 1998. *Religion.* Palo Alto, CA: Stanford University Press.

Dobzhinsky, Sara Rivka Nechama. 2001. *Hitkashrut beChavayah Ishit.* Self-published.

Dodds, E.R. 1951. *The Greek and the Irrational.* Berkley: University of California Press.

Doss, Erika. 1999. *Elvis Culture: Fans, Faith, and Image.* Lawrence: University Press of Kansas.

Doss, Erika. 2005. "Popular Culture Canonization: Elvis Presley as Saint and Savior." In James Hopgood (ed.), *The Making of Saints.* Tuscaloosa: University of Alabama Press, pp. 152–168.

Dow, James. 1986. "Universal Aspects of Symbolic Healing: A Theoretical Synthesis." *American Anthropologist* 88:1, pp. 56–69.

Dundes, Alan. 1976. "Projection in Folklore: A Plea for Psychoanalytic Semiotics." *MLN* 91, pp. 1,500–1,533.

Dundes, Alan. 1980. "Seeing is Believing." In Alan Dundes, *Interpreting Folklore.* Bloomington: Indiana University Press.

Ehrlich, Avrum. 2004. *The Messiah of Brooklyn: Understanding Lubavitch Hasidism Past and Present.* Jersey City, NJ: Ktav.

Elbaz, Sagiv. 2009. "HaKemp: Sadan 'alav Meyatzrim Chasidim." MA thesis, Hebrew University of Jerusalem.

Elior, Rachel. 1993. *The Paradoxical Ascent to God: The Kabbalistic Theosophy of Habad Hasidism.* Albany, NY: SUNY Press.

Elior, Rachel. 1998. "The Lubavitch Messianic Resurgence: The Historical and Mystical Background 1939–1996." In P. Schafer and M.R. Cohen (eds.), *Toward the Millennium.* Leiden: Brill, pp. 383–408.

Elior, Rachel. 2013. "Introduction." In Rachel Elior et al. (eds.), *KaChalom Ya'uf ukeDibuk Ye'achez: 'Al Chalomot veDibukim beYisra'el uva'Amim.* Jerusalem: Magnes, pp. 3–17.

Engelke, Matthew. 2010. "Religion and the Media Turn: A Review Essay." *American Ethnology* 37:2, pp. 371–379.

Epstein, Kalonymus Kalman Halevi. 1994. *Ma'or vaShemesh: 'Al Chamishah Chumshei Torah veRimzei Yamim Nora'im veShalosh Regalim veEizeh Likutim.* Jerusalem: Machon Or haSefer.

Eraqi Klorman, Bat-Zion. 1993. *The Jews of Yemen in the Nineteenth Century: A Portrait of a Messianic Community*. Leiden: Brill.
Etkes, Imannuel. 2004. *The Besht: Magician, Mystic and Leader*. Waltham, MA: Brandeis University Press.
Etkes, Imannuel. 2012. *Ba'al haTanya: Rabbi Shneur Zalman miLiadi veReshitah shel Chasidut Chabad*. Jerusalem: Zalman Shazar Center.
Etkes, Imannuel. 2014. *Rabbi Shneur Zalman of Liadi: The Origins of Chabad Hasidism*. Waltham, MA: Brandeis University Press.
Festinger, Leon, Henry W. Riecken, and Stanley Schachter. 1956. *When Prophecy Fails*. Minneapolis: University of Minnesota Press.
Fishkoff, Sue. 1994. *The Rebbe's Army: Inside the World of Chabad Lubavitch*. New York: Schocken.
Frank, Jerome. 1974. *Persuasion and Healing: A Comparative Study of Psychotherapy*. New York: Schocken.
Freud, Sigmund. 2007 (1900). *The Interpretation of Dreams*. London: Allen & Unwin.
Friedman, Menachem. 2001. "Mashiach uMeshichiyut beChasidut Chabad-Lubavitch." In David Ariel-Joel et al. (eds.), *Milchemet Gog uMagog: Meshichiyut ve'Apologetikah baYahadut ba'Avar uvaHoveh*. Tel Aviv: Yediot, pp. 174–229.
Frow, John. 1998. "Is Elvis a God? Cult, Culture, and Questions of Method." *International Journal of Cultural Studies* 1:2, pp. 197–210.
Garb, Jonathan. 2009. *The Chosen Will Become Herds: Studies in Twentieth-Century Kabbalah*. New Haven, CT: Yale University Press.
Garb, Jonathan. 2011. *Shamanic Trance in Modern Kabbalah*. Chicago: University of Chicago Press.
Geertz, Clifford. 1973. *The Interpretation of Cultures*. New York: Basic Books.
Geiger, John. 2009. *The Third Man Factor: The Secret for Survival in Extreme Environments*. Toronto: Penguin Canada.
Glitzenstein, Avraham Chanoch. 1978. *Sefer haToladot: Admor Rabbi Shneur Zalman miLiadi*. Kfar Chabad: Otzar haChasidim.
Goldberg, Harvey. 1987. "Torah and Children: Symbolic Aspects of the Reproduction of Jews and Judaism." In Harvey Goldberg (ed.), *Judaism Viewed from Within and from Without: Anthropological Studies*, Albany, NY: SUNY Press, pp. 107–131.
Goldberg, Shelly. 2009. *Masa' haNeshamah: Nishmat haTzadik veNitzchiyut haNeshamah beMishnat Chabad*. Jerusalem: Rubin Mass.
Goodman, Yehuda. 2004. "HaChazarah beTeshuvah veZehuyot Datiyot Chadashot beYisra'el beTehilat Shenot haAlpayim." In Aviad Kleinberg (ed.), *Mabat Acher 'al Datiyut veChiloniyut*. Tel Aviv: Tel Aviv University Press, pp. 98–177.
Gotlieb, Jacob. 2009. *Sechaltanut beLvush Chasidi: Demuto shel haRambam beChasidut Chabad*. Ramat Gan, Israel: Bar-Ilan University Press.
Green, Arthur. 1977. "The Zaddik as Axis Mundi in Later Judaism." *Journal of the American Academy of Religion* 3, pp. 327–347.

Grimby, A. 1993. "Bereavement among Elderly People: Grief Reactions, Post-Bereavement Hallucinations and Quality of Life." *Acta Psychiatrica Scandinavica* 87:1, pp. 72–80.

Grunbaum, G.E. von and Roger Caillois. 1966. *The Dream and Human Societies*. Berkeley: University of California Press.

Handelman, Don and Leah Shamgar-Handelman. 1997. "The Presence of Absence: The Memorialism of National Death in Israel." In Eyal Ben-Ari and Yoram Bilu (eds.), *Grasping Land*. Albany, NY: SUNY Press, pp. 85–128.

Harari, Yechiel. 2013. *Sodo shel haRabbi*. Tel Aviv: Yediot.

Harris, Clare. 2004. "The Photograph Reincarnate: The Dynamics of Tibetan Relationships with Photography." In Elizabeth Edwards and Janice Hart (eds.), *Photographs Objects Histories: On the Materiality of Images*. London: Routledge, pp. 139–155.

Heilman, Samuel. 2001. "Still Seeing the Rebbe: Pilgrims at the Lubavitcher Grand Rabbi's Grave in Queens." www.killingthebuddha.com/dogma/still_seeing_rebbe.htm.

Heilman, Samuel. 2004. "A Face to Believe in." In Jack Wertheimer (ed.), *Jewish Religious Leadership: Image and Reality*. Vol. 2. New York: Jewish Theological Seminary Press, pp. 837–878.

Heilman, Samuel and Menachem Friedman. 2010. *The Rebbe: The Life and Afterlife of Menachem Mendel Schneerson*. Princeton, NJ: Princeton University Press.

Hiatt, L.R. 1971. "Secret Pseudo-Procreation Rites among the Australian Aborigines." In L.R. Hiatt and C. Jayawardena (eds.), *Anthropology in Oceania*. Sydney: Angus & Robertson, pp. 77–88.

Hirsch, Orit. 2014. "'Hikonu leVi'at haMashiach-haGever': Nashim Chiloniyot beChabad haMeshichit." *Iyunim Betekumat Yisra'el* 7, pp. 347–370.

Hopgood, James E. 2005. "Saints and Stars: Sainthood for the 21st Century." In James E. Hopgood (ed.), *The Making of Saints*. Tuscaloosa: University of Alabama Press, pp. 124–142.

Horn, Ro'i. 2008. "Ha'Emunah baTzadik 'al pi Sefer Likutei Halakhot leRabbi Natan miNemirov: Mitos, Ritual, veNarativ." MA thesis, Bar-Ilan University.

Horowitz, Shmuel. 2000. *Tzion haMetzuyenet*. Jerusalem: Keren Hadpasah deChasidei Bratslav.

Idel, Moshe. 1988. *Kabbalah: New Perspectives*. New Haven, CT: Yale University Press.

Idel, Moshe. 1992. *Meshichiyut veMistikah*. Tel Aviv: Ministry of Defense Press.

Idel, Moshe, 1995. Hasidism: Between Ecstasy and Magic. Albany, NY: SUNY Press.

Idel, Moshe. 1997. "Shabetai haKochav veShabetai Tzvi: Gishah Chadashah laShabta'ut." *Mada'ei Hayahadut* 37, pp. 161–184.

Idel, Moshe. 2005a. *Enchanted Chains: Techniques and Rituals in Jewish Mysticism*. Los Angeles: Cherub.

Idel, Moshe. 2005b. *Kabbalah and Eros*. New Haven, CT: Yale University Press.

Idel, Moshe. 2007. *Sonship and Jewish Mysticism*. New York: Bloomsbury.

Innis, Robert E. 2004. "The Tacit Logic of Ritual Embodiments." In Don Handelman and Galina Lindquist (eds.), *Ritual in Its Own Right*. New York: Berghahn, pp. 197–212.
Kantor, Ro'i. 2013. *Ha'Akademiyah Mekabelet Pnai Mashiach*. Self-published.
Katz, David S. and Richard H. Popkin. 1999. *Messianic Revolution*. New York: Hill & Wang.
Katz, Yosef. 2015. "Hitkadshuto shel Bayit uMisparo: Tenu'at Chabad ve-'Beit Mashiach' shebeRechov 770 Eastern Parkway beNew York." *Da'at* 78, pp. 107–127.
Kimmerling, Baruch. 1993. Patterns of Militarism in Israel. *European Journal of Sociology* 34:2, 196–223.
Klein, Dan and Hans Teensma. 1997. *Where's Elvis? Documented Sightings Prove that He Lives*. London: Weidenfeld & Nicolson.
Kleinman, Arthur. 1988. *Rethinking Psychiatry: From Cultural Category to Personal Experience*. New York: Free Press.
Kraus, Yitzhak. 2007. *HaShevi'i: Meshichiyut baDor haShevi'i shel Chabad*. Tel Aviv: Yediot.
Kravel-Tovi, Michal. 2009. "To See the Invisible Messiah: Messianic Socialization in the Wake of Failed Prophecy in Habad." *Religion* 39, pp. 248–260.
Kravel-Tovi, Michal and Yoram Bilu. 2008. "The Work of the Present: Constructing Messianic Temporality in the Wake of Failed Prophecy among Chabad Hasidim." *American Ethnologist* 35:1, pp. 1–17.
Lanier, Jaron. 2010. *You Are Not a Gadget: A Manifesto*. New York: Knopf.
Lenowitz, Harris. 1998. *The Jewish Messiahs*. Oxford: Oxford University Press.
Lévi-Strauss, Claude. 1967. "The Effectiveness of Symbols." In Claude Lévi-Strauss, *Structural Anthropology*. New York: Allen Lane, pp. 183–201.
Liebes, Yehuda. 1978–1979. "Mechaber Sefer *Tzadik Yesod 'Olam*: HaNavi haShabta'i R' Liebeli Prosnich. *Da'at* 2–3, pp. 159–174.
Liebes, Yehuda. 1984. "Matzmiach Keren Yeshua'." *Mechkarei Yerushalayim Bemachshevet Yisra'el* 3, pp. 313–348.
Lifko'ach et ha'Einayim: Sipurei Mofet mipi Yehudim sheZachu Lachazot biFnei haMelech haMashiach, Hod K"K Admor Shalita miLubavitch ba'Asor haAcharon. 2007. Brooklyn: Reshet Chabad Lubavitch.
Loewenthal, Naftali. 1990. *Communicating the Infinite: The Emergence of the Habad School*. Chicago: University of Chicago Press.
Loewenthal, Naftali. 1994. "Contemporary Habad and the Paradox of Redemption." In Alfred I. Ivry, Elliot R. Wolfson, and Allan Arkush (eds.), *Perspectives on Jewish Thought and Mysticism*. Sydney: Harwood Academic Publishers, pp. 381–402.
Lorberbaum, Yair. 2015. *In God's Image: Myth, Theology and Law in Classical Judaism*. Cambridge, UK: Cambridge University Press.
Luhrmann, Tanya M. 2004. "Metakinesis: How God Becomes Intimate in Contemporary American Christianity." *American Anthropologist* 106:3, pp. 518–528.
Luhrmann, Tanya M. 2011. "Hallucinations and Sensory Overrides." *Annual Review of Anthropology* 40, pp. 72–85.

Luhrmann, Tanya M. 2012. *When God Talks Back*. New York: Knopf Doubleday.
Magid, Shaul. 2014. *Hasidism Incarnate: Hasidism, Christianity, and the Construction of Modern Judaism*. Palo Alto, CA: Stanford University Press.
Marcus, George E. and Michael M.J. Fischer. 1986. *Anthropology as Cultural Critique*. Chicago: University of Chicago Press.
Marcus, Greil. 1991. *Dead Elvis: Chronicle of a Cultural Obsession*. Cambridge, MA: Harvard University Press.
Marcus, Joel. 1996. "Modern and Ancient Jewish Apocalypticism." *Journal of Religion* 76:1, pp.1–27.
Marcus, Joel. 2001. "The Once and Future Messiah in Early Christianity and Chabad." *New Testament Studies* 47:3, pp. 381–401.
Mark, Zvi. 2009. *Mysticism and Madness: The Religious Thought of Rabbi Nachman of Bratslav*. New York: Bloomsbury.
Mark, Zvi. 2010a. *The Scroll of Secrets: The Hidden Messianic Vision of R. Nachman of Breslav*. Brighton, MA: Academic Studies Press.
Mark, Zvi. 2010b. "Tzadik haNatun beLoa' haSitra Achra: HaAdam haKadosh vehaMakom haTame, 'al ha'Aliyah leRegel leKever R' Nachman miBreslov beUman beRosh Hashanah. *Reshit: Studies in Judaism*, vol. 2, pp. 112–146.
Matter, E. Ann. 2001. "Apparitions of the Virgin Mary in the Late Twentieth Century: Apocalyptic, Representation, Politics." *Religion* 31:2, pp. 125–153.
Melton, J.G. 1985. "Spiritualization and Reaffirmation: What Really Happens When Prophecy Fails." *American Studies* 26:2, pp. 17–29.
Menezes, Adair and Alexander Moreira-Almeida. 2010. "Religion, Spirituality and Psychosis." *Current Psychiatry Reports* 12:3, pp. 174–179.
Meyer, Birgit. 2005. "Remediations: Pentecostal Views in Ghanaian Video-Movies." *Postscripts* 1:2–3, pp. 155–181.
Meyer, Birgit. 2006. "Religious Revelation, Secrecy and the Limits of Visual Representation." *Anthropological Theory* 6:4, pp. 431–453.
Meyer, Birgit. 2014. "Mediation and the Genesis of Presence: Towards a Material Approach to Religion." *Religion and Society: Advances in Research* 5, pp. 205–254.
Meyer, Birgit and Annelies Moors (eds.). 2006. *Religion, Media, and the Public Sphere*. Bloomington: Indiana University Press.
Meyert, William E.H., Jr. 1997. "The Problem of God in a Hypervisual Society." *Journal of American Culture* 20:3, pp. 67–71.
Mirzoeff, Nicolas. 1999. *Introduction to Visual Culture*. London: Routledge.
Mitchell, W.J.T. 2005. *What Do Pictures Want?: The Lives and Loves of Images*. Chicago: University of Chicago Press.
Morgan, David. 1998. *Visual Piety: A History and Theory of Popular Religious Images*. Berkeley: University of California Press.
Morgan, David. 2005. *Sacred Gaze: Religious Visual Culture in Theory and Practice*. Berkeley: University of California Press.
Morris, Bonnie J. 1998. *Lubavitcher Women in America: Identity and Activism in the Postwar Era*. Albany, NY: SUNY Press.

Nelson, Victoria. 2001. *The Secret Life of Puppets*. Cambridge, MA: Harvard University Press.
Newman, Barbara. 1985. "Hildegard of Bingen: Visions and Validation." *Church History* 54:2, pp. 163–175.
Newman, Barbara. 2005. "What Did It Mean to Say 'I Saw'? The Clash between Theory and Practice in Medieval Visionary Culture." *Speculum* 80:1, pp. 1–43.
Niedzwiedz, Anna. 2010. *The Image and the Figure: Our Lady of Czestochowa in Polish Culture and Popular Religion.* Krakow: Jagiellonian University Press.
Noble, David F. 1997. *The Religion of Technology: The Divinity of Man and the Spirit of Invention.* New York: Knopf.
O'Neill, Kevin Lewis. 2009. *City of God: Christian Citizenship in Postwar Guatemala.* Berkeley: University of California Press.
O'Nell, Carl W. 1976. *Dreams, Culture, and the Individual.* San Francisco: Chandler & Sharp.
Orsi, David. 2012. "Material Children: Making God's Presence Real among Catholic Boys and Girls." In Gordon Lynch and Jolion Mitchell (eds.), *Religion, Media, and Culture: A Reader.* London: Routledge, pp. 147–158.
Passariello, Phyllis. 2005. "Desperately Seeking *Something*: Che Guevara as Secular Saint." In James Hopgood (ed.), *The Making of Saints: Contesting Sacred Ground.* Tuscaloosa: University of Alabama Press, pp. 75–89.
Pedaya, Haviva. 2011. *Merchav uMakom: Masah 'el haLo Muda' haTe'ologi-Politi.* Tel Aviv: Hakibbutz Hameuhad.
Peled, Esther. 2012. *LeOrah haTzach shel haMetziyut.* Tel Aviv: Bavel.
Persico, Tomer. 2011. "Chabad vehaNatzrut, haNatzrut veChabad." Minim blog, 3 May. http://7minim.wordpress.com/2011/05/03/habad_christianity_chap_847.
Plasketes, G. 1997. *The Image of Elvis Presley in American Culture, 1977–1997.* Binghamton, NY: Haworth.
Plate, S. Brent. 2002. *Religion, Art and Visual Culture: A Cross-Cultural Reader.* New York: Palgrave Macmillan.
Poll, Solomon. 1995. "The Charismatic Leader of the Hasidic Community: The Zaddik, the Rebbe." In Janet S. Belcove-Shalin (ed.), *New World Hasidism: Ethnographic Studies of Hasidic Jews in America.* Albany, NY: SUNY Press, pp. 257–275.
Price-William, Douglass. 1999. "In Search of Mythopoetic Thought." *Ethos* 27:1, pp. 25–32.
Rapoport-Albert, Ada. 1973. "Confession in the Circle of Rabbi Nahman mi-Braslav." *Bulletin for the Institute of Jewish Studies* 1, pp. 65–96.
Rapoport, Chaim. 2008. "HaTo'elet beRe'iyat Pnei haTzadik beFo'al o Tziyur Demut Deyokano baMachshavah Bichlal ukeHachanah leTefilah Bifrat 'al pi Torat haChasidut." *Heichal Habesht* 21:1, pp. 63–82.
Ravitzky, Aviezer. 1991. "The Contemporary Lubavitch Hasidic Movement: Between Conservatism and Messianism." In Martin E. Marty and R. Scott Appleby (eds.), *Fundamentalism Observed.* Chicago: University of Chicago Press, pp. 303–327.

Ravitzky, Aviezer. 1993. *HaKetz haMeguleh uMedinat haYehudim*. Tel Aviv: Am Oved.
Ravitzky, Aviezer. 1999. *Charut 'al haLuchot: Kolot Acherim shel haMachshavah haDatit*. Tel Aviv: Am Oved.
Reece, Gregory L. 2006. *Elvis Religion: The Cult of the King*. London: I.B. Tauris.
Reinitz, Shlomo. 2001. "Nifla'ot 'Achshav: HaPsichologiyah vehaRetorikah shel haNes beSipurei Nisim baPeleg haMeshichi beChabad." MA thesis, Hebrew University of Jerusalem.
Rheingold, Howard. 1992. *Virtual Reality*. New York: Simon & Schuster.
Rigg, Brian Mark. 2004. *Rescued from the Reich: How One of Hitler's Soldiers Saved the Lubavitcher Rebbe*. New Haven, CT: Yale University Press.
Robbins, Thomas and Susan Palmer. 1997. "Introduction: Patterns of Contemporary Apocalypticism." In Thomas Robbins and Susan Palmer (eds.), *Millennium, Messiahs and Mayhem*. London: Psychology Press, pp. 1–30.
Rosaldo, Renato. 1989. *Culture and Truth: The Remaking of Social Analysis*. London: Beacon.
Rosen-Zvi, Ishay. 2002. "HaCholeh haMedumeh: Tziduk haShoah beMishnat haRav Zvi Yehuda Kook veChugo." *Tarbut Demokratit* 6, pp. 165–209.
Rosman, Moshe (Murray Jay). 1996. *Founder of Hasidism: A Quest for the Historical Ba'al Shem Tov*. Berkeley: University of California Press.
Ruah Midbar, Marianna. 2014. "The Sacralization of Randomness: The Theological Imagination and the Logic of the Digital Divination Results." *Numen* 61:5-6, 619–655.
Sachedina, Abdulaziz Abdulhussein. 1981. *Islamic Messianism: The Idea of the Mahdi in Twelver Shi'ism*. Albany, NY: SUNY Press.
Sagiv, Gadi. 2014. *HaShoshelet: Beit Chernobil uMekomo beToldot haChasidut*. Jerusalem: Zalman Shazar Center.
San Juan, Rose Marie. 2008. "Dizzying Visions: St. Teresa of Jesus and the Embodied Visual Image." In Christine Gottler and Wolfgang Neuber (eds.), *Spirits Unseen: The Representation of Subtle Bodies in Early Modern European Culture*. Leiden: Brill, pp. 245–268.
Sasson, Haim. 2000. *Ata Yada'ati*. Self-published.
Schatz Uffenheimer, Rivka. 1968. *HaChasidut keMistikah: Yesodot Quietistim baMachshavah haChasidit baMe'ah ha-18*. Jerusalem: Magnes.
Scholem, Gershom. 1961. *On the Kabbalah and its Symbolism*. New York: Schocken.
Scholem, Gershom. 1973. *Sabbatai Sevi: The Mystical Messiah*. Princeton, NJ: Princeton University Press.
Scholem, Gershom. 1975. "Lehavanat haRa'ayon haMeshichi beYisra'el." In Gershom Scholem, *Devarim BeGo*. Tel Aviv: Am Oved.
Scholem, Gershom. 1982. *HaRa'ayon haMeshichi beYisra'el*. Jerusalem: Israel Academy of Sciences.
Schwartz, Dov. 1997. *HaRa'ayon haMeshichi baHagut haYehudit biYemei haBenayim*. Ramat Gan, Israel: Bar-Ilan University Press.
Schwartz, Dov. 2011. *Machshevet Chabad miReshit ve'ad Aharit*. Ramat Gan, Israel: Bar-Ilan University Press.

Shaffir, William. 1993. "Jewish Messianism—Lubavitch Style: An Interim Report." *Jewish Journal of Sociology* 35:2, pp. 115–128.
Shaffir, William. 1994. "Interpreting Adversity: Dynamics of Commitment in a Messianic Redemption Campaign." *Jewish Journal of Sociology* 36:1, pp. 43–53.
Shaffir, William. 1995. "When Prophecy Is Not Validated: Explaining the Unexpected in a Messianic Campaign." *Jewish Journal of Sociology* 37:2, pp. 119–135.
Shandler, Jeffrey. 2009. *Jews, God, and Videotape: Religion and Media in America.* New York: NYU Press.
Shapiro, Warren and Uli Linke (eds.). 1996. *Denying Biology: Essays on Gender and Pseudo-Procreation.* Lanham, MD: University Press of America.
Sharot, Stephen. 1982. *Messianism, Mysticism and Magic.* Chapel Hill: University of North Carolina Press.
Shokeid, Moshe. 1988. *Children of Circumstances: Israeli Immigrants in New York.* Ithaca, NY: Cornell University Press.
Sidgwick, H. et al. 1894. "Report on the Census of Hallucinations." *Proceedings of the Society for Psychical Research* 34, pp. 25–394.
Singleton, Andrew. 2001. " 'Your Faith Has Made You Well': The Role of Storytelling in the Experience of Miraculous Healing." *Review of Religious Research* 43:2, pp. 121–138.
Sontag, Susan. 1977. *On Photography.* New York: St. Martin's.
Stadler, Nurit. 2007. "Playing with Sacred/Corporeal Identities: Yeshiva Students' Fantasies of Military Participation." *Jewish Social Studies* 13:2, pp. 155–178.
Stephen, Michele. 1989. "Self, the Sacred Other, and Autonomous Imagination." In Gilbert Herdt and Michele Stephen (eds.), *The Religious Imagination in New Guinea.* New Brunswick, NJ: Rutgers University Press, pp. 4–66.
Sternhartz, Natan. 1984. *Likutei Halakhot.* Jerusalem: Meshech haNachal.
Stolow, Jeremy. 2005. "Religion and/as Media." *Theory, Culture & Society* 22:4, pp. 119–145.
Stone, Jon R. 2000. "Introduction." In Jon R. Stone (ed.), *Expecting Armageddon: Essential Readings in Failed Prophecy.* New York: Routledge, pp. 1–29.
Szubin, Jacob A. 2000. "Why Lubavitch Wants Messiah Now: Religious Immigration as a Cause of Millenarism." In Albert L. Baumgarten (ed.), *Apocalyptic Time.* Leiden: Brill, pp. 215–240.
Taves, Ann. 2009. *Religious Explanation Reconsidered.* Princeton, NJ: Princeton University Press.
Taylor, Julie. 1979. *Eva Peron: The Myths of a Woman.* Chicago: University of Chicago Press.
Taylor, Mark C. 1999. *About Religion: Economies of Faith in Virtual Culture.* Chicago: University of Chicago Press.
Tedlock, Barbara. 1987. *Dreaming: Anthropological and Psychological Interpretation.* Cambridge, UK: Cambridge University Press.
Thompson, Stith. 1966. *Motif Index of Folk-Literature.* Bloomington: Indiana University Press.

Tien, A.Y. 1991. "Distribution of Hallucination in the Population." *Journal of Social Psychiatry and Psychiatric Epidemiology* 26:6, pp. 282–287.

Touminia, Diana G. 2005. *When Prophecy Never Fails: Myth and Reality in a Flying-Saucer Group.* Oxford: Oxford University Press.

Trachtenberg, Joshua. 1970. *Jewish Magic and Superstition.* New York: Atheneum.

Tzarfati, Orly. 1998. "Itona'ut beSherut haMashiach." *Kesher* 24, pp. 16–27.

Varner, Gary. 2009. *Sacred Wells: A Study in the History, Meaning, and Mythology of Holy Wells and Waters.* New York: Algora.

Virilio, Paul. 1994. *The Vision Machine.* Bloomington: Indiana University Press.

Weber, Max. 1978. *Economy and Society: An Outline of Interpretive Sociology.* G. Roth and C. Wittich (eds.). Berkeley: University of California Press.

Weil, Eldad. 2009. "Techilatah shel Tekufat haNashim: Nashim veNashiyut beMishnato shel haRabbi miLubavitch." *Akdamot* 22, pp. 61–85.

Weingrod, Alex. 1993. "Changing Israeli Landscapes: Building and the Uses of the Past." *Cultural Anthropology* 8:3, pp. 370–387.

Weiss, Jeffrey. 2007. "'A River Runs Through Them,' World Religions: How Water Shaped our Beliefs and Rituals." *Science & Spirit* 18:3, pp. 40–43.

Weiss, Joseph. 1974. *Mechkarim beHasidut Bratslav.* Jerusalem: Bialik Institute.

Wiebe, Phillip. 1997. *Visions of Christ.* Oxford: Oxford University Press.

Wiener, Aharon. 1978. *The Prophet Elijah in the Development of Judaism.* London: Routledge & K. Paul.

Wojcik, Daniel. 1996. "'Polaroids from Heaven': Photography, Folk Religion, and the Miraculous Image Tradition in a Marian Apparition Site." *Journal of American Folklore* 109, pp. 129–148.

Wolfson, Elliot R. 1994. *Through a Speculum That Shines: Vision and Imagination in Medieval Jewish Mysticism.* Princeton, NJ: Princeton University Press.

Wolfson, Elliot R. 2009. *Open Secret: Postmessianic Messianism and the Mystical Revision of Menahem Mendel Schneerson.* New York: Columbia University Press.

Wolpe, Sholom Dovber. 2002. *VeTorah Yevakshu miPihu.* Kiryat Gat, Israel: n.p.

Yanover, Yuri and Nadav Ish-Shalom. 1994. *Rokdim uVochim: Ha'Emet 'al Tenu'at Chabad.* New York: Meshi.

Yuval, Israel Jacob. 2007. "Moshe Redivivus: HaRambam ke'Ozer leMelech haMashiach." *Zion* 72, pp. 161–188.

Yuval, Israel Jacob. 2008. *Two Nations in Your Womb: Perceptions of Jews and Christians in Late Antiquity and the Middle Ages.* Berkeley: University of California Press.

Ziff, Trisha. 2006. "Guerrillero Heroico." In Trisha Ziff (ed.), *Che Guevara: Revolutionary & Icon.* London: Abrams Image, pp. 15–31.

Zimdars-Swartz, Sandra. 1989. "Popular Devotion to the Virgin: The Marian Phenomena at Lelleray, Ireland." *Archives de Sciences Sociales de Religions* 67, pp. 125–144.

Zimdars-Swartz, Sandra. 1991. *Encountering Mary.* Princeton, NJ: Princeton University Press.

Zygmunt, Joseph F. 1972. "When Prophecies Fail: A Theoretical Perspective on the Comparative Evidence." *American Behavioral Scientist* 16, pp. 245–268.

INDEX

Note: page numbers in *italics* refer to illustrations. Those followed by "n" indicated endnotes.

abortion, 60, 142, 154, 199–200
absent presence: apparitions and, 158–60, 162, 165; boundary-breaking and, 242; in Bratslav and Chabad, compared, 250–54, 257; cognitive dissonance theory and, 265; Event of Gimel Tammuz and, 222, 236; liminal time and, 24; messianic ecology and, 43, 88; photography and, 220; virtual leadership and, 257; virtual world and, 95–96. *See also* practices of making the Rebbe present
Abuhatzeira, Rabbi Israel (Baba Sali), 275n10
The Academy Welcomes the Messiah (Kantor), 16–17
Adam's rib, 201
admor as title, 256
advertisements, 62–63, 73, 75, 100–101
Afghanistan, 184
Agudas Chassidei Chabad (Association of Chabad Hasidim), 36
Alexander I, Czar, 179
Alkaslasi, Rabbi Shmuel, 194–95
amulets, 60–61, 117–20
Andropov, Yuri, 181

antinomianism, 232–34, 266, 287n27
apocalypticism: catastrophic messianism vs messianism of success, 34, 254; Hurricane Andrew and, 176; messianism and, 3–4, 269n5; Sabbatean movement and, 236; secular, 2; violence of, 24–25; visual idioms and, 164
apotheosis of the Rebbe, 188–96
Appadurai, Arjun, 292n24
apparitions: at "770," 67–68, 137–39, 148, 158–64, 170–71; backgrounds of reporters/witnesses, 147; calling on, 159–60; at Chabad Houses, 160; children and, 163–64; in Christianity compared to Chabad, 155, 168–71, 281n22, 282n27, 283n64; cultural-ecology path vs. distress path, 168–69; cultural factors in, 167–68; expectations and, 283n64; explaining, 149–58; frequency of, 135, 165–66, 167–68; hearing the Rebbe in, 149; *Igrot Kodesh* Oracle and, 66–68; images and, 152–56; messianic ecology and, 147, 150–51, 157, 158–60, 167; photography and video of, 138, 155–57, *156*; principle features of,

147–49; private vs. public events, 154–58; reservations and ambivalence about, 164–67; ritual vs. mundane, 158–64; serial or simultaneous, 147–48, 165–66; technology and, 219. *See also* dreams and dream apparitions
arms-reduction agreement (1992), 284n20
Arush, Rabbi Shalom, 251, 294n34
Ashkenazi, Rabbi Mordechai, 70
Association for the True and Complete Redemption: in Bat Yam, 41; dollar bill auctioned off, 84; haGeula.com, 12; Messiah and Redemption Conferences/Rallies, 15, 17–18, *19*, 82; ruling against referring to the Rebbe's death, 49. See also *Sichat Hage'ulah*
Association of Chabad Hasidim (Agudas Chassidei Chabad), 36
Atah hareta verses, 92
Attachment [to the Rebbe]as a Personal Experience (Dobzhinsky), 59
authority, 57, 70–73, 187, 255–56
Axelrod, Rabbi Gedalia, 70, 274n51, 287n27
Axelrod, Rabbi Shaul, 50, 51
'*ayin*, 127
Azulai, Chaim Yosef David (Hida), 102
Azulai, Rabbi Avraham, 102

ba'alei teshuvah ("masters of repentance" or "those who have returned"): in Bratslav and Chabad, 246; defined, x; Meshichists among, 10; numbers of, 41–43; *Sichat Hage'ulah* and, 48; stories of, 52, 185, 190–91, 193–94, 209
Ba'al Shem Tov, Rabbi Israel, 30, 49, 178, 231, 242–44
Baranes, Meir, 190–93
Bar Kokhba, 4

Barthes, Roland, 220, 278n39
Bat Yam, location of, 41
Baudrillard, Jean, 268n23, 291n23
Beis Moshiach (House of the Messiah) magazine, 12, *14*, 14–15, 107
Benjamin, Walter, 224
Bentall, Richard, 150
Berger, David, 277n36, 286n19
Berland, Rabbi Eliezer, 248
Berland, Tehilla, 248
bibliomancy, 48. See also *Igrot Kodesh* Oracle
"birth-pangs of the Messiah," 32, 35, 287n3
Bistritsky, Rabbi Levi, 191
Black Madonna of Częstochowa, 279n58
blindness, 200, 288n8
Bloom, Harold, 99
Bolter, Jay David, 7, 268n21
border-crossing in Bratslav and Chabad, 242, 243–50
Borochov, Rabbi Herzl, 50–51
Braille, 133
Bratslav and Chabad compared: absent presence and communication channels, 250–54, 257; border-crossing, 242, 243–50; democratization and lack of central authority, 255–57; differences, 241; lack of living *tzadik*, 241–42; lineage and position of Rabbi Nachman and the Rebbe, 242–43; pleasant demeanor and utopian view, 254; system of meaning, all-encompassing, 254–55
Bratslaver Hasidim, 267n2(Pref.)
Brezhnev, Leonid, 181
Buddhas of Bamiyan, Afghanistan, 184
Buyum, Gila, 274n58

cake (*lekah*) handed out, 93–95, 160
Chabad Hasidism: *ba'alei teshuvah* and

INDEX   311

Mizrachim, numbers of, 41–43; "Chabad" as acronym, 30; founding of, 30–31; growth following the Rebbe's death, 271n29; as Israeli Hasidic movement, 38; key elements of, 2–3; messianic idea in, 29–36; moderates and Meshichists within, 9–11, 37

Chabad Houses: apparitions at, 68, 148, 160; Beit She 'an, 143; Bnei Brak, 68; Bratslav Jewish Homes compared to, 246–47; Cusco, Peru, ix–x; first, in Bat Yam, 13; *Igrot Kodesh* and, 66, 72; images of the Rebbe in, 100, 133, 280n3; La Paz, Bolivia, 129; messianic citizenship and, 263; miracles at, 126–27; Mumbai terror attack, 120, 195; Petah Tikva, 71

Chabad.info, 193–95

Chabadinfo.com, 133

Chabad World Center for Welcoming the Messiah, 14

"Chabakuk," 249

chair of the Rebbe, replicas of, 77

charity boxes, 89–90, 276n35

Chavez, Hugo, 279n63

children: apparitions and, 163–64; *Igrot Kodesh* appeals by, 58; immediate connection with the Rebbe, 203; named after the Rebbe or Chaya Mushka, 79, 205, 272n21, 278n48, 289n20, 289n27; socialization of, 96

Chitat "safety kit," 89–91, *92*

"chosen" status of Jewish people, 25

Christianity: apparitions in, 155, 168–71, 281n22, 282n27, 283n64; citizenship, Christian, 295n8; Eucharist, 231; hurricane diversion, 284n3; icons, miraculous preservation of, 279n58; as imitating Judaism, 230; intimacy with God, 295n37; model messianism compared to Chabad, 229–31; visual turn in, 259. *See also* Jesus

Church of Google, 292n26

citizenship, messianic, 263–64

Citizens in the Messiah State (Ezrachim Bimdinat Hamashiach), 109, 196, 263

cognitive dissonance theory, 264–65, 271n28

Cohen, Ge'ulah, 121–22

commandments, annulled, 234

communications technology. *See* technology

communism, 180

companies, blessing of, 186

Conversos, 42, 235

copies. *See* replicas and duplication

cosmology: apotheosis of the Rebbe, 188–96; physical and psychological phenomena, significance of, 54; place and time, holy, 206–14; procreative powers of the Rebbe, 197–205; Schneersoncentrism, 175–87; technology and messianism, 215–25. *See also* theosophy of Chabad

Creator, the Rebbe as, 193–95, 261, 286n3

Crown Heights, 207. *See also* 770

Dahan, Alon, 195–96, 202, 256, 270n25

Dalai Lama, 224

Dan, Joseph, 243

Danin, Rabbi Reuven, 77, 275n6

Danino, Ofer, 90

darshan, 116

Day of Redemption, 210, 211

Days of Awe, 149, 252

Dean, James, 236

decentralized Rebbe, 224–25

Deleuze, Gilles, 222

democratization, 255–57

Derrida, Jacques, 6–7, 269n42

312   INDEX

deus ex machina (divine intervention), 162
Dialing for a Blessing, 218
diaries, personal, 93
Didan Natzach, 210
digital technology. *See* technology
divination. *See Igrot Kodesh* Oracle
divorce, 65, 145
Dobnik, Rabbi Shlomo, 115
dollars distributed by the Rebbe: continuation of, 86, 94; dreams and, 145–46; *Igrot Kodesh* Oracle and, 60, 65; lending of, 85; miracle stories, 84–85, 88–89; obtained miraculously, 86–87; Rebbe's practice of, 84; reproductions, 88–89; time handed out, 85–86; as traces, 77, 84–89
Doron, Rabbi Tuvia, 91, 189, 284n20
Dov Ber, Maggid of Mezeritch, 30, 178
Dovber, Rabbi Shalom (fifth *admor*), 32, 231
Dovber Shneuri, Rabbi (second *admor*), 210
dreams and dream apparitions: connecting disparate people, 144–45; epistemological problem of, 138, 280n6; exegetical framework and, 135–36; fertility stories and, 198–99; good-night blessing for, 143; *Igrot Kodesh* Oracle and, 65–66; images of Rebbe and, 116–17, 123, 136–40; mimetic activity and, 145–46; pictures of the Rebbe and, 136–40; on Sabbath observance, 143–44; wish fulfillment and problems solved, 138–42
Dundes, Alan, 289n15

ecology, messianic: apparitions and, 147, 150–51, 157, 158–60, 167; contrast of Rebbe's presence and absence, 88; defined, 5; epistemology established by, 265; gap between absence and, 158–60; *Igrot Kodesh* Oracle and, 64–65; as matrix, 260; perceptual fields and, 260. *See also* specific aspects, such as images of the Rebbe
Elijah of Vilna, Rabbi, 48
Elijah the Prophet, 281n21
"Elokists," 188, 193–95, 261. *See also* apotheosis of the Rebbe
emissaries: attacks on, in India, 120–21; Chabad's outward orientation and, 245; "consular" functions and transnational governmentability, 263–64; Cusco, Peru, ix–x; dreams and, 143, 145; female, 248; France rectification and, 181; history of, 30; *Igrot Kodesh* and, 83; images of the Rebbe and, 99–100, 117, 129; mainstream and Meshichist, 266; neo-Hasidic identity and, 266; number of, 271n29; operational activities in public spaces, 246; outward-looking vision and, 245; the Rebbe's project of, xi, 34, 204–5; redemption and, 232–33; self-abnegation and, 204; visibility of, x–xi, 38; vocation, sense of, 254, 263; during Yom Kippur War, ix. *See also* Chabad Houses
"Emissary's Letter," 229–30
enchanted world, 220–21, 258, 291n19
Epstein, Rabbi Kalonymus Kalman Halevi, 288n4
eschatology, 24–25
ethnic boundary-crossing, 248–49
etrogim, 75, 160
Event of Gimel Tammuz (departure of the Rebbe, 6/12/94): about, xi, 1; fertility miracles and, 203; holy time and, 211–13; periodicals appearing after, 12
eyes, opening of, 133, 166

eyes of the Rebbe, 121–22
Ezrachim Bimdinat Hamashiach (Citizens in the Messiah State), 109, 196, 263
Ezra youth movement, 71

factionalism, 255–56
fast days, minor, 70, 287n27
fertility stories, 197–205
Festinger, Leon, 231–32, 264–65, 271n28
Festival of Faith and Redemption, 212
film clips, 97, 110–15, 156–57
France, 179, 181–82
Frank, Jacob, 4, 244
Friedman, Menachem, 36

Gaza Strip, Israel's disengagement from, 185, 285n26
gaze, power of, 121–25
Geertz, Clifford, 260
gender and empowerment in Bratslav and Chabad, 248
"Gentlemen! History Repeats Itself!" (Ventura), 213–14
geographical reach of Bratslav and Chabad, 246–47
geopolitical realm: Afghanistan, 184; France, Russia, and Soviet Union, 179–82; Iraq, 184–85; Israel, 184–87; Japan, 178; overview, 177–78; United States, 182–84
Gimel Tammuz. *See* Event of Gimel Tammuz
Ginsburgh, Rabbi Haim Levi Yitzchak, 189
Ginsburgh, Rabbi Levi Yitzchak, 71–72
Givot Olam, 186
Gluckowsky, Rabbi Menachem Mendel, 50
Google, 292n26
Goral HaGR"A (the Oracle of the Vilna Gaon), 48

Gotlieb, Jacob, 270n25
Gourari, Barry, 290n17
Gourary, Rabbi Shmaryahu, 33
graves: Rabbi Nachman (Uman, Ukraine), 247–49, 251, 253; Rabbi Yosef Yitzchak (Queens), 185, 206, 270n19; the Rebbe's grave and Ohel shrine (Queens), 11, 206, 211, 251
Greisman, Nechoma, 248
Grolnik, Rabbi Motti, 71
Grusin, Richard, 7, 268n21
Guevara, Che, 236–39, *237, 239*
Gulf War, First, 177, 185
Gur'el, Aryeh, 186
Gush Emunim settler movement, 2, 256
Gush Katif settlements, Strip, 117

"Ha'aderet Veha'emunah," 182
Haifa, 186
Halperin, Rabbi Israel, 80, 81
Halutz, Dan, 285n26
Hapoel Galil Elyon basketball team, 187, 285n29
Hapoel Safed basketball team, 285n29
Harel, Rabbi Shemariya, 40
Harofeh, Rabbi Tuvia, 292n16
Harris, Clare, 224
Hasidic sects. *See* Bratslav and Chabad compared
Hasidism: "Christian gaze," growth beyond, 188; "disseminating the wellsprings," 181–83, 216, 244; history of, 29–30; images in, 131; inner Torah and, 82, 166, 216; neo-Hasidic identity of emissaries, 266; newcomers, attitude towards, 38, 42; social cohesion of, 265–66; the *tzadik* in, 11. *See also* Chabad Hasidism; sociology, Meshichist; *tzadikim; specific rabbis*
Haskalah (Jewish Enlightenment), 32
Hayun, Rabbi Ilan, 62

healing stories. *See* miracle stories
hearing the Rebbe speak: apparitions and, 149, 153; dreams and, 65–66, 145; in film clips, 97; through images, 129–31, 153
"heretics," 232–36
hermeneutics of suspicion, 31, 151, 166, 250
chevlei mashiach (birth-pangs of the Messiah), 4
"Hidden Scroll" (Rabbi Nachman), 245
Hildegard of Bingen, Saint, 169
Hirschson, Avraham, 285n26
hitbodedut (solo seclusion), 248, 251
Holocaust, 32–33
Holy Letters. See *Igrot Kodesh* Oracle
holy water. See *mikveh* water
Hosea, 293n24
Hoshanah Rabbah, 93
Hoshiar, Rabbi Yigal, 77
hurricanes, 175–76, 177, 184, 262, 284n3
hypermediacy, 8
hypernomia, 233
hyper-realism, 170–71

iconophilia, 101–2, 115–16, 153, 204, 259. *See also* images of the Rebbe
Idel, Moshe, 230
Ifergan, Rabbi Avishai, 185
Igrot Kodesh Oracle (Holy Letters): accessibility of, 59–60, 62, 68–70; advertising and, 62–63, 73; answers before petitions, 64; bibliomancy, 48; book as healing amulet, 60–61; broad circle of petitioners, 52–53, 63–64; children's appeals to, 58; *Chitat* and, 90; creativity of interpretive process, 56; decentralization, democratization, and threat to authority, 70–73; digital and online technologies and, 62, 72; dreams, apparitions, and, 65–68; efficacy of, 53–57; images of Rebbe and, 116, 128; institutionalization of, 50–51, 57, 61–62; instruction pamphlet for, 57; letters to the Rebbe compared to, 47, 54–55, 72; mediated by functionaries, 52, 57; *mikveh* water and, 82–83; ongoing dialogues, 58–60; origins of, 50; other means interwoven with, 64–65; pocket-sized, 68–69, *69*, 262; *Sichat Hage'ulah*, relationship with, 48–49; speed of, 59–60; stories in *Sichat Hage'ulah*, 50–53; virtual Rebbe and, 218
images of the Rebbe: about, 99–101; after his occlusion, 155–57, *156*; as amulet, 117–20; apparitions and, 152–56; on bodies of persons, 99, 111, 119, *199*, 223, 276n44; as catalyst, 116–17; deification of the Rebbe and, 195–96; dreams and, 116–17, 123, 136–40; eyes and power of the gaze, 121–25; famous image with waving hand, 102–7, *103*, *104*, *106*, 119, 198, 237–38; fertility and, 197–98, 200; film clips, 97, 110–15, 156–57; hearing Rebbe speak through, 129–31; history of Chabad's use of images, 98–99; in homes, 111; iconophilia and contemplation practices, 101–2, 115–16; *Igrot Kodesh* Oracle and, 64–65; Meshichist discourse and, 131–34; in Meshichist publications, 105–9; meta-iconization, 110, *112*, *113*; miraculous preservation of, 120–21, 278n58; mirrors paralleled to, 136–37, 280n3; on Partition Wall, *104*; Rabbi Nachman compared to, 251–52; returned gaze and picture as icon, 125–29; silhouette, 121; size of, 109–11; as traces, 77; transformation from image to icon and re-presentation, 115; on variety of items, *104*, 105, *106–8*; virtual Rebbe and, 204, 223

INDEX 315

immediacy, transparent, 7–8
Internet. *See* technology
In the Eye of the Storm (film; Ginsburgh), 176
"An Invisible Hand Is Steering the World into a New Geopolitical Order" (*Beis Moshiach*), 178
Iraq, 184–85
Islam, 29, 233, 259
Israel, state of: establishment of, 2; Gaza Strip, disengagement from, 185, 285n26; Rabbi Yosef Yitzchak's opposition to establishment of, 184; Schneersoncentrism and, 184–87
Israel Defense Forces (IDF), ix, 38–41, 90, 185, 276n35
Israeli-Palestinian conflict, 24–25
Itamar settlement, 118

Jabar, Salim, 25
Jacob, 233
Japan, 178
Jesus: apparitions of, 171, 281n22; Che Guevara as, *237*, 238; comparisons with, 277n36; intimate relationship with, 262; messianic consciousness and name of, 294n6; messianic failure and, 1, 4; subversive and antinomian teachings, 244
Jewish Homes (Bratslav), 246
Jewish Women United for the Redemption of New York, 287n27
Joseph, 288n11
Joshua, 212

Kabbalah: divine creation process, 202; Hasidism and, 30; phallic symbolism, 200, 202; rectification of France and, 181; *sefirot*, 53–54, 201–2, 209; on *tzadikim*, 175, 188, 190, 230; unification with the Godhead in, 286n13; visualization and, 102; women and, 248; the Zohar, 33, 53, 202, 215–16

Kali, Rabbi Boaz, 63
Kaminker, Efraim, 193
Kaminker, Feige, 193
Karadi, Moshe, 285n26
Karlburg, Rabbi Michael, 273n31
Katsav, Moshe, 285n26
Katz, Jacob, 31
Katz, Maya Balakirsky, 98
Kfar Chabad, 14
"The King Messiah's Baby" (story), 198
kipot (skullcaps), 77
Kraus, Rabbi Yoel, 287n27
Kraus, Yitzhak, 16–17, 271n29
Kravel-Tovi, Michal, 166, 282n41

Landa, Rabbi Moshe, 71
Landa, Rabbi Shlomo Zalman, 67, 147–48
Lanier, Jaron, 221–22
La Paz, Bolivia, Chabad House, 129
lawbreakers, 63–64
lekah (cake) handed out, 93–95, 160
Letters, Holy. See *Igrot Kodesh* Oracle
Letters from the Rebbe, 97
Levites, 213–14
library of Chabad (Brooklyn), 210, 290n17
Lifko'ach et ha'Einayim (Open Your Eyes), 146, 154, *155*, 166–67
Likutei Halakhot series, 255
Lithuanian yeshivot, 32
"living water." See *mikveh* water
Loewenthal, Naftali, 32
"Long live our Lord, teacher, and creator," 193–95, 261
lower hemisphere, 183
Luhrmann, Tanya, 170, 171, 262, 281n22, 282n31
Luria, Rabbi Yitzhak, 102
Luskin, Tuvia, 186
Luzzatto, Rabbi Moshe Chaim, 294n6

Machaneh Yehuda *shuk* (open-air market), Jerusalem, 118

Maduro, Nicolás, 279n63
Magid, Shaul, 188
Maimonides, 4, 234, 269n5, 294n6
Malchut (Kingdom), 201–2
male parturition theme, 201
mamash ("in fact"), 10, 73, 270n25
"Marseillaise," 181–82
Mary (Virgin Mary), 155, 169–70, 281n22, 282n27, 283n64
Mashiach Menachem shmo ("Menachem is the name of the Messiah"), 10
Mashour, Lutfi, 63
Mashour, Vida, 63
material religion, 260
Matia ben Harash, Rabbi, 288n8
McLuhan, Marshall, 19
meaning, all-encompassing system of, 254–55, 259
mediation paradigm, 6–9, 151, 216–17, 259–60
medical cures. *See* miracle stories
Menachem Mendel of Lubavitch, Rabbi (the Tzemach Tzedek; third *admor*), 33, 243
mental illness, accusations of, 70, 150, 191–93, 235
Meshichists, as group within Chabad Hasidism, 9–10. *See also specific topics, such as* sociology, Meshichist
Messiah: "birth-pangs" of, 32, 35, 287n3; decentralized, 262; the divine, connection to, 189; immediate accessibility and, 261–62; Menachem as name of, 294n6; the Rebbe's self-identification as, 34–35, 271n25; time and, 262, 295n7
Messiah and Redemption Conferences/Rallies (Association for the True and Complete Redemption), 15, 17–18, *19*, 82
Messiah cards, 118
Messiah's Dance, 153
Messiah's Meal, 144, 231, 292n9
messianic citizenship, 263–64
messianic consciousness, 29, 266, 283n58, 294n6, 294n11
messianic idea: 1990s expectations, 35; apparitions and, 164; border-crossing and, 244–45; Chabad theosophy and, 31–32; democratization and, 256–57; "hot" version of, 24, 263; in Jewish history, 3–4; messianic turn in Chabad, 32–36; the Rebbe's fostering of, 4, 33–34; visual representations and, 131–34
messianism: awakening, messianic, 1–2, 256, 258; catastrophic vs messianism of success, 34, 254; characteristics of, 261–66; Hasidism and, 29–30; naturalism, messianic, 269n5; under Rebbe vs. predecessor, 24–25; religious imagination and, 258–60; technology and, 215–25. *See also* ecology, messianic; redemption
meta-iconization, 110, *112, 113*
Meyer, Birgit, 268n24
mikveh water, 77, 79–83
military discourse, 38–41, 264
miracle stories: *Chitat* and, 90; Derrida on, 269n42; dissemination and material representation in text, 260; dollar bills and, 84–85, 88–89; Elokists and, 194–95; fertility stories, 197–205; gaze of the Rebbe and, 122–23; *Igrot Kodesh* Oracle and, 60; images of Rebbe and, 116–20, 126–28; *mikveh* water and, 80–83; multidimensional intervention, 83; ontological sense, rhetorical framing, and event as experienced, 22–23; technology and, 218
Mirzoeff, Nicolas, 279n78
Mitchell, W.J.T., 278n42, 279n78
Mitzvah Tanks, 38
Mizrachim, 10, 41–43, 191, 235, 248–49
Moses, 186, 213, 243, 281n9

Mumbai Chabad House terror attack, 120, 195
mysticism: aura of the *tzadik*, 121; cognitive dissonance theory and, 150; dialectical, 8, 11, 72, 166; hermeneutics of suspicion, 31, 151, 166, 250; individual nature of, 31; science and, 217; technology and, 72; unification with the Godhead, 286n13; visual images and, 131, 170. *See also* apparitions; cosmology; Kabbalah; New Age mysticism and spirituality; theosophy of Chabad

Nachman of Bratslav, Rabbi, 241–43, 267n2(Pref.)
Nachman of Horodenka, Rabbi, 243
Nahshon, Rabbi David, 40
Na-Nach branch of Bratslav, 247, 251
"Na-Nach-Nachma-Nachman mi'Uman" mantra, 253
Napoleon, 179, 181, 284n11
"Napoleon's March" (song), 181–82
Natan, Rabbi, 251–52
Nathan of Gaza, 286n2
naturalism, messianic, 269n5
nature, Rebbe's control over, 175–77
near-death experiences, 66–67, 192
nesi'im (presidents; sing. *nasi*), 17, 30, 139, 183, 203, 243, 284n20. *See also specific rabbis*
New Age mysticism and spirituality, 62, 73, 249
Newman, Barbara, 168
Noachide laws, 25, 53, 63, 183, 284n20
"noise," 150, 151–52
Now I Knew (Sasson), 107
numerology: "770" and, 127, 129, 208, 295n7; of *'ayin*, 127; calendar and messianic expectations, 35; dollar bills and, 88–89; eleven, 210–11; Gimel Tammuz, 211; *Igrot Kodesh* and, 55, 66; seven, 129, 208; Tzarfat, 182, 208

Odesser, Rabbi Yisroel, 247, 253
Ohalei Keidar prison, Be'er Sheva, 176–77
Oirechman, Rabbi Moshe, 71
Old Montefiore Cemetery, Queens, 11, 206, 270n19. *See also* graves
Olmert, Ehud, 285n26
O'Neill, Kevin Lewis, 263, 295n8
Operation Cast Lead, 117–18
oracle of letters. See *Igrot Kodesh* Oracle
Oro shel Mashiach (Light of the Messiah) summer camp, 39–40, 96, 111, *114*, 179
out-of-body experiences, 66–67, 192

Palestinians, 24–25, 63, 185
Partition Wall, *104*
Peron, Eva, 236
Pesach, 35, 67, 144, 149, 153, 164, 210, 231
phallic symbolism, 200–201, 202, 288nn9–11
photographs. *See* images of the Rebbe
Pizam, Rabbi Yigal, 71
place and time, holy, 206–14
practices of making the Rebbe present: horizontal and vertical factors in, 95–96; imagination and playfulness combined in, 95–97; in life-cycle events, 94, 96–97; ritual practices and holidays, 91–94. *See also* absent presence; images of the Rebbe; traces of the Rebbe
Presley, Elvis, 22, 168, 236–40, 283n82
procreative powers of the Rebbe, 197–205
prophecies, 177, 186, 215–16
Purim, 55, 149

Rabin, Yitzhak, 121
Rashi, 182, 197, 229
the Rebbe. *See* Schneerson, Rabbi Menachem Mendel

rectification, 181–82, 208
redemption: apparitions as "taste of," 164; birth connected to, 197, 287n3; border-crossing and, 244–45; Chabad messianic vision of, 2; conviction of verge of, 2; hastening, 233; holy place, holy time, and, 207–13; the Rebbe's role in disseminating, 4; recognition of Israel and the Jewish people, 185; technology and, 215–16; "years of miracles" (1990–1992) and, 180. *See also* messianism
Redemption Assembly, Bat Yam (2004), 109–10
Redemption Products, 105
Rehovot *Igrot Kodesh* Center, 50–51
remediations, 7, 268n21
replicas and duplication: of "770" (home of the Rebbe), 75, *76, 78*; of dollar bills, 88–89; reproduction, 223–24
resurrection of the dead, 123
revolutionary agenda, 238
revolutions, secular vs. spiritual, 179
Rheingold, Howard, 291n22
Riecken, Henry, 231–32, 264–65
ritual practices. *See* practices of making the Rebbe present
Robertson, Pat, 284n3
Rosh Hashanah, 93–94, 105, 149
Roumani, Shimon, 103, 293n35
Russia, 179–81

Sabbatean movement compared to Chabad messianism, 231–36
Sabbath observance, 143–44
"safety kit," *Chitat,* 89–91, *92*
Samson, 288n8
Sasson, Chaim, 107
Schachter, Stanley, 231–32, 264–65
Schneerson, Chaya Mousiya (Mushka), 33, 146, 289n20, 289n27
Schneerson, Rabbi Menachem Mendel (the Rebbe; seventh *admor*): beliefs about departure vs. death of, 10; birthday of, 68, 149, 210; as childless, 270n25; children named after, 79, 205, 272n21, 278n48; as commander in chief and King Messiah, 39, 41; death or departure of, 35; divine status ascribed to, 109, 188–96; eyes of, 121–22; global presence of, 223; grave of, 11, 206, 211, 251; Hasidic pedigree compared to Rabbi Nachman, 242–43; hidden presence at "770," 162–64; international reputation of, 217; as Messiah and immediately accessible, 261–62; messianic idea and, 34; negligible opposition to, 4–5; path to leadership, 33; self-identification as Messiah, 34–35, 271n25; stroke suffered by, 35, 270n19; studies in science, 216; visiting Rabbi Yosef Yitzchak's grave, 270n19. *See also* Event of Gimel Tammuz
Schneerson, Rabbi Yosef Yitzchak (sixth *admor*): "770" and, 206; candidates for successor of, 33; catastrophic messianism and, 24–25; collected letters of, 48; Day of Redemption and, 211; as embodiment of divine essence, 188–89, 190; envisioning, 153; exile of, 95, 99, 179–80; France and, 181; grave of, 185, 206, 270n19; on Holocaust, 32–33; home of, 142; photos of, 99, 102; the Rebbe as servant and emissary of, 34; release from prison, 210; seventy-year life of, 208; Soviet Union and, 179; "train to the Rebbe," 95; United States and, 183; Warsaw Ghetto, rescue from, 284n11; as Yesod and ninth *nasi*, 202
Schneersoncentrism: companies, 186; forces of nature, control over, 175–77; geopolitical realm, 177–85; mundane world, 186–87; power of

the Rebbe contrasted with predecessors, 175
Schneerson dynasty, 30–31
Schneur Zalman of Liadi, Rabbi (Alter Rebbe; RaShaZ), 30–31, 188
Scholem, Gershom, 231–32, 235–36, 267n7, 292n16
Schwartz, Dov, 31, 269n5
science, theologization of, 215–17
Science and Redemption Conferences, 217
"Seclusion before God/Our Holy Rabbi" webpage, 251
secular public spaces, Bratslav and Chabad in, 246–47
Seder, 231
Sefer Hatanya (Rabbi Schneur Zalman), 30
sefirot: "770" as Chochmah, Binah, and Da'at, 209; as physical experiences, 53–54; Rebbe as Malchut and Rabbi Yosef Yitzchak as Yesod, 201–2
self-abnegation, 202, 204
770 (home of the Rebbe): apparitions at, 67–68, 137–39, 148, 158–64, 170–71; blueprints for, 209; Bratslav's Uman compared to, 253; film clips at, 111–15; as former abortion clinic, 142; hidden presence of the Rebbe at, 162–64; as holy place, 206–10; images of, 75, 208–9; Israel, separation from, 247; as metonymy of the Rebbe, 206; names of, 206–7; numerology and, 127, 129, 208, 295n7; practices of making the Rebbe present at, 91–96; Rebbe continuing to live in, 10; replicas of, 75, *76*, *78*, 208; as Third Temple, 207, 209; visits to grave shrine vs., 11, 206, 211
770live website, 209–10
Shabbat pamphlet (Bratslav), 252
Shabbetai Zvi: children named after, 272n21; comparisons with, 277n36;

conversion to Islam, 29, 233; Conversos and, 42; "I am your God," 234, 286n2; messianic failure and, 1, 4; messianism and, 2; minor fast days and, 287n27; name, messianic consciousness, and, 294n6; procreation and, 287n2; Sabbatean movement compared to Chabad messianism, 231–36; subversive teachings, 244
Shach, Rabbi Elazar Menachem, 190, 255
shalita epithet ("may he have a long and good life"), 49, 238, 239
Shamir, Yitzhak, 285n26
Shandler, Jeffrey, 217, 219, 277n37, 291n13
Sharf, Mira Ruth, 121
Sharon, Ariel, 121, 285n26
Sharon, Rabbi Gidi, 185
Shefa Yamim Exploration and Mining, 186, 285n27
Shemini Atzeret, 148–49
Shimon bar Yochai, Rabbi, 109
Shmulevitz, Rabbi Ya'akov, 143
Shneur Zalman, Rabbi (first *admor*): letter by, 68; Napoleon and, 179, 181, 284n11; painting of, 98–99; release from prison, 210
Sichat Hage'ulah (Discourse on Redemption), *13*; about, 12–14; author in, 19–22; editorial on Gimel Tammuz, 211–12; on Hurricane Andrew, 176; *Igrot Kodesh* Oracle and, 48–49, 50–53, 57, 61–62; image of Rebbe in, 105–7; on male power, 288n10; *mikveh* water foundation myth, 79–80; military language in, 40; soldier with *Chitat* "safety kit," *92*; special issue (no. 1000), 21–22
Sichot Kodesh (collection of the Rebbe's talks), 51, 272n7
signal-detection theory, 150–51
silhouette of the Rebbe, 121

Simchat Torah, 94, 113, 148–49, 181
Sinai, Mount, 131, 213, 280n94, 281n9
social cohesion, 265–66
sociology, Meshichist, 37–43
Sontag, Susan, 220
Soviet Union, 179–81, 212, 262
sports teams, 187, 285n29
Stalin, Josef, 180–81
Stephen, Michelle, 171
sukkah, personal, 93, 94
Sukkot, 94, 123, 148–49, 162–63

Taliban, 184
Tanya (Chabad canonical text), 48, 89, 133
Taylor, Marc, 291n23
technology: "770," use of, 79; in Bratslav and Chabad, 249–50; decentralized Rebbe and, 224–25; enchantment and, 220–21; epistemological status of, 72, 259; *Igrot Kodesh* Oracle and, 62–63, 72–73; mediation and, 6–9; presence of the virtual Rebbe, 217–23; reproduction, issue of, 223–24; theologization of, 215–16, 259; traditional/modern boundary-crossing and, 249–50. *See also* images of the Rebbe
Temimim, Tomkhei, 32
Temple, Third, 207, 209, 247, 295n7
Teresa of Ávila, Saint, 169
theosophy of Chabad: all-encompassing system of meaning and, 254–55; apparitions and, 151, 166; *Igrot Kodesh* Oracle and, 53–54; inconsistent logical systems, 166; material and spiritual, connection between, 53–54, 273n14; messianic idea and, 31–32; technology and, 215
time and place, holy, 206–14
Torah, inner, 82, 166, 216
Torah-portion pamphlet genre, 12, 292n9

traces of the Rebbe: *Chitat* "safety kit," 89–91, *92*; dollar bills as, 83–89, *89*; *mikveh* water as, 79–83; other religions, comparison to, 74–75; variety of objects and signifiers, 74–79; virtual Rebbe and, 223; wedding example, 96–97
transparent immediacy, 7–8, 259–60
tzadikim (righteous leaders or holy men): aura of, 121; as beloved son of God, 230; contemplation of, 102, 277n14; democratization of rank of, 256; divine status of, 188–90, 195; institutionalization and dynastic succession, 29–30, 230; in Kabbalah, 175, 188, 190; mediating between flock and heaven, xi–xii; Yesod, identification with, 29. *See also specific leaders by name*
"*tzadik's* descent," 252
Tzarfat, 182, 208
Tzik, Rabbi Zimroni, 12–14, 19–20, 70–71, 124, 189–90, 287n27
Tzipori, Rabbi Yigal, 40
Tzivot Hashem (Armies of God), 38
Tzurat haBayit (Form of the Home/Temple), 209

Uman, Ukraine (Rabbi Nachman's grave), 247–49, 251, 253
United Nations, 183
United States and Schneersoncentrism, 182–84
utopianism, 2, 254

Vaknin, Yossi, 91
Ventura, Rabbi Tzvi, 213–14
video clips, 110–15, 138–39
videomancy, 115
Virilio, Paul, 222
virtual Rebbe, 204, 217–23
visions. *See* apparitions; dreams and dream apparitions
visual culture. *See* images of the Rebbe
visualization, 102, 135, 146, 152–53

"Waiting for the Messiah" (Hanoch), 290n27
Waronker, Rabbi Ya'akov, 209
water, holy. See *mikveh* water
weather, changing, 176–77
wedding ceremonies, 79, 96–97, 198, *199*, 276n44
"Welcome King Messiah" leaflets, 193
wellsprings, dissemination of, 181–83, 216, 244
Western Wall, 82, 251
When Prophecy Fails (Festinger, Riecken, and Schachter), 231–32, 264–65
Wiesel, Elie, 122
wine distributed by the Rebbe, 145–46, 160
Wolfson, Elliot, 256, 282n58, 288n9, 294n11
Wolpe, Rabbi Sholom Dovber, 102
women, empowerment of, 248

World Redemption Day, 211

"years of miracles" (1990–1992), 180, 220
"Yechi Adoneinu" mantra: at "770," 92; Bratslav compared, 253; dollar bills and, 85; Elokists and, 195; *Igrot Kodesh* and, 52, 61, 66–67; *kipot* embroidered with, 77; *mikveh* water and, 82; at Oro shel Mashiach summer camp, 39; technology and, 218
yehidut (face-to-face audience), 47, 272n1
Yemen, 267n9
Yom Kippur, 93–94, 149, 159
Yomtovian, Rabbi Shneur Zalman, 43

Zionism, 2, 32, 256, 267n7
Zohar, 33, 53, 202, 215–16

SPIRITUAL PHENOMENA
TANYA MARIE LUHRMANN and ANN TAVES, Series Editors

Spiritual Phenomena features investigations of events, experiences, and objects, both unusual and everyday, that people characterize as spiritual, paranormal, magical, occult, and/or supernatural. Working from the presupposition that the status of such phenomena is contested, it seeks to understand how such determinations are made in a variety of historical and cultural contexts. Books in this series explore how such phenomena are identified, experienced, and understood; the role that spontaneity and cultivation play in the process; and the similarities and differences in the way phenomena are appraised and categorized across time and cultures. The editors encourage work that is ethnographic, historical, or psychological, and, in particular, work that uses more than one method to understand these complex phenomena, ranging from qualitative approaches to quantitative surveys and laboratory-based experiments.

David J. Halperin, *Intimate Alien: The Hidden Story of the UFO*

J. Bradley Wigger, *Invisible Companions: Encounters with Imaginary Friends, Gods, Ancestors, and Angels*

Kelly Bulkeley, *Lucrecia the Dreamer: Prophecy, Cognitive Science, and the Spanish Inquisition*

The authorized representative in the EU for product safety and compliance is:
Mare Nostrum Group
B.V Doelen 72
4831 GR Breda
The Netherlands

www.ingramcontent.com/pod-product-compliance
Lightning Source LLC
Chambersburg PA
CBHW031859220426
43663CB00006B/696